Human Geography
CULTURE, SOCIETY, AND SPACE
Harm J. de Blij

John Wiley & Sons

New York   Santa Barbara   London   Sydney   Toronto

Cover and Text Design	EA Burke
Cover Illustration	Mark Smith
Maps	Hammond Incorporated
Illustrations	John Balbalis assisted by John Wiley Illustration Department
Photo Research	Stella Kupferberg
Production	Suzanne Ingrao
Copy Editor	Susan Giniger
Typographer	Progressive
Text Printing	Kingsport Press
Cover Printing	Lehigh Press

World Maps in
this book are based
on a modified Goode's
projection used through
the permission of the
University of Chicago
Department of Geography
"Copyright by the
University of Chicago
Department of Geography."

Library of Congress Cataloging in Publication Data:

De Blij, Harm J
  Human geography.

  Includes bibliographies.
  1. Anthropo-geography.   2. Social history.
3. Culture.   I. Title.

GF41.D4   301.2   76-25994
ISBN 0-471-20047-6

Printed in the United States of America

10 9 8 7 6 5 4 3 2 1

To
the glory of St. Julien
and
Pauillac

PREFACE

Early this year I asked students in an introductory geography class at the University of Miami to identify issues in human geography that interested and concerned them most. Their responses reflected the extent to which they sensed the discomforts and pressures of change in familiar physical, social, and psychological environments; there was also evidence of apprehension about the future. An awareness that circumstances in distant lands could directly affect daily lives brought home the reality of our shrinking world: the drama of the Cuban exodus and its impact on Miami's culture, the growing power of oil-producing states and the recent long lines at gasoline stations, the threat of environmental deterioration and the oil slicks on Florida Keys beaches. With the dislocations and uncertainties of the Indochina nightmare still fresh in memory, the expressed concerns were practical and current: what causes so large a number of countries (then including Cyprus, Lebanon, Northern Ireland, Angola) to be engulfed by conflict? What are the conditions that generate the rise in domestic crime and international terrorism that erode one's sense of personal security? And if a populous, powerful country such as the Soviet Union could experience a serious food deficit while famines struck West Africa and South Asia, could food shortage occur here?

There probably is not a single community in North America that has been left unaffected by the conditions of change. The Cuban exodus is not the only significant migration stream to alter the demographic and cultural fabric of a major city in recent decades. The Florida Keys constitute only one area among many afflicted by severe pollution incidents. Under the circumstances it is perhaps surprising that the list of student responses still included more abstract items such as the debate over the nature of human territoriality (stimulated by recent publicity surrounding the sociobiology issue), theories of climatic reversal, and the politico-geographical future of the world's ocean space.

This book attempts to place a wide range of such current and urgent concerns in a human-geographic context, but without sacrificing major, traditional elements that must also be learned. The issues are addressed in five parts, each consisting of several chapters. In the first part, the population question is discussed under rubrics of numbers, nutrition, health, and mobility. Aspects of cultural geography lie behind several of today's national and regional crises, and cultural differences between societies, even in the present, mobile, interacting world, still remain pervasive. Regional, racial, linguistic, and religious patterns are among those discussed in the book's second part, with some emphasis on art, architecture, and music as elements of the cultural landscape. In the third cluster of chapters, the phenomenon of urbanization is considered from several viewpoints, including the temporal. Part four describes how the fruits of the livelihoods of the world's peoples enter a global distribution and acquisition system that favors some and deprives others. In the fifth and last part of *Human Geography*, a central argument is that the system of states and nations that marks the modern political map is under such ideological and economic pressure that it may not survive. We live in a world of accelerating change, in which the unthinkable should be contemplated.

This book, therefore, contains some chapters not always found in similar volumes, for example "The Coming Crisis," (6), "Architecture, Art, and Music," (11), and "The Distribution of Health" (4).

I am indebted to many colleagues as this volume is completed. Dr. Risa Palm of the University of California, Berkeley, did an exhaustive and enormously productive review of the manuscript and made numerous valuable suggestions. Dr. Karl M. Kriesel of Northeastern Illinois University also wrote a most productive review, as did Dr.

Karl B. Raitz of the University of Kentucky and Dr. Charles F. Bennett of the University of California, Los Angeles. I am deeply grateful for their penetrating and illuminating commentaries. I also thank Dr. Howard G. Roepke of the University of Illinois and Dr. C. W. Dierickx for their assistance and interest.

Dr. Andrew A. Nazzaro of Eastern Michigan University wrote "Malaria and Sickle-Cell Anemia" (page 81) and Prof. Richard K. Kreske of the University of Miami prepared the section on "Histoplasmosis".

I also acknowledge with thanks the work of Editor Paul A. Lee of John Wiley and Sons, Ms. Stella Kupferberg, who did the illustration research, Mr. E. A. Burke, Design Director, Mr. Jerry McCarthy, Manager of Illustration Department, Mr. John Balbalis, Illustration Design, Mr. Terry Rehill, Manager of Production Department, Ms. Suzanne Ingrao, Production Manager, Mr. Malcolm Easterlin, Chief Copy Editor, Ms. Susan Giniger, Copy editor, as well as Ms. Bonnie Doughty and Ms. Kathy DiConza, who aided the progress of the work in many ways.

I wish to thank the Editorial and Cartographic Staff of Hammond Inc. who prepared the maps. Responsibility for the contents, of course, remains mine alone.

Harm J. de Blij

Coral Gables, Florida
May, 1976

CONTENTS

xi

xiv

Boston, Massachusetts from 51,200 feet
(15,600 meters).

1 Preview
a Spatial Orientation

Did you open this book without asking yourself: "What is geography?" If so, you may be in a minority. As long as there has been geography—and geography as a field of study has existed for several thousand years—students and scholars have asked precisely this question. In fact, many geographers themselves often raise this issue, and some of them have spent whole careers trying to define the scope and academic sphere of geography. So if you wondered about this, as you opened *Human Geography*, you were in good company. The question, as we will find, is worth asking.

Somehow we seem to be much more certain that we know what we are talking about when we refer to history or anthropology or psychology than when we speak of geography. If a professor asked you to write an essay to describe exactly what these other disciplines are, you might find it easier than if you were to write a definition of the field of geography. In part this is probably so because other social science disciplines have been more effectively popularized. One way or another we have formed impressions of history as dealing with events of the past, anthropology as focusing on distant, little-known peoples, and psychology as the science of the mind and behavior. But when it comes to geography it is not quite as easy to come up with a similar, brief definition. Some of your friends, when they find out that you are studying geography, will immediately ask you to name the capital of some obscure country. Their impression probably is that geography deals with place names and the kinds of facts you will find in gazetteers. But geography today is something very different.

In these days of intensifying contact and interaction, is there really any point in worrying about the precise nature of academic disciplines? After all, methodologies are borrowed and traded, and it is often difficult to decide whether an article deals with sociology or psychology, political science or public administration. In high school, you may have run into a subject called social studies—a mix-

1

ture of history, civics, and, if you were lucky, perhaps some geography. If we can combine these areas in high school, why separate them now, at the university? There are several reasons. Although there is more interaction among scientists today than ever before, the mass of knowledge is also increasing at a growing rate. it is difficult enough, you will find, to keep up with the new writings in just one discipline, let alone the whole range of the social sciences. Thus we must focus on one area, on a set of ideas we want to study and investigate. Others have done this before us, and we need their findings in order not to repeat ourselves. Obviously we want to build further and to expand our own knowledge. So we concentrate on what interests and concerns us. Geography is such an area of interest and concern.

What is interesting about geography? We should probably add something to this question and ask what is interesting about geography *today*, for if you read about geographers of the past you will find that their pursuits were quite different from ours at present. Geographers such as Alexander von Humboldt (1769–1859) combined their scholarly research with

Alexander Freiherr von Humbolt.

adventurous exploration. Geography, exploration, and the making of maps of unknown lands had virtually the same meaning, and in those days it was still possible for a scientist to become expert in several different fields of science. Von Humboldt in some respects was the last of the Renaissance men: he was an accomplished botanist, geologist, historian, astronomer, cartographer—and geographer. He had unbounded curiosity and his professional life was a sort of scientific treasure hunt. But the age of specialization was approaching. The explosion of knowledge had begun and no individual scholar could hope to contribute in as many areas as Von Humboldt and his colleagues had. And so, during the second half of the nineteenth century, you begin to see the emergence of a new geography. No new continents or peoples remained to be discovered, but some novel questions began to present themselves.

Among these new questions are some that still interest us today, a century later. What is the nature of the relationships between human societies and natural environments? Where will humanity's explosive population growth lead? Why and how do states evolve and decline?

What distinguishes certain areas or *regions* on the earth's surface from other areas? What determines the location and spacing of cities and towns? How are people induced to move, to migrate from their familiar homeland to a totally different part of the world?

Look closely at these questions. They have something in common: they all relate in some way to our living *space*, to the area, the territory on our planet on which we have to accommodate ourselves. Having long explored, described, and mapped areas of the world, geographers today like to theorize about the *spatial* arrangement of people and their institutions. Spatial arrangements, of course, are best represented by maps. If it is true that a picture is worth a thousand words, then a map is worth a million words, and often even more. The U.S. Geological Survey publishes a series of maps called topographic quadrangles, that show elevation of the land, transport routes, and settlements, and it has been estimated that each of these maps contains over 100 million items of information. Even small, simple maps can convey information with great efficiency. Most of us do not spend nearly enough time studying maps and learning from them. Consider how long it took you to read the previous full page of this book. When did you last spend an equal amount of time concentrating on a page-size map?

Maps tell us where places are with respect to other places. True, maps give us the location of places in terms of the earth's latitude-longitude grid, but it really helps you very little to know that Chicago lies at 41 degrees 53 minutes North Latitude and 87 degrees 38 minutes West Longitude. Those figures identify Chicago's *absolute* location, but when you consult a map you are likely to be looking for other details. You may want to know where Chicago lies with respect to Milwaukee, or at what point it touches Lake Michigan, or whether it lies at the mouth of a river, or how it is served by communication lines. Location has meaning only with respect to other locations, and when we consult a map it usually is to discover more about the *relative* location of a place (Fig. 1-1).

Maps show the location of places and areas; they also reveal *patterns*. Geographers, you will find, are always interested in patterns revealed by maps, for behind those patterns may lie processes responsible for their creation. One of the most celebrated cases in point is the map of Dr. John Snow (see p. 85)

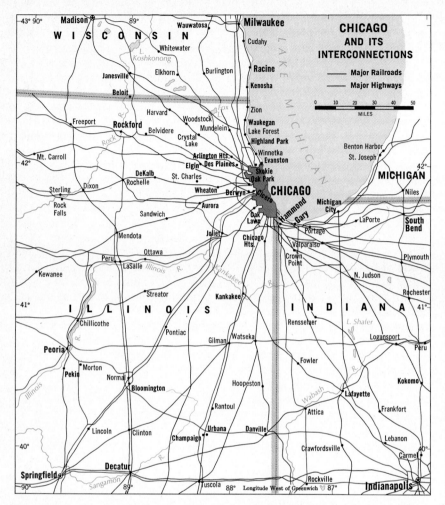

Figure 1-1   Land and water communications converge upon Chicago. The city also lies at the focus of a large number of airline routes.

of the Atlantic Ocean in South America and Africa suggested that those two continents had once been closer neighbors (you can still prove the point by examining a globe or map and tracing the two coastlines). That remarkable, jigsawlike fit was one of the reasons for Dr. Alfred Wegener's pioneering work in continental drift. He just could not believe that what the map showed could be merely an accident of nature (Fig. 1-2).

Maps also provide us with information about *regions*. Everyone has some idea of what the word *region* means: we use regional terms all the time in our everyday conversation. When we talk about conflict in the Middle East, hunger in the Sahel of West Africa, or road construction in the Amazon Basin we have used the regional concept in its broadest sense as a frame of reference. Sometimes we must be more precise than such casual references are, however. If everyone in your class were to draw a map of what is perceived as the region called the Middle East, you might get dozens of versions. What, exactly, is Africa's Sahel region? Where, precisely, are the limits of the Amazon Basin? There will be occasions when we must agree on the dimensions of what we define as a region.

Regions, in the first place, have *location*. When we refer to the Middle East (or to Indochina or the Amazon Basin or the Chicago area, all regions of a kind) we have in mind a region positioned in a particular location somewhere on this globe. We could actually identify that location by using the grid system referred to earlier, by describing it in terms of degrees of latitude

showing the distribution pattern of cholera deaths in the London district of Soho. Using a list giving the victims' addresses, Dr. Snow produced a map that showed a strong concentration near a water pump in public use. He immediately had the pump shut off—and cholera deaths in Soho declined dramatically. What a stack of information piled on a desk cannot reveal, a map can sometimes display impressively.

Sometimes a map can only point to the solution, and suggest the most productive direction of research. Long before physical geographers had proof that our globe's continents are mobile and drifting, the configuration of the opposite coasts

4

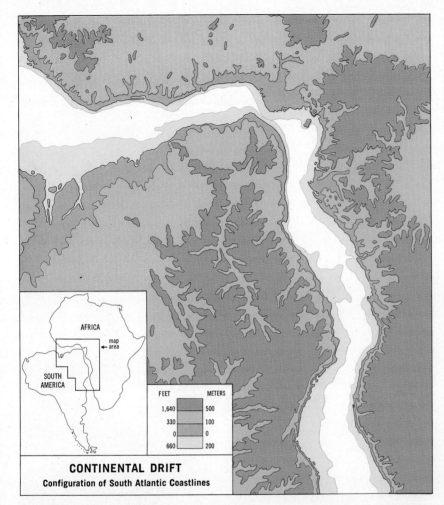

AFRICA

map
← area

SOUTH
AMERICA

FEET	METERS
1,640	500
330	100
0	0
660	200

CONTINENTAL DRIFT
Configuration of South Atlantic Coastlines

Figure 1-2 The remarkable, jigsawlike fit of sections of the South American and African coastlines. When the landmasses were positioned this way, the delta of the Niger River (opposite South America's northeast corner) had not yet formed.

and longitude. But we will be much more interested in our region's relative location: the Middle East relative to the world's oil reserves, Indochina in the context of adjacent cultural areas, the Amazon Basin and its highland margins. Regions interact with other regions, and we are concerned with their relative location.

Regions also have *area*. This seems so obvious as to hardly deserve mention, but herein lie some difficult problems. If a region is to have areal extent, then its limits must be definable. We would probably all agree that the Rocky Mountains form a distinct region in the United States. But taking a map and drawing a line exactly

where the Rocky Mountains end and other regions (such as the adjacent Great Plains) begin is not as simple an exercise as it might seem. The Rocky Mountains form a physical or natural region, but the problem is no easier to solve in human geography. Take a region you might have in mind as "the South." You base your concept of that region on a certain combination of characteristics. But where exactly lies the boundary of "the South" as a region? There is more to a region's area than first appears.

Some regions are defined by a dominant property we call their *homogeneity*. Professor R. Hartshorne, in his book, *Perspective on the Nature of Geography* (1959), defines a region as "an area of specific location which is in some way distinctive from other areas and which extends as far as that distinction extends." We geographers, of course, can decide on the particular distinctive quality we want to regionalize. It could be mountainous terrain, as in the Rocky Mountains, a desert climate, the prevalence of a particular language, or the concentration of a particular racial population group (ghettos are urban regions). Sometimes such regions defined by a certain homogeneity are called *formal* regions, but you should not expect to see this term used a great deal these days.

The boundary of a region: where the Great Plains meet the Rocky Mountains.
The view is south near Boulder, Colorado.

6

A region can also be conceptualized as a system. It may be that what binds a region together is *not* its internal sameness, but an activity or set of activities that connects its various parts. For example, a large city has a substantial surrounding area for which it supplies goods and services, from which it buys farm products, and with which it interacts in numerous ways. The city's manufacturers distribute their products wholesale to regional subsidiaries. Its newspapers sell in the nearby smaller towns. Maps detailing the orientation of road traffic, the source and destination of telephone calls, the readership of newspapers, the audience of radio stations, and other activities will confirm the relationship between the city and this, its tributary region or *hinterland*. Here again we have a region, but this time it is not characterized by homogeneity but, instead, by the city-centered system of interaction that generates it. To distinguish these regions from the formal regions they are referred to as *functional* regions.

It is important to remember that regions exist only on our maps and in our minds—they are mental constructs that help us conceptualize and classify information about the surface of our earth. We will use this concept frequently in this book, since one of our objectives is to learn how our world is regionally different (or "areally differentiated," as some geographers like to say). The regions we use will always be artificial, based on the criteria we set out to define in the first place.

We have referred in passing to the coastlines of continents, to the Rocky Mountains, to desert climate, and to the use of the regional concept in these contexts. These are, obviously, not prominent topics in human geography, but they serve to remind us of two important items: (1) while human geography lies at the heart of the discipline today, and geography is primarily a social science, the discipline also has a tradition in the physical or natural sciences and (2) the regional concept is the strongest of the bonds between human geographers and physical geographers. Geography is, above all, a wide-ranging discipline, and there are geographers whose principal interests lie in the study of landscapes and landforms, in research on climate and weather, or in vegetation and the soil. There are also geographers who concentrate their research and teaching on the relationships between the physical and human worlds. They study the impact of humanity on our globe's natural environments, and the influences of the environment on human individuals and societies. We will refer to these efforts, but our primary interest in this book is the human world—our numbers, our accommodations, our ways of living, our production, and our countries and nations.

Population

We begin by considering the world's population in global terms. Humanity is increasing its numbers at an ever faster rate.

7

There are more than twice as many people on this earth today than there were as recently as 1930, and at present rates of growth the present population of more than four billion will double in only 35 years. Can all those people be accommodated and supplied with food? We study this question in the context of (1) the world distribution of population as it stands at present and (2) concepts of population density. Our globe has huge clusters of concentrated, crowded population, but there still are great empty areas. Why do people not simply move from the overcrowded to the emptier areas? It is, as we shall see, not as simple a matter as that.

In recent years the problem of world hunger has come prominently to our attention. Hunger, as we will find, is largely a matter of geography: of distance from the sources of food, of isolation and migration, of climatic changes and searing droughts. Even the energy crisis contributes to world hunger, for rising prices in oil produce rising costs for fertilizers. In the newspapers and on television we are confronted with the devastating manifestations of hunger and starvation in West Africa, in Ethiopia, in Honduras, in India, in Bangladesh—but still the world's population grows larger as millions of babies are delivered into a world where they will have no chance of survival.

We will examine some possible solutions: the population spiral must be brought under control, we must increase the yield

Regions: The Debate Continues

Is the distinction between a "formal" region marked by homogeneity and a "functional" region generated by process really appropriate? In the simplest terms, the formal region is described as static, uniform, immobile; the functional region, on the other hand, is analyzed as dynamic, active, the manifestation of processes (see text).

But, as R. Symanski and J. Newman point out in a recent article (1973), the "formal" region's internal sameness is *also* the result of processes. The Corn Belt in the Midwest, an urban ghetto, the Amazon Basin—all "formal" regions—have patterns that are generated by processes just as "functional" regions do. Perhaps "formal" regions are less affected by change, more durable, and therefore more visible, but, say many geographers, they are not fundamentally different from "functional" regions, and the distinction is "the product of an intellectual illusion."

Illusion or not, you will see references to "formal" and "functional" regions in much of the geographic literature and it is useful to know what the authors had in mind when they used those terms.

of the world's farmlands and expand the farming areas, and local production must be stimulated. Many parts of the world still await sweeping reforms in the ownership of land, and these must be instituted as rapidly as possible. We need alternative sources of food, and the production of the oceans must be controlled by international agreement.

People who do not eat well do not feel well, and good health, like food, is unevenly distributed over the world. We will examine major problems of health and will discover that nutrition and disease are closely related. It is possible to consume an apparently adequate quantity of calories and still suffer from malnutrition; the role of protein in the development of the body is critical, and many children the world over do not get sufficient proteins as they grow up. Average life expectancy in many countries is still shockingly low, and some diseases that have long been defeated in the Western world still afflict millions in other countries. And, as we will find, the availability of treatment is inadequate even in the richer countries of the world; it is truly dismal in the world of hunger and poverty.

The human migration stream to the city continues the world over, the discomforts of urban slums notwithstanding. The phenomenon of movement is a dominant one in human geography, and Americans are the most mobile people in the world today. In Chapter 5 we find that migration is not just one, but a whole set of different processes, expressed in various ways (e.g., as cyclic, periodic, and permanent movements), and sustained by a whole range

The luxury of space: a sprawling cemetery in the shadow of Manhattan.

Tradition and the crisis of numbers: a funeral pyre being prepared for the cremation of a deceased person in Calcutta, India.

9

of motives. What induces people to leave their homes? The move to the cities is only one manifestation of human mobility, and the perceived attraction of the city is only one motive among many.

The world approaches an era of crises—simultaneous crises that will strain the fabric of societies. In our final chapter dealing with the population question we consider the possibility that world climate is changing and that our living space will be diminished and our farmlands reduced. Our prodigious capacity to pollute and to damage the earth's natural environment is an additional global hazard and one whose consequences are yet unpredictable. Additionally, we may face a crisis of resource availability beyond that of energy sources, and we are not ready to cope with such a situation. Nor are the peoples of the world prepared to begin narrowing the gap between the rich and the poor. As we observe again in Part IV, the rich countries are getting wealthier and the poor countries more poverty stricken. It is a time bomb, and we are not making moves to defuse it.

We also may face new health risks. We have shown our ability to combat polio, cholera, and malaria, but we may find ourselves vulnerable to other maladies. Our drinking water is suspect. Certain preservatives and containers pose apparent health hazards. We do not know yet what the cumulative effects of generations of exposure may be. Nor are we totally sure that we are safe against a cholera-type world epidemic of some new disease that, in our mobile, crowded world, could create havoc. We face an uncertain future.

Culture

Part II deals with cultural geography. First we consider the nature of culture, humanity's many different ways of life in which behavior is learned from parents and others, not biologically inherited. One manifestation of our way of life is the *cultural landscape* we create. The total assemblage of our human works—from skyscraper to junkyard, from billboard to ballpark—all of it goes into the makeup of the cultural landscape. Cultural landscapes in various parts of the world display great individuality, and we identify several in Chapter 7. We also try for the first time to answer some questions about the origins of cultures and their regional expression. Next we view the entire world as 12 *culture realms* and note some of the more prominent properties of each.

Racial origins and human dispersals across and around the world still are shrouded in mystery. We are all members of one race—the human race—notwithstanding the undeniable fact that peoples do differ physically from each other in a number of ways. Mindful of our common origins, we discuss some of our similarities and differences; even today, after countless centuries of human migration and mixture, our differences still have regional expression. When cultures of different strengths make contact, a process called *acculturation* occurs, whereby a culture is changed substantially through contact with another culture.

The relationships between cultural development and natural environment have long been a topic for geographical study, and for a time a dominant theme in this area was *environmental determinism*. This idea, still supported today by a few scholars, holds that human behavior, individually and collectively, is to a large degree controlled or determined by the natural environment. This provides a convenient answer to numerous questions raised by the map of world cultures—but not, we find, a reliable one.

Next, we look at language, a vital and indispensable element of all cultures. After we examine the problems of defining and classifying languages, we take a regional approach and study the language maps of Europe and Africa in detail. The languages of Africa have utility in research in historical and cultural geography, for behind their relationships, and sometimes shared vocabularies, lie past associations that can be unraveled. We also discuss the role of the *lingua franca* in various parts of the world as a means of making and maintaining contact. Finally, in Chapter 9, we examine the problems of countries where more than one language is spoken by sectors of the population.

In many parts of the world, notably in non-Western areas, religion is so central a part of culture that it practically is the whole culture. We study religion in terms of its known sources and dispersals, and in the process we differentiate between universal, cultural, and traditional faiths. Taking a spatial view of this element of human culture, we then consider the development and impact of six major religions of East and West.

Our last chapter of Part II is devoted to expressions we associate closely with the concept of culture: music, art, and architecture. We return briefly to the concept of the cultural landscape to illuminate the role of architecture. Religion has a powerful effect on architecture, for societies over the centuries have poured their resources into the creation of temples and shrines commensurate with the intensity of their faith. Governments, too, have used their power to create the most imposing, impressive headquarters. In the area of art, we have gone from the statues of gods and war heroes to a whole new manifestation of freestanding sculpture, some of it ultramodern and in need of explanation. We cite some examples and look into some other art forms and their impact on the cultural landscape, including dance and theater. Finally, we focus on music, another vital element of culture and one that has strong regional differentiation.

Settlements

In Part III we study places of residence of the world's human population. First we consider the houses themselves: their form, distribution, the materials of which they are made. This gives us our initial view of culture, for the character of people's residence is a basic ingredient of cultural expression. Next we look at the spacing of houses, and discover that some settlement is

best described as concentrated or *nucleated*, while others are spread out or *dispersed*. Small nucleated settlements, hamlets, and villages show a surprising variety of forms, sometimes inherited from a lengthy history.

People everywhere in the world are moving to the cities, or trying to. Ours is truly an urban age, and the world's cities have reached unprecedented dimensions. In Chapter 13 we examine this phenomenal rush to urbanize, and some of the stresses that are imposed on the people who try to accommodate to urban life. In the process we remind ourselves that cities of considerable size already existed long before the Industrial Revolution changed the urban landscape, and we discuss some of the qualities of these *preindustrial* cities. And, familiar as we are with our modern, skyscrapered, Western cities, we should remember that there are also very large, sprawling non-Western cities where some of the principles that govern urban development in our part of the world may not apply.

Cities are built in a particular area whose attributes are those of *site*. A city may lie on an island, or atop an escarpment, or in a swamp: these are site characteristics. A city also has location relative to other cities and towns, farms, mines, transport lines, and this relative location describes the city's *situation*. We take the example of Paris to illustrate these urban assets, and in the process we begin to focus more closely on the spatial relationships between cities, the dominant functions of cities, and, finally, the regional geography of urban centers (for cities have regions just as countries have).

Cities and towns differ in size and, as we soon discover, these size differences have all sorts of implications. Large cities, with their huge factories and other installations, can dominate, overwhelm, and even absorb smaller towns in their hinterland. After we examine the size *hierarchy* of urban places we turn to the classification of cities on grounds other than size. Cities, we find, perform different functions: some are ports, others are mining towns, still others are capitals. Many other functions can be identified, and this helps in the effort to classify urban centers according to the role they play. Still, we discover, classifying cities is no simple matter and no system yet devised is totally satisfactory.

Cities are spaced certain distances from each other, and it is difficult to look at any map of an area's urban centers without wondering how that urban network came to be. Some urban centers are larger and provide more services than others; they appear to have greater *centrality*. By ranking urban places according to their degree of centrality, it is possible to derive a theoretical network that would account for the distribution of cities of various sizes, given certain assumptions. We consider the beginnings of *central place theory*, long a major concern of urban geographers.

In our final segment on urban centers we become regional geographers and try to discern the internal structure of cities in various parts of the world. We all know some of these urban regions as a matter of general reference: when we speak of "downtown" or "the suburbs" we have made a regional reference just as we did with the "Midwest." But how do the regions of cities relate to each other? When cities grow larger, as they continue to do, what happens to the regional geography? How do regions change over time? These are the kinds of questions that are less easily answered. We conclude our look at urbanization with an essay on the current crisis in the American city.

Livelihoods

Beginning with Chapter 15 we view the changing use mankind has made of the earth's resources, and the disparities that exist to this day between societies in this respect. The processes whereby food is produced, distributed, and consumed form a fundamental part of every culture, and these processes have ancient origins. First we account for the way people managed to survive before farming was learned, and where they found the best locations for doing so. Then we theorize about the way cultivation may have been learned, and about the regions in the world where this new capacity may have taken root. After adding animal domestication to the range of human means of sustenance, we discuss *shifting cultivation*, still a way of life for some millions of the world's population even in this day of dwindling space. A far larger proportion of humanity survives on *subsistence farming*, an often risky way of life in which the threat of hunger is never far away and malnutrition is common.

Next we consider how the modern world has been transformed by modern farming methods, the power and capital of the advantaged, rich nations, and the realities of current economic geography. After reminding ourselves that much of our earth is not suitable farmland, we turn the clock back to the days of a remarkable scholar named Von Thünen. He owned an estate in what is now Germany during the first half of the nineteenth century, and he took an interest in the way the soil is allocated by farmers given certain market conditions. We find that Von Thünen's arguments still have some validity today—and that they can be expanded to fit today's world in general. After considering some local and regional examples of Von Thünen's ideas we put the present world pattern of agriculture in this context, and find that much of our modern world is oriented to serve the markets of the wealthy, well-fed nations.

In order to support such an argument we must have some knowledge of the distribution of world agriculture, and we conclude Chapter 16 with an outline of the plantation phenomenon, the livestock herds, and grain crops of today. We follow this with a brief essay on the way land is owned and occupied in various cultures.

The Industrial Revolution has yet to invade parts of our world, it is changing other areas, and already there is evidence in still other regions that we are past the industrial age and entering what will be known as the age of technology. In the final chapter of Part IV we

argue that the present change (to the technological age) may be more radical even than was the so-called Industrial Revolution (which, we suggest, was really a case of industrial *intensification*).

Since we take a spatial view of the industrializing world, we must account for the factors that influence the location of industries, old and new. While we do so, we differentiate between primary, secondary, and tertiary industries; the *secondary* industries are those that make their mark most strongly on the landscape. Finally, we identify the world's major industrial regions and find that four such regions (Europe, North America, the Soviet Union, and Japan-China) stand out far above any and all other nuclei of industrial development. Following Chapter 17 is an essay reminding us of the divisive effects of the insular development we have just examined.

Politics

In Part V we examine the many manifestations of political behavior that have spatial expression. First we trace the rise of statelike political entities in the Middle East in conjunction with the emergence of urban settlements. Having enumerated some of the characteristics of these *feudal* societies, we identify other regions of the world in which urban growth and political development (the two are closely associated) began early. Thus we focus on the Indus Valley of what is today Pakistan, on ancient Egypt, on Northern China, on West Africa, Middle America, and the South American Andes.

But the state system that has spread all over the world is the

Excessive crowding is a condition of many of the world's large cities. A street
bazaar has evolved near a housing development in Hong Kong.

13

one that evolved in Europe, and so we next deal with the evolution of the European model, beginning with the *city-states* of ancient Greece, the remarkable achievement of the Roman Empire, and ending with the infusion of wealth that brought Europe unprecedented power. This infusion came while Europe's internal order was changing radically, and we focus on the case of France to discover what a combination of internal revolution and external colonial acquisition produced. Inevitably, the European political system was exported to the colonial empires forged by Europe's states.

The state is a system. In Chapter 19 we dissect the system and look closely at the geography of its individual elements. Here we view the "four pillars" of the state: its territory, population, organization, and power. Each has spatial expression: territory has size and shape (morphology, to use the appropriate term); population has distributional as well as quantitative aspects; organization in many spheres can be interpreted from the map itself (in transportation, for example); and power is reflected in the state's external relationships. In the course of our scrutiny of the elements of the state system we focus on the nature and evolution of boundaries as we know them today, the "heart" of the state we shall call the core area, and the role of the capital city as the state's center of gravity.

We are witnessing, at this very moment, a significant stage in the evolution of the world map. States have occupied all the available space on the world's landmasses, and now they are extending their sovereignty over the adjacent seas and over the nearby *continental shelf*. In Chapter 20 we identify the timid beginnings of this process and watch it accelerate during the twentieth century, to reach its present state of almost frenzied acquisition reminiscent of the days when states grabbed colonies in Africa and Asia. As the hope for international agreement and the survival of free and open oceans recedes, the motives for the acquisition of "territorial seas" multiply: to protect fishing industries, to secure minerals on and beneath the continental shelf, to prevent pollution of beaches. In Chapter 20 we describe the oceans as the earth's last frontier and we observe this frontier invaded and parceled out. In the process we learn about the character of coastlines, the nature of maritime boundaries, and the potential of the submerged continental shelf. Even the deepest ocean floor, we find, contains promising mineral deposits.

In our final chapter we view the state as a body and study its behavior toward other states. Several geographers (among many other scholars) have tried to account for the apparent life cycle of states: their growth, maturing, and, frequently, their decay and collapse. We examine some of these theories and find that they have, at times, led to dangerous prescriptions.

An especially interesting aspect of political geography relates to the colonial period. European states acquired huge overseas empires, and in due course they began to imprint their cultural heritage on those distant lands. But they did so in different ways. Some of these efforts can be seen on the colonial (and even present-day) map: the centrality and primacy of French-colonial capital cities, the fervent railroad building in the German colonial realm, the attempt made by the Belgians to create a political framework in the Congo that would minimize regional contrasts, the federal map of Nigeria at the time of independence from Britain. We study these cases in some detail.

A prominent twentieth-century phenomenon is the cooperative behavior of states today: their willingness to associate in *supranational* organizations for economic benefit, military protection, or for the promotion of shared objectives of other kinds. Although alliances are nothing new, modern interstate organizations appear to be of a more permanent nature than has ever been the case, and in Europe the map is being transformed. We discuss this multinational phenomenon and then another, even more recent, and ultimately perhaps even more significant reality: the rise of the so-called multinational corporation as an influence in world political geography. The boardrooms of corporations based in New York or elsewhere may exert more political power in distant countries than the parliament buildings of those countries themselves.

This brief preview of *Human Geography* gives you an idea of the directions we take as we study the cultures, societies, and life-styles of our modern world. Whenever we can, we focus on the spatial expressions of human activity. Remember: the maps tell much of the story.

PART ONE
population

Sampan houses in the Aberdeen
floating colony, Hong Kong: even on the
water congestion develops.

2 Population and Space

In August, 1974, representatives of nations from all regions of the
world met at the World Population Conference in Bucharest, Romania, to discuss a problem of global importance: the explosive
growth of this planet's human population. The conference dele-
gates were addressed by scientists specializing in population
studies, and they were reminded of some frightening realities.
Every day of the year the world's population increases by 200,000.
Every month, there are 6 million more mouths to be fed. Every
year witnesses the addition of nearly 80 million people to our
already crowded world. Less than three years from the moment
you read this, a population the size of the United States' will have
been added to our numbers.

And yet, people by the hundreds of thousands—even millions—are dying of hunger in places as far apart as South Asia
and West Africa, Bangladesh and Ethiopia. If there is not enough
food even now, why does the growth of world population continue?
Can new sources of food be found and developed? Can countries
be persuaded to reduce their growth rate? These and other questions confronted the Bucharest conference.

In the United States and Canada, and in the Western world generally, those staggering figures do not yet seem to affect us much.
We hear that high-rise apartments encroach on some area that con-
servationists are trying to save, and there is the occasional story of
a developer pushing streets and sewers into a beautiful forest.
Bumper stickers in Oregon tell visitors that they are welcome—temporarily. A letter in the *Miami Herald* proposes that Florida discour-
age further immigration from other parts of the United States because crowding is becoming a problem there. Traffic jams seem to
be worse, and waiting lines may appear longer than ever. But no
one need die of hunger, and while our population also grows, its
rate of increase is much less than that of many non-Western countries. We may sense some discomfort, but not disaster.

17

Nevertheless, our future is inextricably tied to those other parts of the world where population growth is truly explosive. No country can exist in isolation, no matter how varied and rich its resources. India relies heavily on shipments of U.S. grain, just as the United States depends severely on import of Middle East oil. The United States does not send its wheat to India as a humanitarian gesture. It is strictly business—commercial and political. The specter of world disorder arising from political pressures that result from widespread hunger and hopelessness hangs heavily over the comparative comfort of Western nations. In the fall of 1974, after parts of Ethiopia had been afflicted by years of hunger and starvation, the direct result was a political upheaval that terminated more than 40 years of stable (if not progressive) rule under Emperor Haile Selassie. What could not be achieved by attempted coups, religious conflicts, and regional insurrections was accomplished by the desperation of famine. On a larger scale, such a sequence of events could have global implications. Western grain shipments are intended in large measure to diffuse the pressure.

Small wonder, then, that Western nations at the World Population Conference pushed hardest for concrete action on means to reduce the rate of growth of the world's population. In the long run, the West has as much to gain from such a slowdown as do the populations of such hungry countries as India and Bangladesh.

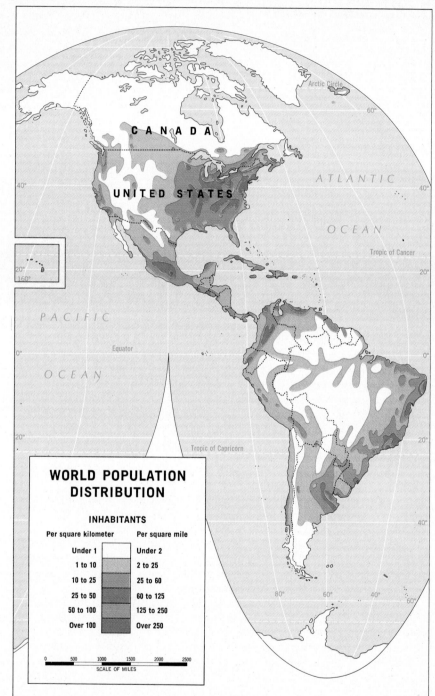

WORLD POPULATION DISTRIBUTION

INHABITANTS

Per square kilometer	Per square mile
Under 1	Under 2
1 to 10	2 to 25
10 to 25	25 to 60
25 to 50	60 to 125
50 to 100	125 to 250
Over 100	Over 250

SCALE OF MILES
0   500   1000   1500   2000   2500

Figure 2-1.

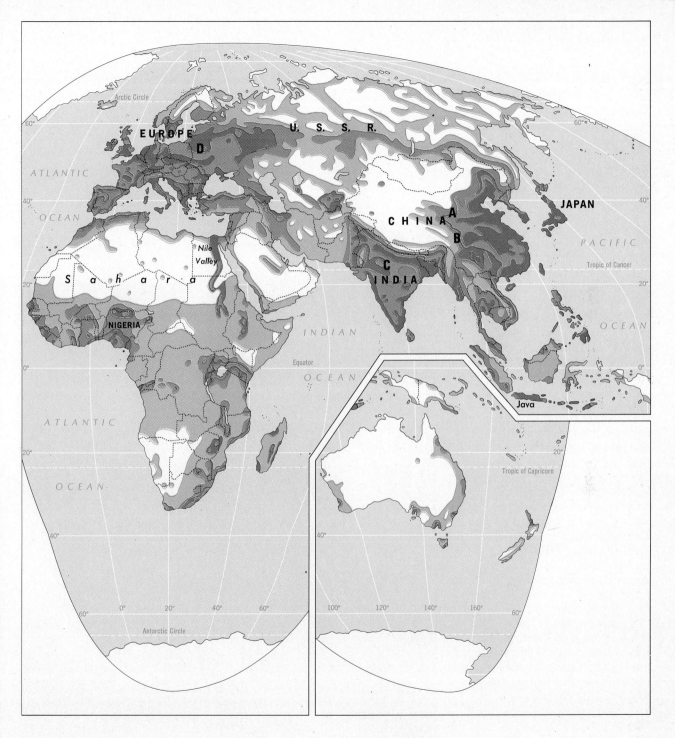

Concentrations and Clusters

Before returning to the problem of population growth and its related issues, we should consider the distribution of the world's four billion people. That milestone—four billion—was reached in early January, 1975.

Of course, the world's population is not distributed evenly over the continents. Even the most densely inhabited countries still have comparatively empty areas. As our map (Fig. 2-1) shows, parts of Western China are as empty as the Sahara Desert. And in India, where crowding is such a serious problem, you can still travel through miles of sparsely peopled territory. The map depicts population distribution through levels of shading to indicate density per unit area: the darker the colors, the larger the number of people clustered in an average unit area. The most extensive area of such dark shading lies in East Asia, principally China but extending into Korea and Vietnam and leapfrogging to Japan. More than a quarter of the entire world's population is concentrated in this East Asian cluster, some 900 million in China alone.

Observation of the dimensions of the East Asian population cluster reveals that it adjoins the Pacific Ocean from South Korea to North Vietnam, and that the number of people per unit area tends to decline from

Rivers are lifelines; populations cluster in their valleys. These farmlands lie along the Euphrates in Iraq.

this coastal zone toward the interior. Also visible are several ribbonlike extensions of dense population, penetrating the interior (Fig. 2-1 *A* and *B*). A reference to a physical map of East Asia tells us that these extensions represent populations clustered in the basins and lowlands of China's major rivers. This serves to remind us that the great majority of the people in East Asia are farmers, not city dwellers. True, there are great cities in China, and some of them, such as Shanghai and Peking, rank among the largest in the world. But the total population of these and the other cities is far outnumbered by the farmers—those who need the river valleys' soils, the life-giving rains, and the moderate temperatures to produce crops of wheat and rice to feed not only themselves but also those in the cities and towns.

The second major concentration of world population also lies in Asia, and it displays many similarities to that of East Asia. At the heart of this South Asia cluster lies India, but it extends also into Pakistan and Bangladesh, and onto the island of Sri Lanka. Again, note the coastal orientation of the most densely inhabited zones, and the fingerlike extension of dense population in Northern India (Fig. 2-1 *C*). This is one of the great concentrations of people on earth, in the valley of the Ganges River.

The South Asia population cluster numbers as many as 800 million people, and at present rates of growth it will reach the one billion mark by the end of the 1970s. Our map shows how sharply this region is marked off by physical barriers: the Himalaya Mountains rise to the north above the Ganges lowland, the desert takes over west of the Indus River valley in Pakistan. This is a confined region, whose population is growing more rapidly than it is almost anywhere else on earth, and whose capacity to support it has, by all estimates, already been exceeded. As in East Asia, the overwhelming majority of the people are farmers, but here in South Asia the pressure on the land is even greater. In Bangladesh, some 75 million people are crowded into an area about the size of Iowa. Nearly all of these people are farmers, and even fertile Bangladesh has areas that cannot sustain as many people as others. Over large parts of Bangladesh the rural population is several *thousand* per square mile. To compare: the 1976 population of Iowa was about 2.9 million, of whom just 43 percent (by the 1970 Census) lived on the land rather than in cities and towns. Rural density in Iowa: 22 per square mile.

Further inspection of Figure 2-1 reveals that the third-ranking population cluster also lies in Eurasia—and at the opposite end from China. An axis of dense population extends from the British Isles into Soviet Russia, and includes large parts of West and East Germany, Poland, and the Western U.S.S.R.; it also incorporates the Netherlands and Belgium, parts of France, and Northern Italy. This European cluster counts nearly 700 million inhabitants, which puts it in a class with the South Asia concentration—but there the similarity ends. A comparison of the population and physical maps indicates that in Europe, terrain and environment appear to have less to do with population distribution than in the two Asian cases. See, for example, that lengthy extension marked *D* on Figure 2-1, which protrudes far into the Soviet Union. Unlike the Asian extensions, which reflect fertile river valleys, the European population axis relates to the orientation of Europe's coal fields, the power resources that fired the Industrial Revolution. If you look more closely at the physical map, you will note that comparatively dense population occurs even in rather mountainous, rugged country, for example along the boundary zone between Czechoslovakia and Poland. In Asia, there is much more correspondence between coastal and river lowlands and high population density than there generally is in Europe.

Another contrast lies in the number of Europeans who live in cities and towns. Far more than in Asia, the Europe population cluster is constituted by numerous cities and towns, many of them products of the Industrial Revolution. In the United Kingdom, about 80 percent of the people live in such urban places; in West Germany, nearly 80; in France about 70. With so many people concentrated in the cities, the rural countryside is more open and sparsely populated than in East and South Asia, where fewer than 20 percent of the people reside in cities and towns.

The three world population concentrations discussed (East Asia, South Asia, and Europe) account for over 2.7 of the world's approximately 4 billion people. Nowhere else on the globe is there any population cluster with dimensions even half of any of these. Look at the dimensions of the landmasses on Figure 2-1 and consider that the populations of South America, Africa, and Australia combined total *less* than that of India alone. In fact, the next-ranking cluster, comprising the East-Central United States and Southeastern Canada, is only about one-quarter the size of the smallest of the Eurasian concentrations. As Figure 2-1 shows, this region does not have the large, contiguous high-density zones of Europe or East and South Asia.

The North American population cluster displays European characteristics, and it even outdoes Europe in some respects. Like the European region, much of the population is concentrated in several major cities, while the rural areas remain relatively sparsely populated. The major focus of the North America cluster lies in the urban complex along the Eastern Seaboard, from Boston to Washington, which includes New York, Philadelphia, and Baltimore. This great urban agglomeration is called *megalopolis* by urban geographers who predict that it is only a matter of time before the whole area coalesces into an enormous megacity. But there are other urban foci in this region: Chicago lies at the heart of one, and Detroit and Cleveland anchor a second. If you study Figure 2-1 carefully, you will note other prominent North American cities standing out as small areas of high-density population, including Pittsburgh, St. Louis, and Minneapolis-St. Paul.

Still further examination of Figure 2-1 leads us to recognize substantial population clusters in Southeast Asia. It is appropriate to describe these as discrete clusters, for the map confirms that they are actually a set of nuclei rather than a contiguous population concentration. Largest among these nuclei is the Indonesian island of Djawa (Java), with some 75 million inhabitants. Elsewhere in the region, populations cluster in the lowlands of major rivers, some of which came frequently to our attention during the Vietnam conflict, for example the Mekong. Neither these river valleys nor the rural surroundings of the cities have population concentrations comparable to those of either China to the north or India to the west, and under normal circumstances Southeast Asia is able to export rice to its more hungry neighbors. Decades of strife have, however, disrupted the region to such a degree that its productive potential has not been attained.

South America, Africa, and Australia do not sustain population concentrations comparable to those we have considered. Africa's less than 400 million inhabitants cluster in above-average densities in West Africa (where Nigeria has a population of some 82 million) and in a zone in the east extending from Ethiopia to South Africa. Only in North Africa is there an agglomeration comparable to the crowded riverine plains of Asia: the Nile valley and delta with its 36 million residents. Importantly, it is the pattern—not the dimensions—that resembles Asia. As in East and South Asia, the Nile's valley and delta teem with farmers who cultivate every foot of the rich and fertile soil. But the Nile's gift is a miniature compared to its Asian equivalents. The Ganges, Yangtze, and Hwang Rivers' lowlands contain many times the number of inhabitants that manage to eke out a living along the Nile.

South America does not contain population concentrations comparable to those of
East and South Asia, but its cities include slums that are among the world's worst.
The photograph shows a part of a slum development in Rio de Janeiro, Brazil. These
accommodations are by no means the least comfortable in town.

Distribution and Density

The large light-shaded spaces in South America and Australia, and the peripheral distribution of the modest populations of these continents, suggest that here remains space for the world's huge numbers. And indeed, South America could probably sustain more than its present 200 million, as Australia can undoubtedly accommodate more than 13 million. But the population growth rate of South American countries is among the highest in the world, and Australia's environmental limitations hardly qualify that continent as a relief valve for Asia's millions.

In our discussion of world population distribution, we have used population *density* figures as the measure. On the face of it, this is a good index to use when comparing world areas. From each country's national census we obtain the total population. The country's area is a matter of record, and all that is required is to calculate the number of people per unit area (per square mile or kilometer) in the world's countries.

But we already know—and Figure 2-1 reminds us—that the people of any country are not evenly distributed over the national territory. Thus the result of any calculation may be misleading. The United States, with 3,615,122 square miles (9,363,123 square kilometers) has a 1975 population of over 215 million, and its average population density would, therefore, be figured as 59 per square mile (23 per square kilometers). This is the *arithmetic* density of the United States, and this is the figure that appears alongside those enormously high averages for Asian countries such as Bangladesh (1360 per square mile), Japan (751), India (483), and others. These averages do not, however, take account of the internal clustering of people within countries. In the case of the United States, it fails to reflect the emptiness of Alaska, the sparseness of population in much of the West, the concentration of people in the Eastern cities. To take an even clearer example of the misleading nature of average density figures, consider the case of Egypt, with its 39 million inhabitants. As noted earlier, nearly all these people live in the Nile valley and delta. But Egypt's total area is 387,000 square miles, so the average density is just about 100 per square mile. You will agree that this figure is rather meaningless when all those people are crowded onto the Nile's irrigable and cultivable soils and the rest of the country is desert! It has been estimated that 98 percent of Egypt's population occupies just 3 percent of the country's total area.

Can we arrive at a more meaningful index of population density in individual countries? Yes—by relating the total population to the amount of cultivated land in the country rather than its whole area. In those overpopulated Asian countries, after all, it is the productive land that matters, not the dry areas or the inhospitable mountains. Instead of the arithmetic density, we calculate the *physiological* density, the number of people per unit area of productive land. In the case of Egypt, while the arithmetic density is 100, the physiologic density is 3898—nearly 4000 people per cultivable square mile. In Japan the physiologic density is even higher, 4515 per square mile. In Europe, the country with the higher physiologic density is the Netherlands, with the far lower figure of 3048.

Even these calculations are subject to error, however. In every country there are farmlands of different productivity. Some acres produce high crop yields (more than once a year, in many Asian countries), while others are marginal or can sustain only livestock. All these variable levels of production are treated equally in our calculation of physiologic density. Still, the measure is much more useful than the arithmetic density index. Table 2-1 provides an indication of the usefulness of the concept of physiological density. Note, for example, that the United States and Colombia have about the same arithmetic density, but Colombia has a physiologic density more than twice that of the United States. Egypt's arithmetic density of 100 does not look especially high, but its physiologic density tells us what the real situation is in terms of cultivable land and the pressure on it. Argentina is the only country on the list with both a low arithmetic and a low physiologic density, while Iran is one of those countries where the arithmetic density looks quite low—lower than the United States—but the physiologic density is quite high. Also note that India's physiological density, while rather high, is still moderate compared to Japan's and Bangladesh's.

Table 2-1

Country	Population (millions)	Area (000 sq.m.)	Acres/ Capita	Arithmetical Density	Physiological Density
United States	216.0	3615	5.0	59	128
Argentina	27.4	1072	18.0	26	36
Colombia	25.7	440	2.3	58	278
Egypt	39.1	387	0.17	100	3898
Iran	33.5	636	1.5	53	427
Ethiopia	30.3	472	8.0	64	80
Nigeria	60.2	357	2.1	182	305
Japan	110.1	143	0.16	769	4515
Bangladesh	75.1	55	0.19	1360	3368
India	593.0	1262	0.8	469	807

Before returning to the issues associated with the growth of the world's population, we should remind ourselves of a reality that affects all our calculations and figures: the unreliability of the information we are compelled to use. When calculating the arithmetic density of a country, we must depend on population counts that may very well be inaccurate (but at least we can be fairly sure of the country's total area). When it comes to figuring the physiological density, we divide population data of which we are often uncertain and "cultivable area" data about which we are not sure either. Since population problems are so vital to the world's nations and their future, there has been a major effort in the United Nations to help countries organize their census and to increase the effectiveness of data-gathering systems. But taking a census is an expensive business, and countries that cannot even afford enough food cannot be expected to place a very high priority on census accuracy, which is viewed as a costly luxury. And so, in the statistics we have just used and those we will use later, we should realize that many are subject to considerable error.

Growth

If there is reason to doubt the validity of some population statistics, there is no question about another dimension of world population: its accelerating growth. Not only is the world's population growing: the *rate* at which it is growing increases all the time. This is dramatically illustrated when we take a backward look. At the time of the birth of Christ, the world population probably was about 250 million. It took until about 1650 A.D. to reach 500 million. Then, however, the population grew to one billion by 1820, and in 1930 it was two billion. As we said at the beginning of this chapter, it reached four billion early in 1975.

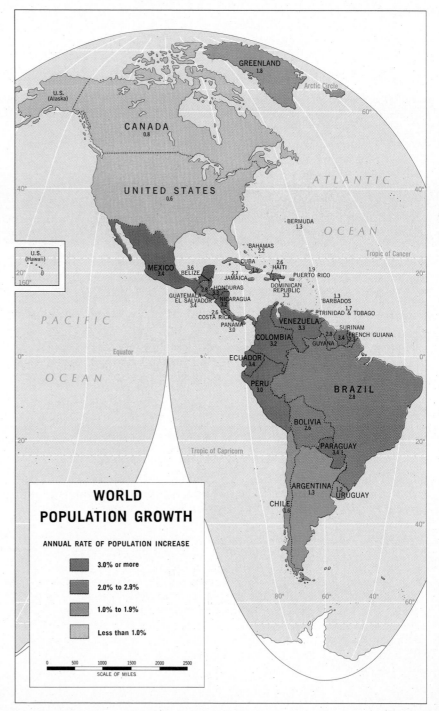

WORLD POPULATION GROWTH

ANNUAL RATE OF POPULATION INCREASE

- 3.0% or more
- 2.0% to 2.9%
- 1.0% to 1.9%
- Less than 1.0%

0 500 1000 1500 2000 2500
SCALE OF MILES

Figure 2-2

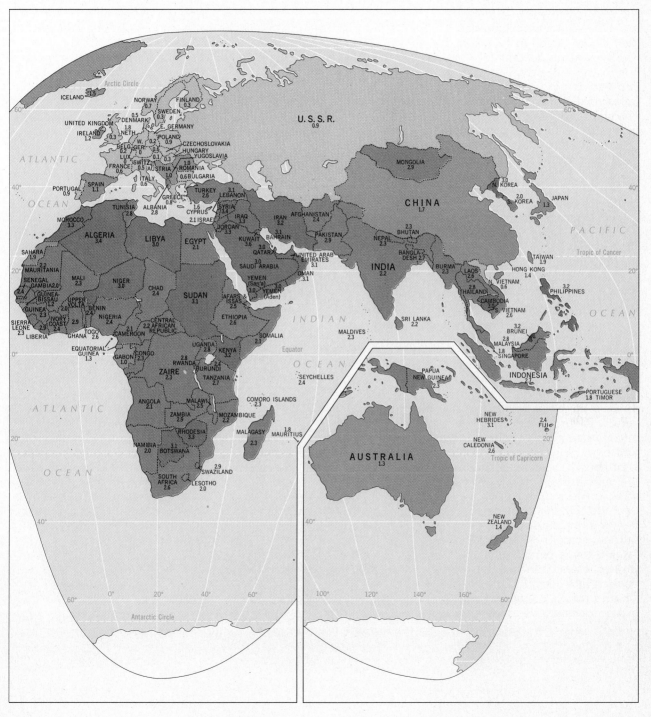

ICELAND 1.5

Arctic Circle

NORWAY 0.7
SWEDEN 0.3
FINLAND 0.3

UNITED KINGDOM 1.8
DENMARK 0.5
E. GERMANY 0.2
IRELAND 1.2
NETH.
BELG. W. GER. 1.0 0.2
POLAND 0.9
CZECHOSLOVAKIA 0.5
LUX.
SWITZ. 0.1
AUSTRIA 0.5
HUNGARY
YUGOSLAVIA
FRANCE 0.6
ITALY 0.6
ROMANIA 1.0
BULGARIA 0.6
PORTUGAL 0.9
SPAIN 1.1
GREECE 0.8
TURKEY 2.6
LEBANON 3.1
TUNISIA 2.8
ALBANIA 2.8
CYPRUS 1.6
SYRIA 3.4
ISRAEL 2.1
IRAQ 3.3
IRAN 3.2
AFGHANISTAN 2.4

MOROCCO 3.3
ALGERIA 3.4
LIBYA 3.0
EGYPT 2.1
JORDAN 3.3
KUWAIT 3.6
BAHRAIN
QATAR 3.0
SAUDI ARABIA 3.0
UNITED ARAB EMIRATES
OMAN 3.1

SAHARA 1.9
MAURITANIA 2.2
SENEGAL 2.4
MALI 2.3
NIGER 3.0
CHAD 2.4
SUDAN 3.1
YEMEN (San'a) 3.0
YEMEN (Aden) 3.0

GAMBIA 2.0
GUINEA-BISSAU 1.7
UPPER VOLTA 2.0
GUINEA 2.3
BENIN 2.4
NIGERIA 2.4
CENTRAL AFRICAN REPUBLIC 2.1
ETHIOPIA 2.6
AFARS & ISSAS 2.5
SOMALIA 2.4

SIERRA LEONE 2.3
IVORY COAST 2.4
GHANA 2.6
TOGO 2.6
CAMEROON 2.2
UGANDA 2.8
KENYA 3.2

LIBERIA
EQUATORIAL GUINEA 1.3
GABON 1.0
CONGO 2.4
ZAIRE 2.3
RWANDA 2.8
BURUNDI 2.4
TANZANIA 2.7

ANGOLA 2.1
ZAMBIA 2.8
MALAWI 2.8
MOZAMBIQUE 2.3
COMORO ISLANDS 2.3

NAMIBIA 2.0
BOTSWANA 2.8
RHODESIA 3.3
MALAGASY 2.3
MAURITIUS 1.8

SOUTH AFRICA 2.6
SWAZILAND 2.9
LESOTHO 2.0

U.S.S.R. 0.9

MONGOLIA 2.9

CHINA 1.7

N. KOREA 3.0
S. KOREA 2.0
JAPAN 1.3

NEPAL 2.3
BHUTAN 2.3
PAKISTAN 2.9
BANGLA-DESH 2.7
INDIA 2.2
BURMA 2.3
LAOS 2.6
N. VIETNAM 0.6
THAILAND 3.1

TAIWAN 1.9
HONG KONG 1.4
CAMBODIA 3.0
S. VIETNAM 2.6
PHILIPPINES 3.2

SRI LANKA 2.2
MALDIVES 2.3

BRUNEI 2.6
MALAYSIA 1.8
SINGAPORE
INDONESIA
PORTUGUESE TIMOR 1.8

SEYCHELLES 2.4

PAPUA NEW GUINEA 2.3

NEW HEBRIDES 3.1
FIJI 2.4
NEW CALEDONIA 2.6

AUSTRALIA 1.3

NEW ZEALAND 1.4

ATLANTIC OCEAN
PACIFIC OCEAN
INDIAN OCEAN
ATLANTIC OCEAN

Tropic of Cancer
Equator
Tropic of Capricorn
Antarctic Circle

27

We can look at these figures in another way. It took nearly 17 centuries for 250 million to become 500 million, but then that 500 million grew to one billion in just 170 years. One billion doubled to two billion in 110 years, and two billion became four billion in only 45 years. The population's *doubling time* at present growth rates is only 35 years. The shorter the doubling time, the higher the rate of population growth. The doubling time has been decreasing steadily, and the growth rate has been rising without letup. This is what mathematicians call *exponential* growth—growth along an upward curve rather than along a straight line (Fig. 2-3).

Importantly, the world's population is not increasing at the same rate in all regions. The overall growth rate, producing a doubling time of 35 years, is 2 percent. But, as Figure 2-2 shows, the population of many Middle and South American countries is growing more rapidly than this, in excess of 3 percent (which produces a doubling time of just 23 years). In Africa, too, a number of countries have very high birth and high growth rates. And the enormously populous countries of South Asia also have growth rates far above the world average. On the low side of the average are many countries in Europe, some of which grow at rates below 1 percent, the United States, Canada, the Soviet Union, and Japan. China's rate of growth, always a matter for speculation since the Chinese have not been liberal

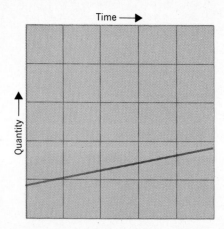

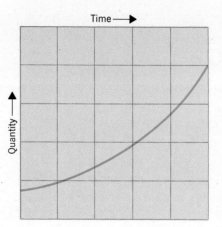

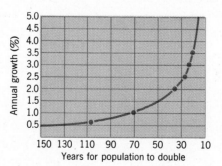

Figure 2-3   Linear or arithmetic growth (top), exponential growth (middle), and doubling time at various growth rates (below).

with information about their country, is estimated to have been 1.7 percent during the period 1950 to 1975. Thus the contribution by the world's various regions to global population growth differs markedly.

Annual population growth is calculated as the number of excess births over deaths recorded during a given year, and usually expressed as a percentage, as on Figure 2-2. In Brazil, for example, the annual growth rate is given as 2.8. The birth rate in Brazil is currently 37 per thousand, and the death rate 9 per thousand. Thus, each year for every thousand Brazilians, there are 28 excess births over deaths, or 2.8 percent. In the United States, the population growth rate in the late 1970s is 0.6 percent, with 15 births per thousand population and 9 deaths. (Figs. 2-4, 2-5.) To compare what these figures mean in terms of doubling time, the doubling time of Brazil's population is just 25; for the United States, it is 116. Some populations are doubling even faster than Brazil's: Mexico, with a population approaching 60 million, has an annual growth rate of 3.4 percent and a doubling time of only 20 years. In just two decades, at present growth rates, there will be twice as many people in Mexico as there are now.

The population explosion on a farmstead in Paraguay: a couple with 14 of their 15 children. The husband is 42, the wife 37; their oldest child is 19, the youngest is 1, and the mother is pregnant.

The Role of Migration

Occasionally a country's annual rate of population growth does not match, exactly, the difference between birth rates and death rates. U.N. statistics often reveal discrepancies that are not attributable to a rounding off of the figures. In such cases, the cause may lie in the movement of people into (or out of) the countries involved. For years, Jewish immigrants have been journeying to Israel to start a new life there. In recent years more than 50,000 Asians, as well as several thousand others, have left Uganda. Cuba has seen a substantial out-migration during the 1960s; Australia has received many thousands of new immigrants.

We will consider the phenomenon of migration in more detail in Chapter 5, but we should take note of the process in the context of population growth and decline as well.

The map of world population growth confronts us with an inescapable reality: the countries with high growth rates tend to be those variously identified as the "have-not" countries, the "underdeveloped" countries, or, more optimistically, as the "developing" countries. These are the world's poorest countries, least able to afford to feed and house additional millions of people. The economic gains made by these countries are all but wiped out by the demands of their mushrooming populations, and reduced growth rates are an essential ingredient in any formula for improvement. As we will see later, high population growth rates form only one element in the overall condition of underdevelopment—but it is the critical one.

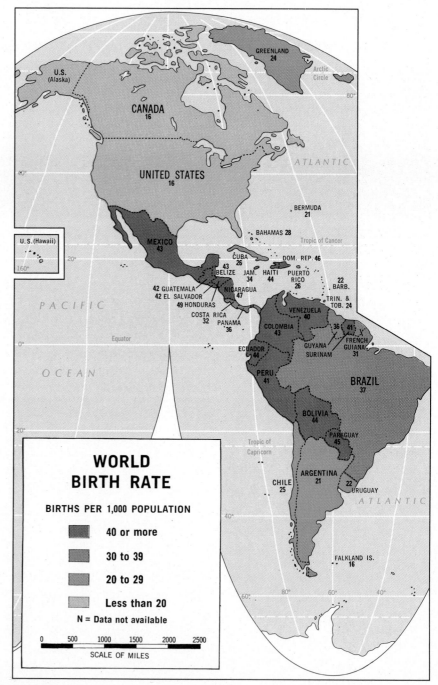

WORLD BIRTH RATE

BIRTHS PER 1,000 POPULATION

- 40 or more
- 30 to 39
- 20 to 29
- Less than 20
- N = Data not available

0 500 1000 1500 2000 2500

SCALE OF MILES

Figure 2-4

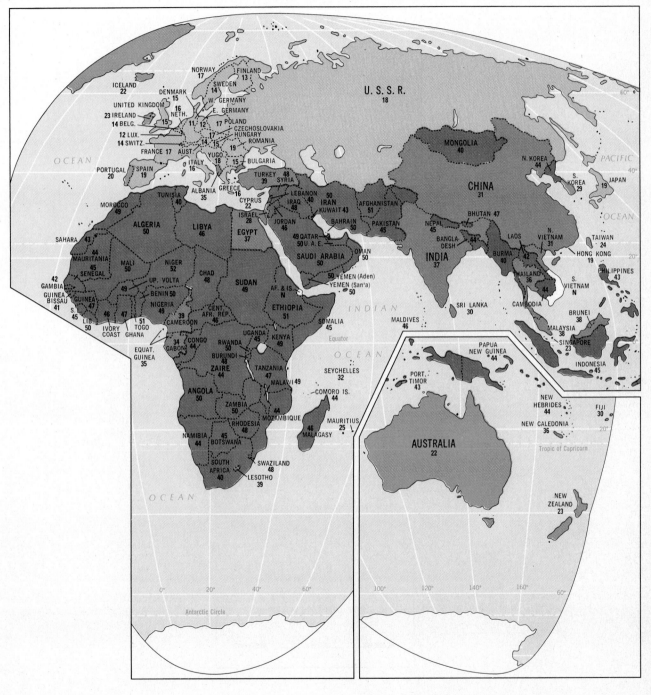

ICELAND
22

NORWAY
17

FINLAND
13

SWEDEN
14

DENMARK
15

W. GERMANY
16

E. GERMANY

UNITED KINGDOM
16

NETH.

23 IRELAND
14 BELG.

POLAND
17

CZECHOSLOVAKIA
17

12 LUX.

11. 12

HUNGARY

14 SWITZ.

14.

ROMANIA

FRANCE 17

AUST.

YUGO.
18

19

U. S. S. R.
18

PORTUGAL
20

SPAIN
19

ITALY
16

15

BULGARIA

MONGOLIA
40

N. KOREA
44

PACIFIC

S.
KOREA
29

JAPAN
19

ALBANIA
35

GREECE
16

TURKEY
39

48

CYPRUS
22

SYRIA

LEBANON

CHINA
31

OCEAN

TUNISIA
40

ISRAEL
28

IRAQ
48

IRAN
40

AFGHANISTAN
51

TAIWAN
24

MOROCCO
49

JORDAN
46

KUWAIT 43

BHUTAN 47

HONG KONG
19

EGYPT
37

BAHRAIN

PAKISTAN
45

NEPAL
45

N.
VIETNAM
31

PHILIPPINES
43

ALGERIA
50

LIBYA
46

49 QATAR
50 U. A. E.

BANGLA-
DESH
44

LAOS

SAHARA
43

SAUDI ARABIA
50

OMAN
50

INDIA
37

BURMA
40

S.
VIETNAM
N

BRUNEI
38

MAURITANIA
44

MALI
50

NIGER
52

CHAD
48

SUDAN
49

YEMEN (Aden)
50

THAILAND
36

44

42
GAMBIA

SENEGAL
45

YEMEN (San'a)
50

CAMBODIA

MALAYSIA
38

GUINEA
BISSAU
41

GUINEA
47

UP. VOLTA
49

BENIN 50

NIGERIA

AF. & IS.
N

SINGAPORE
23

S.
45 LIB.
50

46

47

CENT.
AFR. REP.
46

39

ETHIOPIA
51

SOMALIA
45

INDIAN

MALDIVES
46

INDONESIA
45

IVORY
COAST

51
TOGO
GHANA

CAMEROON

SRI LANKA
30

34

EQUAT.
GUINEA
35

GABON

CONGO
44

RWANDA

UGANDA
45

KENYA
49

Equator

PAPUA
NEW GUINEA
44

BURUNDI
48

OCEAN

ZAIRE
44

TANZANIA
47

SEYCHELLES
32

PORT.
TIMOR
43

ANGOLA
50

MALAWI 49

ZAMBIA
50

44

COMORO IS.
44

NEW
HEBRIDES
44

FIJI
30

RHODESIA
48

MOZAMBIQUE

MAURITIUS
25

NEW CALEDONIA
36

NAMIBIA
44

BOTSWANA
45

46
MALAGASY

AUSTRALIA
22

Tropic of Capricorn

SOUTH
AFRICA
40

SWAZILAND
48

LESOTHO
39

NEW
ZEALAND
23

OCEAN

0°

20°

40°

60°

100°

120°

140°

160°

60°

Antarctic Circle

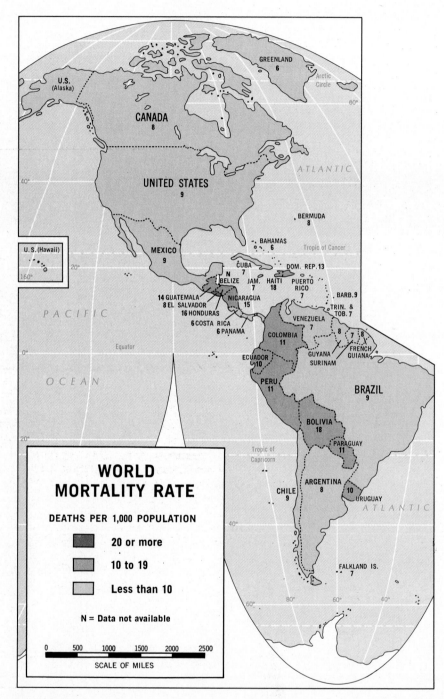

WORLD
MORTALITY RATE

DEATHS PER 1,000 POPULATION

20 or more

10 to 19

Less than 10

N = Data not available

0   500   1000   1500   2000   2500
SCALE OF MILES

Figure 2-5

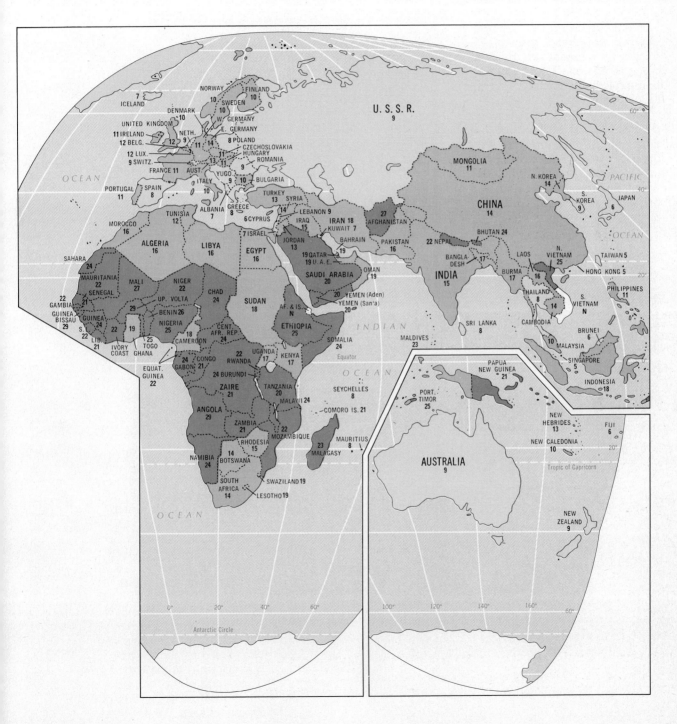

ICELAND 7
NORWAY 10
SWEDEN 10
FINLAND 10
DENMARK 10
UNITED KINGDOM 11
IRELAND 11
BELG. 12
NETH. 9
W. GERMANY 11
E. GERMANY 14
POLAND 8
CZECHOSLOVAKIA 13
HUNGARY
ROMANIA 9
LUX. 12
SWITZ. 9
FRANCE 11
AUST.
YUGO. 9
ITALY 9
BULGARIA 10
PORTUGAL 11
SPAIN 8
ALBANIA 8
GREECE 8
TURKEY 13
SYRIA 14
LEBANON 9
CYPRUS 6
IRAQ 15
ISRAEL 7
IRAN 18
KUWAIT 7
AFGHANISTAN 27
MOROCCO 16
TUNISIA 12
SAHARA
ALGERIA 16
LIBYA 16
EGYPT 16
JORDAN 13
QATAR 19
U.A.E. 19
BAHRAIN
SAUDI ARABIA 20
OMAN 19
YEMEN (Aden) 20
YEMEN (San'a) 20
MAURITANIA 22
MALI 27
NIGER 22
CHAD 24
SUDAN 18
SENEGAL 21
GAMBIA 22
GUINEA BISSAU 29
GUINEA 24
S. 22
LIB. 21
IVORY COAST 25
UP. VOLTA 29
BENIN 26
NIGERIA 25
TOGO 19
GHANA 25
CAMEROON 18
CENT. AFR. REP 24
AF. & IS. N
ETHIOPIA 25
SOMALIA 24
EQUAT. GUINEA 22
GABON 21
CONGO 24
ZAIRE 21
RWANDA
BURUNDI 24
UGANDA 22
KENYA 17
TANZANIA 20
ANGOLA 29
ZAMBIA 21
MALAWI 24
MOZAMBIQUE 22
RHODESIA 15
NAMIBIA 24
BOTSWANA 14
SOUTH AFRICA 14
SWAZILAND 19
LESOTHO 19
MALAGASY 23
MAURITIUS 8
COMORO IS. 21
SEYCHELLES 8
MALDIVES 23
U.S.S.R. 9
MONGOLIA 11
N. KOREA 14
S. KOREA 9
JAPAN 6
CHINA 14
BHUTAN 24
NEPAL 22
BANGLA-DESH 17
INDIA 15
PAKISTAN 16
LAOS
N VIETNAM 25
TAIWAN 5
HONG KONG 5
BURMA 17
THAILAND 8
S. VIETNAM 14
CAMBODIA
PHILIPPINES 11
BRUNEI 6
MALAYSIA 10
SINGAPORE 5
INDONESIA 18
SRI LANKA 8
PAPUA NEW GUINEA 21
PORT. TIMOR 25
NEW HEBRIDES 13
NEW CALEDONIA 10
FIJI 6
AUSTRALIA 9
NEW ZEALAND 9

Equator
INDIAN OCEAN
PACIFIC OCEAN
OCEAN
Tropic of Capricorn
Antarctic Circle

0° 20° 40° 60° 100° 120° 140° 160°
60° 40° 20°

Exploding Populations

It is not surprising that the rate of world population growth during the present century has come to be called the "population explosion," for the process is indeed rapid, still quickening, uncontrollable, threatening, and expansive. Consider the implications of Figure 2-6: from the dawn of history to 1975 the world population grew to four billion. The next four billion, at present growth rates, will be added in 35 years.

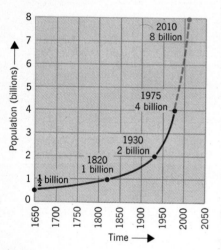

Figure 2-6

Some Demographic Shorthand

CBR *Crude Birth Rate*	The number of births (given per thousand or as a percentage) for the total population.
NRR *Net Reproduction Rate*	Index that reflects the number of female births against the number of potential mothers in a population (women aged 15 to 45). Below 1.0, the rate indicates a reduction in the number of potential mothers in future generations (and hence a future slow-down in population growth). Over 1.0, an increase in the number of potential mothers signals a higher future growth rate.
ZPG *Zero Population Growth*	Both a concept and a slogan. Technically, zero population growth would involve a condition of stability and a "growth rate" of 0.0, deaths per thousand per year matching births. "ZPG" became the name of an activist organization formed in 1969 by a group of concerned citizens including the biologist Paul Ehrlich, author of *The Population Bomb* (1968). ZPG's rapid growth (it counted 10,000 members after just one year of existence) reflects the growing awareness of the negative consequences of crowding on our planet.

34

As Figure 2-6 reveals, the 1650 population was only about 500 million; not until 1820 did the world accommodate one billion inhabitants. Even then, a century and a half ago, there were scientists who realized that the world was headed for trouble. The most prominent among these was Thomas Malthus, an English economist who sounded the alarm as early as 1798 in an article entitled *An Essay on the Principle of Population as It Affects the Future Improvement of Society*. In this essay, Malthus reported that population in England was increasing faster than the means of subsistence; he described population growth as geometric and the growth of the means of subsistence as arithmetic (see Fig. 2-3). Inevitably, he argued, population growth would be checked by hunger. Malthus' essay caused a storm of criticism and debate, and between 1803 and 1826 he revised it several times. He never wavered from his basic position, however, and continued to predict that the gap between the population's requirements and the soil's productive capacity would ultimately lead to hunger, famines, and the cessation of population growth.

We know now that Malthus was wrong about several things. The era of colonization and migration vastly altered the whole pattern of world production and consumption, and worldwide distribution systems made possible the transportation of food from one region of the world to another. Malthus could not have

foreseen this; nor was he correct about the arithmetic growth of food production. Expanded acreages, improved seed strains, and better farming techniques have produced geometric increases in world food production, but Malthus was correct in his prediction that the gap between need and production would widen. It has—and there are areas in the world in the 1970s where population growth rates are being checked in the way he predicted, as famines claim the lives of hundreds of thousands in Africa and Asia.

Even today there are scholars and specialists who adhere essentially to Malthus' position, modified, of course, by modern knowledge and experience. These people are sometimes referred to as prophets of doom by those who take a more optimistic view of the future. They are also called neo-Malthusians, tying their concerns to those of that farsighted Englishman who first warned that there are limits to this earth's capacity to sustain our human numbers.

Demographic Cycles

In view of the prospects we have so far encountered, how can anyone confront the population question with any optimism? Part of the answer, again, lies in the map (Fig. 2-2). Note that the countries whose rate of population growth is comparatively low are those we call the "have" countries—the rich, "developed" countries, including the United States, Europe, the Soviet Union, and Australia. These countries, however, did not always have such low rates of population growth. They, too, went through a period of explosive growth, until the rate began to level off for many reasons associated with the processes of development: industrialization, urbanization, modernization in general. We will view this phenomenon of development in more detail later, but those optimists who see declining world population growth rates argue that the explosive increases of today are only temporary stages that will be followed by lowering birth rates as development takes hold everywhere. Besides, they say, the world still has potential for vastly increased food production, and all that is needed is greater investment in research on agriculture and improved world food distribution systems. On a television program on October 27, 1974, U.S. Secretary of Agriculture Earl Butz denied that a world food crisis existed as yet.

Figure 2-6 indicates that it took countless centuries for the earth's human population to reach one-half billion; the unprecedented population explosion really began during the nineteenth century and is now climaxing during the twentieth. What kept population growth so slow before the nineteenth century? Famines, epidemics, and plagues periodically ravaged peoples everywhere to such a degree that populations in some regions actually declined for certain periods. That curved line on Figure 2-6, prior to 1820 or so, is really an average of many ups and downs. In Europe during the middle years of the fourteenth century, the bubonic plague struck and killed fully one-quarter of the population, nearly half of the people in England. When the Europeans reached the Americas and introduced their diseases to the Indian peoples, millions of them died, having no natural defenses against the white man's ills. In India and China there are records of fearful famines during

Thomas Robert Malthus was born in 1766 on the Surrey (England) estate owned by his father. He went to private schools and entered Cambridge University's Jesus College. Early in his career he pursued theology, and his first job was as clergyman at the parish of Albury in Surrey. But even during that beginning period of his career he was already at work on his famous *Essay*. Its first version appeared just one year after his Albury appointment. The *Essay* gained considerable notoriety, and soon Malthus was writing and lecturing so much that he decided to leave the clergy. In 1805 he took a job that was more appropriate to his interests: professor of modern history and political economy at the Haileybury College, an institution financed and operated by the East India Company.

Malthus did have his critics. One of them was Karl Marx, who suggested that the poverty of the masses foreseen by Malthus had less to do with their growing numbers than with the capitalist system governing them. Far from supporting the idea that population growth be limited, Marx wanted to alter the control and use of the country's natural resources by taking them from the hands of the few and distributing them among the many. Charles Darwin, on the other hand, related Malthus' concept of the struggle for existence to his principle of the survival of the fittest, and he acknowledged that Malthus had contributed to his theory of evolution.

Malthus died at Haileybury in 1834.

the eighteenth and nineteenth centuries. And, of course, wars took their toll also. Birthrates during these centuries were high, but death rates were high as well. Frequently there were more deaths than live births, and population numbers decreased—an almost unheard of phenomenon these days.

The second half of the eighteenth century brought the beginnings of permanent change in this sequence of ups and downs. In Europe, the agricultural revolution had begun, with improved farming techniques, increased yields, and better storage and distribution facilities. Then the Industrial Revolution began to wipe out the old Europe as well. Sanitation facilities made the cities and towns safer from the epidemics that used to ravage them; disease prevention through vaccination introduced a whole new era in public health. Soap became generally

available. Soon, death rates began to decline markedly. Before the mid-eighteenth century, death rates probably averaged about 35 per 1000 (with births averaging under 40), but by the middle of the nineteenth century death rates in Europe were around 16. Consider what this means in terms of growth rate: if in 1750 the birthrate was 39 and the death rate 35 per thousand, then the natural increase was 4 per thousand or 0.4 percent. In 1850 births were still high, perhaps 36 per thousand, but the death rate was down to 16. Thus the natural increase was at a rate of 2.0 percent. In terms of doubling time, Europe went from 150 years in 1750 to only 35 years in 1850.

But when we look again at Figure 2-2, we note that Europe's countries today are by no means growing at 2.0 percent; many are not even growing at 1.0 percent. What has become of those high growth rates of the late nineteenth century? Let us examine the sequence of events in the United Kingdom, where fairly reliable statistics were kept from quite early times. In the period before the Industrial Revolution, birth and death rates were both high, as reflected by Stage 1, Figure 2-7. Then, as Britain industrialized and urbanized, and as health and medical facilities improved, the death rate began a sharp decline, carrying it far below the birthrate, as in Stage 2. This, of course, produced an increasing growth rate (*A*), leading to a period of explosive growth (*B*). However, the birthrate also began to decline

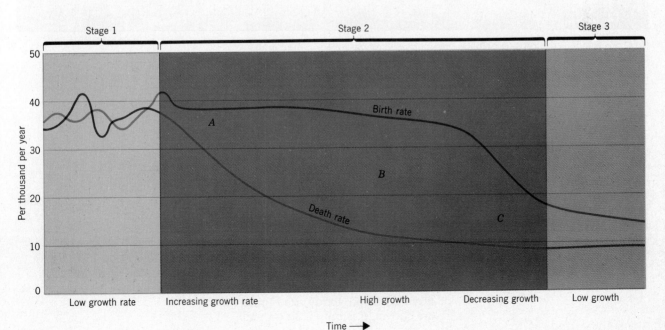

Figure 2-7

Nowhere is India's explosive population growth more strongly reflected than in the country's teeming, congested cities. The scene shown here is from Poona.

as the United Kingdom modernized during period (C), leading to sharply reduced growth rates. Finally, population growth rates are once again low during Stage 3, the stage in which the United Kingdom finds itself today.

In terms of real figures, the period from 1750 to about 1900, illustrated by Figure 2-7, saw the population of the United Kingdom grow from about 6.5 million to 35 million. Since shortly after the beginning of the twentieth century, growth rates have declined; today, as Figure 2-3 shows, it is only 0.3 percent.

Here we have one of those reasons for the optimism of some population experts: on the basis of examples such as this, they predict that eventually all countries will experience declines in their population growth rates, and that the present explosion is but a temporary phase—just as the one in England was. When the underdeveloped countries progress toward development, they reason, population growth rates will go down. It may take time, but the world population will stabilize.

Several indicators suggest that we should approach such optimistic predictions with caution. First, the population in Britain when the rapid-growth stage began was well under 10 million. Two doubling periods still produce only 40 million on this base. But the present population totals in countries such as Mexico, Nigeria, Bangladesh, and India are of a very different order. In two doubling periods, Mexico and Nigeria would go from 60 to 240 million, Bangladesh from 75 to 300, India from 600 to 2400 million. "Exploding" Europe never experienced such increases.

Second, there is a real question whether development will ever be possible in some countries. Here is how biologists Paul and Anne Ehrlich view the situation in their book *Population, Resources, Environment* (1970):

Look for a moment at the situation in those nations that most of us prefer to label with the euphemism "underdeveloped," but which might just as accurately be described as "hungry." In general underdeveloped countries (UDCs) differ from developed countries (DCs) in a number of ways. UDCs are not industrialized. They tend to have inefficient, usually subsistence agricultural systems, extremely low gross national products and per capita incomes, high illiteracy rates, and incredibly high rates of population growth . . . most of these countries will never, under conceivable circumstances, be "developed" in the sense in which the United States is today. They could quite accurately be called "never-to-be-developed" countries. . . .

Thus the European model may be irrelevant to many countries, and if we wait for the cure of development to solve the world population crisis, we may do so in vain.

Third, there looms the frightening prospect that the world population crisis may become an issue in ideological struggles. At the Bucharest Conference of 1974, the representative from China argued that Western-led efforts to stem the tide of population growth constitute a plot to deprive the developing countries of the one area in which they have strength, that is, population numbers. He urged developing countries not to follow advice from the developed world in the adoption of policies designed to reduce the growth rate. If the attack on the world population crisis is blunted by disunity, our prospects are bleak indeed. We repeat: there may be long-range grounds for optimism, but at present there is no effective machinery to defuse the population "bomb."

3 Population and Nutrition

We live in a society in which advertising space for weight reduction clinics and various remedies for obesity exceeds that given to
reports about the prevailing condition of this world's inhabitants,
their malnutrition. We occasionally see a magazine article about
an especially severe famine, such as the one afflicting the African
Sahel in the early 1970s, but hunger, to most of us, is an unknown, remote experience.

Nevertheless, we live in a world where malnutrition is commonplace. Even in this modern decade of the 1970s, hundreds of millions of people are afflicted from childhood until death by gnawing
hunger, incomplete mental and physical development, lack of energy, and susceptibility to diseases. Even in the United States, the
richest large country in the world, there are people who go hungry.
Go to a government food-stamp office in a large city on the first
day of any month and people in those seemingly endless lines will
tell you that they and their families ran out of food before the end
of the last month, and that three well-balanced meals per day is
the exception rather than the rule for their children.

Adequate nutrition is not only a matter of eating enough food.
The diet must also be balanced, and in large parts of the world
that balance is lacking. A balanced diet includes carbohydrates
(derived from staples such as rice, corn, wheat, and potatoes), proteins (from meat, poultry, fish, eggs, and dairy products), vitamins
(from fruits and vegetables as well as other sources), fats, and minerals. Proteins, a critical element in the diet, also are derived from
plant sources, including soybeans, peas, peanuts, and wheat. The
amount of food intake is measured in terms of calories, which are
units of energy production in the body. It is impossible to generalize
about the number of calories we need without adding many qualifi-
cations. People in desk jobs need fewer calories than people
engaged in manual labor. Young adults need more calories than
old persons or children. People of large stature require more calo-

41

ries than smaller people. Men
need more calories, on the
average, than women. But even
with these considerations taken
into account, it is clear that there
are whole countries whose populations are badly underfed. The
per person daily calorie intake
in the United States, Canada,
Australia, and New Zealand exceeds 3100, but in India, the Philippines, Ethiopia, and
Ecuador—to identify just a few
among many countries—the
average is under 2360 calories.
This figure, 2360 calories, is
given as the minimum daily requirement by the Food and Agricultural Organization (FAO) of
the United Nations. Actually,
even 2500 calories is a pretty
meager intake, but, if we can
rely on official published figures,
about half of the people of the
world survive on fewer calories
than this.

The situation would not be
so bad if the people who must survive on too little food could at
least have a balanced diet. But
they are not so fortunate. With
few exceptions, the countries
where there is a low calorie intake are also the countries
where protein is in short supply.
Recent studies have indicated
that the first six months of life
are critical in this respect: inadequate protein intake can damage brain and body for life. And
the food sources that are richest
in proteins, meat, fish, dairy
products, are all too often in
short supply where they are
most needed. It takes food to
raise the animals that produce
meat, and that food cannot be

Figure 3-1

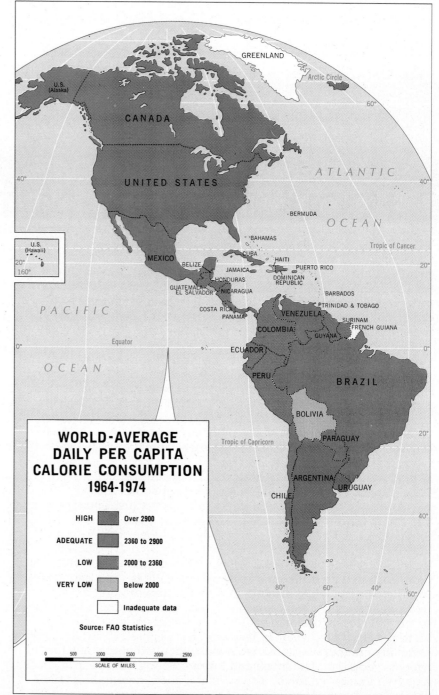

WORLD-AVERAGE
DAILY PER CAPITA
CALORIE CONSUMPTION
1964-1974

HIGH   Over 2900

ADEQUATE 2360 to 2900

LOW   2000 to 2360

VERY LOW Below 2000

          Inadequate data

Source: FAO Statistics

0   500   1000   1500   2000   2500
SCALE OF MILES

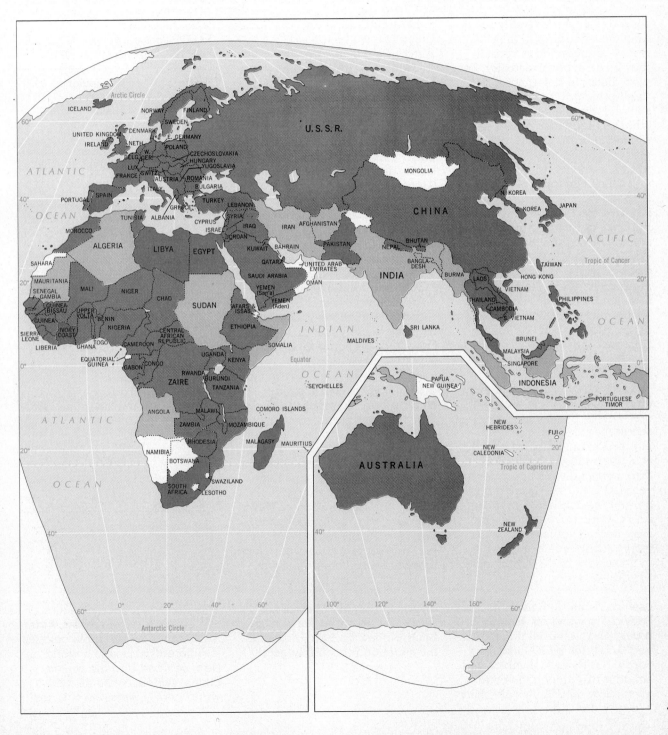

ATLANTIC OCEAN

ICELAND
NORWAY FINLAND
SWEDEN
UNITED KINGDOM DENMARK
IRELAND NETH. E. GERMANY
BELG. W. POLAND
GER.
LUX. CZECHOSLOVAKIA
FRANCE SWITZ. HUNGARY
AUSTRIA YUGOSLAVIA
PORTUGAL SPAIN ITALY ROMANIA
BULGARIA
TUNISIA GREECE TURKEY LEBANON
MOROCCO ALBANIA CYPRUS SYRIA
ISRAEL IRAQ IRAN AFGHANISTAN
ALGERIA LIBYA EGYPT JORDAN
KUWAIT BAHRAIN PAKISTAN
SAHARA QATAR UNITED ARAB
MAURITANIA SAUDI ARABIA EMIRATES
SENEGAL MALI NIGER YEMEN OMAN
GAMBIA (San'a)
GUINEA- CHAD YEMEN
BISSAU UPPER SUDAN (Aden)
GUINEA VOLTA BENIN AFARS &
SIERRA NIGERIA ISSAS
LEONE IVORY CENTRAL ETHIOPIA
LIBERIA COAST GHANA TOGO AFRICAN
CAMEROON REPUBLIC SOMALIA
EQUATORIAL UGANDA
GUINEA GABON CONGO KENYA
ZAIRE RWANDA
BURUNDI
TANZANIA
ANGOLA MALAWI
ZAMBIA MOZAMBIQUE
RHODESIA MALAGASY MAURITIUS
NAMIBIA
BOTSWANA
SWAZILAND
SOUTH LESOTHO
AFRICA

U.S.S.R.

MONGOLIA
N. KOREA
S. KOREA JAPAN
CHINA
BHUTAN TAIWAN
NEPAL HONG KONG
BANGLA- BURMA LAOS
DESH VIETNAM
INDIA THAILAND
CAMBODIA
S. VIETNAM PHILIPPINES
SRI LANKA
MALDIVES BRUNEI
MALAYSIA
SINGAPORE
SEYCHELLES INDONESIA
PORTUGUESE
TIMOR

COMORO ISLANDS

PAPUA
NEW GUINEA

NEW
HEBRIDES
FIJI
NEW
CALEDONIA

AUSTRALIA

NEW
ZEALAND

Arctic Circle
60°
40°
20°
Equator
20°
40°
60°
Antarctic Circle

Tropic of Cancer
Tropic of Capricorn

PACIFIC OCEAN
INDIAN OCEAN
ATLANTIC OCEAN

0° 20° 40° 60°
100° 120° 140° 160°

spared; fish is not readily available either in distant, interior areas, and canned or dried it may be an expensive luxury. People's diets are determined by three principal factors: what the soil and climate can produce, what the economic circumstances are, and what the people's traditions are. There are places in the world where certain taboos limit people's access to the meat products that might improve their dietary imbalance, but most of all it is a shortage of surplus feed that creates the barrier. The result is that even persons whose calorie intake is marginally adequate are actually malnourished. There is "hidden hunger" even in the areas identified as "Adequate Calories" (Fig. 3-1).

The map of daily average calorie consumption in the world's countries in recent years (Fig. 3-1) is based on data that are not always reliable, so it should be taken as a general impression only. Published statistical information about calorie intake, especially for the underdeveloped countries, is often based on estimates rather than accurate counts. Nevertheless, the map reveals rather clearly the world distribution of hunger and malnutrition. In the Americas, the United States, Canada, Uruguay, and Argentina are best fed; Haiti, El Salvador, and Bolivia are worst off. Mexico, Brazil, and Venezuela have adequate calories by FAO standards, but Peru, Colombia, and Ecuador are among the countries below the FAO-established

minimum. Europe and the Soviet Union are well supplied, but in Africa not a single country in the decade 1964–1974 reached the European standard (Egypt came closest). In fact, all but six countries in Africa were below FAO minimum standards, and five were in the lowest possible category . Our map depicts averages for the decade, but the drought in Africa's Sahel during the early 1970s caused even lower food supplies than normal for those poor countries. Late in 1974 the FAO identified the following African countries as being in a food crisis: Upper Volta, Niger, Mali, Chad, Mauritania, and Senegal (the Sahel countries), and Somalia, Angola (both shown on our map as inadequately fed) as well as Tanzania. Regional famine was occurring in Ethiopia.

In Asia, Figure 3-1 reveals, a whole tier of countries including Iran, Afghanistan, India, Bangladesh, Burma, and Indonesia, have a per-capita daily consumption of calories below 2000. In addition, the Philippines faced a food crisis in 1974; together these countries account for nearly one billion people. This is the world's worst hunger zone. Very few Asian countries are in the "adequate calories" category; those that are better off, such as Thailand, Japan, and China, are still below the 2360-calorie level. Only in the Malaysian sector of Borneo, in Taiwan, in South Korea, and in Pakistan is the situation reasonably good.

Table 3-1 Average Daily Calorie Consumption in Selected Countries (1964–1974)

High Calories	New Zealand	3330
	United States	3290
	United Kingdom	3180
	Soviet Union	3180
	Argentina	3160
	Romania	3010
	Italy	2940
Adequate Calories	Brazil	2820
	South Africa	2730
	Taiwan	2620
	Mexico	2570
	Cuba	2500
	Venezuala	2490
	Costa Rica	2370
FAO Minimum for Adequate Nutrition 2360 Calories		
Low Calories	Peru	2340
	Nigeria	2290
	Thailand	2220
	Colombia	2190
	Tanzania	2140
	Zaire	2040
	Laos	2000
Very low Calories	Bolivia	1980
	Algeria	1950
	India	1940
	Iran	1890
	Somali Republic	1770
	Haiti	1720
	Indonesia	1700

Source: FAO statistics.

Table 3-1 reveals how wide is the range of available calories in different parts of the world. In New Zealand and the United States, people consume food worth nearly twice the calories available to people in Haiti and Indonesia. Again, the table should be read with caution. All seven countries in the "High Calories" category have a combined population of the same magnitude of that of India (Very Low Calories) alone. It is worth comparing Figure 3-1 and Table 3-1 to the map of world population distribution, Figure 2-1. Malnutrition is the rule, not the exception in this world.

It is especially tragic that undernutrition and malnutrition affect so many of the world's children. A child's brain grows to about 80 percent of its adult size in the first three years of life, and an adequate supply of protein is crucial in this development. If there is not enough protein, brain growth is inhibited and mental capacities are permanently impaired. There can be no subsequent recovery of the loss. Both mental capacity and physical growth are adversely affected by inadequate nutrition, and so the unfortunate youngster born into an environment of deprivation faces a lifelong handicap. United Nations experts report that vitamin-A deficiency is a principal cause of blindness in India, Indonesia, Bangladesh, Vietnam, the Philippines, Northeastern Brazil, and El Salvador.

In Eastern Asia alone, some 100,000 children go blind every year.

We return again to the world distribution of health and disease in the next chapter, but in order to understand the nature of the impact of world hunger we should examine not only the present and future distribution of world population (as we did in Chapter 2), but also the *structure* of populations in various countries and regions, for this reveals much about the position of various groups (children and oldsters, for example) in each.

The structure of a population involves the number of people in various age groups, and it is represented by an age-sex pyramid. The age-sex pyramid for India in 1970 (Fig. 3-2) shows how great is the number of chil-

Figure 3-2   Age-sex pyramid for India, 1970.

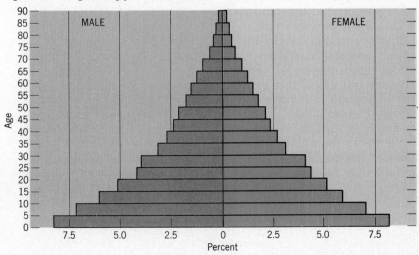

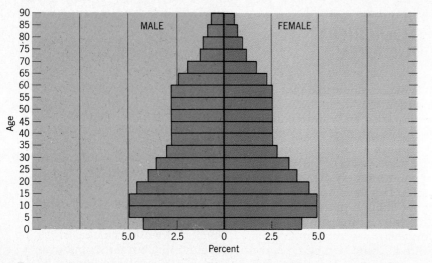

Figure 3-3 Age-sex pyramid for the United States, 1970.

dren in the lowest three age categories (0–4, 5–9, 10–14) compared to people in the older groups. In an age-sex pyramid such as that shown in Figure 3-2, males are customary recorded to the left of the center line, females to the right. India's population structure as reflected by Figure 3-2 reveals a rapid rate of population growth. India in 1972 still had a birthrate of 37 per thousand and a death rate of 15; fully 42 percent of all India's 600 million people are under 15 years old. Mexico, whose age-sex pyramid has a structure quite similar to India's, has 48 percent of its population below 15 years of age. Families in countries such as Mexico and India are large, with five to six children per couple the average.

When family size decreases, and with it the overall population growth rate, the age-sex pyramid shows lower percentages in the younger age groups, as in the case of the United States (Fig. 3-3). This pyramid, for 1970, reveals the baby "boom" after the end of World War II (the step-like increase below the stable "waist" of the pyramid). Then, beginning in the late 1950s, the increase levels off, and the most recent category (0–4 years, born 1966–1970) shows a decline. Compared to the population structure of India, note how much greater is the percentage of older people in the United States.

When, therefore, we see that there is hunger and malnutrition in India, in Bangladesh, in Ethiopia, and in the Sahel, we know that it is the children who are hungry—the children who cannot fend for themselves and

the old people who no longer can do so. And the young children and the old people make up a huge percentage of the populations of countries that are under the stress of the population explosion. In 1974, an estimated 10 million people died of starvation, most of them children; nearly 500 million people faced the threat of starvation in the near future.

When drought and famine struck the Sahel, no coordinated relief programs existed. Planes were sent to drop bags of food, which burst open upon impact; people crowded on the desert surface to collect the scattered beans.

47

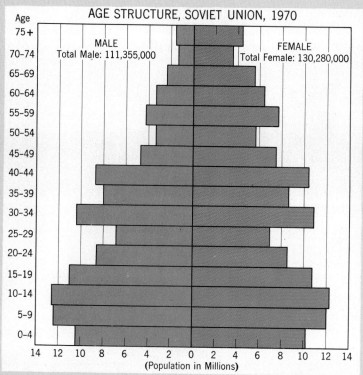

AGE STRUCTURE, SOVIET UNION, 1970

MALE
Total Male: 111,355,000

FEMALE
Total Female: 130,280,000

(Population in Millions)

Figure 3-3

Consider this highly irregular population pyramid for the Soviet Union (1970) in the context of what you know of that country's turbulent past. Note how disproportionately few males there are over 44 years of age, especially in the 50–54 category (the Revolution). Major population loss is also evident, and on both sides of the line, in the 25–29 age category (World War II). The most recent decline in the two-lowest age groups relates to the reduction in the number of females in the 20–29 age groups, and to the country's growing urbanization and industrialization. Also, Soviet authorities have in recent years phased out the campaign for large families, started after the heavy losses of World War II.

Hunger as a Regional Phenomenon

As Figure 3-1 indicated, some of the world's countries suffer severely from malnutrition while others still enjoy comparative plenty. In South America, for example, Bolivia has been chronically malnourished, but Brazil, right next door, has been adequately fed. In Asia, India suffers while China manages. If you took a trip eastward from Western Europe, you would find the food situation getting steadily worse. Patches of malnutrition occur in Eastern Europe (where Albania is poorly fed), it gets worse still in the Middle East and Iran. India's position is again poorer, but the most severely afflicted country is Bangladesh.

Our map (Fig. 3-1) shows the situation as it averaged out over the decade of 1964–1974 when recorded country by country. Groups of countries in Africa and Asia were hungry, and individual countries in Middle and South America. What the map does not show is that regions within countries are also hungry, even though the average for the country conceals that reality. In Brazil, for example, the northeast always is badly malnourished, and sometimes the scene of devastating famines. In 1877, a drought and consequent famine cost an estimated half million people their

48

lives. Even now, a century later, Brazil's interior Northeast still remains an area where calorie consumption is insufficient, protein availability is inadequate, and malnutrition takes its heavy toll. But go to the large cities of southeastern Brazil, and there the situation is far different, and more like that in the better-fed countries of the world.

Regional hunger is a reality even in India. Malnutrition, hunger, and starvation are much more severe in eastern India, in the region that merges into Bangladesh, than they are in the Punjab, to the west. If you were to arrive in Delhi and travel about the city, you would see large areas of poor housing and ill-fed and poorly clothed people. But if you next went to Calcutta, the horror of starvation and poverty would obliterate all you saw in Delhi. The Punjab is India's major region of economic development, and optimistic projections for India's future hold that when that development extends across the majority of the country, the population crisis will begin to recede. But it is difficult to be optimistic after seeing the hopeless masses of people that crowd Calcutta's slums.

Daily they struggle in from the city's surrounding countryside, unable to find food on the land and hoping for help at the government's food kitchens. Endlessly they stand in line for a daily bowl of gruel. Many never make it to the city, and die along the way. And yet, even in Calcutta there are waiters serving martinis before steak lunches in good hotels, and there is waste.

Make no mistake; regional hunger is not a monopoly of the poorest underdeveloped countries. Brazil is not poor, nor is the United States, and even here in North America there are pockets of people who are not fed well enough. Compared to those who die in the streets of Calcutta, or along the roadways of Bangladesh, we do not see real hunger. But even in the United States there is malnutrition. Hundreds of thousands of families cannot afford to spend on food what would be required to balance daily diets adequately. People surviving on food stamp allocations often run out of food before the next allotment is made, and the matter of dietary balance hardly comes up. Inflation has downgraded the nourishment of millions of people. It was recently estimated that nearly 15 percent of all the pet food made in the United States was eaten by people, not cats and dogs, as the cheapest way to add some meat to the diet. In the United States the regional contrasts are not as sharp as they are in Brazil or India, but there are regional differences in nutrition nevertheless. A map of the distribution of income per family is a good guide to where the people are eating well—but our regional hunger is also in regions of cities, in ghettos and slums.

The luxury of an American supermarket: anomaly in a hungry world.

We in North America are quite used to visiting supermarkets where there are potatoes from Idaho, oranges from Florida, cereals from the Midwest, and plenty of products from other countries—bananas, raisins, beef, and so on. Thus it is difficult to comprehend the factors that maintain the regional concentrations of hunger in the world. If Southeast Brazil is better fed than the Northeast, why not distribute the food differently so the Northeast is better fed? How can one part of India be reasonably well fed while people die in the streets in another area of the same country? One huge problem is exactly that: getting the food to the people who need it most immediately and urgently. When hunger and starvation overcame the people of Africa's Sahel, there simply was not the necessary distribution system to get relief supplies to the people. Airplanes were used to drop bags of grain to people far removed from highways, roads, and trucks. But no armada of planes could bring enough food to the people, the cost was enormous, the loss factor high, and many people simply found themselves too far from where the planes brought the supplies, and never saw the food.

Even when the machinery for distribution exists, the failure rate is high. Let us follow a short ton (2000 pounds) of wheat from a Midwestern farm, destined for people near a village in the countryside some miles from Calcutta. First, the grain is harvested and put in storage. If you have traveled through Kansas and other Midwestern states, you have seen those huge, high

Chaos and loss in the distribution of food to hungry countries: broken bags, too many feet, ineffective organization. Dacca, Bangladesh.

storage facilities whose combined contents make up the reserves with which we and other peoples have to reckon. From those storage facilities, the grain is sold on the market to India, a big buyer of this commodity on the world's markets wherever it is available. Next, our ton of grain is taken by railroad car to the port, where it is transferred to a freighter for the month-long journey to Calcutta's docks. At this point a few pounds may have been lost in the transfers, but our ton of grain is still essentially intact. Now, however, serious losses begin. In Calcutta, the grain is stored in large sheds that are often leaky and wet and frequently overrun with rats. Between them, the rats and the moisture can destroy as much as 400 pounds of each arriving ton of grain—sometimes more, depending not only on the conditions of storage but also on the length of time it lies there, awaiting removal. Eventually, the remainder of our ton of grain is loaded on a train or a truck and transported to a distribution

51

point in a town some distance from Calcutta. There, it is once again unloaded and stored. Some of it is now sold to consumers in the town, and some is again transported away, this time to a village grain shop, with accompanying loss (theft becomes a factor too). What remains of the ton of grain—less than half of it, perhaps only a quarter—reaches that village, but it is far too little by now to save the people for whom it was most urgently bought (Fig. 3-4).

Various grains—rice, wheat, corn, and others—produce about 53 percent of the world's food supply by direct consumption. Additional amounts of grains are fed to livestock and thus indirectly consumed. (Thus the distinction is drawn between the *food* grains and the *feed* grains). In the United States and Canada, we consume as much as one ton of grains per person per year, but only 150 pounds of this comes to the table in the form of bread or cereal. All the rest is consumed indirectly, in the form of meat and dairy products. In the food-poor countries, on the other hand, only about 400 pounds of grains, less than one-fifth the U.S. supply, is available for each person. Obviously, little of this meager amount can be spared for livestock raising. As a result, dairy products and meat are in short supply in the food-poor countries, and protein deficiencies compound poor nourishment. Comparing the situation in another way, it takes five times as much soil, water, and fertilizer to sustain a person in the United States as it does to feed someone in India, Ghana, or Peru. And the wealthier a nation gets, the greater its demands on the food market. In the United States, people were eating an average of 55 pounds of beef in 1940. In 1974, Americans consumed more than twice as many pounds. The consumption of poultry nearly tripled over the same period. Consider the increased investment in livestock in terms of feed grains to meet this demand—feed grains that could have been food grains available for export to hungry regions of the world!

Figure 3-4

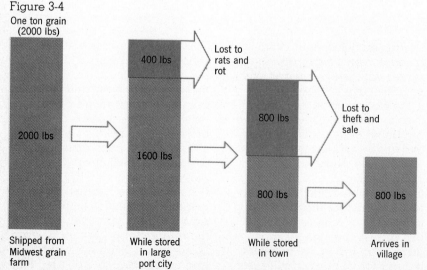

One ton grain
(2000 lbs)

2000 lbs

Shipped from Midwest grain farm

400 lbs

Lost to rats and rot

1600 lbs

While stored in large port city

800 lbs

Lost to theft and sale

800 lbs

While stored in town

800 lbs

Arrives in village

Regional to Global Hunger

In years past, you rarely heard expressed the concern that the world might be running out of food. A few scholars and specialists made dark predictions, but our general attention remained focused on other issues, such as Vietnam and the Middle East. But the decade of the 1970s brought the global food situation sharply into focus. It was not simply a passing phase, a temporary worsening of a condition we had always known afflicted parts of this earth. A combination of circumstances produced a world food crisis of truly unprecedented magnitude and uncertain implications. Terms such as "sea of hunger" came into use, and in November, 1974 the first World Food Conference was convened in Rome, Italy, to face the rising food crisis and to devise ways to cope with it.

Certainly a comparison of Figures 3-1 and 3-5 produces an alarming picture. In the mid-1970s Africa's regions of hunger coalesced into nearly continentwide malnutrition and large zones of famine and starvation, not only in the Sahel but on

Figure 3-5

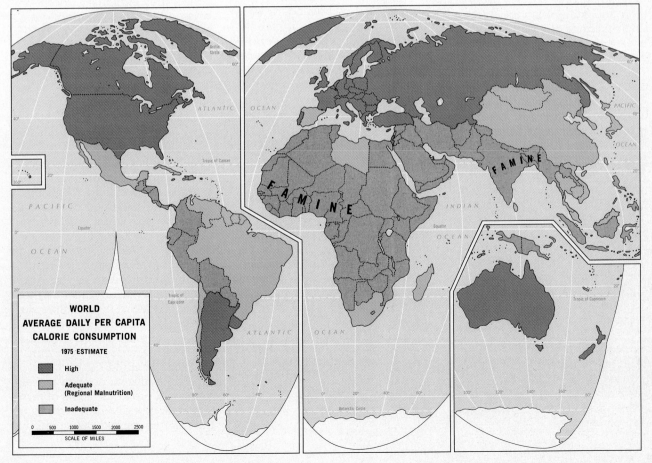

WORLD
AVERAGE DAILY PER CAPITA
CALORIE CONSUMPTION
1975 ESTIMATE

High

Adequate
(Regional Malnutrition)

Inadequate

0   500   1000   1500   2000   2500
SCALE OF MILES

an as yet smaller scale in Ethiopia and Somalia. From the Middle East to Bangladesh, hunger prevailed, with death-dealing famines in India's West Bengal and in neighboring Bangladesh. In Southeast Asia, serious hunger affected more people than at any time in recent memory. In Middle and South America, limited areas of malnutrition and hunger had spread to encompass the Andean countries and the Central American republics south of Mexico. Could the unthinkable happen—could serious malnutrition and hunger invade even those islands of plenty still unaffected by the specter of global food shortages?

The answer is yes, and many Americans have already felt the comparatively minor discomforts of shortages, fast-rising prices putting items beyond budgets' reach, less-well balanced diets, and, as we noted earlier, real hardship in a growing number of cases. This threatening world food crisis, of course, is not the result of one condition alone. It is not due only to the continued increase of the world's human population, for this would have generated a more gradual intensification of the problem. Instead, the situation has worsened quite suddenly, and the dimensions of the emergency are unprecedented. And so we should identify the causes of the crisis before seeking solutions. The present situation can be traced to the following conditions.

Harvest Failures

Perhaps the most ominous of all factors is the repeated failure of grain crops in the world's bread-baskets. The 1972 crop year was a poor one, 1973 was adequate, but 1974 produced another short crop. World reserves, which a decade ago held enough grain to feed the world for over 90 days, had dwindled to about 20 days in 1974 and might be less than 10 days in 1977. In the American Midwest, in the Soviet Union, in Canada, and in China the crops were far below normal, and climatologists were warning that this might be only the beginning of major, worldwide climatic changes. We will return again in Chapter 6 to the possibility that the environmental zones of the earth are changing, and that the world's most productive farmlands may lose their capacity to yield as they have done.

Globe-Girdling Droughts

The rich farmlands were not the only regions affected by climatic adversity. Searing droughts dessicated the Brazilian Northeast, Africa's Sahel, Ethiopia's eastern lowlands, and regions of South Asia. Peoples who had always coped with limited rainfall and marginally productive soils found themselves without hope for survival when the rains

failed altogether, dustbowl conditions developed, and their livestock died by the thousands. Seasonal streams failed to flow, oases and wells dried up, and countless people just wandered into the encroaching desert to die. Some were sustained by emergency relief supplies, but others succumbed to newly rampant disease. To some peoples trapped in the Sahel, disease came almost as a relief, and there were reports that tribespeople were refusing U.N.-sponsored immunization because, they explained, there was no hope that their children would grow up normally anyway; even if they did survive they would always be afflicted by the ravages of malnutrition and near starvation.

The Energy Crisis

At first glance, the energy crisis of the early 1970s might not seem to have much to do with food shortages. But consider this: the same petroleum that drives our cars also forms the base for essential fertilizers. The reduced output that marked the energy crisis also shrank the quantity of available fertilizer. Those higher prices we see at the gasoline stations are paralleled by enormously increased costs of fertilizers. The underdeveloped countries simply could not afford to buy the fertilizers needed merely to sustain previous levels of farm production; individual farmers in the poor countries could not buy them either. But those fertilizers were needed to grow the improved, more productive strains of grain agricultural researchers had introduced. Now the farmers turned to older, less productive strains that could be cultivated. The result: a double loss of yield. And the high cost of oil itself had a negative effect on farm production in the underdeveloped countries. Irrigation pumps are run on gasoline, but the gasoline became so expensive that the pumps came to a halt.

The Failure of Alternative Sources

One major hope for the alleviation of world malnutrition has long focused on the oceans as an inexhaustible source of a direly needed commodity: protein. And indeed, during the 1950s and 1960s the harvest from the seas rose from just over 20 million tons to nearly 70 million. But then, the effects of overfishing began to be felt, and during the early 1970s, coinciding with all the other food problems, the upward trend in world fish catches was checked. Once-dependable fishing grounds failed to produce. Some species even faced extinction. Another world food source fell short of expectations.

The Failure of Social Reform

All these conditions are superimposed on the continuing population spiral, the failure of population control where it is most urgent, the absence of land reform where it is most needed, the continued inadequacy of distribution networks, the unconcerned acceptance by so many of the world's people that millions of their cohabitants on this earth simply have to starve, and that nothing can be done about it. Only now, when the rising sea of hunger threatens to engulf the remaining islands of plenty, have the first efforts at collective, concerted action begun.

If the rising tide of world hunger is to be stemmed, the first requirement is that all countries cooperate in the effort. The developed, food-producing countries must replenish the depleted emergency reserves. The oil-rich countries must support the hungry countries through loans or preferential oil prices. The underdeveloped countries must spend their resources on agriculture and family planning, not atomic bombs and tanks. As we will see, global cooperation on the food question will involve sacrifices—which not all countries may be willing to make.

The present food crisis may well mark the beginning of a whole new era in world consumption that could take decades to stabilize. Thus we should think in terms of long-range solutions, principally the reduction of population growth rates, but such long-range programs do not help the millions of people in trouble now. Hence we also must embark on short-range schemes to combat the crisis of the next several years. Such short-range programs, naturally, depend on the willingness of the richer, surplus-producing countries to take massive action. The highest priority would be the growing and harvesting of the largest possible grain crops by the United States, Canada, Australia, and Argentina, and the redevelopment of a substantial emergency reserve.

Another short-term boost for the underdeveloped, food-poor countries would be the creation of a scaled system of oil prices, permitting the underdeveloped countries to buy oil more cheaply than the richer countries, thus making fertilizers cheaper and making it possible to run irrigation pumps more economically. Alternately, some of the huge income from increased oil prices might be made available to the hungry countries in the form of cheap loans. Of course, those underdeveloped countries can help themselves by cutting expenditures on arms and diverting the freed funds to food production. A worldwide decrease in investment in the machinery of war of just 10 percent would make available tens of billions of dollars for the war on hunger, the ultimate poverty.

Another immediate objective is the repair of world food distribution systems. When as much as one-third of the emergency relief supplies rot away or are eaten by rodents, a major attack is obviously needed. Storage facilities must be restored, and rodent plagues should be combated. Furthermore, the food-poor countries must improve the efficiency of their allocation systems. In India, the emergency supplies are first made available in the cities, where government-subsidized sales divert a large part of the available quantity; often very little remains to be sent into the hungry rural areas. But then, the cities is where the political pressures are strongest.

We in the well-fed countries also can do our share to combat

Food distribution: waiting for bread in the Howra section of Calcutta, India.

world hunger. Many of us eat too much—not just in terms of total calories but also in terms of the *kinds* of food we consume. It takes a huge investment in soil, fertilizer, feed grains, and more to allow each of us to eat more than 110 pounds of meat per year. We could live well on much less. And we could waste less. It is estimated that between one-quarter and one-third of all food put on tables in American homes and restaurants is thrown away uneaten, as garbage. Just by eating 10 percent less meat and wasting 10 percent less food, we could free enough food to sustain 100 million people. And, if everyone cooperated, it could be done right away. This would not be some fuzzy, long-range program of uncertain effectiveness.

But more permanent, long-range programs are needed as well, for unless the population explosion is contained, no sacrifices will suffice. These long-term projects will require slow development, research, experimentation, and the application of pressure on governments. We can recognize seven urgent areas for long-range development.

Population Policies

The control of population growth remains the most important objective, for no program of increased food production and distribution can indefinitely keep up with the population spiral. Nor can population growth be permitted to run its course, to await the constraining impact of economic development. Quite simply, that impact may never come in those cases where the food shortage is most critical, and population planning is the only recourse there.

Effective population policies are not easily established, however. Still the prime example of success is Japan, a country that experienced explosive population growth after the end of World War II, when medical services and public health improved. Families were reunited after the conflict, a baby boom occurred, and the rate of population growth increased to 2 percent. This represents, as we know, a doubling time of just 35 years, and Japan already had 70 million inhabitants in the mid-1940s.

In 1948, the Japanese government took action. The so-called Eugenic Protection Act legalized abortions for "social, medical, and economic reasons." Contraceptives were made available, and family planning clinics were set up throughout the country. Although contraception and female sterilization (also made possible) helped reduce the birth rate, it was the enormous number of abortions that really brought it down. In fact, so many abortions were performed, perhaps 7 or 8 million in a decade, that the Japanese authorities began to worry about the effect on the well-being of the nation. Now there was emphasis on contraception rather than abortion, with an extensive propaganda campaign and educational programs. And the birthrate, which in 1947 had been over 34 per thousand, was down to 18.0 just one decade after the implementation of the Eugenic Protection Act. It has been between 17.0 and 19.0 since. With the death rate declining from 14.2 in 1948 to 7.5 in 1958 and 6.0 in 1973, the population increased for a time at little over 1 percent per year. Today Japan's population of 110 million is growing at 1.3 percent annually.

But what was accomplished in Japan has not proved easy to achieve elsewhere. China has reportedly reduced its growth rate by supporting late marriage, encouraging two-child families, sterilization, and abortion. India, too, has begun to promote birth control and family planning, as has Pakistan. Neither India nor Pakistan, however, is able to invest as much money into birth control clinics and educational efforts as is needed. India began a modest program in 1952, based on education about the rhythm method. This program had little impact, but in 1976 the Indian government moved to enact legislation that would limit families to three children, with incentives to have only two.

In Africa, and in Middle and South America, there has been comparatively little progress in the adoption of population control. In Africa this has to do with nationalist ideologies that in the colonial aftermath equate strength with numbers. In Middle and South America the Roman Catholic Church continues to militate against birth control, but here, too, the concept of strength in numbers still prevails. In European countries dominated by the Roman Catholic Church, but where birthrates have nevertheless declined, it has happened through late marriage, illegal abortions, and permitted (rhythm) and forbidden means of control.

All this suggests that population control is least effective where the crisis is greatest and where what little progress is made annually is consumed by the additional mouths that must be fed. But it is difficult to disseminate the required information and devices to illiterate populations that live in places where there has been little or no change in ways and means of living, and where there is often a fatalistic acceptance of death as common company. Still, the effort must be made, and the surplus-exporting countries may well tie their assistance to the condition that the hungry countries intensify their efforts to stem the population tide.

Greater Crop Yields

In the 1960s the optimists among demographers, who argue that technological advances will overcome world food crises, scored a point when there was a real breakthrough in the search for new, more productive strains of cereals. "Miracle rice," as one such new variety aptly came to be called, permitted the Philippines to end more than 50 years of dependence on rice imports, and Ceylon's production rose by 32 percent in two years. Wheat, too, shared in this revolution: Pakistan and India in three years increased their wheat harvests by

50 percent. Over a longer period, Mexico (where the wheat experiments first proved successful) tripled its production of this grain. The miracle rice, developed at a research station in the Philippines, has a short maturing time, a high-yield capacity, and a high response to fertilizers.

But even the Green Revolution could not eradicate hunger in our world. While the gap between population numbers and food needs closed temporarily (as reflected by Fig. 3-1), what the world got was a reprieve, not a solution. Nor was the Green Revolution without its negative side. The greatly increased yields depended on substantial use of fertilizer and on ample water supplies. While large-scale agricultural projects could afford such requirements, the local subsistence farmer could not. Still, more and more farmers were encouraged to try the new strains, to invest in some fertilizer. And then, after some years of good rainfall and success, the roof fell in on the Green Revolution. Population numbers caught up to the new level of supply. The droughts of the 1970s ended the period of good rains that had marked the 1960s in general. And the price of oil went up fivefold, putting fertilizer out of the reach of many farmers who had been persuaded to try the new strains of grain.

Does this mean that the search for better yields holds no further promise? On the contrary; experts hold out hopes for still more productive strains than we now have. The need is for drought-resistant strains, perhaps even for wholly new

cereals. In the meantime, the world's soils now under cultivation often do not produce nearly the yield they could. Soils differ in quality, of course, and some soils simply cannot produce as much as others. But careless farming, lack of attention, wasting of natural fertilizer, and other practices cost millions of tons of lost harvests every year. China's massive attack on such problems contributed substantially to that country's success in overcoming the threat of hunger.

Expanded Farmlands

There are always dreams that vast, warm, well-watered parts of this earth still covered by natural vegetation can some day be converted to productive farmlands. Not much more than 10 percent of the earth's lands are under crops at present, and agricultural specialists are always looking for ways to increase that amount. If the Amazon Basin and the well-watered expanses of Zaire in Africa can sustain dense forests, could they not support our food crops? Some experts believe that the present cultivated area could be . . . tripled!

This is not simply a matter of cutting down the trees and planting crops, however. Those tropical forests support themselves not only by absorbing nutrients from the soil; they also feed on their own dead leaves and branches. Disturb that cycle of self-rejuvenation, and everything dies. Many a farmer has tried cutting down the tropical trees and planting new seedlings. For a little while they would grow, and then die off. To save them, such massive doses of fertilizer are needed that the soil is practically reconstructed artificially. The cost, of course, is astronomical, and no peasant farmer could afford it. In fact, the governments of the world cannot afford it. It has been estimated that the cost would be $2000 per acre ($5000 per hectare) to convert unproductive land to farmland, on the average. Imagine what millions of needed acres would cost.

Again, there are areas that would not require such massive doses of fertilizer, but which would need huge supplies of water to be made productive. Australia, Africa, and the Americas all have such areas, and again the matter is one of cost. Irrigation systems are enormously expensive, and most of the soils that could be irrigated given present technologies and investment capacities are already under irrigation. To add to the acreage would require the kind of financing even the rich countries have difficulty with, let alone the underdeveloped ones. Still, the need is great enough for new irrigation systems to be under development in some parts of the world. Egypt, for example, is in the middle of a massive project designed to add millions of hectares to its cultivable area—a project that extends over a period of several decades.

Stimulate Local Production

An urgent concern should be the increased productivity of areas in and near chronic hunger zones. People are streaming to the cities in West Bengal and Bangladesh, not because their lands will not produce at all but because yields are depressed by drought, a lack of affordable fertilizer, and often the physical weakness of the farmers, exhausted by hunger and sickness. While help should come from the surplus-exporting countries, this is not a desirable long-range solution. It would be much better for the grains to be produced much nearer the crisis areas. The governments of the underdeveloped countries must encourage local productivity and reduce waste. This involves attacks on costly traditions (in India, the sacred cow eats huge quantities of food needed by humans), diversion of investments from prestige-building heavy industries to agriculture, and changing priorities in other spheres (armaments purchases) as well.

Land Reform

It has been proven many times that farmers farm their own land more carefully and productively than they cultivate someone else's soil. Again a prime example comes from Japan, where, at the close of World War II, huge tracts of land were in the hands of absentee landlords, farmed by tenants. Among the changes introduced by the U.S. occupation was a land reform measure that put the farms in the hands of the individual tillers as owners, not

tenants; the landlords were expropriated. Many of the farms thus assigned were small, but production rose enormously. Today Japanese farmers, meticulous in their care of the land and its crops, produce up to four times as much grain per unit area as do other Asian farmers.

Land reform programs in other parts of the world have had similar, if not quite as dramatic, impacts on yields. Mexico began major land reform after the revolution, Egypt after the overthrow of King Farouk, Taiwan after World War II. On a more modest scale, land reform programs have been started in many other countries. Almost without exception, this has resulted in increased productivity and much better care of the soil. In the Soviet Union, workers on collective farms are assigned a small parcel of land for their own use. Anyone who has traveled through the U.S.S.R. will have been struck by the intensive use made of these tiny plots and their huge output given their size.

In China, the hunger crisis has been overcome not by allocating farmers individually owned land, but by collectivization and an intensive campaign of persuasion that good farming contributes to national well-being. In the absence of such an alternative, land reform aimed at individual ownership is the prime requirement for countries where absentee landlords still own most of the farmland. There are still dozens of countries where most of the farmers are tenants, without interest in the condition or output of their acreages, and kept in a state of serfdom. For the good of the soil as well as the farmer, there must be long-range concern for the condition of the land, and the capacity to make the necessary investment to maintain it well. Tenants cannot make such decisions. Even where land is ostensibly in communal ownership, as in much of traditional Africa, the situation is not good. Tribal chiefs can assign farmland to individuals for temporary use to sustain them and their families, but this discourages the kind of careful concern the soil needs. The need for land reform is nearly worldwide, and progress in this area is much too slow.

Search for Alternative Food Sources

The hope that the oceans might provide an almost limitless supply of high-protein food has recently diminished. There are, after all, limits to the oceans' harvests just as there are on land. What is urgently needed is another aspect of global cooperation: the oceans' resources must be protected while they are used. Until quite recently, only a few species of marine fauna were endangered by over-fishing, as whales are today. But now radar-equipped, machine-driven vessels can secure such enormous hauls that there are already areas where such common fish as sardines, herring, salmon, tuna, and cod are being depleted beyond the level

of potential recovery. Larger fish eat smaller fish. When a whole region is cleared of small fish, larger fishes can be expected to die out.

Many observers predict that rational harvesting of the oceans, if it ever comes about, will be achieved only after permanent damage has been done. The seas remain open to all comers. And who are the comers? The countries that need protein most desperately? Or the technologically advanced countries that have floating factories and huge fleets plying all the oceans?

If the oceans present a dark picture, there is hope in another direction. Aquaculture, the raising of fish in enclosures, is in its infancy, but it could be a form of protein production that will attain importance in the future. It has developed considerably in Japan, where several hundred thousand tons of fish are produced annually this way. This is still a drop in the bucket when the annual world catch is over 50 million tons, but fish contribute importantly to the protein supply in Japan's unbalanced diets, and as world fishing grounds fail, the aquaculture industry is likely to grow.

Food scientists also pursue the alternate food potential in another direction: in the laboratory. Attempts are made to make food from grass and leaves, from algae of the sea, even from oil. If only a single pill could be given once a day to all hungry people, fulfilling their most urgent food needs! Unfortunately, there is not even the prospect that success in the laboratory will guarantee success among the people. Traditions and preferences (not to mention cost) tend to make people hold to conventional, known foods.

Reduce the Cultural Predominance of the Male

In substantial areas of the world, women are more severely malnourished than men—the women who must bear the children and raise them under the most difficult of circumstances. This is so because the male predominates in these traditional societies to such a degree that he demands and takes a disproportionate share of the family's food supply. Among the children, already severely disadvantaged in their competition with adults for food, the male is again in a better position than the female.

The prevalent desire to have male offspring, furthermore, is a powerful factor in sustained high birth rates. When a couple has produced two daughters, the father is likely to want to continue enlarging the family until two or more sons have been born.

In traditional societies of Africa, it is not uncommon for women not only to be more severely malnourished than men, but to be responsible for hoeing the croplands, making the family's clothing, walking endless miles for water and firewood, cooking the meals, and numerous other tasks, in addition to bearing the children. Men do not perform nearly the share of work they could; not infrequently they abandon the family and go to the city. It is obviously impractical to expect rapid change in traditions that are nearly as old as those societies themselves. But it is possible to direct remedial programs to the women and the children primarily, and to begin an attack on the maldistribution of responsibilities.

We stand at the beginning of a new era in the world food situation, requiring action on a series of fronts and global cooperation in several areas of concern. The rising tide of hunger threatens world order. Even the most selfish interests in the well-fed countries have a stake in the war on malnutrition.

A village in Ivory Coast, West Africa: women pound the grain.

Patients at the Lambarene Hospital, Gabon.

4 The Distribution of Health

Good health, like good and adequate food, is unevenly distributed across the world. People who are inadequately fed are susceptible to many debilitating diseases. Hunger and malnutrition produce dangerous weaknesses in the body, and lower the resistance to all kinds of disease organisms. Here in North America, where our food is generally adequate and inspected for quality, and where our water is purified and treated, we have far less trouble with disease than most of the rest of the world. We read how cities of Europe were devastated, centuries ago, by such killer diseases as the bubonic plague, and victims were carted away by the wagonload—but this is history. We have no such fears in the Western world today. Those days are not over, however, in the hungry world. There, too few people are protected by vaccination, and too many are weak and susceptible to serious illness. Just a few years ago, an estimated 50,000 people died within a single region of India during a cholera outbreak. Surveys of cities in the hungry areas of the world indicate that millions of people have never been vaccinated against some of the most severe diseases prevailing there, including smallpox.

Disease and Nutrition

World regions where malnutrition prevails are also areas of poverty, inadequate medical services, inadequate sanitation, and substandard housing. It is difficult, therefore, to discover the specific effects of malnutrition on people's susceptibility to disease, because so many other factors are present at the same time. But there is little doubt about the effects of malnutrition on the growth and development of the body. The impact on children, especially, is devastating. In the protein-poor tropical and subtropical countries kwashiorkor ravages the children. The child's belly grows disproportionately large in a grotesque irony, while the skin loses its tone and discolors. The hair develops a reddish tinge and begins to fall out. Later liquids begin to collect in swelling limbs, the digestive system fails, and total apathy overcomes the child. Death may not be far away. Many children die young, in the very first years of life, and in these countries the high infant-mortality rate is related directly to the incidence of kwashiorkor, the greatest killer of small children there. More importantly, a child can develop kwashiorkor even when enough total calories are available. Kwashiorkor is a result of malnutrition, not necessarily undernutrition. Often it develops when a mother stops breast feeding her child (perhaps because a new baby has been born), and the child is put on a starchy diet (Fig. 4-1).

An example from Africa indicates what may happen. In a region in Zaire, the staple diet is the tropical banana. This fruit is filling enough, but it contains only about 1 percent protein by weight, and thus a child would have to eat about 20 pounds (10 kilograms) of bananas each day to satisfy its protein requirements! When the adults eat the banana, they dip it into a sauce made of meat, vegetables, and spices, and this sauce contains enough protein to make up for the banana's deficiency. The small child, however, is unable to do as well as the adults, and cannot dip the banana and then turn it while putting it in his or her mouth, to avoid spillage. All too often the banana winds up in the child's mouth without any sauce at all. In this way the child eats enough not to feel hungry, but is still seriously malnourished, and the symptoms of kwashiorkor appear.

Where both deficiencies—lack of protein and insufficient calories—prevail, a child is likely to develop marasmus. The body is thin and bony, the skin shrivels, and the eyes appear huge in the tiny, drawn face. Staple foods do exist whose protein content is less even than the banana, notably the cassava, a root crop grown in the tropics. The sweet potato, another staple in tropical areas, also has a very low protein content. Marasmus and kwashiorkor occur in these areas, and as many as half the children never reach their fifth birthday as a result.

Kwashiorkor and marasmus are among a host of other threats facing the malnourished. Calorie inadequacy and protein deficiency usually go hand in hand with vitamin insufficiency, and vitamin shortages are directly related to diseases of various kinds. Low vitamin A intake is related to diseases affecting the eyes, and these, too, take a heavy toll of children. Beriberi, which affects the nervous and digestive systems as well as the heart, is related to vitamin B deficiency, and it prevails in South and East Asia. Insufficiency in vitamin C contributes to the development of scurvy, and vitamin D is needed to ward off rickets.

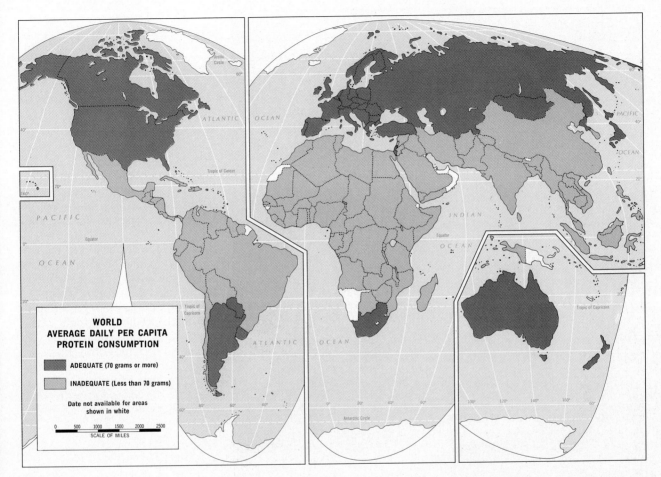

WORLD
AVERAGE DAILY PER CAPITA
PROTEIN CONSUMPTION

ADEQUATE (70 grams or more)

INADEQUATE (Less than 70 grams)

Date not available for areas
shown in white

SCALE OF MILES

Figure 4-1

65

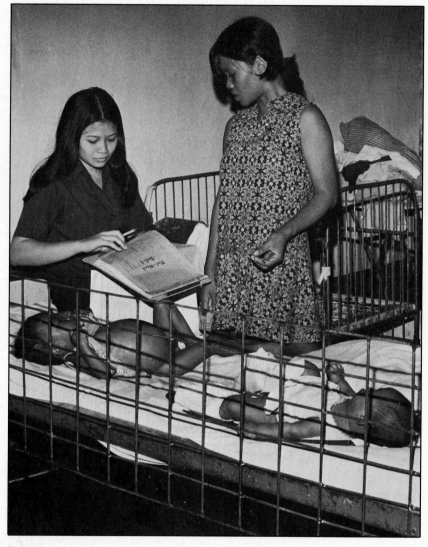
The effects of malnutrition: tiny patients in a hospital in the Philippines.

This depressing (and far from complete) list of diseases directly related to hunger and malnutrition does not include the many other infectious and chronic diseases that prey on the ill-protected, malnourished body. Cholera, yellow fever, hookworm, malaria, and numerous other maladies ravage people already weakened by their imbalanced diets, and they take a heavy toll if not of life, then of energy and longevity. Later in this chapter we investigate some of these diseases and their diffusion. In the meantime, let us take note of the well-fed tourists and travelers from the comfortable world of plenty, who see people sleeping on sidewalks, resting on their jobs, or working at a snail's pace, and who conclude that those people are not better off because they are lazy, there in Guatemala, in Chad, in India, in the Philippines. And let us not be among them.

Life Expectancy

Diseases diminish not only the quality but also the length of life. A child born in the United States or Canada in the early 1970s could expect to live to the age of 71 or 72. Just two centuries ago, life expectancy in Western European countries was little more than half that figure, and in the young United States of the late eighteenth and early nineteenth centuries it was also in the vicinity of 40 years. Today, life expectancy at birth in Sweden is 75, and it is over 70 in many other countries of the Western world. But, as Figure 4-2 shows, life expectancy is still dismally low in numerous countries of the poor world. In Haiti it is 47 years, in Indonesia 48, in India just 51. Some African figures suggest the Middle Ages: Ethiopia, 40 years; Upper Volta, 35 years.

These life expectancy figures do not mean, of course, that everyone in those countries lives to that age. The figure is an average that takes account of the children who die young and the people who survive well beyond that level. Thus the dramatically lower figures for the underdeveloped countries reflect primarily the high rate of infant mortality. A person who has survived beyond the childhood years is likely to survive well beyond the recorded expectancy. Those low figures for the hungry countries remind us again how hard hit are the children in the underdeveloped world.

In the United States and Canada, only 19 babies per thousand die at birth. This is by no means the lowest average in the world: in Finland it is only 11; in the Netherlands, 12; in Australia and New Zealand, 17. But compare these totals to those of underdeveloped countries such as Bolivia, where it is 108; Nicaragua, 123; Nigeria, 180; India, 131. In Angola in the early 1970s, one in five live-born babies died very shortly after birth. In some ways Figure 4-3 reflects more realistically than any of our other maps the variations in the well-being of world societies. It is an index of sanitary conditions, medical services, the state of health of the mothers, and general welfare. When you compare the life expectancies of populations at advanced ages (say at 20 and at 40 years), the contrasts between the developed and the underdeveloped countries are much less dramatic.

Modernization and development have had their most far-reaching impact on infant mortality, which has been reduced enormously. Less progress has been made, however, in the suppression of the diseases of middle age. Thus the differences between conditions in the developed and the underdeveloped countries are most sharply defined by the map of life expectancy at birth.

Figure 4-2

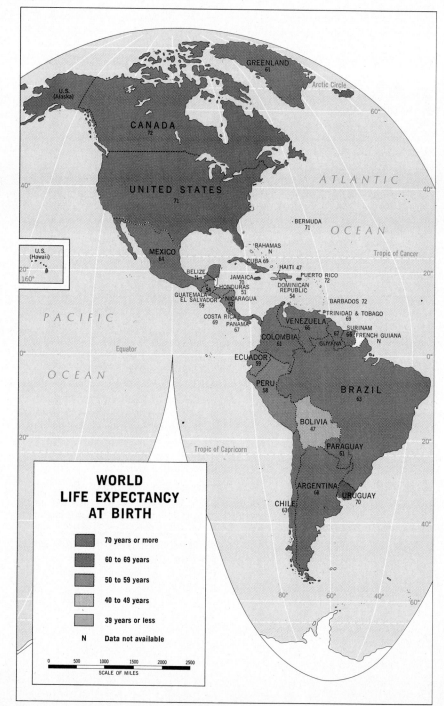

**WORLD
LIFE EXPECTANCY
AT BIRTH**

- 70 years or more
- 60 to 69 years
- 50 to 59 years
- 40 to 49 years
- 39 years or less
- N   Data not available

0   500   1000   1500   2000   2500
SCALE OF MILES

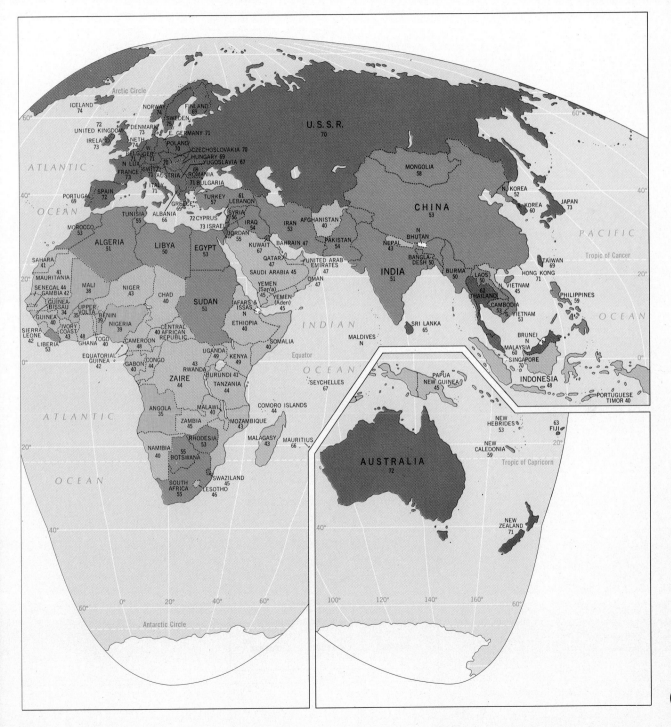

ICELAND 74
NORWAY 74
FINLAND 69
SWEDEN 75
72
UNITED KINGDOM
DENMARK 73
E. GERMANY 71
IRELAND 73
NETH. 74
W. GER. 71
POLAND 70
U.S.S.R. 70
BELG. 71
N LUX.
FRANCE 73
CZECHOSLOVAKIA 70
SWITZ. 70
AUSTRIA 71
HUNGARY 69
YUGOSLAVIA 67
ROMANIA 69
ITALY 71
BULGARIA
PORTUGAL 69
SPAIN 72
GREECE 69
TURKEY 57
LEBANON 61
MONGOLIA 58
TUNISIA 55
ALBANIA 66
CYPRUS 72
SYRIA 56
IRAQ 54
IRAN 53
AFGHANISTAN 40
CHINA 53
MOROCCO 53
ISRAEL 73
JORDAN 55
N. KOREA 52
S. KOREA 60
JAPAN 73
SAHARA 41
ALGERIA 51
LIBYA 50
EGYPT 53
KUWAIT 67
BAHRAIN 47
PAKISTAN 54
NEPAL 43
N BHUTAN
TAIWAN 69
41 MAURITANIA
QATAR 47
UNITED ARAB EMIRATES 47
BANGLA-DESH 50
BURMA 50
HONG KONG 71
SENEGAL 44
MALI 38
NIGER 43
SAUDI ARABIA 45
INDIA 51
LAOS 50
N. VIETNAM 45
GAMBIA 42
CHAD 40
OMAN 47
THAILAND 52
PHILIPPINES 59
GUINEA-BISSAU 34
UPPER VOLTA 35
YEMEN (San'a) 45
YEMEN (Aden) 45
CAMBODIA 50
GUINEA 40
BENIN 39
NIGERIA 39
SUDAN 51
AFARS & ISSAS N
S. VIETNAM 53
SIERRA LEONE 42
IVORY COAST 43
GHANA 48
TOGO 40
CENTRAL AFRICAN REPUBLIC 40
ETHIOPIA 40
SRI LANKA 65
BRUNEI N
LIBERIA 53
CAMEROON 48
SOMALIA 40
MALDIVES N
MALAYSIA 60
SINGAPORE 70
EQUATORIAL GUINEA 42
GABON 40
CONGO 44
UGANDA 49
KENYA 49
SEYCHELLES 67
INDONESIA 48
ZAIRE 44
RWANDA 43
BURUNDI 41
TANZANIA 44
PORTUGUESE TIMOR 40
ANGOLA 35
MALAWI 41
ZAMBIA 45
MOZAMBIQUE 43
COMORO ISLANDS 44
PAPUA NEW GUINEA 45
NEW HEBRIDES 53
63 FIJI
RHODESIA 53
MALAGASY 43
MAURITIUS 66
NEW CALEDONIA 59
NAMIBIA 40
BOTSWANA 55
AUSTRALIA 72
SOUTH AFRICA 55
SWAZILAND 45
LESOTHO 46
NEW ZEALAND 71

69

Figure 4-3

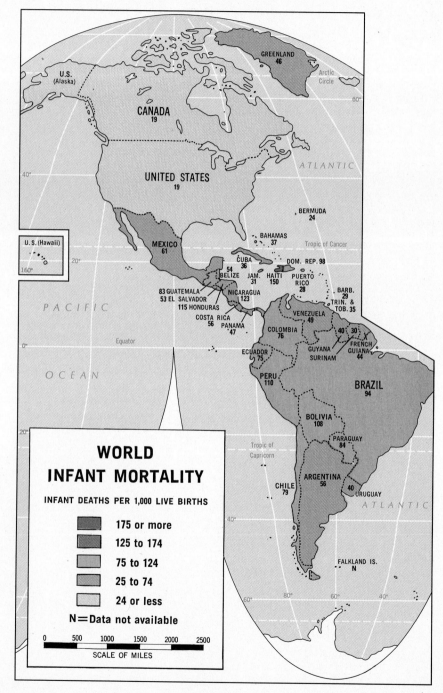

GREENLAND 46

U.S. (Alaska)

Arctic Circle

CANADA 19

ATLANTIC

UNITED STATES 19

BERMUDA 24

U.S. (Hawaii)

MEXICO 61

BAHAMAS 37

Tropic of Cancer

CUBA 36

DOM. REP. 98

54 BELIZE

JAM. 31

HAITI 150

PUERTO RICO 28

83 GUATEMALA
53 EL SALVADOR
115 HONDURAS

NICARAGUA 123

BARB. 29
TRIN. & TOB. 35

COSTA RICA 56

PANAMA 47

VENEZUELA 49

COLOMBIA 76

40 30

FRENCH GUIANA 44

PACIFIC

ECUADOR 75

GUYANA SURINAM

Equator

PERU 110

BRAZIL 94

OCEAN

BOLIVIA 108

Tropic of Capricorn

PARAGUAY 84

CHILE 79

ARGENTINA 56

40

URUGUAY

ATLANTIC

FALKLAND IS. N

WORLD INFANT MORTALITY

INFANT DEATHS PER 1,000 LIVE BIRTHS

175 or more

125 to 174

75 to 124

25 to 74

24 or less

N = Data not available

0   500   1000   1500   2000   2500

SCALE OF MILES

70

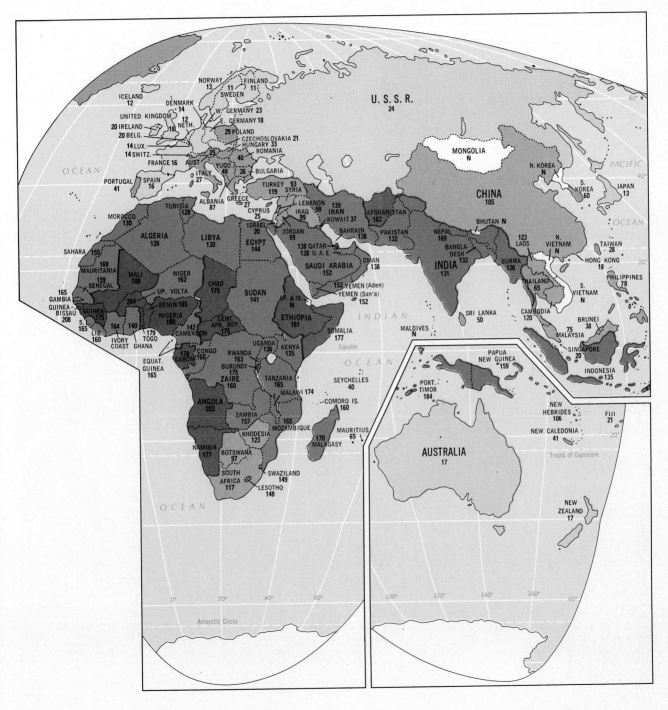

ICELAND 12

NORWAY 13
FINLAND 11
SWEDEN 11
DENMARK 14
W. GERMANY 23
E. GERMANY 18
POLAND 29
CZECHOSLOVAKIA 21
HUNGARY 33
ROMANIA
AUST
YUGO. 40
ITALY 27
BULGARIA
26

UNITED KINGDOM
IRELAND 20
20 BELG.
14 LUX.
14 SWITZ.
FRANCE 16
12 NETH.
18

PORTUGAL 41
SPAIN 16

U.S.S.R. 24

MONGOLIA N

N. KOREA N

PACIFIC

S. KOREA 60

JAPAN 13

CHINA 105

OCEAN

TURKEY 119
SYRIA 93
GREECE 27
CYPRUS 25
ALBANIA 87

LEBANON 59
IRAQ 99
ISRAEL 20
JORDAN 99

IRAN 139
AFGHANISTAN 182

BHUTAN N

TUNISIA 128

MOROCCO 130

ALGERIA 128

LIBYA 130

EGYPT 144

KUWAIT 37
BAHRAIN 138
QATAR 138
138 U.A.E.
SAUDI ARABIA 152
OMAN 138

PAKISTAN 132

NEPAL 169
BANGLA-DESH 132
INDIA 131

LAOS 123
N. VIETNAM N
BURMA 126
THAILAND 65
S. VIETNAM N

TAIWAN 28
HONG KONG 18

PHILIPPINES 78

SAHARA 155
MAURITANIA 169
159 SENEGAL
165
GAMBIA
GUINEA-BISSAU 208
S. 165
LIB. 160

MALI 188

NIGER 162

UP. VOLTA 204

CHAD 175

SUDAN 141

YEMEN (Aden) 152
YEMEN (San'a) 152

AF. & IS.

ETHIOPIA 181

INDIAN

SRI LANKA 50

CAMBODIA 120

BRUNEI 38
MALAYSIA 75
SINGAPORE 20

INDONESIA 135

GUINEA 175
164 140
IVORY COAST 179
TOGO
GHANA

BENIN 185
NIGERIA 180
142 CAMEROON
CENT. AFR. REP. 175

EQUAT. GUINEA 165

178 CONGO
GABON 160

UGANDA 136
RWANDA 163
BURUNDI 175
ZAIRE 160

KENYA 135

SOMALIA 177

MALDIVES N

OCEAN

SEYCHELLES 40

PAPUA NEW GUINEA 159

NEW HEBRIDES 106

FIJI 21

TANZANIA 165
MALAWI 174
ANGOLA 203
ZAMBIA 157
MOZAMBIQUE 165
RHODESIA 123
NAMIBIA 177
BOTSWANA 97
SWAZILAND 149
SOUTH AFRICA 117
LESOTHO 148

COMORO IS. 160
MALAGASY 170
MAURITIUS 65

Equator

PORT. TIMOR 184

NEW CALEDONIA 41

AUSTRALIA 17

Tropic of Capricorn

NEW ZEALAND 17

OCEAN

Antarctic Circle

0° 20° 40° 60°

100° 120° 140° 160° 60°

Age, Disease, and Location

In Chapter 3 we noted the youthfulness of populations in the underdeveloped countries. The structure of a population has important implications for the spread of diseases and the seriousness of their effect on people in the various age categories. Certain diseases affect some age groups more severely than others. When a child gets the measles, it is usually a much less severe case than when an adult has this disease. On the other hand, an adult can normally cope better with diarrhea than a child, and many of the children in the world's mal-

A World Health Organization team at work on a malaria-eradication program in Southeast Asia. In this region, the method used is the distribution of kitchen salt that contains 0.05 percent pyrimethmine, which stops the fever and prevents development of the malaria parasite.

nourished countries die of diarrheic diseases.

Obviously, when the age structure of a population is such that a large proportion are children, as in many of the underdeveloped countries, that population has many more susceptible individuals than an older population. This is because people tend to develop immunities to various diseases as they grow older; children have not attained such immunities yet. In addition, huge numbers of children in underdeveloped countries remain unvaccinated for a long time, since medical systems do not reach them. This means that, despite all the efforts of various organizations attempting to improve the health of populations in the poor countries, the reservoir of susceptibilities to epidemic-scale disease outbreaks is growing with the population explosion.

It is alarming to realize that even an intensive vaccination campaign that reaches as many as 90 percent of the children still leaves enough individuals untouched to sustain a disease outbreak of epidemic proportions. And that total—9 out of 10 children—is rarely attained even during well-organized immunization campaigns in underdeveloped countries. In West Africa, following a massive effort to vaccinate against smallpox during the 1960s, subsequent surveys indicated that only 40 percent of the intended population had been reached. Thus we may expect reports of epidemics in the underdeveloped countries

(as with the cholera outbreak in India in 1972), and there will be crisis regions for health as there are for nutrition.

The tendency of people to move and migrate adds to the health risks. As we will see in more detail later, people all over the world are moving from the countryside to the cities and towns. The reasons for this process are many; in South Asia, people are driven off the land and into the cities by hunger. In Africa, males often leave their families in the rural area and go to the city in search of work. This migration to the urban areas usually involves younger people—many young adults and children. Older people have a greater tendency to stay put. The young adults and their youngsters bring with them a greater susceptibility to various diseases, and so the cities contain not only the hungry but also the vulnerable. The threat of epidemics grows as the numbers rise. For example, children who spent their early years in the countryside may not have been exposed to the tubercle bacillus, as city-dwelling children mostly are. In childhood, the effects are usually mild, but the impact is much more severe when the individual is older. Thus many of the teenage and young adult immigrants are struck by tuberculosis and have no resistance. The cities are real markets for disease.

Distribution and Diffusion of Diseases

Medical geographers are interested, among other matters, in the regional distribution of diseases and in the processes whereby diseases spread or diffuse. Much can be learned from maps, and maps make possible certain important predictions. For example, a map showing the location and extent of an outbreak of diarrheal diseases can serve as an early alert for the development of kwashiorkor, often a successor of such an epidemic. Maps showing the distribution of unvaccinated susceptibles in urban areas can assist in preparations for crisis situations.

Our susceptibility to diseases is a reminder that we humans, technologically capable as we may be, remain only an element in the earth's larger ecological system. We are part of an intricate food web, and because we eat meats and vegetables (animals and plants) we also ingest organisms that establish colonies in our bodies. Some of these tiny organisms exist in permanent adjustment with our system, and do it no damage. Others, however, attack and ravage part or parts of the body, and continue to multiply and grow unless checked in some way. Infectious diseases are caused by the entry and expansion of foreign organisms in our bodies.

When we are afflicted by an infectious disease, we are the *host* to that disease organism.

The disease-causing organisms or *agents* include viruses, bacteria, and larger animals such as parasitic worms and insects. Diseases can be transmitted from one person directly to another, by contact, or they can be carried by *vectors*. The malaria mosquito, for example, is such a vector, and insects are the most common disease vectors. But animals (including house pets) can also function as vectors. Disease organisms can also be transmitted via water, soil, or food. These nonanimal conveyors of disease are called *vehicles*, to distinguish them from the vectors.

Diseases can be grouped according to whether they are vectored (carried from one host to another by some vector), nonvectored (transmitted directly), or chronic (disease of long duration). These categories are not absolutely exclusive, of course. Some diseases can be transmitted directly or via a vector, another human serving as the vector. There is uncertainty about the way some diseases are transmitted, such as cancer, a chronic disease. Examples of vectored diseases include malaria, African sleeping sickness, and schistosomiasis. The malaria mosquito carries malaria, the tsetse fly is the vector for sleeping sickness, and the snail is an intermediate host in the role of a vector for schistosomiasis, a disease marked by a worm infestation of veins with attendant blood loss and tissue damage. Examples of nonvectored diseases include the common cold, smallpox, the measles, cholera, infectious hepatitis, and venereal diseases. Vehicles such as water, milk, or

The map (page 75) shows the distribution of a disease called *histoplasmosis* in the United States. Histoplasmosis is a respiratory infection resembling pneumonia, but it frequently occurs in a very mild form and can be mistaken for a cold. Occasionally, however, histoplasmosis fungi spread through the body, beginning with the lungs but also destroying the liver, spleen, heart, and attacking the brain; death follows.

Histoplasmosis was first identified by Dr. Samuel Darling in 1906, but the fungus *histoplasma capsulatum* was not cultured and recognized as the cause of the disease until 1934. The fungus thrives in moist, dark areas in forests, caves, basements, and similar places. Chickens are often infected and their droppings contain large quantities of the parasites; when manure of this type is used as fertilizer the risk of infection is great. Places such as bat-infested caves and accumulations of bird guano anywhere also promote exposure, and the fungi can be ingested directly, by hand contact, or inhaled as they are wafted into the air.

The map shows a remarkable concentration of histoplasmosis in the Mississippi Valley and adjacent areas. In a part of Kentucky the incidence is as high as 97 percent, and in other areas as well the disease may be considered endemic. The pattern shown on the map has been only partially explained through correlations with maps of soil quality, moisture capacity, the incidence of suitable environments such as caves, and the prevalence of birds of various kinds. Among the questions the map does not answer is this: why are areas with apparently similar, favorable conditions elsewhere in the country not nearly as severely affected as might be expected?

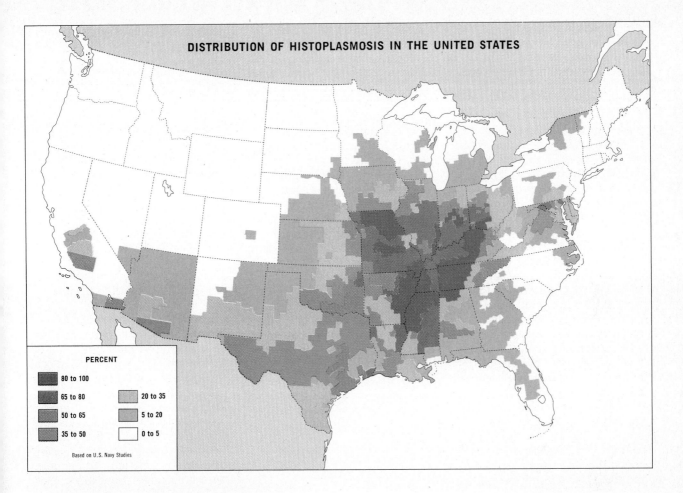

DISTRIBUTION OF HISTOPLASMOSIS IN THE UNITED STATES

PERCENT

- 80 to 100
- 65 to 80
- 50 to 65
- 35 to 50
- 20 to 35
- 5 to 20
- 0 to 5

Based on U.S. Navy Studies

**ENVIRONMENTAL CONDITIONS,
CONDITIONS CONDUCIVE TO
NATURAL CULTURE OF
HISTOPLASMOSIS CAPSULATUM**

1. Alluvial soils.
2. Red-yellow podzolic soils under certain conditions of temperature, humidity, winds, and enriched by bird guano.
3. Loamy and loam-humus types of soil.
4. Soil moisture levels should be up to 85 percent of the water holding capacity of the soil.
5. Soil temperature must be within the range of 72 to 104°F. (22 to 40°C.)
6. Soil pH level must be between 5 and 10.
7. Grows primarily in the upper 2 in. (5 cm.) of soil cover—especially in the upper one-half inch—although it has been found in soil depths as great as 25 in (50 cm)

**VEHICLES AND
VECTORS**

1. Airborne Histoplasma capsulatum fungus.
2. Direct contact.
3. Guano and dung of pigeons, starlings, domestic fowl and bats—airborne or direct contact.
4. Well water, used for drinking supply and untreated.

MAN

INGESTION OR INHALATION OF HISTOPLASMA CAPSULATUM SPORES VIA RESPIRATORY SYSTEM

eating utensils play a role in the diffusion of nonvectored infectious diseases. Among chronic diseases, several rank as major killers in the United States: heart disease, cancer, stroke.

We all know that some diseases can cause large numbers of deaths, as India's recent cholera outbreak did, but that other diseases can be carried by a large part of the population without causing such devastation. Today, many people in the United States have syphilis, whose incidence is still rising; some have the disease without knowing it. Such a disease, carried by many hosts in a condition of near equilibrium and without leading to a rapid and widespread death toll, is *endemic* to that population. This is not to suggest that the disease has no effect on the well-being of the people it affects. General health does deteriorate, and energy levels are lowered. But there is no immediate threat of death. Mononucleosis is another disease that is endemic to our population, and many people on university and college campuses have it without being aware of it.

When there is a sudden and severe outbreak of a disease, leading to a high percentage of afflictions in a population and a substantial number of deaths, there is an *epidemic*. An epidemic is a regional phenomenon, as was the typhoid outbreak in Bangladesh following the 1970 cyclone that ravaged the low-lying countryside, killed 600,000 persons, and polluted water and food for the survivors.

In Brazil in 1973 and 1974 there was an epidemic outbreak of meningitis, but the disease did not spread to other South American countries.

Occasionally an outbreak begins regionally and then spreads worldwide, as various forms of influenza have done since the beginning of the present century. When this happens, the outbreak has *pandemic* proportions. Many diseases, however, have a limited range, determined by the restricted habitat of their vectors. There is no fear that African sleeping sickness will suddenly become pandemic: the tsetse fly, its vector, is restricted to an area approximately within 14° of the equator in tropical Africa, and at elevations below about 4000 feet (1300 meters).

Vectored Infectious Diseases

A substantial number of the world's most severe infectious diseases have tropical, warm-climate origins. This is no surprise, because high temperatures accelerate and intensify biological processes. We associate yellow fever with tropical Africa and South America, sleeping sickness (*trypanosomiasis*) with tropical Africa, malaria with tropical regions from where it has spread into other areas.

The distribution of yellow fever (Fig. 4-4) indicates that this disease is confined to tropical and near-tropical areas, but in past centuries it extended far beyond these confines. The disease is caused by a virus that is transmitted by various kinds of mosquitoes, and it has been one of the great killers of world population. In the Americas, there were devastating epidemics and serious outbreaks in the Caribbean islands, in tropical Middle and South America, and serious outbreaks as far from the tropics as Boston. The Southern United States were repeatedly invaded by yellow fever, always a dreaded disease; the last major outbreak struck coastal cities, especially New Orleans, as recently as 1905. Europe, too, experienced severe attacks of yellow fever; not even England and France were spared.

Today the disease has been driven back to the areas where it has been endemic, and there is a vaccine available that can provide long-term immunity. Eradicating it is a difficult proposition, however, since yellow fever also affects monkeys and several species of small forest animals.

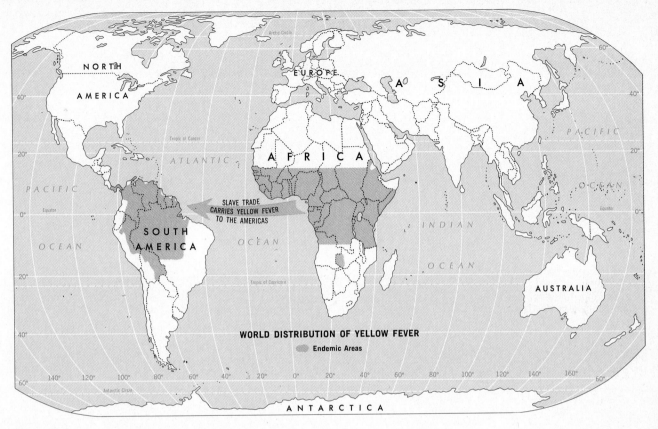

SLAVE TRADE
CARRIES YELLOW FEVER
TO THE AMERICAS

WORLD DISTRIBUTION OF YELLOW FEVER

Endemic Areas

Figure 4-4

In the tropics, then, immunization of humans is the only solution. It was yellow fever that contributed importantly to the failure of Ferdinand de Lesseps, builder of the Suez Canal, in his attempt to cut a canal across Panama's mosquito-infested swamps in 1876. Not until a massive campaign of eradication had been waged could a second attempt at a Panama Canal be made in 1905.

As the name of the disease suggests, its onset, some days after the bite of the vector mosquito, is marked by high temperatures. Head- and backaches accompany the fever, as does vomiting. Sometimes unchecked vomiting leads to death. In less acute cases, and since the virus attacks the liver, jaundice occurs, and the deposition of bile pigment colors the eyes and skin quite yellow. Once the disease has been contracted, there is no treatment, and it has to run its course. Where the disease is endemic, the local population has developed a degree of immunity. Still, there always is a sufficient reservoir of susceptibles to sustain a high-intensity outbreak, and the threat of yellow fever still prevails for millions of people.

The diffusion of African sleeping sickness is thought to have begun about 1400 A.D. from a source area in West Africa (Fig. 4-5A). The tsetse, of which Africa has many

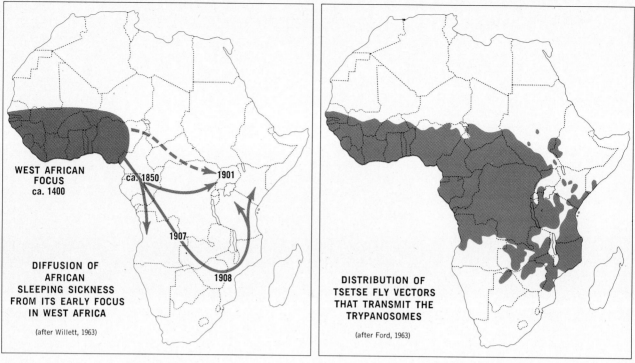

WEST AFRICAN
FOCUS
ca. 1400

ca. 1850

1901

1907

1908

DIFFUSION OF
AFRICAN
SLEEPING SICKNESS
FROM ITS EARLY FOCUS
IN WEST AFRICA

(after Willett, 1963)

Figure 4-5A

DISTRIBUTION OF
TSETSE FLY VECTORS
THAT TRANSMIT THE
TRYPANOSOMES

(after Ford, 1963)

Figure 4-5B

species, is the vector; its distribution indicates the extent of occurrence of the disease (Fig. 4-5A). The fly sucks blood from an infected animal or person, and in so doing ingests the single-celled agents or *trypanosomes*. In the fly's body, these trypanosomes undergo reproduction, and eventually they reach the insect's salivary glands. When next the fly bites a person or an animal, it spreads the infection to new hosts.

Africa's wildlife population forms a veritable reservoir for sleeping sickness, for many of its great herds of antelope are carriers of the disease (Fig. 4-6). The fly infects not only people, but also their livestock, and its effect on Africa's human population

has been incalculable. It has inhibited the development of livestock herds where meat and milk would provide crucial elements in seriously imbalanced diets. It had prevented the adoption of the animal-drawn plow and cart in Africa before the Europeans arrived there. It channeled the diffusion of cattle into Eastern and Southern Africa through tsetse-free corridors, destroying the herds that moved into nearby, infested zones. But most of all, it ravaged the population, depriving it not only of potential livelihoods but also of its health.

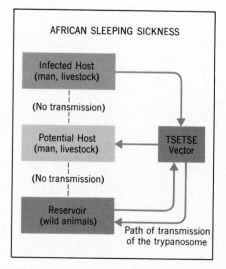

Figure 4-6

In humans, sleeping sickness begins with a fever, followed by a swelling of the lymph nodes. Next, the inflammation spreads to the brain and the spinal cord, producing the lethargy and listlessness that give the disease its name. Death may follow. When livestock get the disease, called nagana, the consequences are similarly severe, as the animal either withers away to die within a year of infection; in some areas the disease is accompanied by a grotesque swelling of the limbs, of which control is lost before long. The animal stumbles helplessly about, is eventually crazed, then dies.

Sleeping sickness is one of the tropics' real scourges, and while progress has been made in combating this dreaded disease, much of Africa still is afflicted by it. The most promising line of attack is at the vector—killing the flies in massive eradication campaigns. Sometimes whole villages have been moved from infested to tsetse-free zones. The killing of infected wildlife, destruction of the bush the tsetse fly needs as its habitat, and other methods have been attempted. But Africa is large—some 4.5 million square miles (over 11.5 square kilometers)—and over much of the continent, the tsetse fly still rules.

Disease and Development

Among the most widespread tropical diseases in Africa and other tropical areas is *schistosomiasis*, also called *bilharzia*. This is a vectored infectious disease, and an intermediate host vector is the snail, which carries the parasites between human hosts. In humans, the parasites travel in the blood vessels and lay their eggs in the walls of various organs; these eggs perforate the tissues and cause internal bleeding. Pain and loss of energy are the major consequences of infection, though schistosomiasis is not a killer disease.

The environment of the snails requires standing or slowly moving water, which is contaminated with the parasites they carry. Just bathing in the water, standing or walking in it, or drinking it, can infect the human host. The World Health Organization estimates that perhaps as many as 200 million people are victims of this debilitating disease.

In several areas of Africa, when development plans and irrigation projects were introduced, an unexpected and unfortunate by-product was the simultaneous introduction, in the slowly moving and standing waters of the irrigation ditches, of the parasite-carrying snails. The projects were designed to help the local people, and certainly the crops grew better and local economies were stimulated . . . but at the unanticipated cost of the further spread of schistosomiasis. Development, in this case, contributed to disease rather than containing it.

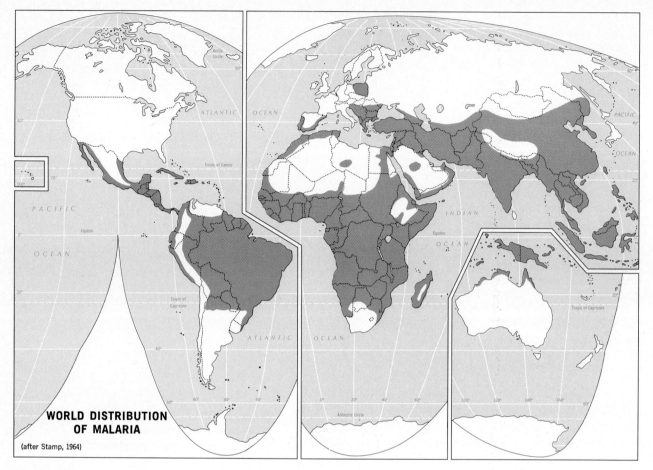

WORLD DISTRIBUTION OF MALARIA

(after Stamp, 1964)

Figure 4-7

Malaria, another vector-transmitted disease, has a world-wide distribution (Fig. 4-7), affecting Middle and South America, Africa and Mediterranean Europe, much of Asia, and northern margins of Australia. Several different types of malaria exist, some more severe than others; not only human beings, but also various species of monkeys, rats, birds, and even snakes can be affected by it. Malaria's vector is the mosquito, but although this is among the oldest recorded maladies in human history the role of the mosquito was not discovered until near the end of the nineteenth century. The pattern is now familiar: one of several species of the anopheline mosquitoes stings an infected host and sucks up some of the disease agents. In the mosquito's stomach, the parasites reproduce and are transmitted to the saliva. When the mosquito stings another person, some of the parasites are injected into the blood stream.

Malaria has killed and incapacitated countless millions of people, and continues to ravage human populations today. It is endemic over large areas—indeed, over most of the regions shown as infected on Figure 4-7. During the 1950s it was estimated by health authorities that malaria was responsible for one million deaths *per year* in India alone. Most of the victims are children who sustain their first attack of the disease; if they survive, they develop a certain degree of immunity, although someone infected by malaria is

Sickle-Cell Anemia and Malaria

When a person is infected with malaria, the parasite *Plasmodium* invades the walls of the red blood cells and, once inside, advances to the next stage in its life cycle. But under certain circumstances the red blood cells do not accommodate malaria's parasites. This occurs when the red cells in large numbers have begun to lose their normal, concave-disc shape and assume a sickle shape. Sickle-cell anemia, as a result, confers a degree of resistance to certain types of malaria on the stricken individual—but it is a high price to pay for such partial immunity.

Sickle-cell anemia in parts of Africa and India afflicts as high as 15 percent of the population (map); among black people in the United States the incidence ranges regionally from 6 to 10 percent and averages about 8.

This is *not* a contagious disease, so there is no vector: it is a disease of genetic origin and is, therefore, inherited. When one parent has sickle-cell anemia and the other does not, a child may be only slightly affected and often has a chance to lead a nearly normal life with occasional sickle-cell related crises. When both parents have the disease, the child is likely to suffer much more acutely and death frequently comes at an early age.

When red blood cells "sickle," they loose their capacity to deliver oxygen-carrying hemoglobin to the body's organs. They become prone to clotting in veins and arteries, causing failure of such vital organs as the liver and spleen. The overall effect of the anemia is devastating, ranging from extreme

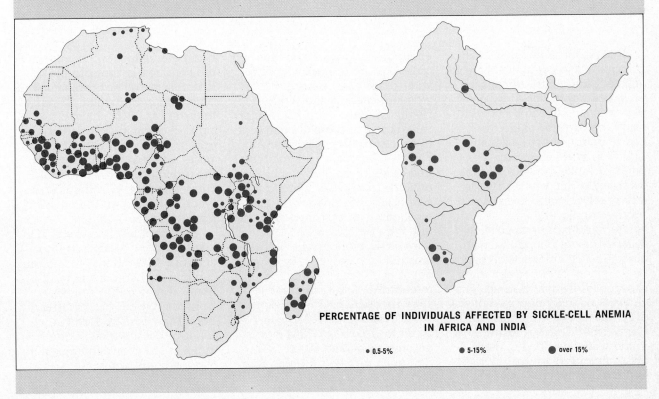

PERCENTAGE OF INDIVIDUALS AFFECTED BY SICKLE-CELL ANEMIA IN AFRICA AND INDIA

● 0.5-5%   ● 5-15%   ● over 15%

pain in the back and joints as a result of oxygen stress to malformation of limbs and organs in growing children.

Sickle-cell anemia has a strong tropical concentration, although migrations have carried it to other world areas including the United States and Mediterranean Europe. In the absence of its particular relationship with malaria, sickle-cell anemia's incidence might have declined over time. But through their higher immunity to malaria's ravages, sickle-cell victims have had a key to survival in regions where malaria is the great killer. As a result, sickle-cell anemia continues to prevail and, in areas where malaria is still endemic, the disease continues to spread.

In part because the disease is not vectored and no agent can be attacked, scientists have not been able to arrest sickle-cell anemia. The search for a substance that might inhibit the sickling of the red blood cells has led to the use of zinc and urea, but so far there is hope only of treating the symptoms, not the cause. In early 1976 it was reported that West Africans may have serendipitously discovered a helpful drug. Many Africans make use of a chewing stick as a dental hygiene measure, and in Nigeria they use the fibrous root of the *fagara* tree for this purpose. Synthesis of the active reagents in the *fagara's* roots produced a chemical that appears able to arrest the sickling of red cells, ameliorating the painful sickle-cell crises victims undergo. Again there is hope for the millions of stricken.

—after A. A. Nazzaro

likely to be debilitated and lacking energy. Whole populations are so afflicted, and entire regions have been abandoned by peoples who simply could not withstand the ravages of the disease. The abandonment of extensive irrigation systems and apparently fertile lands, sometimes ascribed to climatic change, is more probably due to the advance of malaria.

Malaria manifests itself as a recurrent fever and chills, with associated symptoms such as the enlargement of the spleen and, practically always, anemia. The victim is not only deprived of energy; there is also an increased risk of other diseases taking hold in the weakened body. There are antimalarial drugs, but to defeat malaria it is necessary to eliminate the vector, the mosquito. In 1955 a massive, worldwide program against malaria was launched by the World Health Organization, following a remarkably successful campaign in Sri Lanka (then Ceylon). As Figure 4-7 shows, Sri Lanka is free of malaria. This was not so until the mid-1940s, when a massive, islandwide attack on the mosquito was launched with the aid of a pesticide called DDT. The results were dramatic: the mosquito was practically wiped out, and so was the high death rate attributable to malaria. In 1945 the death rate had been 22 per thousand; in 1947 it was down to 15, and by 1954 it was an unprecedented 10. In 1972, Sri Lanka reported a death rate of only 8 per thousand. Malaria had been defeated. Of course, the conquest of malaria produced some other problems. The birth rate in Sri Lanka, 32 per thousand in 1945, showed no signs of declining proportionally, and in 1972 it was still 30. Thus while malaria was diminished, the growth rate rose to double what it had been. There is no solution yet to the problems arising from that new situation.

The malaria-free areas in low-latitude, low-altitude locations are yet few (Fig. 4-7). Malaria is being pushed back in Northern South America (Venezuela-Columbia), in Southern Africa, and in the Eastern Mediterranean. But the battle against malaria still shows the mosquito a widespread winner.

Nonvectored Infectious Diseases

Nonvectored infectious diseases, as we noted earlier, are caused by agents that are transmitted directly from person to person, normally without an intermediate live carrier. Such vehicles as contaminated food or water can, of course, transmit the disease. When direct transmission takes place, several possibilities exist: (1) close bodily contact, through which such maladies as venereal disease and mononucleosis are transmitted; (2) the contamination of water and food by fecal material, which spreads cholera and infectious hepatitis, for example; and (3) the contamination of air when tiny droplets of saliva are expelled by infected persons and then inhaled by others, as in the case of tuberculosis, influenza, and the common cold.

Perhaps the most frightening disease in this group is cholera, also called Asiatic cholera, a term used to denote a set of diseases in which diarrhea and dehydration are chief symptoms. Cholera is an ancient disease, with its focus in India, and it remained confined there until the beginning of the nineteenth century. Then, in 1816, it spread to China and Japan and to East Africa and Mediterranean Europe in the first of several devastating pandemics. This first wave abated by 1823, but by then the very name cholera struck fear in people worldwide. People in communities everywhere had died by the hundreds, even thousands; death was horribly convulsive and would come in a matter of days, perhaps a week; and no one knew what caused the disease and how to avoid it when it

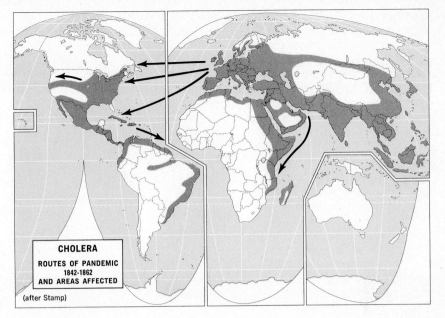

Figure 4-8A

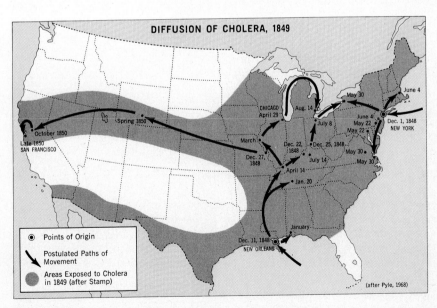

Figure 4-8B

83

invaded. And it was not long before a second pandemic struck, from 1826 to 1837, when cholera crossed the Atlantic and attacked North America.

During the following pandemic, 1842 to 1862, England was severely hit, and the cholera again spread into North America (Fig. 4-8). During this period the vehicle for cholera was discovered (see box) and for the first time, it was possible to take evasive if not yet preventive action. As Figure 4-8A shows, cholera during the 1842-1862 pandemic spread southward along the East African coast and reached what is today northern Mozambique and Madagascar; it spread through the Middle East to Europe and was carried across the Atlantic to North America. The disease diffused across the United States in patterns displayed on Figure 4-8A. It arrived in December, 1848 at New York and New Orleans, and soon spread into the interior, mainly northward along the Mississippi valley. It reached Chicago on April 29, 1850; about the same time it was traveling westward to San Francisco, where it struck late in the same year.

There was only a brief respite before the last great world cholera pandemic began, in 1865. But now people knew to take precautions against contaminated water, and although the advance was worldwide (Fig. 4-9A) this was to be the last of the great cholera waves. In the United States, cholera reached the east coast in May, 1866 (Fig. 4-9B), and spread rapidly into the interior, reaching Detroit on May 29 and Chicago on July 21. This time it moved southward through the Mississippi valley,

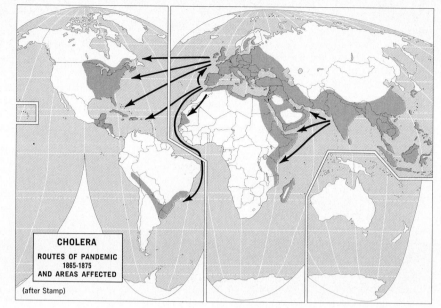

Figure 4-9A

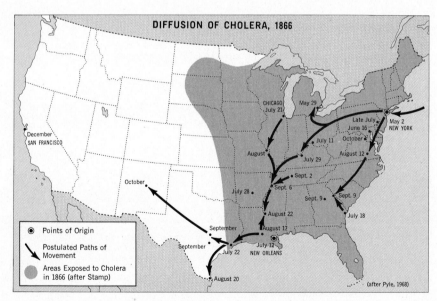

Figure 4-9B

meeting a northward attack that had originated in New Orleans in July as well. But the disease failed to reach the West Coast during the 1865-1875 pandemic.

Although there were later advances of cholera, it has for decades been confined to its South Asian endemic zone. Nevertheless, predictions that it had been defeated except in Asia proved premature. Europe, after being free from cholera for 50 years, had an outbreak in 1972 in Naples, Italy, causing deaths; also in the 1970s parts of Africa not recently affected reported cholera cases.

Cholera is defeated when sanitation and health conditions improve, and vaccines exist. Unfortunately the cholera vaccine does not remain effective for very long (about six months), and if it is difficult to vaccinate an entire population even once, you can imagine the prospects of vaccinating twice every year. So the disease remains rampant in South Asia, where it kills still today. There is much to be learned about the causes and course of cholera, but the symptoms are well known. Within a half day of infection, the host's small intestine is invaded and its functions blocked; diarrhea and vomiting follow, and the body becomes rapidly dehydrated. Unless countermeasures are taken, the skin shrivels, blood pressure falls, muscular cramps and coma follow. The sequence of events can be over in two days, but may last for seven. The countermeasures include the replacement of fluids and salt, and antibiotics to combat the infection. But these luxuries are not available in the slums of Asia's crowded cities where cholera lurks.

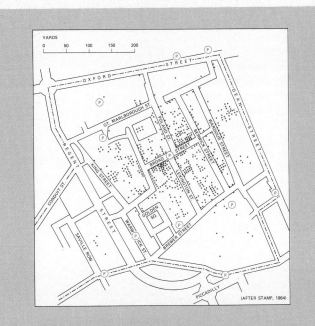

The map above was drawn by Dr. John Snow in 1854. It represents the streets and squares of Soho, a district of London. In those days, people still drew their water at municipal pumps and carried it home; each Ⓟ symbol on the map represents the location of such a pump.

Dr. Snow had been working on the problem of cholera for many years, and he had become convinced that contaminated water was to blame for carrying the disease to its victims. When the pandemic that began in 1842 reached England, the Soho district was severely hit. Dr. Snow, on the street map above, located every cholera death in Soho by marking the place of residence of each with a dot. Some 500 deaths occurred in Soho, and as Dr. Snow's map took shape, it became evident that an especially large number of those deaths were clustered around the pump on Broad Street. At the doctor's request, city authorities removed the handle from that pump, making it impossible to draw water there. The result was dramatic: the number of reported new cases declined almost immediately to near zero. Dr. Snow's theory about the role of water in the spread of cholera was confirmed.

Chronic Diseases

In the United States at the end of the nineteenth century, the leading causes of death were such illnesses as tuberculosis, pneumonia, diarrhea and associated diseases, and heart disease. Today, cancer and heart disease head the list, with cerebral hemorrhage next and accidents and violence high on the list. Tuberculosis and pneumonia, at the turn of the century, caused 20 percent of all deaths; today they cause less than 5 percent. The diarrheal diseases that are so high on the old list are primarily children's maladies, and infant mortality in the United States in 1900 was still quite high. Today these diseases are not even on the new list of 10 leading causes of death in this country. The modern list of deadly diseases is a list of the afflictions of middle and old age, reflecting our increased life expectancy.

The list reflects some other realities, some not so pleasant. Although the diseases of infancy have been defeated to a large extent, and such infectious diseases as tuberculosis and pneumonia are lesser threats than they were, the battles against cancer and heart disease are far from won. Modernization has brought with it new life-styles, new pressures, new consumption patterns, and we do not know exactly how these circumstances affect our health. People often smoke cigarets because they find it relaxing, but lung cancer—a major modern killer—has been linked to heavy smoking. In order to distribute adequate food supplies to populations concentrated in huge urban areas we add various kinds of preservatives, without being sure of just how, in the long run, those preservatives in bread, milk, and other foodstuffs will affect our health. In our overfed society we substitute artificial flavoring for sugar and other calorie-rich substances, but some of those substitutes have been proved to be dangerous. The map of cancer and heart disease shows as heavy a concentration in our modernized part of the world as some of the major infectious disease focus on the underdeveloped regions (Fig. 4-10).

And some new dangers confront even the children. As everyone knows, children will chew on almost anything—toys, utensils, and whatever is in reach. In the poorer areas of the cities and towns, where many families live in substandard housing, the paint peels off the walls, and the children pull at the slivers and chew on them. But the paint contains lead, and now it is known that many children sustain lead poisoning this way. Lead poisoning has sev-

She will wake up and be tempted to pull on the peeling wall paint. If she chews on the slivers, as thousands of children do, she risks lead poisoning and brain damage, and the effects will be with her for life.

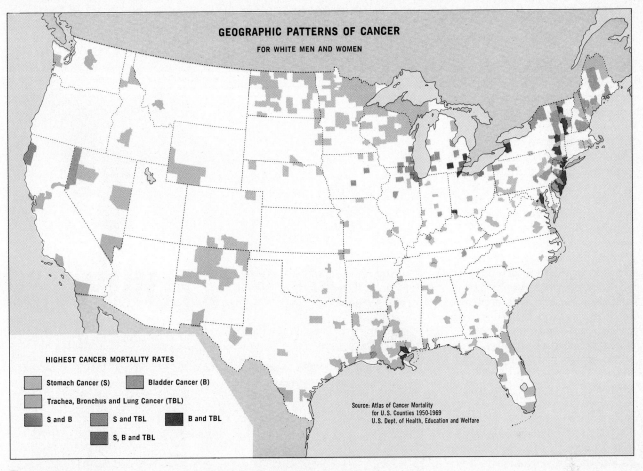

GEOGRAPHIC PATTERNS OF CANCER

FOR WHITE MEN AND WOMEN

HIGHEST CANCER MORTALITY RATES

Stomach Cancer (S)   Bladder Cancer (B)

Trachea, Bronchus and Lung Cancer (TBL)

S and B   S and TBL   B and TBL

S, B and TBL

Source: Atlas of Cancer Mortality
for U.S. Counties 1950-1969
U.S. Dept. of Health, Education and Welfare

Figure 4-10

eral negative effects on the body, and one of them is brain damage. Again, there are rising fears that the water of many areas in the United States contains substances conducive to the development of various forms of cancer. Chlorine and fluoride are added to water to re-duce the risk of contamination, and other chemicals are used to treat water pollution of various kinds. We are not sure of the long-term effect when we consume water over the years, however, and we may be substituting one risk for another. It is one thing to start using treated water at middle age, but it is another to begin consuming it virtually at birth. Any damaging substances have a long time to build up. Water treatment on the scale at which it occurs today is a rela-tively new phenomenon, and only the most recent generation has been using chemically modi-fied water all along. The results in terms of disease and mortality are yet to be ascertained.

Distribution of Treatment

Most of us, when the need arises, have access to a physician or to a hospital. We may find the treatment to be very expensive, and insurance costs are high, but treatment and expertise are available to almost everyone. During the twentieth century the United States and several other countries developed extensive and complex health care systems, with facilities ranging from small private physicians' offices to huge medical schools complete with research laboratories and hospitals. The richer, developed countries could afford such luxuries: Sweden, the Netherlands, the United Kingdom, Canada, and Australia are among countries with well-developed health care systems.

As we noted previously, many people in the poorer countries do not receive essential vaccinations and never or only rarely see a medical facility of any sort. The contrast between the "have" and the "have-not" countries in this context is vividly illustrated by a single statistic: the number of people per doctor. In the United States in the early 1970s, there was one doctor for every 618 persons, and one hospital bed per 124 people. Compare these figures to those of India, where there is one doctor for every 4900 people and more than 2000 people per hospital bed. In Egypt, the situation is still worse: 15,000 persons per doctor and 464 people per hospital bed. And in Nigeria, there are some 29,000 persons for

Millions of ill people still come no nearer a hospital bed than this. Bombay, India.

every doctor and nearly 2300 per hospital bed. Such figures make a strong case for the position that the underdeveloped countries need highly trained, specialized doctors less than they need medical technicians capable of coping with the most urgent and widespread health

problems—technicians who can be trained more rapidly and far more cheaply than physicians.

Such comparisons suggest that the developed countries have achieved satisfactory health care delivery systems—but when we examine these modern systems in some

detail, we discover that even in the United States and in certain other Western countries those elaborate medical systems are not doing the job as well as they should. And some of the major problems involved are geographical in nature. Even with our favorable doctor/people ratio,

Even in the hospitals of Western countries, waiting rooms are often overcrowded, delays very long, and treatment incomplete.

Far from the neediest patients: a hospital in Pennsylvania, positioned on the outer edge of town, near an affluent suburb and expressways, but remote from the majority of the people who need it most.

there is a shortage of physicians in the United States. Perhaps even more importantly, those doctors now available are not distributed as well as they could be; there are too many doctors in some areas and too few in others. And what is true of doctors' offices is true of hospitals as well: hospitals are frequently located in places that make them inaccessible to many potential patients. Studies have shown that distance is an important factor in the use made by sample populations of hospital facilities. An important criterion in the locational planning for hospitals, therefore, should be their closeness to the largest possible number of people they are intended to serve. But there has not been enough cooperation between planners of cities and regions and planners of the nation's health facilities.

Another major shortcoming of our health delivery system lies in its unequal availability to the various population groups that constitute our nation. While some of us can go to a doctor's office and be treated within an hour, others wait for half a day or longer in understaffed clinics. As with nutrition, it is the poor people who are least adequately served by the system, and the statistics tell the results. In a study of the health situation in Chicago in the 1960s, the contrasts between the poor and the well-off were revealed by some dramatic figures. In the poor areas, infant mortality was 100 percent greater than in the wealthier areas; syphilis-related deaths 300 percent higher; gonorrhea-connected mortality was over 1600 percent higher. More than four times as many children died

from pneumonia; diarrheal diseases afflicted 60 percent more children than in the wealthier areas. Some of the details in that study would seem to apply to distant underdeveloped countries rather than sections of our own society. And so, again, where the need is greatest, the system frequently fails to deliver. Those favorable statistics on doctors and hospital beds conceal some serious inequities here at home.

This chapter focused on only a few of the topics related to the state of health of the world's population. But the problems of medical geography should not be viewed in isolation from the issues raised in the earlier chapters on population. Improved medical systems in underdeveloped countries may prevent diseases from claiming as many lives as in the past—only to add to the numbers dying later of starvation. Even developed countries still have not achieved satisfactory health delivery systems, but the underdeveloped countries need something very different: integrated programs that combine planning efforts in areas of nutrition, sanitation, health services, and family planning. The tasks ahead are numerous and enormous, and the future of the world depends on those who will tackle them.

"Link to the city."

5 Movement and Migration

Every year, millions of the world's people make what is often a momentous decision: to move to a new abode. Perhaps the move is across town, or possibly to another part of the country. Sometimes it involves emigration, leaving one's homeland to seek a new life in another part of the world. We should know—the United States was born of an era of immigration. Even today, Americans are perhaps the most mobile people in the world. On the average we move every five years, which means that fully one-fifth of the American population is involved each year in a change of address. Well over 45 million Americans will find new residences in 1980!

Although human mobility increases all the time, large-scale population movements are nothing new. The emergence of the first human communities occurred in East Africa and perhaps elsewhere; soon they migrated into unoccupied parts of a zone extending from Africa through Southwest, South, East, and Southeast Asia, and into Australia. While the most recent glacial advance still prevailed, these migrations were confined to low-latitude areas of the world. But beginning about 15,000 years ago, glacial retreat opened up areas in higher latitude for human penetration and settlement. Improved weapons (spears and harpoons) made it possible to hunt the giant mammoth and other animals on the plainlands of what is today Western Europe and in the waters offshore; soon people ventured out in primitive boats. Human populations entered North America, probably via Alaska from Asia, although this postulated migration route raises some questions about the pattern of Indian development in the Americas, as we note in Chapter 18.

The development of the earliest states led to new kinds of migrations. No longer was human migration only a search for better hunting grounds or protection from competitors or enemies: those early states stabilized local population, but they stimulated the movement of traders, administrators, slaves, armies, and others. During ancient Greece's golden age, thousands of boats plied the Mediterranean and nearby waters. Rome imported slaves and war prisoners and disseminated armies and government representatives from Britain to the Persian Gulf and from the Black Sea to Egypt. In West Africa, warriors from Morocco threatened the stability of states in the Niger region. In Middle America, the Aztecs herded thousands of people from farflung areas to be sacrificed to the sun god. In China, governments ordered the building of walls to keep Mongols out and Chinese in.

Inevitably the breakdown of states would be followed by sometimes massive population readjustments. In Europe after the Roman Empire fractured, a major *völkerwanderung* occurred—a momentous stirring and movement of peoples that saw the Anglo-Saxons invade Britain from Danish shores, the Franks enter France, the Allemanni reach Germany, and Burgundians, Vandals, and Visigoths attain new positions in what was Rome's Western Empire. Meanwhile the Huns threatened the east from the steppes of Asia, while the Moors penetrated Europe from North Africa.

When we take note of more modern movements and migrations, therefore, we observe phenomena that are by no means novel in world history. And yet the past five centuries have witnessed human migration on an unprecedented scale, much of it generated by events occurring in Europe. Major modern migration flows include (Fig. 5-1): from Europe to North America (1); from Southern Europe to South

and Middle America (2); from Britain to Africa and Australia (3); from Africa to the Americas during the period of slavery (4); from India to Eastern Africa, Southeast Asia, and Caribbean America (5); from China to Southeast Asia (6); from the Eastern United States westward (7); and from the Western U.S.S.R. eastward (8). The last two migrations are internal to the United States and the Soviet Union, and our map does not show some other internal migrations of significance, for example the south-to-north movement of black Americans during the present century. We return to these great population shifts later in this chapter.

Migratory movements such as we have just discussed are not the only kinds of movement that affect populations and communities. Consider your own life-style in this context. You may go to classes every weekday, and perhaps to a job as well. This is a form of *cyclic* movement: you leave your room or apartment, travel to class or work, and return daily, taking approximately the same route each time. But you may also have come from another town, even another state to study at the college or university you now attend. Your arrival for the fall quarter or semester and your return trip after the spring is a different form of movement—*periodic* movement, involving a lengthy period of residence following your trip. And after you graduate, you may decide to take a position in a foreign country, say Australia or the United Kingdom. If you decide to move there permanently, as did some who refused to fight in the war in Vietnam and took up residence in Canada and Sweden, your move is a form of *migratory* movement. As we observe below, these are only three of many other possibilities under each of these major types of movement, and we now examine them in some detail.

Cyclic Movement

Cyclic movement involves journeys that begin at and bring us back to our home base. In farming villages around the world, the farmers walk or ride

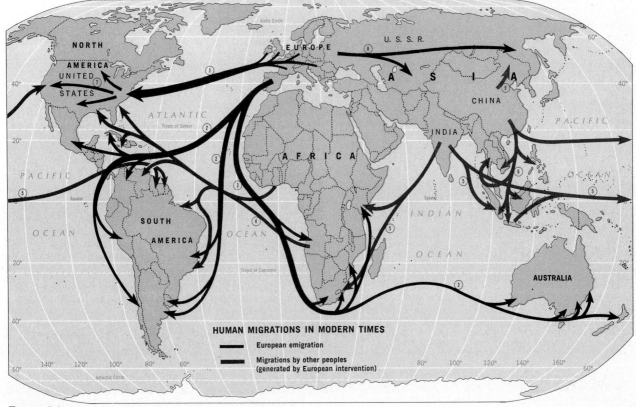

Figure 5-1

HUMAN MIGRATIONS IN MODERN TIMES

European emigration

Migrations by other peoples
(generated by European intervention)

to the fields each morning, spend the day at work on the land, and return to the village at night. This *daily* cyclic movement has its equivalent in our urbanized society in the daily journey to work, a trip that sometimes involves hours of travel in automobiles, buses, trains, or subways. People working in the central business districts of large cities such as New York and Chicago are prepared to travel an hour or more each way every working day. Thus these cities have huge drawing power over the surrounding labor force; thousands of people, for example, travel from New Jersey into and out of New York every day for work purposes.

Your trip to classes each day may be shorter, but it is nevertheless a form of cyclic movement. So, too, are your shopping trips; if you would keep a record of those journeys you would find yourself returning time and again to the same store or gasoline station. Again, your visits to friends and other trips for social purposes are usually done during the same day and with some frequency during the week or month.

More time-consuming and less frequent are *seasonal* forms of cyclic movement. Many of us take our vacations and holidays during the same period each year. Then we undertake a trip that may cover thousands of

95

Commuting to work: a form of cyclic movement. Rush hour traffic on the approach to the San Francisco Bay Bridge.

Some cyclic movements are, by contrast, *irregular* in their timing. A common form of movement in this category is the business trip. People involved in sales and marketing take numerous long-distance trips per year, but not normally according to regular and recurrent schedules. This is a form of movement whose intensity is surely a hallmark of our particular society; every day tens of thousands of salespersons are in transit by air and automobile, traveling from one prospective buyer to another before returning to the home base for record keeping and restocking.

Quite another form of irregular, yet cyclic movement is nomadism in various forms. We may envisage nomadic groups of people as wandering aimlessly across steppe or desert, but in fact most nomadic movement takes place according to travel patterns that are repeated time and again. Often the climate and its seasonal changes influence the nomads' decisions to break camp and move, and in that sense this is in some degree a seasonal form of cyclic movement. But in those arid areas where nomadic peoples trek, year-to-year climatic patterns can vary enormously. And nomadic peoples frequently do have a base to which they return for a period each year. The Masai of East Africa, for example, establish a village where they remain while the rains permit a sedentary life; they even try to grow some crops nearby. When the rains begin to fail and drought encroaches, everyone packs belongings on the back of donkeys and the cattle and goats are driven in pursuit of the essential ingredient of life: water. Eventually the group

miles and extend over several weeks. Each spring, thousands of college and university students find their way to Fort Lauderdale and nearby Florida towns on the warm Atlantic coast; every winter skiers from all over the country try the slopes of Colorado. Many people, of course, cannot afford the luxury of vacation travel. Still the flood of tourists in search of winter warmth or the challenge of ski slopes has the magnitude of a small-scale migration!

Not all seasonal travel is for fun and recreation, however.

The herring fleets of Western Europe wait in port until the fish run, then fan out into the North Sea and adjacent waters to pursue their catches. Again, such fishing trips may take one or more days, but the boats return to the port that is their home base, thus engaging in cyclic movement.

The cyclic movements so far discussed occur on given days (working days) or during given seasons (the Christmas and New Year's holidays, for example).

Nomadism usually takes place according to established travel plans, with some variation in the overall patterns. A desert caravan near Ur in Iraq.

will return to the village, and, if the rains permit, remain at the site for some months. In some years, there is hardly any rain and the stay at the village base is but brief.

Periodic Movement

Some forms of movement involve a longer period or periods of residence away from the home base than cyclic movements normally do. When you leave home to go to college, you are likely to be away for nine months of the year, except perhaps for a few brief vacations. And while you may have gone off to college intending to return eventually to your home town, that may never happen. Employment opportunity elsewhere, graduate school—the chances are numerous that you will go on to still another location rather than return. In the United States alone, some 2 million students are attending colleges and universities, a majority of them away from home. For them, a new residential location is established for a substantial period of time.

Other hundreds of thousands of people are relocated through their military service. This, too, is periodic movement—to military bases, training schools, and, of course, combat. At the height of the Indochina War, the United States had a half million people in Vietnam, truly a mass movement involving a force numbering more than twice the whole population of Iceland. In a given year in the United States, perhaps as many as 10 million persons, including people in service and their families, are in one way or another moved because of their association in some capacity with the military. Many of them become familiar with the area to which they are moved, and remain after their period of duty has expired.

The movement of migrant laborers and their families is also periodic, although more cyclic than that of college students or military personnel. The migrant labor force moves from place to place as crops ripen in different areas and a temporary demand for labor arises there. This happens according to recurrent cycles, but climate in various parts of the country does vary and sometimes there is less work in certain areas during a particular year. If the crops are late, the migrants may arrive too early, and must wait until they are needed; if the crops fail or if the harvest is poor, there may not be enough demand for labor to put everyone to work. It is a precarious and difficult existence, and poverty is the rule among migrant farm workers. Unlike the college graduate and the discharged military personnel, migrants do not have the opportunity of choice of residential location when they work temporarily in an area. They are trapped in a system of transience from which escape is very difficult.

Another form of periodic movement is one we identify as *transhumance*. The term is used to denote a system of pastoral farming whereby livestock and their keepers adjust their abodes to the seasonal availability of pasture. Switzerland's mountainous areas are best known for this practice, but it occurs elsewhere as well. In the summer, the herd is driven up the slopes to high, fresh pastures in zones cleared of winter snow. Sometimes the whole farm family takes up residence in cottages built especially for this purpose near the summer snow line. With the arrival of the colder weather in the fall, the cattle and goats and their keepers abandon the high pastures and summer cottages and descend to the lower valleys to await the winter. In some respects, this is a seasonal cyclic movement, but there is a far longer period of residence at the two bases with very brief actual movement. This resembles the college-bound and military-dictated movement patterns rather than seasonal movements such as tourism.

Migratory Movement

Migratory movement is the most consequential of all the forms of movement we discuss here: it involves permanent relocation, a leaving behind of the old, a new beginning. It has numerous causes and many manifestations—so many that it is often impossible to discern the exact reasons underlying people's decisions to seek new abodes. Obviously there are factors that *push* people away from their homes, and other forces that *pull* them to new, promising locations. Determining or measuring these forces is a difficult proposition. Oppression, discrimination, the threat of war or natural catastrophe can drive people away. The attraction of better economic opportunity, greater freedom, or security can pull them to new homelands. But always, some of the people will move, others will stay behind.

What motivates those who move, and those who decide to remain where they are?

Among the greatest human migrations in recent centuries has been the human flow from Europe to the Americas. When, in Part I, we discussed the period of explosive population growth in nineteenth-century Europe, we did not fully account for this process, which kept the total increase far below what it might have been. The great emigration from Europe [(1) and (2) on Fig. 5-1] began slowly. Over the several centuries prior to the 1830s, perhaps 2.75 million Europeans left to settle overseas in newly acquired spheres of influence and colonial dependencies. But then the rate of emigration increased sharply, and between 1835 and 1935 perhaps as many as 75 million departed for the New World and other overseas territories. Britishers went to North America, Australia, New Zealand, and South Africa. From Spain and Portugal many hundreds of thousands emigrated to Central and South America. Early European colonial settlements grew to substantial size even in such places as Angola, Kenya, and Java. True, some millions of Europeans eventually returned to their homelands, but the net outflow from Europe was enormous.

This European emigration has had no counterpart in modern world history in terms of scale and numbers, but it is not the only major migration flow to have occurred in recent centuries. The Americas were the destination of another mass of immigrants: Africans, transported in bondage, but migrants nevertheless. This migration began during the sixteenth century,

The lure of the Americas pulled millions of Europeans across the Atlantic. Many tra-
velled in discomfort on decks of ill-equipped ships. The photograph was taken on an
emigrant ship in 1902.

when Africans were first brought
to the Caribbean. In the early
decades of the seventeenth century they arrived in small
numbers on the plantations that
were developing in coastal Eastern North America, and so they
were among the very first
settlers in this country.

It will never be known how
many Africans were forced to
travel to the Americas; estimates
range from 12 to 30 million. As
the plantation economy evolved,
labor was needed. Prior to the
1830s, the European population
in the Americas remained quite
small, and so the flow of African
slave labor grew. There was a
time, before the flow of European immigration intensified,
when there were five or six
times more blacks in the
Americas than whites. The heaviest concentration of Africans in
bondage was in the Caribbean
and Northern and Eastern South
America. Today, the descend-
ants of these people form the
overwhelming majority in several Caribbean countries' total
population. Actually, despite the
substantial black population of
the United States at present, the
number of enslaved Africans
who were taken to this country
was quite small compared to the
mass that went as forced immigrants to the Caribbean and
South America. By 1800 the
black population of the United
States was just one million (Fig.
5-2).

It is appropriate to reflect on
the consequences the quest for
slaves had in Africa itself (Fig.
5-3). Europe's emigrants mostly
were able to leave by their own
choice (some did go as exiled
prisoners or as indentured laborers), and by their departure they
relieved to some extent the very

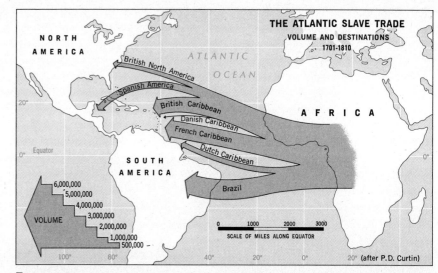

Figure 5-2
Figure 5-3

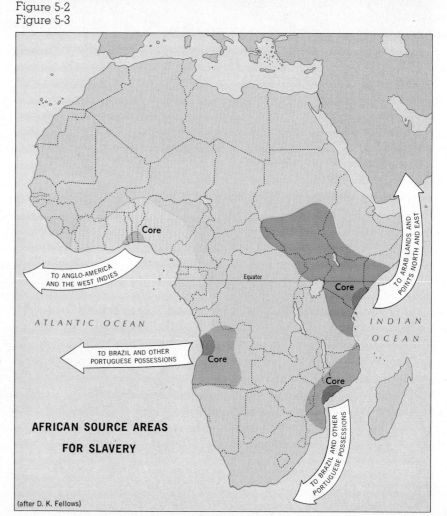

100

pressures that forced them to leave. In Africa, on the other hand, there was no such freedom of choice, and far from improving the situation, the forced emigration greatly damaged the societies involved. From Europe, families left as a whole and joined communities in America that could to some degree cushion the effects of migration shock; in Africa, families were destroyed, children were orphaned, communities were disrupted—and in America the African slaves faced not only terror but loneliness as well. In Africa the communities subjected to slave raiding, if they survived at all, found themselves without most of their younger men; in America, there long was a shortage of women even after freedom came. It took generations to repair the damage.

The properties of these two great migration flows—of Europeans to overseas settlements and of Africans to the Americas—indicates that there are different *types* of migratory movements. The most obvious classification to be derived is that there are voluntary and forced migrations. But within each of these categories there are different cases. Those African slaves were captured and transported in bondage like prisoners, then sold and placed in servitude. Other migrants who were forced to move faced quite different circumstances. To use a modern case: during the early 1970s the African leadership of Uganda decided to oust nearly all the Asians in that country, many of whom were shopkeepers, traders, or otherwise engaged in commerce. They had no choice, and were given very little time to get out of a country in which many of them were born. As some 50,000 Asians were transported out of Uganda with only the belongings they could carry, this was obviously a forced migration—but still a very different sort of forced migration than that of the African slaves to America. We should, therefore, focus more closely on our two classes of migratory movement and examine their contents.

Voluntary Migration. Among the millions of Europeans who came to the Americas, most arrived with the hope of material improvement, greater opportunity, and better living standards. These same motives carried others from Europe to the African and Asian colonies—Portuguese and British to new farmlands in Angola and Kenya, Belgians and Hollanders to the riches of the (then) Congo and Netherlands East Indies. Some of the emigrants, among them many Irish families, left for the New World in the face of declining harvests and the specter of hunger, so that an element of force does

The promise of cheap land and an independent future attracted many imigrants to the American West. Here a public land drawing is taking place near Hollister, Idaho, in the early 1900s.

enter the picture. But the prevailing force was the "pull" of beckoning opportunity elsewhere. Today, as we note later, this is the force that leads people to abandon their rural abodes and head for the cities.

Another kind of voluntary migration involves people's search for places where they can be with their own kind. The world is a mosaic of languages, religions, and ways of life, and there are minorities everywhere. Most of these minorities have become adjusted to life under their particular circumstances, but times do change. When independence came to Africa's European colonies, some of the white settlers were able to adjust to the new situation; they remained through the transition. Others could not confront it, and they departed, some to South Africa, others to Europe. Unlike the Asians forced out of Uganda, these Europeans were not ousted. If there was a "push" factor, it often was more in what they perceived might happen than did actually occur. Theirs was a voluntary emigration. Similarly, communities may decide to seek new abodes where they will enjoy better religious adjustment, as many Moslems did when India and Pakistan were partitioned. People move for linguistic reasons, for reasons of social and psychological adjustment. It is all a matter of perception and choice.

In the United States, we see another considerable migration flow in the movement of people who reach retirement age, and who leave their long-time homes for Florida, Arizona, or another locale where the weather may be milder and where costs may

be lower (many move to Mexico). Again, this is mainly a voluntary migration, often planned for many years before the move is actually made. There are elements of cultural migration here, similar to those discussed in the preceding paragraph; older people perceive that they will find themselves living in places where other retirees also reside, so that they may share that group's interests and activities. The impact of this migration flow can be seen in Florida's high-rise condominiums and Arizona's sprawling retirement villages.

Forced Migration. While the African slave trade prevailed, European countries also were busy deporting convicted criminals and other undesirables to distant colonies. Such deportation—or "transportation" as it was called—had long been bringing British convicts to American shores until the Revolutionary War of the 1770s interrupted this process. When British jails began to overflow, Australia became the dumping ground for those convicted of their crimes and sentenced to "transportation."

For those of us who have learned of the horrible treatment of black slaves transported to America, it is revealing to find that European prisoners sentenced to be deported were no better off, despite the fact that their offense often was the simple inability to pay their debts. The story of the second dispatch of deportees to Australia gives an idea: more than a thousand prisoners were crammed aboard a too-small boat, and 270 died on the way and were thrown overboard. Of those who arrived at Sydney alive, nearly 500 were sick, and

another 50 died within a few days. The toll in human life during Europe's colonial period is immeasurable.

Large-scale slavery and "transportation" no longer contribute to world population migrations, but other kinds of forced migration still occur. We have already taken note of the expulsion of Asians from Uganda (most of those families went to Europe); the exodus of Palestinians from areas designated to become part of the State of Israel was similarly a forced migration. So was the ouster of Germans from Eastern Europe following the end of World War II. Political decisions often lead to forced migrations. Cultural oppression—religious, linguistic, and racial—has the same effect.

Another cause of forced migration is the threat of a natural disaster. People do move away from places where such threats exist, especially after a catastrophic event has taken place. Earthquake-prone regions drive people away; there is a measurable flow away from California following each significant quake, for example. Volcanic activity and the threat of floods also can dislocate populations, although it is always amazing to observe the large number of people who will remain where they are despite the evident and obvious risks they are taking. And as we noted earlier, a severe and persistent drought cycle is as much a natural disaster as an earthquake, and can kill as many people. Population patterns in the African Sahel have been affected by drought-induced migrations.

The end of Portuguese rule in Angola led to the departure of hundreds of thousands of Portuguese, most of whom went to Portugal under difficult circumstances. It was a case of forced migration in the early 1970s.

Intercontinental, Regional, and Internal Migrations

Another way to approach the study of migration relates to spatial properties including distance and political boundaries. Among the examples we used in the previous pages, some migration flows extended between continents (Europeans to America); some affected adjacent countries within a particular region (Germans ousted from East European countries); and still others prevailed within individual countries (movement from rural areas to the cities).

Intercontinental migrations took Europeans to America and other parts of the world; the Europeans in America, Africa, and Asia generated the migration of other peoples. We have already considered the movement of Africans to the Americas, but other peoples were induced to move as well. Indentured Indian labor was brought to Natal, South Africa, and to areas of East Africa by the British. This intercontinental migration [(5) on Fig. 5-1] substantially changed the ethnic mosaic of Eastern Africa from Kenya to the Cape. Free Asian entrepreneurs followed the stream of indentured laborers, and eventually much of the local trade and commerce along the East African coast was in the hands of Asians. The British were also instrumental in relocating Asians, mainly from India, to such Caribbean countries as Trinidad and Tobago and Guyana [the trans-Pacific stream marked (5) on Fig. 5-1]. The Hollanders brought Javanese from what is today Indonesia to their former dependency

Figure 5-4

of Surinam along the same route. Meanwhile, the colonial occupation of Southeast Asia presented opportunities for the Chinese to function as middlemen, and a considerable immigration of Chinese to this region

occurred (6). Chinese minorities in Southeast Asian countries (Fig. 5-4) represent substantial sectors of national populations: 12 percent in Thailand, 30 percent in Malaysia, 14 percent in North Vietnam, 8 percent in

104

South Vietnam. The Chinese minority in Indonesia accounts for only 3 percent of the total population, but Indonesia has over 130 million people, so that the Chinese minority is one of Southeast Asia's larger clusters. Several governments in Southeast Asia during the twentieth century have discouraged and restricted Chinese immigration. Like the Asians in East Africa, the Chinese minorities are urban-based and disproportionately influential in trade, commerce, and finance in the Southeast Asian states.

A modern intercontinental migration, albeit on a smaller scale, is the flow of Jewish immigrants to Israel. This has been mainly a twentieth century development; at the turn of the century there were probably less than 50,000 Jewish residents in what was then Palestine. From 1919 to 1948 the United Kingdom held a mandate over Palestine under the auspices of the League of Nations, and Britain encouraged the immigration of Jews from Europe. By 1948 there were perhaps three-quarters of a million Jewish residents in Palestine, and an independent state of Israel was established through U.N. intervention and the partition of Palestine. The immigration continued, and Jewish migrants came from Europe, from South Africa, from America—even from the Soviet Union, where obstacles were raised to the emigration of Jews to Israel. The population of Israel now approaches 3.5 million, of whom more than 85 percent are Jewish and nearly half are immigrants who arrived after independence.

Jewish emigrants leave Europe after World War II, boarding a ship at Marseilles bound for Haifa, Israel.

Migration and Demographic Structure

The age-sex pyramid of individual countries summarizes the structure of the population as a whole, but it conceals internal differences. Age-compositions of cities often differ markedly from rural areas: families in cities tend to be smaller, and there are fewer children, proportionally, than in the countryside. Even within cities, contrasts occur, for the population pyramid of the white sector may differ substantially from that of the black. Obviously the migration process that brings people to the cities from the countryside has an impact on their respective population structures, for many of the migrants are young adults in search of work. This age-selective migration can be discerned on the charts.

Migration also can be sex-selective, whether forced or voluntary. Far more male than female Africans were taken to the New World as slaves; in modern times the number of male emigrants from European countries to America was much larger than the female total. At the beginning of the century there were about 107 males in the United States for every 100 females, but time has eliminated that disparity, and now the statistics show women to be in a slight majority. Greater male wartime losses and the longer life expectancy of women have contributed to the reversal. In cities of India and Africa males continue to outnumber females, sometimes overwhelmingly—a result of sex-selective migration and the cause of serious problems of social adjustment.

Regional migrations often follow major political changes or periods of war. After the end of World War II, as many as 15 million Germans migrated from their homes in areas of Eastern Europe westward, either voluntarily or under expulsion. Several million fled Soviet-controlled East Germany and crossed into West Germany. During the 1950s and continuing to the present, Europe's economic unification under the EEC (European Economic Community, the "Common Market") made it possible for workers to seek jobs in countries other than their own, often at higher wages than they could earn at home. Millions of workers moved from Spain, Italy, Greece, even Ireland and Turkey into the European industrial heartland. Today, Italian labor serves German factories, Greek waiters work in Dutch restaurants, Spanish workers take jobs in French industries. In general the direction of this regional migration is from Southern Europe to the north, and from all directions to the European core area, especially to West Germany and to France. Although many workers leave their families at home and send money to support them, perhaps more than half eventually settle permanently in their new abode and bring their families over. In Greece during the 1960s, nearly three out of four workers who emigrated to seek work elsewhere in Europe failed to return. Portugal, too, experienced a substantial exodus. In Italy, the emigrant flow has subsided somewhat in recent years. But the postwar period in Europe has been a

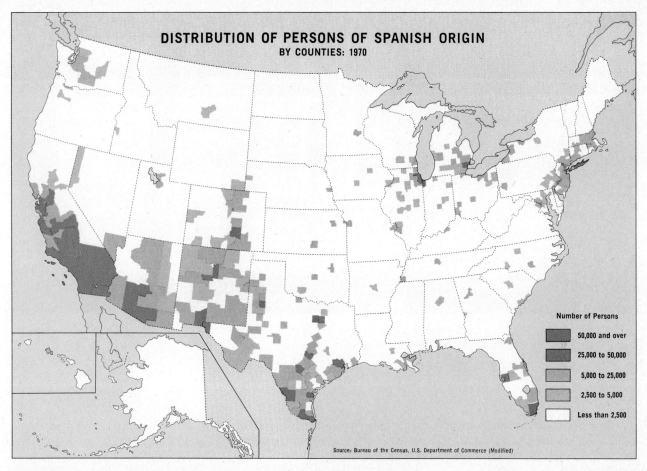

DISTRIBUTION OF PERSONS OF SPANISH ORIGIN
BY COUNTIES: 1970

Number of Persons

50,000 and over

25,000 to 50,000

5,000 to 25,000

2,500 to 5,000

Less than 2,500

Source: Bureau of the Census, U.S. Department of Commerce (Modified)

Figure 5-5

time of major readjustment and mixing.

The United States has also experienced a regional migration in recent years, one that followed a major political change. When the Castro regime took control of Cuba, its policies led several hundred thousand Cubans to leave. This migration commenced even before the Cuban socialist course was set, but during the 1960s it intensified and was formalized as the "Cuban Airlift." Although some

of the Cuban families went to Spain, the overwhelming majority came to the United States—and most of those settled in the nearest urban area and their initial point of immigration, Miami. There, they developed a southeastern core of Spanish-speaking people, whose concentration has always been strongly oriented to the Southwest (Fig. 5-5).

Regional migrations also occur when a substantial labor force is needed in a concentrated area in an underdeveloped region. In West Africa,

prevailing directions of regional migrations are coastward, from the interior (where drought is likely to be the "push" factor) to coastal zones where cities and productive agricultural areas lie. In Southern Africa, migration directions have been focused on the mining-industrial-urban zone that extends from Zaire's Southeastern region through Zambia's Copperbelt and Rhodesia's Great Dyke (that country's mineral-rich backbone) all the way to the Witwatersrand and its focus, Johannesburg (Fig. 5-6).

107

Regional migration in Europe: a large group of Italian workers wait to board a train for West Germany, where they are to be employed in industry.

Internal migrations can also involve significant population shifts, even though no political boundary, sea, or ocean is crossed by the migrants. During the last decades of the Czarist period in Russia, the great Siberian expanses east of the Urals were invaded by growing numbers of peasant farmers in search of new lands and new opportunities. This flow was strengthened by the construction of the Trans-Siberian Railroad to Vladivostok, started in 1892. Eventually World War I and subsequently the Revolution stemmed the tide of eastward migration, but after the reorganization of the 1920s it became Soviet policy to stimulate the development of Siberia once again. Natural resources were opened up, industrialization was supported, and various incentives were used to induce people to move eastward to places such as Novosibirsk and Krasnoyarsk. The invasion from the west during World War II further strengthened Soviet resolve to develop Eastern regions of the realm, and more than 2 million people were resettled east of the Urals. Today, although the center of Soviet population still lies far to the west in the great Eurasian realm, there are more than twice as many people east of the Urals than there were just 50 years ago—some 60 million, with 20 million in Western and Eastern Siberia, 5 million in the Soviet Far East, and more than 30 million in the Central Asian Republics. This great internal migration is identified as flow (8) on Figure 5-1.

If the Soviet Union had an interest in peopling and consolidating its Far East, so did the Chinese—who lost territory to Russian imperialism. Manchuria was a prize in the inevitable war between Russia and Japan (1904–1905), and following Russia's defeat the region became a Japanese sphere of influence. During the interwar period the Japanese developed Manchuria, but it was the Chinese who peopled the area. At the time of the Russian-Japanese War, Manchuria contained a small sedentary Chinese population in the south and a mainly nomadic Manchu population elsewhere, totaling perhaps 10 million. The Japanese needed the Chinese labor force, and in the 1930s Manchuria's population passed the 30-million mark, by now overwhelmingly Chinese.

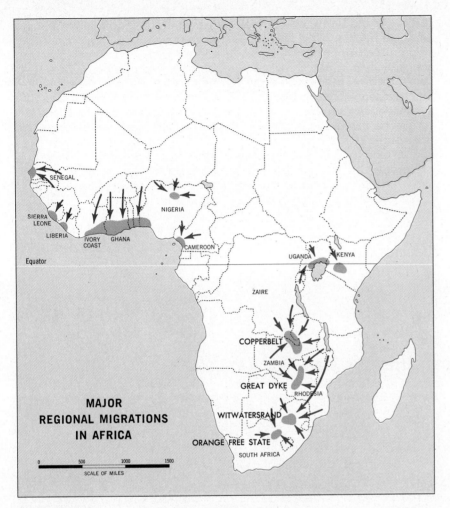

Figure 5-6

Japan's defeat in World War II and Manchuria's incorporation into modern China further stimulated Chinese consolidation there. Manchuria has become China's industrial heartland and a not inconsiderable agricultural region; its population today is probably near 75 million. This is among the larger internal migrations in recent decades.

Several simultaneous internal migrations have occurred in the United States. The first of these is our well-known west-ward expansion. The second involves the migration of black Americans from the South to the North. The third is a process that takes place not only in the United States but in nearly all countries: the movement from rural areas to the cities. In the United States, however, there is a special relationship between these last two internal migrations, for the great majority of the black Americans who migrated northward moved to northern cities, and there stimulated large-scale intracity migration by whites.

The northward migration of blacks from the South was a mere trickle until the years of World War I, when the immigrations from Europe were cut off. Industries continued to expand and required more labor. Now a campaign began to recruit black workers from the South, and blacks responded by leaving the South by the hundreds of thousands. Most moved to the cities of the American heartland. The flow continued after the end of the war and, indeed, increased

109

during the 1920s; after a decline during the depression years of the 1930s it resumed its upward climb. At the turn of the century, only 10 percent of the black population lived outside the South; in 1970 it was nearly 50 percent. This means that the black population of the United States became urbanized even more rapidly than the white population did, for the vast majority of those who went to the industrialized North came from rural areas in the South. Today, about 90 percent of black Americans living in rural areas remain in the South; of those in the North, over 90 percent live in cities. This helps explain the apparent Southern concentration of black population shown on Figure 5-7: the Southeastern core area is extensive, but substantially rural. The urban concentrations of the north show less spatial extent, but their numbers are great.

We have referred previously to the fate of new arrivals in the cities of underdeveloped countries and the inadequacy of their housing and facilities. What were the circumstances confronting these black Americans when they came to the cities of the North? They usually settled in one of the few areas in the city where black people already were living; mostly in areas where rents were low. Crowding soon became a problem, and the increasing densities had two immediate consequences: the expansion of the black residential areas in the city, and their rapid deterioration. Black people could

Figure 5-7

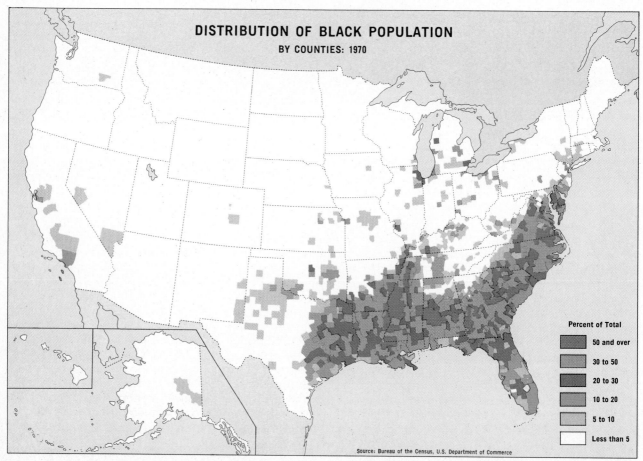

DISTRIBUTION OF BLACK POPULATION
BY COUNTIES: 1970

Percent of Total

50 and over

30 to 50

20 to 30

10 to 20

5 to 10

Less than 5

Source: Bureau of the Census, U.S. Department of Commerce

110

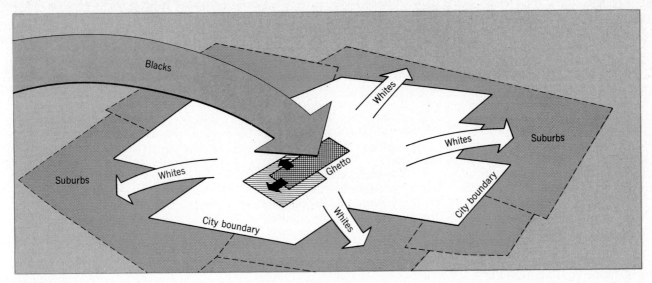

Figure 5-8

not simply move to any part of town and buy a house; most could not afford it, and those who might be able to purchase a modest home found that their choices were limited to few areas. Thus a pattern of residential segregation evolved, quite similar to that with which the black people had been acquainted in the South. It is, we know, a persistent feature of the American city still today. When Burgess wrote about his concentric zone theory, he described the city in America as the great assimilator, the unifying force. The city has not been the equalizer some anticipated it to be.

As the immigration of black residents swelled the population of the inner cities, it also generated an out-migration of white residents (Fig. 5-8). Eventually the suburbs began to sprawl beyond the municipal boundaries, producing administratively separate communities. This had several implications. First, the flight of the white inhabitants of the interior regions of the city reduced the opportunities for constructive contact between the cultures of the city. Second, those white residents who moved beyond the city's boundaries took with them their substantial taxable incomes. The city suffered the loss of the taxes—and many businesses followed their customers out of the city as well. Now the city proved still less able to provide for its remaining inhabitants the services that were already inadequate and under the pressure of growing numbers. The ripple effects of the internal migration of black Americans have not subsided.

The Migration Process

Earlier in this chapter we asked this question: what makes people decide to move or migrate? Studies focusing on the migration-decision indicate that the intensity of the migration flow varies with such factors as (1) the degree of difference between the known location (the source) and the perceived goal (the destination), (2) the effectiveness of the information flow from those who migrated to those who remained behind but were receptive, and (3) distance. Obviously it is easier to study internal migration than regional or intercontinental movements, and as long as a century ago the British social scientist E. G. Ravenstein researched internal migration in England with the aim of deriving laws governing the process. Ravenstein concluded that there is an inverse relationship between the incidence of migration and the distance between source and destination—that is, the quantity of migrants declines as the distance they know they must travel to reach their objective increases. Subsequent studies of internal migrations in several countries have modified this model as well as some of the other laws Ravenstein derived from his data. The concept of intervening opportunity, for example, reminds us that people's perception of the advantages of a far-away destination are changed when there are opportunities nearer by. The distant destination does not look nearly so attractive when a closer one exists. In the days when Britishers emigrated to Africa and beyond, many chose South Africa rather than cross still another ocean to go to Australia.

The character of information flow—feedback—also has been studied in detail. People who migrate write family members and friends who remained behind, telling them of their experiences, opportunities, achievements, and problems; they encourage them to come, but describe problems faced as well. This information flow tends to channel the migration flow, and researchers have found that migrations tend to be concentrated along rather well-defined routes. Of course, people's information is not always correct—in fact, most migrants probably move on the basis of partially distorted perceptions of reality, including distances, costs, opportunities and advantages, and most other aspects of the adventure. Again, research suggests that there is a certain knowledge decay that varies directly with distance: the greater the distance between source and destination, the greater the degree of distortion, the more severe the decay in knowledge. It is not difficult to identify people who migrate today, even with our world's improved communications, and find themselves victims of knowledge-decay. Ask some of those Russian Jewish emigrants who wait in Austria, asking to be allowed to return to the very Soviet Union they left under such difficult circumstances, and who found Israel to be quite unlike what they had imagined.

Restrictions on Migration

People have moved and migrated across our globe since the dawn of history—and attempts to stem various tides and flows of migration are just about as old. It is appropriate for us to consider some of these efforts, for they continue to trouble our modern world.

Among the most massive efforts to limit the movement of peoples are the huge walls built by the Chinese before and during the Han period, walls built not only to keep the Mongol "barbarians" out of the sedentary farming areas of China, but also to stop Chinese farmers from being absorbed into the nomadic ways of the drier steppes beyond. More recently we have seen wall building in Berlin, there to stop the departure of East Germans and others to the West via the "window" of West Berlin.

More frequently, however, the obstacles placed in the way of would-be migrants are legal, not physical. As early as 1882, the United States by an act of Congress restricted the immigration of Chinese to California; when the composition of European immigrants began to change in what many considered undesirable directions, a quota system was established for them as well by acts passed in the 1920s. This system continued until 1966, but restrictions on immigration still continue. In recent decades the sources of immigration to the United States have changed. Europeans come in smaller numbers, but immigration from Middle and South American countries has increased to nearly half the overall total. In addition, illegal immigration has become a major problem, and in the 1970s voices were being raised in the U.S. government in favor of stronger control measures over the inflow of aliens.

The United States is not the only country to grapple with immigration problems. A small but significant intercontinental migration from the West Indies, Africa, and Asia has begun to change the population mix in Britain, and the United Kingdom weighs limitations on this flow from Commonwealth countries. The Soviet Union places barriers in the way of Jewish citizens who want to emigrate to Israel (and makes other emigrants' exits problematic too) under the rule that requires such emigrants to pay the state back for the education and other amenities received free during their residence. The Soviet restrictions on emigration are unusual in today's world: most countries are quite willing to see emigrants leave if they prefer an alternate abode. This does not apply to some Southern European countries that have lost significant elements of their labor force in Europe's recent regional migration, or, for example, to Britain's "brain drain" of the 1950s and early 1960s. But those countries hardly made emigration practically impossible, as has happened in the U.S.S.R. and several Eastern European countries. Restrictions on migration have normally involved keeping would-be immigrants out—as in Australia's now-revised all-white policy, South Africa's restrictions on the internal migration of Asians, Thailand's limitation on Chinese immigration, Burma's efforts to limit immigration from India, Ethiopia's attempts to stem the tide of periodic migration along the Somali border. Human population will stop moving no more than it will stop multiplying.

Act of faith and hope.

6 The Coming Crisis

It is likely that we stand, today, at the threshold of a period of critical change in the course of world history. Not since the onset of the Industrial Revolution, 200 years ago, has the potential for change been greater. But unlike the years when technological innovations and products transformed much of the world, and change meant progress and expansion, we face the reality that we are approaching our earth's limits. For more than a century humanity has grown like a biological culture in an ideal environment, consuming space and resources and energy at exponentially increasing rates. And now, during the last quarter of the twentieth century, we are at a turning point in more ways than one. The natural environments under which we multiplied are changing, and those disastrous harvests of the 1970s may signal worldwide climatic reversal. The artificial environments we have created for ourselves in crowded cities are leading to stress and social dislocation. By our pollution of the environment we contribute to local as well as global environmental deterioration. We are exhausting our earth's resources and do not have substitutes ready; the 1973 energy crisis was just a hint of what lies ahead. The prospect of global hunger and deteriorating nutrition even in the world's richer countries looms for the first time. As the gap between the developed and underdeveloped countries grows, the hopes for a lasting world order recede. The frustrations of the disadvantaged are expressed not only in rising local crime rates associated with recession and unemployment but also in the dislocations caused by international terrorism. And our medical victories are still not absolute: some experts warn that we are possibly vulnerable to new disease epidemics through our use of antibiotics and other medicines. Never before has the world confronted such a set of actual and potential crises.

In this chapter, we examine the world's prospects under five rubrics, keeping in mind that we have already considered the popula-

115

tion crisis in other contexts in the previous chapters. As you will see, we refer in later chapters to some of the issues we are about to raise; it would be impossible to discuss our cities without referring to the problems associated with their living environments, for example. Presently we focus on (1) world climate and the indications that it is changing from both natural and human causes; (2) our pollution of local and possibly even global environments, contributing further to permanent change; (3) world resources and their exploitation, especially the energy-producing resources; (4) the threat to a lasting world order created by the widening gap between poor and rich; and (5) the potential for reverses in our fight for better world health.

The evolution of human societies to the level of today has taken place in a very brief period, when measured against the lifetime of the earth itself. The emergence of Homo Sapiens from a series of predecessors involves, at the most, a period of perhaps 10 million years; the development of complex human societies has taken place in the last 10,000 years. Consider this in the framework of an earth that may be five *billion* years old!

The natural environments of our planet change continuously. In a human lifetime we tend not to perceive such changes, except that we sometimes feel that winters are getting colder, or rainfall seems to be less plentiful than it used to be. But over

longer periods those changes are very real. During the earth's lifespan, mountain ranges have been built and worn away, seas have formed and dried up again. Even the continents themselves drifted across the face of our planet, coalescing during one period of earth history and then splitting apart again. And most important to us, the earth's climates also changed over time. Places where rain and moisture were once plentiful are now the driest of deserts. Areas that were cold and under permanent ice are now fertile farmlands. In the rock layers of the continents we can read the endless cycles of climatic change.

One of the remaining mysteries of our planet relates directly to climatic change. At in-

For them, the crisis is already here. Bombay, India.

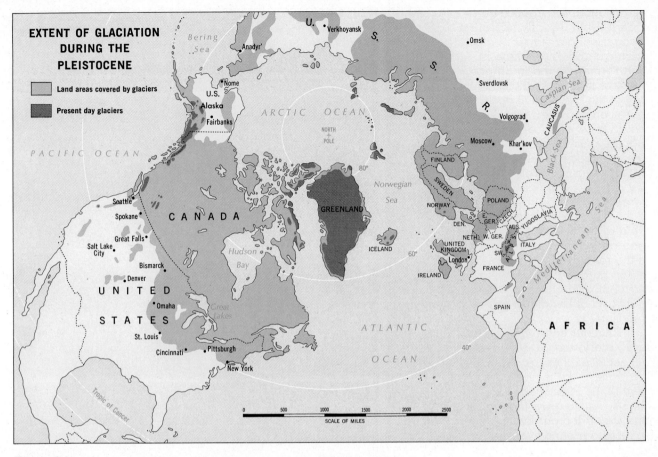

EXTENT OF GLACIATION DURING THE PLEISTOCENE

Land areas covered by glaciers

Present day glaciers

SCALE OF MILES
0   500   1000   1500   2000   2500

Figure 6-1

tervals, our globe becomes colder, and the ice and snow usually locked up in the Arctic and Antarctic polar areas begins to advance toward the equator. Enormous ice sheets develop, eventually covering whole regions of continents. Correspondingly, the temperate, subtropical, and tropical zones of the earth also become cooler. World climatic patterns shift in response; forests disappear, green grasslands turn into deserts. Then the glacial advance stops, and the ice retreats. During the warming trend, ice-covered areas are exposed, vegetation takes a hold, soils develop anew. But the warming trend also is only temporary, and a new glacial advance begins. The ice sheets come back. Glacial epochs are marked by a series of such cyclic advances and retreats of the ice sheets.

The most recent of these glacial epochs is called the Pleistocene, and what started during the Pleistocene is still going on today. The Pleistocene glaciation began about three million years ago, and humanity has been described as the product of the Pleistocene epoch, because it was during the cycles of glacial advance and retreat that the final

117

stages of our emergence occurred. Until recently, scientists recognized four stages of glacial advance and retreat here in North America and in Europe, but now it appears that the history of the Pleistocene epoch is more complex than that. What we do know with certainty is that the most recent retreat of the ice occurred just 10,000 to 20,000 years ago. Think about it: just a matter of thousands of years ago, the ice sheets stood to the banks of what is today the Ohio River, covering all of Michigan and Wisconsin and most of the rest of the Midwest. (Fig. 6-1) In Europe the ice covered most of England, much of Germany, all of Denmark, Sweden, and Norway.

Thus our entire modern culture history, the development of our societies, has taken place in the wake of the most recent retreat of the Pleistocene ice sheets. As we grew in numbers and expanded our living spheres, we found ever more habitable space. The earth was warming up: snows turned into rainfall, tundra areas developed good soils, growing seasons lengthened. And, as we will see in Chapter 14, this period—the past 20,000 years—also witnessed the domestication of animals and plants, the increasing use of the earth's natural resources, and the evolution of ever more complex human societies. Eventually the Industrial-Technological Revolution occurred, followed by the explosive growth of human population discussed in Chapter 2, and the livable space on this earth was occupied as never before.

But the most recent retreat of the Pleistocene's ice sheets probably was not the *last* retreat of those glaciers. Compared to the

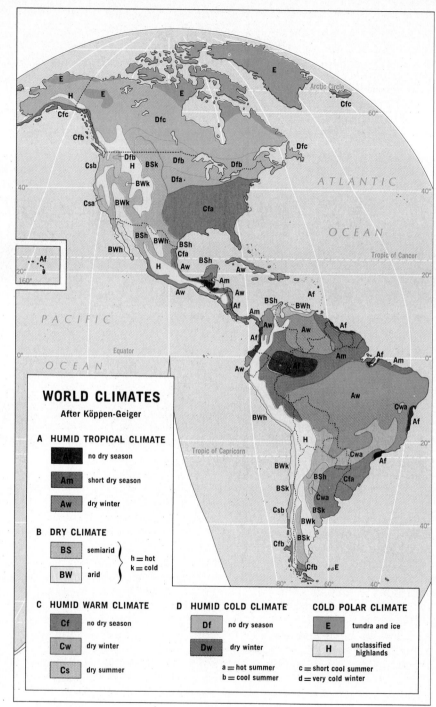

Figure 6-2

118

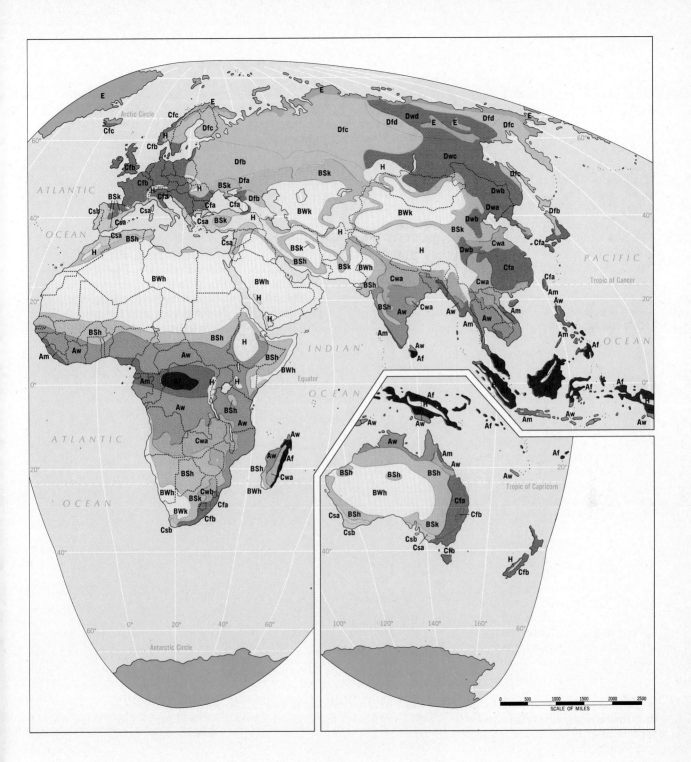

119

duration of earlier glacial epochs in earth history, the Pleistocene glaciation has been brief indeed; three million years is not much in the time frame of a planet as old as ours. What has optimistically been described as the Pleistocene's final advance (the Wisconsin glaciation in North America, the Würm glaciation in Eurasia) was very likely not the concluding phase of the Pleistocene at all. Humanity's modern evolution has taken place not *after* the Pleistocene, but *during* one of the Pleistocene's warmer periods—during an *interglacial,* to use the appropriate term for such a spell between ice advances. And this means that our familiar map of world climates (Fig. 6-2) represents but a very temporary situation, and perhaps the most optimistic and positive one that the Pleistocene could produce. This is the ideal environment during which humanity, as we stated it earlier, has grown like a biological culture. There are signs that we are already past the midpoint of the present interglacial.

In places where human settlement hangs precariously on the margins of a frigid landmass (Greenland) and where temperature records have been kept for centuries (Iceland) there are indications that the next glacial advance may be about to begin. It is always possible, of course, that these signs are false, and represent only a minor oscillation within the interglacial we are now enjoying. Reliable climatic statistics are not available for past centuries; Iceland is one of the few places in Europe where systematic information was recorded and kept for a very long time. So we can still only guess about worldwide climatic fluctuations, but when the available evidence is pieced together the indications are that we are at the threshold of a new glacial advance.

The results of a renewed encroachment of the ice sheets will be barely imaginable. The climatic zones on Figure 6-2 will be compressed into a much narrower segment of the globe. In the Northern Hemisphere, summers and growing seasons will disappear from Canada and the Midwest; Europe will cease to be a temperate region and Siberia will be an Arctic area as far south as the Himalayas. The Sahara Desert will migrate southward and reach the West African coast. As the jet stream fails to make its annual northward, trans-Himalayan migration, India's monsoon will cease. Northern China will become tundra country. The world's granaries will be destroyed. Other areas may become productive; North Africa and the Middle East may experience again the fertility they enjoyed in pre-Roman times. Equatorial Africa and the Amazon Basin of South America also may be transformed.

None of this will occur over-

The Sahara encroaches, the Sahel dies.

120

night, of course, but, on the other hand, it may not take as long as you might believe. It may be that the Sahara's southward march, already underway and directly related to the current food crisis in the Sahel, is another piece of evidence that the coming change is already in progress. The worldwide crop failures to which reference was made in Chapter 3 are likely to be more than a coincidence. They may signal worldwide climatic reversals as well.

It is important, then, to recognize present-day world climates as temporary and transitional. Natural forces that we cannot control are at work. At the same time, we are contributing to changes in world climates ourselves, and we do not know the consequences of our actions. We are filling the atmosphere with smoke and gases, and quite possibly we are in the process of interfering with the course of nature. We may hasten the onset of the next ice age; some scholars believe that we may be slowing it down. Whatever we are doing (and we will consider this in the next section) there is one overriding reality: our global living space will be reduced, and the earth's productivity restricted, by climatic change at the very time when we are yet unable to solve the world's population problems. Even the slightest hint of the beginning of a return to another Pleistocene glacial epoch could have an impact on the world of the twenty-first century that is beyond imagination.

The earth has six continents and seven seas—but it has only one atmosphere, a thin layer of air that lies on the lands and oceans. On this atmosphere we all depend for our survival. We breathe its oxygen. It shields us from the destructive rays of the sun, and moderates temperatures everywhere. It carries moisture from the oceans over the land (Fig. 6-3), sustaining crops and forests and replenishing soils and wells. It is the essence of life on this planet.

But by our growing numbers and our drive for "progress," we are making a giant sewer of our atmosphere (and our oceans as well). Somehow the atmosphere seems always to be able to cleanse itself, even when we blacken the skies with soot. In the end, however, that may prove to be an illusion. True, the air disperses even the densest smoke and the most acrid of chemical fumes. Nevertheless, some of the waste pouring into the atmosphere is producing irreversible changes in the troposphere (our eight- to nine-mile thick, lowest atmospheric layer). These changes may ultimately affect the radiation balance, that is, the type and intensity of the sun's rays that reach the earth, and thus modify the whole life support system on this earth.

We experience pollution of

Figure 6-3 The hydrologic cycle constitutes a circulation system that brings moisture from ocean surfaces to land areas in humidity–laden airmasses. Condensation, cloud formation, and precipitation occur over the land, and runoff, seepage, and evaporation return the moisture to the oceans.

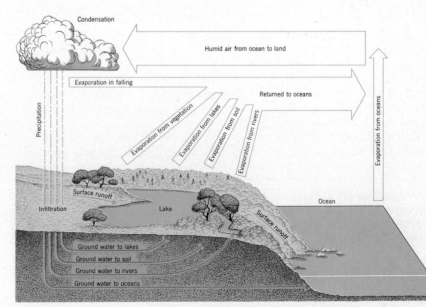

Oil spills around the world have done enormous ecological damage. The breakup of giant tankers and the failure of precautions on offshore drilling rigs have fouled water and beaches from Spain to Santa Barbara. A cleanup is under way following a recent oil spill near San Francisco.

the air and its consequences in our personal lives (e.g., when someone smokes in our home), at work (in an office or a factory), and in our community in general. In our North American society, automobiles in the 1970s were contributing about 60 percent of all the pollutants sent into the atmosphere, and factories about 20 percent. Automobiles contribute a great deal of carbon monoxide as well as hydrocarbons and nitrogen dioxide; these last two are the main elements in a now-familiar urban phenomenon, smog. Industries such as steel mills, refineries, and chemical plants produce a

different gas, that is, carbon dioxide, among many pollutants. Power generators, many of which still burn coal and oil, spew huge quantities of sulfur dioxide into the atmosphere—some two million tons annually in the New York area alone, for example. When you add up all the places around the globe where this is happening, around the clock, every day, the total tonnage of pollutants we send into the atmosphere is truly staggering. Like the population explosion, it cannot go on without producing a worldwide crisis.

It is possible that the cumulative effect of all this pollution is already changing the climates of the earth as a whole. At least two processes may be going on. In the first place, the sun's rays may be reflected back into space by all those particles suspended in the atmosphere to an ever greater degree. This means that less radiation from the sun reaches the surface of the earth, less heating therefore takes place, and we may be helping the ice age come back even faster than nature would have done. On the other hand, those pollutants in the air may also serve to retain heat in the atmosphere, for they also interfere with heat that radiates outward and would otherwise be lost. You may have noticed, if you live in a city, how the evening weather report predicts colder nighttime winter temperatures in the suburbs than in the downtown area. In large measure this is due to the concentration of pollution in the heart of the city, and the clearer air in the outlying areas. Scholars are not sure whether the pollution in the atmosphere will ultimately contribute to a more rapid cooling of the earth or to a retention of heat, slowing the cooling rate associated with the new ice-sheet advance. But this very point—that we are affecting the atmospheric processes without knowledge of what the consequences may be—underscores the dangers inherent in our pollution of the air.

For example, there are scientists who believe that increasing pollution will cause such heating of the atmosphere that, rather than precipitating an ice age, we will cause the polar ice caps to melt and sea level to rise, slowly at first, then more rapidly to a level perhaps 300 feet above what it is today. They argue that this will occur not in some distant future geologic period, but soon—beginning in about 80 years or so. And, they say, we had better start getting used to a map showing new continental outlines (Fig. 6-4).

Compare that map to the world population map: it shows the living space of hundreds of millions of people inundated. Whether through a new ice age or by inundation, we should be prepared for a reduction of our habitat on this planet. And through our pollution of the atmosphere we may be contributing to its relatively rapid diminution.

Figure 6-4

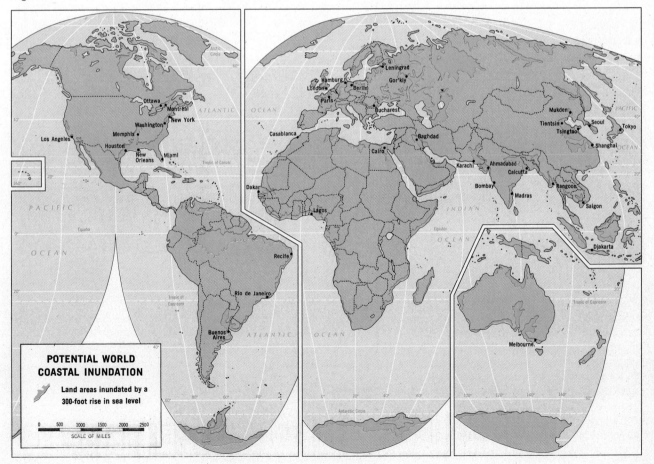

POTENTIAL WORLD COASTAL INUNDATION

Land areas inundated by a 300-foot rise in sea level

0 500 1000 1500 2000 2500
SCALE OF MILES

This map represents a critical element of our earthly environment: the distribution of precipitation, mainly in the form of rainfall. It shows the large quantity of rainfall during an average year in India and Bangladesh, and over large parts of China and Southeast Asia, where the rains must water the rice paddies and are a matter of survival for the population. It also reveals large annual rainfall totals in less densely peopled areas of the tropics in Africa and Asia. Compared to these equatorial and tropical totals, often in excess of 80 inches (200 centimeters) per year, the fertile lands of the United States and Canada, Europe, and other midlatitude regions of the world receive relatively little precipitation. Here we must remember that *evapotranspiration* (that is, the return of moisture to the air by evaporation from soils and by transpiration from leaves) is far greater in the warm tropics than in the cooler temperae regions. Thus 40 inches (100 centimeters) of annual rainfall in a midlatitude region may be more ample than 60 inches (150 centimeters) in a tropical area, and, other things being equal, crops may do better in the less moist— but cooler—temperate zone.

This world precipitation map is the product of all the complex processes going on in the atmosphere—processes that may, according to scientists, be undergoing modification by human actions. If the map of 25 years from now shows a global reduction in total precipitation, the effect in terms of lost productivity would be disastrous.

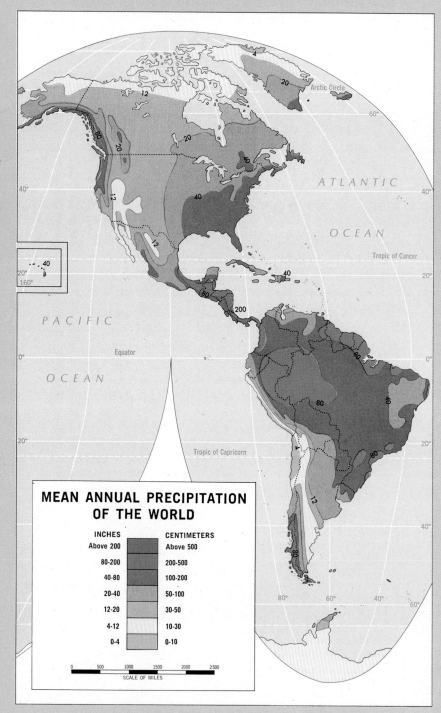

MEAN ANNUAL PRECIPITATION OF THE WORLD

INCHES		CENTIMETERS
Above 200		Above 500
80-200		200-500
40-80		100-200
20-40		50-100
12-20		30-50
4-12		10-30
0-4		0-10

0   500   1000   1500   2000   2500
SCALE OF MILES

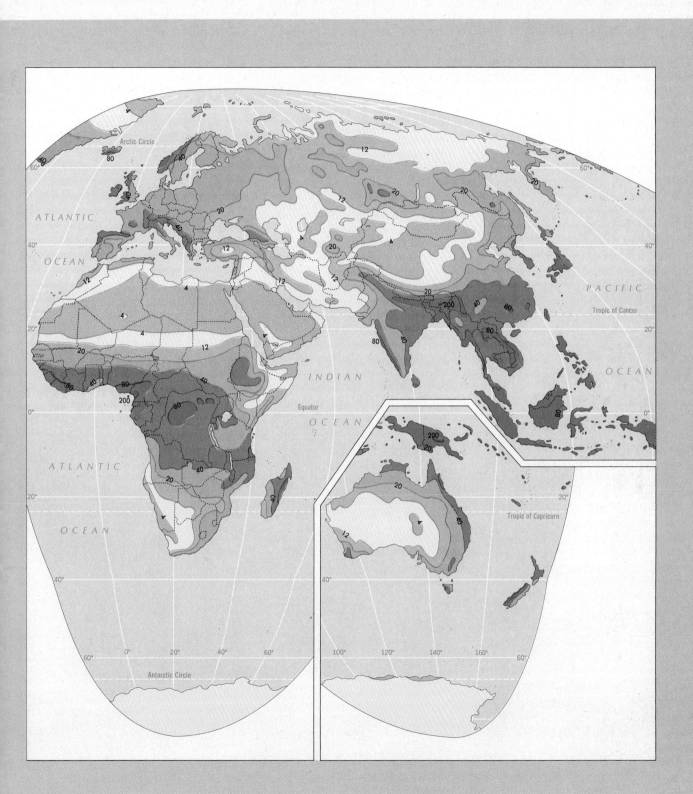

Scarcer Resources

Even as our earliest human ancestors led a hunting and gathering existence, they began to make use of the earth's rocks and minerals. From those beginnings, when spear- and arrowheads were chipped from fine-grained flint (a kind of quartz), our search for this planet's mineral wealth has intensified. Since the onset of the Industrial Revolution we have consumed the earth's resources at a very rapid rate.

Perhaps we should define the term resource—what is a resource and what is not? To the earliest, forest-dwelling people, copper and tin were not resources. Copper did not become a resource until it was deemed to have value as a malleable substance for the creation of various implements; its worth increased when, in combination with tin, it produced the harder metal bronze. To the ancient Egyptians, petroleum was not a resource. Uranium did not become a resource until the twentieth century. There may be substances in the earth that will become resources in the future, but that are not resources today. In other words, human development determines and defines the nature of resources; what is and what is not a resource is a cultural matter. Each civilization, in human history, has depended on its own set or complex of resources. In ours, at present, the power resources dominate, and the earth's mineral fuels (coal, petroleum, natural gas) are the critical elements of this complex. As everyone knows, we are in the middle of an energy crisis. Our resource complex is running short.

Sign of the first phase of the energy crisis: long lines at gasoline stations. Here motorists wait their turn at a station in Manhattan.

126

It is important to distinguish between *renewable* and *nonrenewable* resources. Our soils, for example, are a resource, and they are renewable. They can regenerate after they have been exhausted or overused. Forests will grow again after having been cut down. Water supplies, too, constitute renewable resources, for the rains come to replenish dry wells. But coal, natural gas, and petroleum are nonrenewable resources, as are iron ores, copper deposits, and other metallic and nonmetallic minerals. They can be used up—and humanity has an enormous appetite. There are fears that the known supply of iron ore may be exhausted early in the twenty-first century, and that other metals will soon follow. But ours is an age of energy, and it is the energy picture that has resource specialists worried.

It is not likely that we will run out of oil, gas, and coal suddenly some summer (although some observers have gone so far as to predict such a doomsday); the problem is that demand is skyrocketing and the supply appears on the verge of falling seriously short. The most accessible reserves have been worked out, costs are rising fast, and technological developments are not coming as fast as they are needed (Fig. 6-5). The effect of all this is felt especially strongly on electricity, the form of power for which demand is rising most rapidly of all.

Strip mining can do great damage to local and regional ecology. The photo shows what has been done to the mountain landscape near Santa Barbara by strip mining operations.

127

Electric power is manufactured from oil, coal, and gas; it is also produced by hydroelectric plants, and it is generated more and by the power plants of the future, the nuclear reactors. Today, the United States still uses 25 percent of its energy resources for the production of electricity. Industry uses most of the output (more than 40 percent), and private homes and commercial establishments consume most of the rest. The problem with the conversion of oil and coal into electric power is that it is a very dirty process. Just over one-third of the fuel is made into electricity, and the rest becomes wasted smoke and heat. An increase in electricity supply, therefore, requires a disproportional increase in fuel supply and consumption, which means more landscape-destroying strip mining, more ocean-polluting oil spills, and more atmosphere-befouling soot and poisonous gases. Has the technological revolution finally failed?

Perhaps not, but the makings of a crisis are at hand. Even now, while industrialized countries are still converting their power plants from coal to oil and gas, preparations are already underway to switch again to nuclear reactors. Today the nuclear plants produce a mere 4 percent of U.S. electricity requirements. Predictions are, however, that by 1990 that figure may be 50 percent or more. If the nuclear plant is to be the generator of the future, why not convert directly and more quickly to these plants? The answer, again, lies in our mushrooming population numbers and their

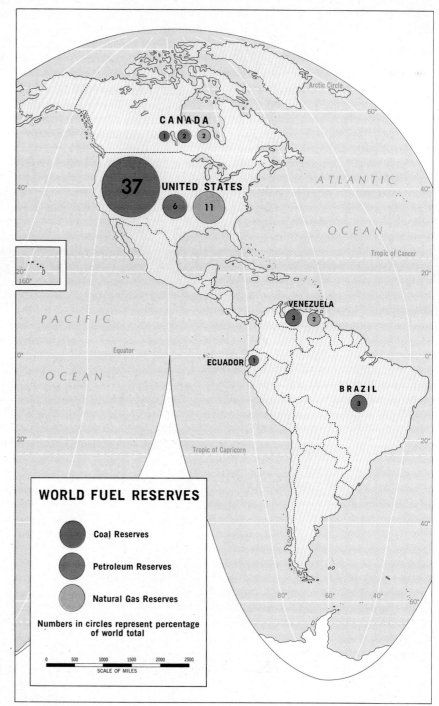

Figure 6-5

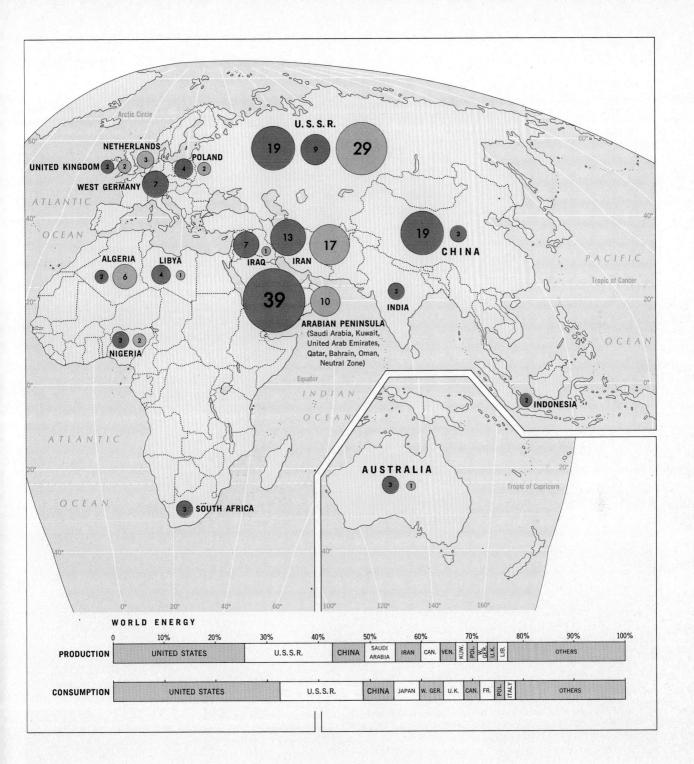

U.S.S.R.

19 9 29

NETHERLANDS

POLAND

UNITED KINGDOM 2 2 3

WEST GERMANY 7 4 2

CHINA

19 3

ALGERIA 2 6

LIBYA 4 1

7 13 17 1

IRAQ IRAN

39 10

INDIA 3

ARABIAN PENINSULA
(Saudi Arabia, Kuwait,
United Arab Emirates,
Qatar, Bahrain, Oman,
Neutral Zone)

NIGERIA 3 2

INDONESIA 2

SOUTH AFRICA 3

AUSTRALIA 3 1

WORLD ENERGY

	0	10%	20%	30%	40%	50%	60%	70%	80%	90%	100%

PRODUCTION: UNITED STATES | U.S.S.R. | CHINA | SAUDI ARABIA | IRAN | CAN. | VEN. | KUW. | POL. | W. GER. | U.K. | LIB. | OTHERS

CONSUMPTION: UNITED STATES | U.S.S.R. | CHINA | JAPAN | W. GER. | U.K. | CAN. | FR. | POL. | ITALY | OTHERS

129

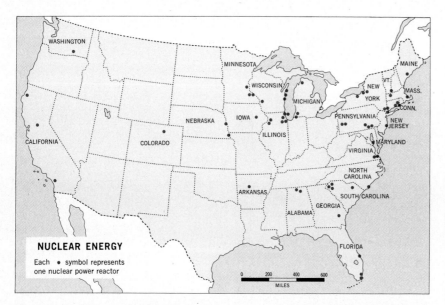

NUCLEAR ENERGY

Each • symbol represents
one nuclear power reactor

0   200   400   600
MILES

Figure 6-6 This map of the distribution of nuclear reactors in the United States shows that many of the new reactors lie near large population clusters—a matter of concern among experts who believe that the nuclear power plants are potential hazards. Radiation leakage or explosion, they argue, could endanger millions in a single accident. Proponents of nuclear power cite safeguard systems and the existing safety record in support of their position.

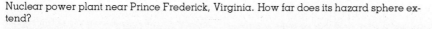

Nuclear power plant near Prince Frederick, Virginia. How far does its hazard sphere extend?

burgeoning needs; the technology is not yet available to mass produce nuclear plants. In addition, there are fears that lethal radiation pollution will occur around nuclear plants just as surely as soot emanates from coal-using plants. Dangers of catastrophic explosion, problems with radioactive waste and its disposal, and other obstacles confront the conversion to nuclear reactors (Fig. 6-6). Not surprisingly, interest has recently begun to focus on the potentials of harnessing and storing solar energy, perhaps a safer prospect.

The energy crisis may be temporary, since an ultimate solution is in sight, but it could

have far-reaching, perhaps permanent impact on our society. We are overstraining the world's remaining conventional energy resources. When this occurred in the past, human resourcefulness and innovative capacity managed to overcome the problem. But today, our capacity for technological innovation is being overtaxed by spiraling demand and inhibiting cost factors. Look at those glass-and-steel greenhouses that line the downtown streets of modern U.S. cities and which, without winter heating and summer air conditioning, would be freezers in one season, ovens in the other. Consider what the impact might be on our far-flung suburbs if the automobile were to be forced into disuse. Adequate mass transit in U.S. cities is still as much a dream as are safe and adequate nuclear reactors. The ultimate solutions are apparently in sight, but the need is here and now: a gap looms. In these terms, our age of energy is clearly on a crisis course.

The widening gap between the developed and the underdeveloped countries has implications beyond those of malnutrition and hunger. The period following the end of World War II brought new hopes and expectations to peoples that had long been shackled and silenced: the United Nations provided a world forum for the expression of their aspirations, and decolonization brought independence to numerous new nations. Where colonial powers were slow to grant independence, revolutions and rebellions hastened the process: in Indonesia against the Netherlands, in Algeria against France, in Kenya against the British. It was natural for those "emerging" states, as the new countries came to be called, to anticipate better times, and to expect that the end of colonial occupation would bring improved living conditions for their peoples. In fact, many politicians in those "developing" countries promised just such better conditions to their new constituents.

But the past two decades have seen conditions get worse, not better, in many underdeveloped countries. Greater numbers of people suffer from hunger and disease, national development plans are not working out, and while the world's poorer countries may have a strong voice in the forums of the United Nations, they have very little actual power. Compared to what the hungry countries had hoped, for example, the United States committed very little concrete assistance to the crisis-struck countries at the First (1974)

Rome Conference on the world food situation. It is not that the U.S. could not have committed more: it was a decision made on the basis of conditions and prospects in the United States itself, and the Administration decided that food costs in America could not be permitted to rise even more than was already the case. Assistance on the scale requested by the hungry countries would have driven the prices up markedly. And so the starving countries could demand and denounce, but they could not force the United States to consider the starvation of millions to be a matter more serious than the price level here at home.

Depending on how you calculate things, the United States consumes between 30 and 40 percent of the world's available resources each year. But the U.S. population, of course, is only about 5 percent of the world total. This combination of figures is all too well known to the governments of countries that have raw materials needed and used in large quantities by the United States. Some of these countries have begun to form organizations designed to create a united front, to make the United States and other Western countries pay more for their resources and change their international political roles. The most successful has been the Organization of Petroleum Exporting Countries (OPEC). Member states are able to demand much higher prices for their crude oil,

131

and they are also capable of influencing the United States' role in the Middle East as it relates to the state of Israel. A good measure of a country's power is its ability to influence and modify the behavior of other countries, and in combination, the OPEC organization has achieved some power in the international scene. Now, the richer countries face the prospect that other groups of countries will establish similar unions—for example, those exporting bauxite (the source of aluminum) to the United States and Europe.

Comparatively few of the underdeveloped countries have the kinds of critical resources that might force the richer countries into a redistribution of the world's wealth, however—and there lies the threat to world order. To the richer states, and to the governments and better-off people in the poorer countries, the most hoped-for future is one of stability, during which solutions can perhaps be found for the critical problems facing the modern world. But such stability means something very different to the starving millions of India and Bangladesh, the landless Palestinians in the Middle East, the Jews trapped by the Soviet establishment, the Africans still subjugated by alien regimes. There are many millions of frustrated people in the world, to whom change—any change—appears preferable to the kind of stability governments hope for.

OPEC, 1976

The following states were members of the Organization of Petroleum Exporting Countries in January, 1976:

Algeria	Qatar
Ecuador	Saudi Arabia
Gabon	United Arab Emirates
Indonesia	Venezuela
Iran	Iraq
Kuwait	Libya
Nigeria	

Airports as widely distributed as Rome, Tel Aviv, and New York have been the targets of terrorist attacks. This is the terminal building at La Guardia Airport, New York, as it looked the day after a bomb exploded without warning, killing 12 and injuring more than 70 persons.

There have always been op- pressed, deprived, landless, and hopeless people in the world. Mostly, they have been voiceless and powerless. Modern times, however, are bringing change to that. The world's poor and their representatives know much better than ever before how underprivileged they really are, and what the widening gap between developed and under- developed means for the future. And they are beginning to dis- cover that while arguments at conferences may have no effect, well-directed terror tactics can and do. In 1974 alone, activists for the Palestinian peoples car- ried on a worldwide campaign of terrorism; the conflict in Northern Ireland spilled terrorist tactics into England; Argentina continued in the grip of several simultaneous terror campaigns; Israel repeatedly witnessed ter- rorist attacks. Modern weapons can be obtained by almost any- one who can produce the money, and we are now at the point where it is conceivable that an airport, a town, even a city can be threatened by any group claiming to represent one or more of the world's numerous causes. Chief among these is the growing contrast between this world's rich and poor—locally in cities with slums and affluence, regionally in countries with developing and depressed areas, globally in states as dif- ferent as the United States and Haiti. The events of Munich, Rome, Buenos Aires, and Tel Aviv may be merely the begin- ning of a wave of terror that could reach crisis proportions.

Modern medicine and im- proving health delivery systems have had an enormous impact on world death rates (and, as we noted, contributed substan- tially to the population explo- sion). In the developed coun- tries, the greatest success has been in the reduction of infant mortality. Progress in the battle against the diseases of middle and old age has been less spec- tacular. Still, there are predic- tions of breakthroughs in the fight against cancer and heart disease, and it is possible that life expectancies in the devel- oped countries, which have been more or less stable for some time now, may rise again.

Some medical geographers warn that new threats to the health of the population of the world loom behind this veneer of success. We alluded to some of these potential threats: we know far too little about the cumula- tive, long-term effect of medica- tions we are taking and food ad- ditives we are consuming. Even our modern vaccination pro- grams may contain the elements of trouble. As Professor John L. Girt wrote recently in *The Geog- raphy of Health and Disease*:

. . . Are we creating a serious health risk for the future by inade- quate vaccination programmes? For example, measles vaccination has been promoted in North America for a number of years and, in the short run, the number of measles cases

may show a downward trend. How- ever, not everyone is being vacci- nated nor becoming immune. The vaccinated and immunes protect many susceptibles from the disease, but it remains to be seen whether the reservoir of susceptibles will reach some unknown threshold size necessary to support a reinfection. If such an epidemic comes, it could be very serious, for not only will it affect children but adults with per- haps serious consequences.

Another area of medical risk is creating increasing concern today—our modification of the earth's atmospheric environ- ment. The atmosphere acts as a shield against damaging forces from beyond our planet. Frag- ments of meteoric material are burned up before they can hit the surface and perhaps do serious damage; destructive rays from the sun are reflected back into space. The atmosphere con- sists of several distinct layers, and each of these layers per- forms a particular function in shaping our environment. One of these layers is the ozone layer, which lies from 10 to 30 miles above the earth's surface and protects us against the sun's ultraviolet rays (Fig. 6-7).

The earth's ozone layer, ac- cording to scientists, is being destroyed by a safe-looking little gadget—the spray can from which we get our deodorants, in- secticides, paints, and many other products. These cans send into the atmosphere a quantity of fluorocarbons, a substance that reacts chemically with the ozone and destroys it. One can produces only a small amount of

133

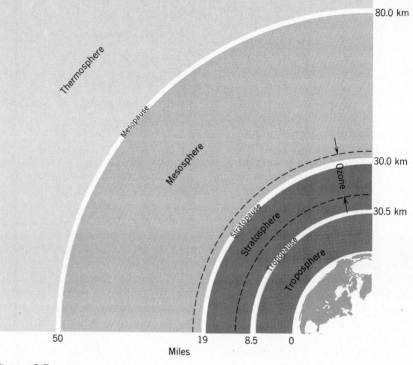

Figure 6-7

this gas, but when you consider the countless millions of cans in use, the threat to the atmosphere appears more serious. There is, of course, no way to measure just how much of these fluorocarbons has already been sprayed into the air, or what the effect on the ozone layer will be even if we stopped using aerosol cans today. But scientists warn that we have already pumped enough fluorocarbons into the atmosphere to continue eroding the ozone layer for 10 to 15 years to come. And now a new, more massive threat is on the scene: the exhausts of the engines of new supersonic airliners and jet transports that will fly at 60,000 to 65,000 feet, there dumping nitrogen oxide, another destroyer of ozone. Unlike our spray cans, the new aircraft send their pollutants into the upper layer of the atmosphere, right where the ozone layer lies, thereby causing immediate chemical changes.

What will the effect be on earth if we do not limit all this pollution? If ultraviolet rays from the sun increase by 20 percent, there will be a large increase in the incidence of skin cancer and substantial climatic changes described by scientists as potentially catastrophic in their effects on world agriculture. If the destruction of the ozone layer were to approach 40 percent, and were to occur very quickly, nearly all life on this planet would be destroyed. Again, this is not some distant, far-away threat, but an immediate prospect that will reach crisis proportions during the last quarter of *this* century. We do not know how much damage we have already done, and although scientists are warning governments, collective action had still not been taken as late as 1976. We are indeed in an age of crisis.

134

Pollution cloud hangs over Denver, Colorado, January 9, 1974.

Reading

The development of geography as a discipline is described by Preston E. James in *All Possible Worlds* (Odyssey, New York, 1972), a readable and often absorbing book that traces the history of geographical ideas from classical to contemporary times. In that book you will find numerous references to the regional concept, and to prove that this whole idea remains a matter for debate among geographers, see the article by R. Symanski and J. L. Newman, "Formal, Functional, and Nodal Regions: Three Fallacies," in the *Professional Geographer*, Vol. XXV, November, 1973. For an indication of the range and potentials of geography see the volume edited by D. A. Lanegran and R. Palm, *An Invitation to Geography* (McGraw-Hill, New York, 1973).

On the population problem, you will want to consult the publications of the Population Reference Bureau, Washington, D.C., whose *Bulletins* include statistics, maps, and commentaries on current questions. Also see S. Johnson, Ed., *The Population Problem* (Wiley, New York, 1973), and John I. Clarke's excellent introduction to the field of *Population Geography* (Pergamon, New York, 1972). Some interesting readings were assembled by Q. H. Stanford in *The World's Population: Problems of Growth* (Oxford, New York, 1972), and you will want to spend an evening with the Ehrlichs' *Population, Resources, Environment* (Freeman, San Francisco, 1975), a book whose first edition of 1970 aroused considerable debate. If you are writing a paper and need recent statistics, remember the United Nations Yearbooks in your library.

A general introduction to world population distribution is G. T. Trewartha's *A Geography of Population: World Patterns* (Wiley, New York, 1969), and you will find some disturbing details in a book by D. H. Meadows, D. L. Meadows, J. Randers, and W. W. Behrens entitled *The Limits to Growth* (Universe Books, New York, 1972).

The food question was summarized by G. Borgstrom in *The Hungry Planet* (Macmillan, New York, 1965). A more recent discussion of the world situation is by L. R. Brown and G. W. Finsterbusch in *Man and His Environment: Food* (Harper, New York, 1972). The importance of protein in diets and the problems of production are described by A. Jones in *World Protein Resources* (Wiley, New York, 1974). J. Hutchinson discusses the interdependence of countryside and town in *Farming and Food Supply* (Cambridge, 1972).

A fascinating introduction to the field of medical geography is edited by J. M. Hunter, *The Geography of Health and Disease* (University of North Carolina, Chapel Hill, 1974). A collection of readings that will provide many insights is edited by N. D. McGlashan and entitled *Medical Geography* (Methuen, London, 1972). If you want to go into the technical problems of health delivery, see D. Dewey, *Where The Doctors Have Gone* (Illinois Regional Medical Program, Chicago, 1973) and G. W. Shannon and G. E. Alan Dever, *Health Care Delivery* (McGraw, New York, 1974). Examples of detailed studies by geographers include J. M. Hunter, "River Blindness in Nangodi, Northern Ghana: a Hypothesis of Cyclical Advance and Retreat," in *The Geographical Review*, Vol. 56, July, 1966, and C. G. Knight, "The Ecology of African Sleeping Sickness," *Annals* of the Association of American Geographers, Vol. 61, March, 1971. Also see G. F. Pyle, "The Diffusion of Cholera in the United States in the Nineteenth Century," *Geographical Analysis*, Vol. 1, 1969.

On migration, consult B. du Toit and H. Safa, editors of two books entitled *Migration and Urbanization* and *Migration and Development* (Mouton, The Hague, 1975) which contain a wealth of information and insight. Also look up a volume by D. Ward, *Cities and Immigrants* (Oxford, New York, 1971), subtitled "A Geography of Change in Nineteenth Century America." R. M. Prothero's *Migrants and Malaria* (Longmans, London, 1965) deals with African migrations, and in a useful book by W. A. Hance the topics we have so far discussed are assembled in an African context as well: *Population, Migration, and Urbanization in Africa* (Columbia, New York, 1970). Another valuable source is a book edited by L. Kosinski and R. Prothero, *People on the Move* (Methuen, London, 1975).

Rising concern over the condition of world environments has generated a large number of volumes that deal with various aspects of the question. Under the auspices of the Association of American Geographers, I. R. Manners and M. W. Mikesell edited *Perspectives on Environment* (A. A. G., Washington, 1974). Editor D. L. Wheeler's *The Human Habitat* (Van Nostrand-Reinhold, New York, 1971) includes writings by observers including former Supreme Court Justice William O. Douglas, Rachel Carson, and Stewart Udall. G. E. Frakes and C. B. Solberg produced the *Pollution Papers* (Appleton-Century-Crofts, New York, 1971), and you will want to consult the book by W. H. Mason and G. W. Folkerts, *Environmental Problems* (Wm. C. Brown, Dubuque, 1973). Various aspects of the energy issue are addressed in *Perspectives on Energy* (Oxford, New York, 1975), a volume edited by L. C. Ruedisili and M. W. Firebaugh.

PART TWO
culture

Eight centuries of Amsterdam: a cultural landscape of permanence and continuity.

7 Culture and Society

More than four billion people inhabit the limited space on this earth, and they live their lives in thousands of different ways. Their racial sources and ancestries vary. Their religious beliefs are not the same. Their languages are mutually unintelligible. They build their houses in different ways. In their technologies, their systems of education, and in countless other ways the societies of the world reveal their contrasts and differences. Societies, large and small, all occupy a part of the earth's surface—and all have, in some special way, exploited their particular physical resources and environments. They have, in the process, developed different kinds of spatial organization. In cultural geography we focus on these spatial aspects of human cultures.

141

Culture as Concept

In Chapter 1 we discussed an important organizing concept in geography, the region. We noted that the regional concept is subject to constant debate and modification, but that it has been a central intellectual construct in geography for many decades. Similarly, the concept of culture is also under continuous debate. In a sense, the culture concept is to anthropologists what the regional concept is to geographers, and endless pages have been written in the search for acceptable definitions. Where culture is of interest to geographers involves its spatial expression. If it is possible to establish physical (physiographic) regions, climatic regions, and urban regions, then we should be able to identify world culture regions as well. But before we try, we should know something more about culture itself.

A culture is the way of life of a people. But right away even as simple a definition as this causes trouble: is it their *actual* way of life (the "way the game is played") or the standards whereby they give evidence of *wanting* to live, through their statements of beliefs and values (the "rules of the game")? Anthropologists differ on this, and in the process their own definitions become quite involved and complicated. Consider this one by A. L. Kroeber and C. Kluckhohn, writing in an article that comments on the problems of definition: "Culture consists of patterns, explicit and implicit, of and for behavior and transmitted by symbols, constituting the distinctive achievements of human groups, including their embodiments in artifacts . . . the essential core of culture consists of traditional (that is, historically derived and selected) ideas and especially their attached values; culture systems may, on the one hand, be considered as products of action, and on the other as conditioning elements of further action." Note that these anthropologists carefully insert elements of time and tradition, the tangible and the intangible into their definition. They also refer to culture *systems*, indicating that the culture concept, like that of the region, involves a set of components from the simple (the culture *trait* or element) through combinations (the culture *complex*) to the comprehensive culture *system*, which we would express spatially as the cultural region.

A culture, then, is the way of life of a population, all their ways of doing things, all the kinds of behavior they have learned and transmitted to successive generations. Language, religion, architecture, music—even food preferences and taboos form part of a culture. Culture consists of people's beliefs and values (religious, political), institutions (legal, educational, governmental), and technology (skills, equipment). It is expressed in the ways people communicate, in the way they perceive and exploit their resources, in their architecture and art—and, most important for geographers, in the way they organize that part of the earth that is theirs.

We should also remind ourselves of what culture is *not*. Culture is not the result of biological inheritance, it is not genetically predetermined, and it is not the result of some primitive, basic instinct. In other words, if you are born in one culture area and immediately taken to another culture and raised there, you will acquire the cultural attributes of the culture in which you were raised, not the one in which you were born.

Cultural Landscape

Culture is expressed in many ways. Culture gives character to an area. Aesthetics play an important role in all cultures, and often a single scene, in a photograph or a picture, can reveal to us in general terms in what part of the world it was made. The architecture, the mode of dress of the people, the means of transportation, perhaps the goods being carried reveal enough to permit a good guess. This is because the people of any culture, when they occupy their part of the earth's available space, transform the land by building structures on it, creating lines of contact and communication, tilling the fields, parceling out the soil. There are but few exceptions: nomadic people may leave a minimum of permanent evidence, and some people living in desert margins (such as the Bushmen) and in tropical forests (the pygmies, for example) alter their natural environment but little. But most of the time, there is change: asphalt roadways, irrigation canals, terraced hill-slopes, fences and hedges, villages and towns.

This composite of human imprints on the surface is called the *cultural landscape*, a term that came into general use in geography in the 1920s. Carl O. Sauer, for several decades professor of geography at the University of California, Berkeley, developed a school of cultural geography that had the cultural land-scape concept as its focus. Among his numerous books and articles on the subject is a paper written in 1927 entitled "Recent Developments in Cultural Geography," and there he proposed his most straightforward definition of the cultural landscape. This constitutes, he said, "the forms superimposed on the physical landscape by the activities of man." He stressed that such forms result from cultural processes prevailing over a long time period, so that successive generations contribute to their development. Sometimes these successive groups are not of the same culture; consider the European migrations we discussed in Chapter 5. Villages built by Germans are now occupied by Poles. Minarets of Islam rise above the townscape of Eastern European cities, evincing the former hegemony of the Ottoman Empire. D. Whittlesey introduced the principle of *sequent occupance* to account for these successive contributions to the evolution of a region's cultural landscape.

A cultural landscape consists of buildings and roads and fields and more, but it also has an intangible quality, an "atmosphere" that is often so easy to perceive and yet so difficult to define. The smells and sights and sounds of an African traditional market are unmistakable, but try to record those qualities on maps or in some other way for comparative study! Geographers have long grappled with this problem of recording the less tangible characteristics of the cultural landscape, which are often so significant in producing the regional personality. This is the regional version of the *Gestalt*, as a school of German psychologists in the early part of this century came to call a mentally perceived configuration involving many different impressions received by our several senses. Jean Gottmann, a European geographer, put it this way in his *Geography of Europe*:

. . . To be distinct from its surroundings, a region needs much more than a mountain or a valley, a given language or certain skills; it needs essentially a strong belief based on some religious creed, some social viewpoint, or some pattern of political memories, and often a combination of all three. Thus regionalism has what might be called *iconography* as its foundation: each community has found for itself or was given an icon, a symbol slightly different from those cherished by its neighbors. For centuries the icon was cared for, adorned with whatever riches and jewels the community could supply. In many cases such an amount of labor and capital was invested that what started as a belief, or as the cult of or even the memory of a military feat, grew into a considerable economic investment around which the interests of an economic region united . . .

Gottmann is trying here to define some of the abstract, intangible qualities that go into the makeup of a cultural landscape. The more concrete properties are a bit easier to observe and record. Take, for example, the urban "townscape" (a prominent element of the overall cultural landscape), and compare a major United States city with, say, a leading Japanese city. Visual representations would reveal the differences quickly, of course, but so would maps of the two urban places. The U.S. city, with its rectangular layout of the central business district (CBD) and its far-flung, sprawling suburbs contrasts sharply with the clustered, space-conserving Japanese city. Again, the subdivision and ownership of American farmland, represented on a map, looks unmistakably different from that of an African traditional rural area, with its irregular, often tiny patches of land surrounding a village. Still, the whole of a cultural landscape can never be represented on a map. The personality of a region involves not only its prevailing spatial organization but also its visual appearance, its noises and odors, even the pace of life.

Culture Hearths

Where and how did it all begin? What are the origins of the world's cultural landscapes? The 143

Sequent Occupance

A search of the modern literature of geography indicates that the concept of sequent occupance, introduced by D. Whittlesey in a 1929 article in the *Annals of the Association of American Geographers* and vigorously pursued for a time, now is rarely mentioned. And yet this is a useful organizing construct, for it provides a framework for the study of an area that is inhabited—and transformed—by a succession of residents, each of whom leave lasting cultural imprints. A place and its resources are perceived differently by peoples of different technological and other cultural traditions, and these contrasting perceptions are reflected in their respective cultural landscapes. Whittlesey himself used an area in New England to illustrate: to its Indian occupants it was a virgin forest to be used for hunting and gathering. To the immigrant European farmers it afforded lowlands suitable for plowing and farming and hillsides where livestock could graze. Modern times and changing economies saw the area covered once again by a (second-growth) forest, with some livestock still present. Whittlesey predicted that a fourth stage in the sequence would bring forestry as the main activity.

But the idea of sequent occupance is also applicable in urban areas. Take the faraway example of Dar es Salaam, long the coastal capital of the East African country now known as Tanzania (the government's headquarters were recently moved to Dodoma, in the interior). The site of Dar es Salaam was first chosen for settlement by Arabs from Zanzibar, to serve as a mainland retreat. Next it was selected by the German colonizers as a capital for their East African domain, and given a German layout and architectural imprint. Upon the German ouster following their defeat in World War I, a British administration took over Dar es Salaam, and the German-built city began still another period of transformation. In the early 1960s it became the capital of newly independent Tanzania, under African control for the first time. Thus Dar es Salaam in less than one century experienced four quite distinct stages of cultural dominance, and each stage of the sequence remains imprinted in the cultural landscape. Such imprints, as Whittlesey said, can only result from true "stages" of occupance during which "the human occupance of an area remains constant in its fundamental aspects."

Perhaps the idea of sequent occupance became dormant because too much attention was paid to the stages of history and not enough to the spatial expressions of geography. In any case, the concept still survives and its opportunities remain available.

beginnings of human culture and its development are undoubtedly related to those earliest experiments in sedentary agriculture to which we referred when discussing the rise of the first towns and cities. Professor Sauer developed hypotheses about the areas where this progress in agriculture was first made, and he also introduced the concept of *diffusion* to account for the spread of what was learned to other areas over time.

It is not unreasonable to assume that the places where human societies first achieved sedentary agriculture were also the earliest *culture hearths*.

When there was relatively ample food supply, society generated a segment of population that could afford to engage in activities other than the production and distribution of food—people who could develop their skills in the arts, science, and other fields. Not everyone agreed with Sauer's conclusions

144

about the location of these ancient culture hearths, or about the routes by which the ideas generated there were diffused to other regions. Sauer himself attached more significance to the Southeast Asian hearth (Fig. 7-1) than other scholars did, and the degree to which the West African hearth was truly an area of innovation has also been open to debate. But the map undoubtedly shows the major areas of opportunity and early development, and there can be no such doubts about Mesopotamia or Mesoamerica, for instance.

The directions of early diffusion (Fig 7-1) are also somewhat speculative. Unquestionably, innovations, ideas, and goods radiated outward from Southwest Asia and the Nile Valley—into Europe, to West Africa, perhaps also to China. There was interaction with the developing culture in the Indus Valley, and some scholars believe that Egyptian influences reached Central America long before the first Europeans saw the Caribbean.

We can perhaps learn a good deal about these early developments of culture hearths, and about ancient diffusion processes, by studying more recent cases. Agricultural regions (such as the Corn Belt) and cultural regions (such as the Mormon region) have developed comparatively recently, and their origins and evolution are rather easier to trace than the growth of those ancient culture hearths of some thousands of years ago. Quite possibly the mechanics of the processes have changed rather little, so that what we learn of modern cases may be applicable to ancient regions of human growth. In 1963, J. E. Spencer and R. J. Horvath pub-

Figure 7-1

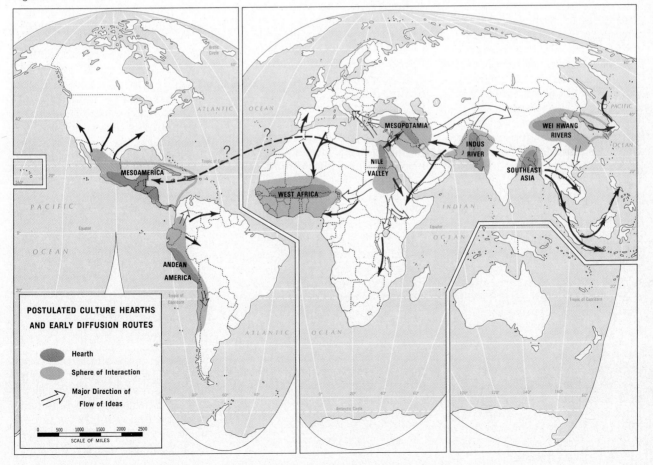

lished an article entitled "How Does an Agricultural Region Originate?" They studied agricultural development and cultural evolution in three comparatively modern farming regions: the U.S. Corn Belt, the Phillippine coconut-palm region, and the Malaysian (then Malayan) region of rubber plantations. The two scholars concluded that six cultural processes are at work when such regions take shape. At the top of the list are *psychological* processes, including prevailing perceptions of the physical environment and pressures to "do things the way your neighbors do." *Political* processes involve the allocation and subdivision of land, and the imposition of price structures. *Historical* processes often include a resistance to change and a conservatism that we know to be quite characteristic of rural populations. *Technological* processes have to do with the limitations imposed by whatever equipment is available. The development of agriculture in the ancient culture hearths was attended by inventions designed to improve the capacity to turn the soil, but those farmers had neither the wheel nor hard metals from which to forge plows. *Agronomic* developments in the culture hearths were momentous as discoveries were made in seeding and planting; those processes of agronomic discovery are still going on, as the Green Revolution of the 1960s proved. Finally, Professors Spencer and Horvath identified *economic* processes operating in agricultural regions. These involve modern factors of supply and demand and economies of scale, but undoubtedly economic processes also began to operate as soon as the first surpluses were created in the Fertile Crescent.

Obviously we cannot be sure of the circumstances under which ancient agricultural-culture hearths developed. But we can structure our thinking according to the conclusions Spencer and Horvath drew from their research. Perceptual obstacles had to be overcome by the ancient farmers who, very likely, combined their efforts in agriculture with some other pursuit (fishing in some localities, gathering and hunting in others). The stabilization of farming communities brought about really momentous political changes, and the political processes affected the course of agricultural development as the cultivation, storage, and distribution of food became matters of policy and strategy. The new needs of agriculture brought on pressure for inventions to facilitate the process. For example, it is believed that cattle in Southwest Asia were used to pull platforms during religious ceremonies (the milk-producing cow was a holy animal); then someone thought of the possibility of using cattle to pull plows to turn soil hitherto turned by hand hoe. In the agronomic area, we should remind ourselves that the first farmers probably planted roots and cuttings from forest areas long before they learned to use seed. It is believed that root crops may have grown spontaneously from food remnants thrown on refuse heaps in places where settlement was fairly lengthy (as in a fishing camp), and so the idea that root crops could be planted came about. Seeding involved more deliberate activity: the gathering of grains from plants, the preparation of the land, then the

sowing, followed perhaps by some weeding and general attention to the crop. And it is not difficult to see that food, once cultivated, harvested, and stored, would set economic processes in motion—even thousands of years ago.

Culture Regions

So far we have tied the development of cultural identity to the evolution of agriculture. Spencer and Horvath used comparatively modern agricultural regions in their effort to discern the leading processes that give character to agricultural landscapes; can the same be done with cultural regions? Professor D. W. Meinig answered this question affirmatively in an article published in 1972 entitled "American Wests: Preface to a Geographical Introduction." Meinig pointed out that no less than six discrete cultural nuclei developed in the U.S. West, generating cultural regions. He identified these on a map (Fig. 7-2) and suggested that such culture regions evolve through four coincident stages of development. First, *population* increases and an original settlement grows by expansion. Second, *circulation* patterns change as internal communications intensify and external connections become more effective. Third, *political organization*, rudimentary at first, grows more complex and involves a greater number of spheres. Fourth, *regional culture* emerges and then begins to become submerged in a developing national culture. It is important to keep in mind that these are not successive but parallel developments. Thus population influx continues as circulation patterns intensify, while political organization

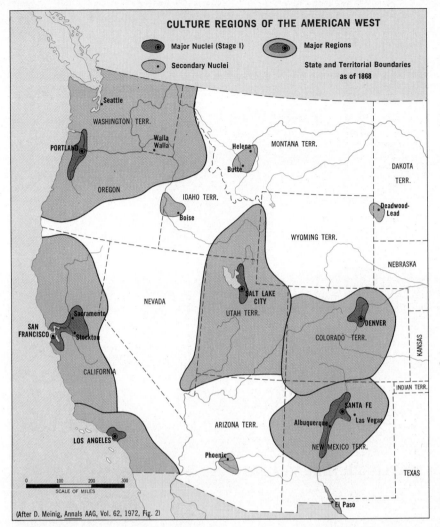

CULTURE REGIONS OF THE AMERICAN WEST

Major Nuclei (Stage I)   Major Regions

Secondary Nuclei   State and Territorial Boundaries
                            as of 1868

Seattle
WASHINGTON TERR.
Walla Walla
PORTLAND
Helena   MONTANA TERR.
OREGON   Butte   DAKOTA TERR.
IDAHO TERR.
Boise   Deadwood-Lead
                WYOMING TERR.
                                         NEBRASKA
                SALT LAKE CITY
Sacramento   UTAH TERR.   KANSAS
SAN FRANCISCO   Stockton   DENVER
                                COLORADO TERR.
CALIFORNIA   NEVADA   INDIAN TERR.
                                SANTA FE
LOS ANGELES   Albuquerque Las Vegas
                ARIZONA TERR.   NEW MEXICO TERR.
                Phoenix   TEXAS
0 100 200 300
SCALE OF MILES   El Paso

(After D. Meinig, Annals AAG, Vol. 62, 1972, Fig. 2)

Figure 7-2

grows more complex and cultural identity strengthens. Of course, it is possible for a regional culture *not* to be submerged in a national culture, through isolation by distance or inaccessibility, through racial or linguistic separateness, or perhaps by religious discreteness. Thus the Mormon culture region retains some sharper identities than some of the other culture regions of the American "Wests." To go a bit farther

afield, France lies at the heart of a culture region in Europe (the culture region extends somewhat into Belgium, Switzerland, and Italy). Although still quite strong, the French culture region is in the process of being submerged in a developing European culture complex. Even when regional culture coincides spatially with a political unit or

state, it may be absorbed in a greater complex.

The case of South Africa's Cape Province provides an excellent illustration of the Meinig hypothesis. The original Dutch settlement on the shore at Cape Town became the cultural nucleus, first implanted to create a way station for passing ships but soon expanding because of its own attractive qualities. The population influx brought not only greater numbers but also new contributions, including a sizeable French component that brought to the Cape a new language and new agricultural abilities: Cape Town's hinterland soon displayed vineyards and small chateaus. The Dutch language began to change under the influence of the French presence, and the hinterland's circulation system developed rapidly as roads were pushed into the valleys. Before long the administration centered in Cape Town was unable to cope with the problems of an expanding colony, and local autonomy grew, although against opposition from Amsterdam. Eventually the Cape achieved a most distinctive cultural landscape and regional identity, expressed in an architecture still known as "Cape Dutch," a language that eventually evolved into Afrikaans, a religious mosaic quite different from that of the source areas, and an agricultural scene that is still unmistakably "Cape." This is so despite the colony's ultimate incorporation into what has become the national culture region of South Africa, and the submergence and dilution of much of its original distinctiveness. South Africa today is a culture complex, in which the Cape nevertheless remains a discrete element.

147

Culture Realms

The study of culture landscapes and culture regions involves so many factors and criteria that it is best carried on at a manageable scale. The larger the area, the greater is the complexity of detail, and the more difficult do the inevitably necessary generalizations become. Still there can be no question about it: the world as a whole remains divided into a number of huge *culture realms*, even today in our age of mobility and interaction. In our everyday language we use terms that reveal our awareness of this world framework of cultures, as when we refer to news items from "The Arab World" or from "Latin America." But it is one thing to have a general impression of such world realms, and quite another to specify their location and boundaries on a map. At this level of generalization, we must submerge details that at a different level of scale would have required modifications of our scheme. For example, we identify a realm variously called the "Arab world," the "Islamic realm," and the "dry world." When we focus on the contents of that culture realm (Fig. 7-3), we find that many of its inhabitants are *not* Arabs (Israelis and Iranians, for example); many do not adhere to Islam (Lebanon's Christians, for instance), and important parts of the realm are not arid, but well watered and green. Nevertheless the dominant, distinguishing combination of historical, cultural, and physiographic factors leads us to outline the realm as on our map:

Figure 7-3

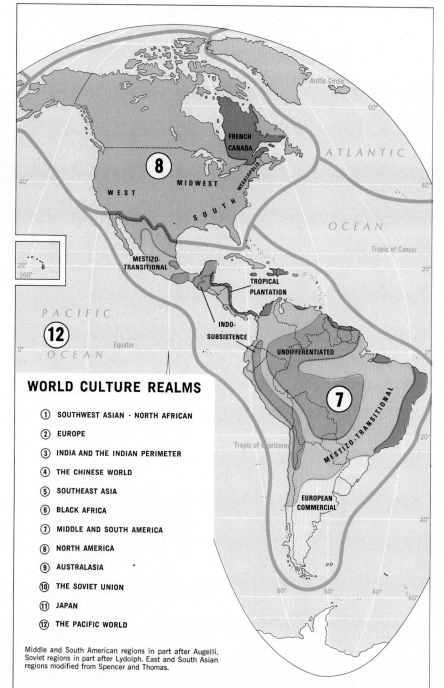

WORLD CULTURE REALMS

1. SOUTHWEST ASIAN · NORTH AFRICAN
2. EUROPE
3. INDIA AND THE INDIAN PERIMETER
4. THE CHINESE WORLD
5. SOUTHEAST ASIA
6. BLACK AFRICA
7. MIDDLE AND SOUTH AMERICA
8. NORTH AMERICA
9. AUSTRALASIA
10. THE SOVIET UNION
11. JAPAN
12. THE PACIFIC WORLD

Middle and South American regions in part after Augelli. Soviet regions in part after Lydolph. East and South Asian regions modified from Spencer and Thomas.

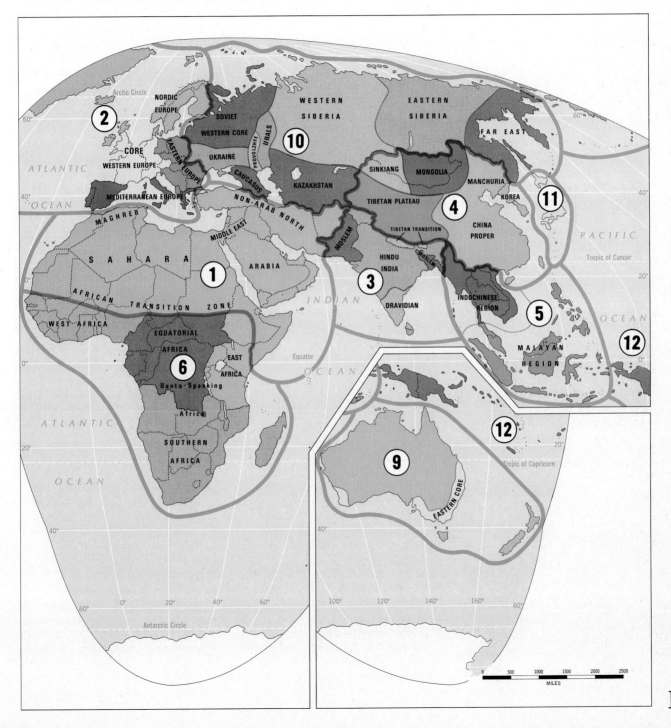

NORDIC EUROPE

CORE
WESTERN EUROPE

EASTERN EUROPE

MEDITERRANEAN EUROPE

MAGHREB

MIDDLE EAST

SAHARA

ARABIA

AFRICAN TRANSITION ZONE

WEST AFRICA

EQUATORIAL AFRICA

EAST AFRICA

Bantu-Speaking Africa

SOUTHERN AFRICA

ATLANTIC OCEAN

ATLANTIC OCEAN

Arctic Circle

Equator

Antarctic Circle

SOVIET WESTERN CORE

UKRAINE

CAUCASUS

NON-ARAB NORTH

POVOLZHYE

URALS

KAZAKHSTAN

WESTERN SIBERIA

EASTERN SIBERIA

FAR EAST

SINKIANG

MONGOLIA

MANCHURIA

KOREA

TIBETAN PLATEAU

CHINA PROPER

TIBETAN TRANSITION

MOSLEM

MOSLEM

HINDU INDIA

DRAVIDIAN

INDOCHINESE REGION

MALAYAN REGION

INDIAN OCEAN

PACIFIC OCEAN

Tropic of Cancer

Tropic of Capricorn

EASTERN CORE

0   500   1000   1500   2000   2500
MILES

① ② ③ ④ ⑤ ⑥ ⑨ ⑩ ⑪ ⑫

149

the exceptions are not sufficient to disrupt the whole.

Naturally we should give attention to historical and physical as well as cultural realities (and we take the term cultural in its broadest sense, to include not only language and religion but also politics and economics). The historical context is useful in that it protects us from the assumption that today's situation is somehow permanent and entrenched. Without it we might, for example, be tempted to identify parts of Southern Africa as a sector of Western, European culture, when in fact South Africa is part of the Black African culture realm. In the context of time, the white domination of Rhodesia and South Africa will prove to be merely interludes. Similarly, the Soviet domination of Eastern Europe is likely to be only another stage in that area's succession of foreign dominations. This episode does not mean that Eastern Europe is now part of the Soviet culture realm.

Our map (Fig. 7-3) shows culture-realm boundaries coinciding substantially with political boundaries (the Arab-African boundary is a significant exception). This is as much a matter of convenience and expedience as it is a reflection of our criteria. We know, for example, that Spanish-Mexican influence extends well into the Southwestern United States, and U.S. influence of various sorts penetrates Mexico. Yet our boundary runs along the Rio Grande and then along the U.S.-Mexico political boundary. This is *not* to suggest that the boundaries of our culture realms are in fact sharp lines; they are transition zones within which the sharpest break may well lie along the political boundary. Culture realms merge into each other, in general, and the boundary lines on Figure 7-3 represent wider zones of transition.

When you compare our framework to that of others who have attempted to delimit world culture realms, you will discover that differences frequently are matters of detail—but the major outlines of the world's culture realms are matters of substantial agreement and consensus. And not only geographers have developed such outlines; historians and other social scientists have also approached the problem, and with surprisingly similar results. We now concentrate on our framework as represented by Figure 7-3.

Southwest Asian-North African Realm (1)

This culture realm, as we noted earlier, is known by several names, none of them satisfactory: the Islamic realm, the Arab world, the dry world. Undoubtedly the all-pervading influence of the Islamic religion is this realm's overriding cultural quality, for Islam is more than a faith: it is a way of life. The contrasts within the realm are underscored when we note its contents, extending as it does from Morocco and Mauritania in the west to Iran and Afghanistan in the east, and from Turkey in the north to Ethiopia in the south. Huge desert areas separate strongly clustered populations whose isolation perpetuates cultural discreteness, and we can distinguish regional contrasts within the realm quite clearly.

The term "Middle East" refers to one of these regions, countries of the Eastern Mediterranean (Fig. 7-3); the *Maghreb* is a region constituted by the population clusters in the countries of Northwest Africa and centered on Algeria. Still another region extends along the transition zone to Black Africa, where Islamic traditions give way to African lifestyles. In the realm's northern region, Turkey and Iran dominate as non-Arab countries.

Rural poverty, strongly conservative traditionalism, political instability, and conflict have marked the realm in recent times, but this is also the source area of several of the world's great religions and the site of ancient culture hearths and early urban societies. Had we drawn Figure 7-3 several centuries ago, we would have shown Arab-Turkish penetrations of Iberian and Balkan Europe and streams of trade and contact reaching to Southeast Africa and East Asia. So vigorously was Islam propagated beyond the realm that, to this day, there are more adherents to the faith outside the "Arab world" than within it.

Europe (2)

Europe merits identification as a culture realm despite the fact that it occupies a mere fraction of the total area of the Eurasian landmass—a fraction that, moreover, is largely made up of that continent's Western peninsular extremities. Certainly Europe's size is no measure of its world significance; probably no other part of the world is or ever has been so packed full of the products of human achievement.

150

The Golden Mosque in Baghdad, Iraq, and the nearby townscape.

Innovations and revolutions that transformed the world originated in Europe. Over centuries of modern times the evolution of world interaction focused on European states and European capitals. Time and again, despite internal wars, despite the loss of colonial empires, despite the impact of external competition, Europe proved to contain the human and natural resources needed for rebounding and renewed progress.

Among Europe's greatest assets is its internal natural and human diversity. From the warm shores of the Mediterranean to the frigid Scandinavian Arctic and from the flat coastlands of the North Sea to the grandeur of the Alps, Europe presents an almost infinite range of natural environments. An insular and peninsular West contrasts against a more continental East. A resource-laden backbone extends across Europe from England eastward. Excellent soils produce harvests of enormous quantity and variety. And the population includes people of many different stocks, peoples grouped under such familiar names as Latin, Germanic, Slavic. Europe has its minorities as well, for example the Hungarians and the Finns. Immigrants continue to stream into Europe, contributing further to a diversity that has been an advantage to Europe in uncountable ways. Today Europe is a realm dominated, especially in the West, by great cities, intensive transport networks and mobility, enormous productivity, dynamic growth, a large and in many areas very dense population, and an extremely complex technology.

India and the Indian Perimeter (3)

The familiar triangle of India is a subcontinent in itself, a clearly discernable physical region bounded by mountain range and ocean, inhabited by a population that constitutes one of the greatest human concentrations on earth. The scene of one of the oldest civilizations, it became the cornerstone of the vast British colonial empire. Out of the colonial period and its aftermath emerged four states: India, Bangladesh, Pakistan, and Sri Lanka.

Europe was a recipient of Middle Eastern achievements in many spheres; so was India. From Arabia and the Persian Gulf came traders across the sea. The wave of Islam came over land, across the Indus, through the Punjab, and into the Ganges valley. Along this western route had also come the realm's modern inhabitants, who drove the older Dravidians southward into the tip of the peninsula.

Long before Islam reached India, major faiths had already arisen here, religions that still shape lives and attitudes. Hinduism and Buddhism emerged before Christianity and Islam, and the postulates of the Hindu religion have dominated life in India for several thousands of years. They include beliefs in reincarnation and the *karma* (see p. 197), in the goodness of holy men and their rejection of material things, and in the inevitability of a hierarchical structure in life and afterlife. This last quality of the Hindu faith had expression in India's caste system, the castes being social strata and steps of the universal ladder. It had the effect of locking people into social classes, the lowest of which—the untouchables—suffered a miserable existence from which there was no escape. Buddhism was partly a reaction against this system, and the invasion of Islam was facilitated by the alternatives it provided. Eventually the conflicts between Hinduism (primarily India's religion today) and Islam led to the partition of the realm into India and Pakistan, an Islamic republic.

If the realm is one of contrasts and diversity, there are overriding qualities nevertheless: it is a region of intense adherence to the various faiths, a realm of thousands of villages and several teeming, overpopulated cities, an area of poverty and frequent hunger, where the

Street scene in Calcutta, India.

difficulties of life are viewed with an acquiescence that comes from the belief in a better new life, later.

The Chinese World (4)

China is a nation-state as well as a culture realm. The Chinese world may be the oldest of continuous civilizations. It was born in the upper basin of the Hwang Ho (Yellow River) and now extends over an area of over 3½ million square miles and has some 900 million inhabitants. Alone among the ancient culture hearths we discussed earlier, China's spawned a major, modern state of world stature, with the strands to the source still intact. Chinese people still refer to themselves as the "People of Han," the great dynasty (202 B.C. to 220 A.D.) that was a formative period in the country's evolution. But the cultural individuality and continuity of China were already established 2000 years before that time, and perhaps even earlier.

In the lengthy process of its evolution as a regionally distinctive culture and a great nation-state, China has had an ally in its isolation. Mountains, deserts, and sheer distance protected China's "Middle Kingdom" and afforded the luxury of stability and comparative homogeneity. Not surprisingly Chinese self-images were those of superiority and security; the growing Chinese realm was not about to be overrun. There were invasions from the steppes of inner Asia, but invaders were repulsed or absorbed. There would always be China. The European impact of the nineteenth century finally ended China's era of invincibility, but it was held off far longer than in India, it lasted far shorter, and it had less permanent effect.

Unlike India, China's belief system always was concerned more with the here and now, the state and authority, than with the hereafter and reincarnations. The century of convulsion that ended with the communist victory witnessed a breakdown in Chinese life and traditions, but there is much in the present system of government that resembles China under its dynastic rulers. China is being transformed into a truly communist society, but Chinese attitudes toward authority, the primacy of the state, and the demands of regimentation and organization are not new.

View over the old and new town in Peking, China.

153

China is moving toward world-power status once again, and there are imposing new industries and growing cities. But for all its modernization, China still remains a realm of crowded farmlands, carefully diked floodplains, intricately terraced hillslopes, cluttered small villages. Crops of rice and wheat are still meticulously cultivated and harvested; the majority of the people still bend to the soil.

Southeast Asia (5)

Southeast Asia is nowhere nearly as well-defined a culture realm as either India or China. It is a mosaic of ethnic and linguistic groups, and the region has been the scene of countless contests for power and primacy. Even spatially the realm's discontinuity is obvious: it consists of a peninsular mainland, where population tends to be clustered in river basins, and thousands of islands, which form the archipelagoes of the Philippines and Indonesia.

During the colonial period the term "Indochina" came into use to denote part of mainland Southeast Asia. The term is a good one, for it reflects the major sources of cultural influence that have affected the realm. The great majority of Southeast Asia's inhabitants have ethnic affinities with the people of China, but it was from India that the realm received its first strong, widely disseminated cultural imprints: Hindu and Buddhist faiths, architecture, arts, and aspects of social structure. The Moslem faith also arrived via India. From China came not only ethnic ties but also culture elements: Chinese modes of dress, plastic arts, boat types and other qualities were adopted widely in Southeast Asia. In recent times a strong immigration from China to the cities of Southeast Asia further strengthened the impact of Chinese culture on this realm.

Black Africa (6)

Between the southern margins of the Sahara Desert and South Africa's Cape Province lies the Black Africa culture realm. As we noted, its boundary with the realm of Islam is generally a zone of transition, and this is a case where coincidence with political boundaries cannot be employed. In Sudan, for example, the north is part of the Arab world, but the south is quite distinctly African: So strong are the regional contrasts within Sudan that it would be inappropriate to include the entire country in either the Islamic realm or the Black Africa realm. Therefore, the Sudan (and Ethiopia, Chad, Niger, Mali) are bisected.

The African realm is defined by its mosaic of hundreds of languages belonging to specific African language families, and by its huge variety of traditional, local religions that, unlike world religions such as Islam or Christianity, remained essentially "community" religions.

With some exceptions, Africa is a realm of farmers. A few people remain dependent on hunting and gathering, and some communities depend primarily on fishing. But otherwise the principal mode of life is farming. Nor was this subsistence way of life much changed by the European colonialists. Tens of thousands of villages all across Black Africa were never brought

Bustling Lagos exemplifies emerging Africa.

Contrasting urban landscapes of Rio de Janeiro, Brazil.

into the economic orbits of the European invaders. Root crops and grains are grown in ancient, time-honored ways with the hand hoe and the digging stick. It is a backbreaking, low-yield proposition, but the African farmer does not have much choice.

Middle and South America (7)

Middle and South America constitute the realm often called "Latin" America because of the Iberian imprint placed on it during the European expansion, when the ancient Indian civilizations were submerged and destroyed. Portugal in Brazil, and Spain in most of the remainder of this realm, founded vast colonial empires. Later these dependencies freed themselves from Iberian control, but the cultural impress was there to stay. Spanish is spoken from Mexico and Cuba to Argentina and Chile, and Brazil's 100 million people speak Portuguese. The Catholic religion prevails throughout "Latin" America. Systems of land ownership, tenancy, taxation, and tribute were transferred from the Old World to the New. Still today, the realm carries the culture of its source region, in the architecture of its cities, the visual arts, music. Against these assets there are liabilities involving the allocation and ownership of land and the means of production, and the region's recent political conflicts reflect the problems involved in the processes of change.

Notwithstanding the realm's essential unity, some rather strong regional differentiation exists, as reflected by Figure 7-3. The clearest of these separates Middle America from South America. Middle America is dominated by Mexico but includes also the Central American republics and the island states and territories of the Caribbean. Non-Latin influences were always stronger in Middle than in South America, as attested by the non-Iberian heritage of such countries as Belize, Jamaica, Haiti, and numerous smaller Caribbean island territories.

Regional differences can also be observed in South America, where Andean and Amazonean Indian areas stand in contrast to the Europeanized South and Southeast. As in Middle America, an early, coast-oriented plantation economy developed, segments of which still persist along South America's northern and north-eastern margins. The strongest mixture of European and Indian-American traditions exist in the regions marked "mestizo-transitional."

Large-scale, highly productive agriculture is one of North America's pervasive qualities. Here, a single farmer and one piece of equipment work a huge piece of land in California's Imperial Valley.

North America (8)

The North American culture realm consists of two of the most strongly urbanized and industrialized countries in the world. In the United States there are more than 60 cities with populations in excess of half a million, within which live fully 50 percent of all the people in this country. The vast majority of the remainder, moreover, live in urban places larger than 10,000.

The North American realm is characterized by its large-scale, massive technology; its enormous consumption of the world's resources and commodities; and its unprecedented mobility and fast-paced life-styles. Suburbs grow toward each other as cities coalesce, surface and air transport networks intensify, skylines change. Skyscrapers, traffic jams, waiting lines, noise, pollution of air and water—these are some of the attributes of our American technocracy.

Both the United States and Canada are plural societies, Canada's cultural sources lying in Britain and France and those of the United States in Europe and Africa. In both Canada and the United States, minorities remain separate from the dominant culture: Quebec is Canada's French province, and, in the United States, patterns of racial segregation persist, with black Americans concentrated strongly in particular urban areas. The problems associated with cultural pluralism are prominent modifiers of this culture realm.

Transplanted Europe: the spacious luxury of Australia's Gold Coast.

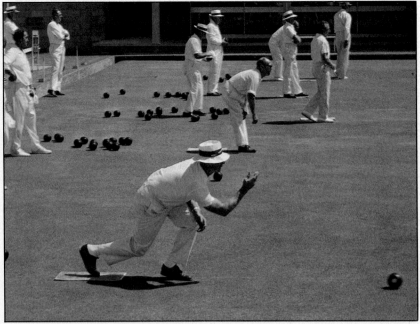

Australia's favorite sports include cricket, rugby, and (pictured here) lawn bowling—all part of the realm's British heritage.

Australia (9)

Just as Europe merits recognition as a continental realm although it is merely a peninsula of Eurasia, so Australia has achieved identity as the island realm of Australasia. Australia and New Zealand are European outposts in an Asian-Pacific world, as unlike Indonesia as Britain is unlike India.

Although Australia was spawned by Europe and its people and economy are Western in every way, Australia as a continental realm is a far cry from the crowded, productive, populous European world. The image of Australia is one of impressive, large, open cities, wide expanses, huge herds of livestock (perhaps also the pests, rabbits and kangaroos), deserts, and beautiful coastal scenery. There is much truth in such a picture: 9 of Australia's 13 million people are concentrated in the country's seven largest cities! In this as well as other respects, Australia is more like the United States than other realms. With its British heritage, its homogeneous population, single language (excepting only the small indigenous minority), and type of economy, Australia's identification as a realm rests on its remoteness and spatial isolation.

The Soviet Union (10)

The Soviet Union—the world's largest country territorially—constitutes a culture realm not just because of its size. To its south lie the Japanese, Chinese, Indian, and Southwest Asian realms, all clearly different culturally from the realm that Russia forged. The Soviet realm's Western boundary is always subject to debate, but neither Finland nor Eastern Europe have been areas of permanent Soviet or Russian domination.

The events of the twentieth century have greatly strengthened the bases for the recognition of the Soviet Union as a culture realm. Russian expansionism was halted, the Revolution came, and a whole new order was created, transforming the old Russia and its empire into a strongly centralized state whose hallmark was economic planning. The new political system awarded the status of Soviet Socialist Republic to areas incorporated into the Russian empire, including those inhabited by Moslems and other minorities. In the economic sphere, the state took control of all industry and production, and agriculture was collectivized.

Notwithstanding the disastrous dislocation of World War II, the past half century has seen much progress in the U.S.S.R. The state has risen from a backward, divided, near-feudal country to a position of world power with a strong, individualistic (and also centrally directed) culture, a highly advanced technology, and a set of economic and social policies that have attracted world attention and, in some instances, emulation.

Urban scene in the Soviet Union: Lenin Street in Irkutsk, Siberia.

Rebuilt Nagasaki, one of Japan's leading cities.

Japan (11)

On Figure 7-3, Japan hardly seems to qualify as a culture realm. Can a group of comparatively small islands qualify as a culture realm? Indeed it can—when 100 million people inhabit those islands and when they produce there an industrial giant, an urban society, a political power, and a vigorous nation. Japan is unlike any other non-Western country, and it exceeds many Western-developed countries in many ways. Like its European rivals, Japan built and later lost a colonial empire in Asia. During its tenure as a colonial power Japan learned to import raw materials and export finished products. Even the calamity of World War II, when Japan became the only country ever to suffer atomic attack, failed to extinguish Japan's forward push. In the postwar period Japan's overall economic growth rate has been the highest in the world. Raw materials no longer come from colonies, but they are bought all around the world. Products are sold practically everywhere. Almost no city in the world is without Japanese cars in its streets, few photography stores are without Japanese cameras, many laboratories use Japanese optical equipment. From tape recorders to television sets, from ocean-going ships to children's toys, Japanese manufacturers flood the world's markets. The Japanese seem to combine the precision skills of the Swiss with the massive industrial power of prewar Germany, the forward-looking designs of the Swedes with the innovativeness of the Americans.

Japan constitutes a culture realm by virtue of its role in the world economy today, the transformation, in one century, of its national life, and its industrial power. Yet Japan has not turned its back on its old culture; modernization is not all that matters to the Japanese. Ancient customs still are adhered to and honored. Japan is still the land of *Kabuki* drama and *sumo* wrestling, Buddhist temples and Shinto shrines, tea ceremonies and fortune-tellers, arranged marriages, and traditional song and dance. There is still a reverence for older people, and despite all the factories, huge cities, fast trains, and jet airplanes, Japan is still a land of shopkeepers, handcraft industries, home workshops, carefully tended fields, space-conserving villages. Only by holding on to the culture's old traditions could the Japanese have tolerated the onrush of their new age.

The Pacific World (12)

Between Australasia and the Americas lies the vast Pacific Ocean, larger than all the land areas of the world combined. In this great ocean lie tens of thousands of islands, large (such as New Guinea) and small (some even uninhabited). This fragmented, culturally complex realm defies effective generalization. Population contrasts are reflected to some extent in the regional diversification of the realm. Thus the islands from New Guinea eastward to the Fiji group are called *Melanesia* (*mela* means black). The people here are black or very dark brown and have black hair and dark eyes. North of Melanesia, that is, east of the Philippines, lies the island region known as *Micronesia* (*micro* means small), and the people here evince a mixture between Melanesians and Southeast Asians. In the vast central Pacific, east of Melanesia and Micronesia and extending from the Hawaiian islands to the latitude of New Zealand, is *Polynesia* (*poly* means many). Polynesians are widely known for their good physique; they have somewhat lighter skin than other Pacific peoples, wavier hair, and rather high noses. Their ancestry is complex, including Indian, Melanesian, and other elements. Anthropologists recognize a second Polynesian group, the Neo-Hawaiians, a blend of Polynesian, European, and Asian ancestries.

Culture in the Pacific realm is similarly complex. In their songs and dances, their philosophies regarding the nature of the world, their religious concepts and practices, their distinctive building styles, their work in stone and cloth, and in numerous other ways the Polynesians built a culture of strong identity and distinction.

We have defined the 12 realms depicted in Figure 7-3 on the basis of a set of criteria that include not only cultural elements but also political and economic circumstances, relative location, and modern developments that appear to have lasting qualities. Undoubtedly our scheme has areas where it is open to debate, and such a debate can itself be quite instructive. We have indicated some locations where doubts may exist; there are others, as further reading and comparisons of our framework to others will prove. In the process of making up your mind on the problem areas, and as you gather the evidence, you learn much about diverse regions of the world.

159

8 Race and Culture

When you, as a traveler, enter a country for a visit you are asked to fill out a questionnaire to be presented, with your passport, to the immigration officer. As often as not, one of the questions will be "what is your race?" And the appropriate answer, of course, is "human." All the people of this world belong to the same species. We all have far more features in common than there are differences between individuals or groups.

But the answer "human" on the questionnaire is not the one that is wanted (in fact, it may get you into trouble). The term "race" has come to refer to an undeniable reality of our human existence: people differ physically from each other. And what is more, those differences have regional expression. Even after centuries of movement and migration, mixing, and intermarriage, and even in our mobile world, peoples with distinct physical traits remain clustered in particular areas of the world. Thus we use the term "race" in quite a different way: we speak of the European, African, Polynesian *races* of humanity. It may not be quite correct to do so (indeed, some anthropologists have proposed that the whole concept of race be abandoned) but it is an inescapable fact of life.

Race, then, is first and foremost a biological concept, for it refers to people's physical features. A racial group such as those mentioned in Chapter 7 (European, African) is recognized because it has a distinctive combination of such physical traits, the product of a particular genetic inheritance. This inheritance has been determined by many centuries of isolation and inbreeding, during which a certain dominant set of genes—a gene pool—evolved for each racial group. Humanity may be presumed to have evolved from a common stock, but after radiating outward from the source area (perhaps Southwest Asia, Northern, and Eastern Africa) spatial and social isolation began to play their role in generating discrete gene pools and racial groups in Asia, Australia, Africa, Europe, and the Americas. And so humanity differentiated into what used to be called the white, black, red, yellow, and brown races. As the concept of race was refined, other terms emerged: Caucasoid, Negroid, Amerindian, Mongoloid, Australian. Classifications are still changing. Anthropologists have recently been using a nine-unit racial classification of man; (1) *European*, (2) *Indian*, peoples of the Indian subcontinent, (3) *Asian*, peoples of China, Japan, inner Asia, Southeast Asia, Indonesia, (4) *African*, peoples of African south of the Sahara, (5) *American*, the indigenous, Indian populations of the Americas, (6) *Australian*, the original peoples of Australia, (7) *Micronesian*, (8) *Melanesian*, (9) *Polynesian*. The last three groups, as we have noted, are peoples of the Pacific Ocean's islands. The European race includes not only Scandinavians, Russians, Germans, and Italians, but also the peoples of Southwest Asia (such as the Iranians, Syrians, Saudi Arabians) and North Africa (Egyptians, Algerians, Moroccans).

What are these physical traits that form the bases for racial classification of this kind? They are quite familiar to us, especially one: the cloak of color we all wear. Skin color is the most pervasive of physical traits, and our differentiation by color has bedeviled human relationships for uncounted centuries. Skin color is a matter of pigmentation, a protective element against strong radiation. The more pigment, the darker the skin. But there are internal variations within groups: there are dark-skinned northern Europeans and light-skinned Africans. The first image in the perception by one race or culture of another, however, is still likely to be one of skin color. This despite the fact that the color of human

Figure 8-1   Various theories have been advanced to account for the world distribution of skin color shown on this map, which reveals that tropical populations in South America have lighter skins than peoples of the African tropics. One modern theory holds that long–term vitamin D deficiency and natural selection have played roles in creating this pattern. Vitamin D deficiency produces rickets (Chapter 4), but sunlight stimulates the body to produce Vitamin D. Excessive sunlight, however, causes softening and calcification of bones in people who cannot withstand the high intensity of ultraviolet radiation. Over long periods of time those susceptible to bone calcification have been eliminated by natural selection in favor of those who now combine their resistance with the obvious adaptation to intense radiation: dark skin.

It is reasoned that the lighter skin of American Indians living in tropical areas adds proof to the idea that their arrival in those regions has been comparatively recent, and there has not been time for the selective and adaptive processes to run their course.

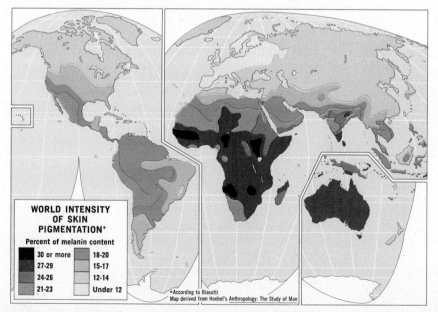

WORLD INTENSITY OF SKIN PIGMENTATION*

Percent of melanin content

30 or more	18-20
27-29	15-17
24-26	12-14
21-23	Under 12

*According to Biasutti
Map derived from Hoebel's Anthropology: The Study of Man

skins varies from nearly white to nearly black, through all the intermediates (Fig. 8-1).

Another somewhat obvious physical feature is the character of people's hair: whether it is straight or woolly, fine-textured, or thick. Asians tend to have straight hair, Europeans, often curly hair, and Africans, woolly hair. Again, there are differences in people's stature or height. Although this factor is obviously related to adequacy of nutrition, it is clear that there are genetic forces at work as well: under similar living conditions, peoples have developed quite different average heights. In eastern Zaire and neighboring areas, three peoples of different stature live together or nearly so: the tall Watusi, the small pygmy, and the medium-height Bahutu. Still another, less obvious physical trait lies in the shape of the head. Anthropologists for a long time thought that the *cephalic* index (which is the ratio of the breadth and length of the skull) might yield substantial insights into the evolution of races. But although it was possible to record a clustering of prevailing head shapes (Japanese have round heads; Western Europeans have long heads), it did not prove possible to use the data for much more than speculation.

Indian (Sri Lanka)

Pacific (Polynesian)

163

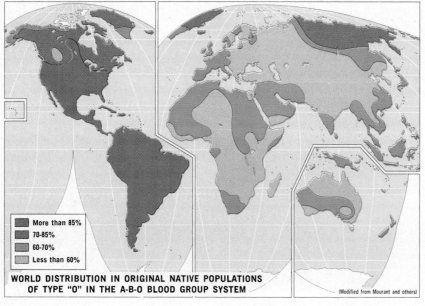

More than 85%
70-85%
60-70%
Less than 60%

WORLD DISTRIBUTION IN ORIGINAL NATIVE POPULATIONS OF TYPE "O" IN THE A-B-O BLOOD GROUP SYSTEM

(Modified from Mourant and others)

Figure 8-2

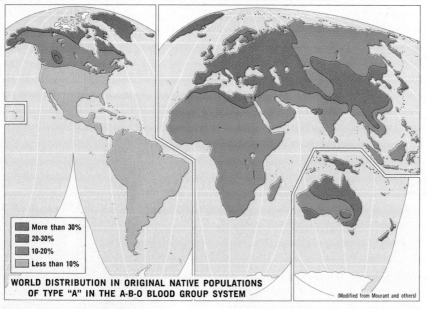

More than 30%
20-30%
10-20%
Less than 10%

WORLD DISTRIBUTION IN ORIGINAL NATIVE POPULATIONS OF TYPE "A" IN THE A-B-O BLOOD GROUP SYSTEM

(Modified from Mourant and others)

Figure 8-3

Other physical traits, including the shape of the eye, of the nose, of the lips, and the degree of protrusion of the jaw, all provide data to compare, but little in the way of evidence for the racial differentiation of humanity. Anthropologists could do little more than classify peoples according to individual traits and map their distribution; meaningful covariances were difficult to find. But, more recently, another physical feature has been studied with more success. This is one we cannot normally see at all—the blood and blood types.

We all know that various blood types exist. The classification is based on the presence or absence of agglutinative (clotting) agents, which cause a clotting of red blood cells when mixed with alien blood that does not contain them. There are four blood types: A, B, AB, and O. The letters A and B denote blood carrying those two types of agents, AB carries both, and type O does not have either. When the existence of blood types was discovered, data soon began to accumulate from all over the world on this newly recognized trait. And since a person has only one blood type, the resulting statistics were a great deal less hazy than "skin color" or "height." A population might vary from 5 feet 1 inch to 6 feet 4 inches in stature, with 5

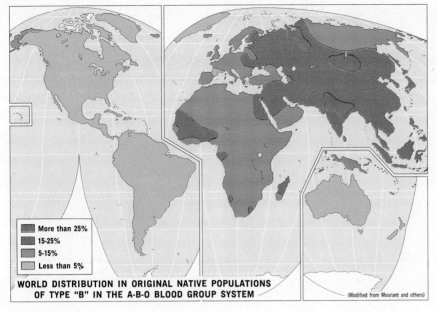

More than 25%
15-25%
5-15%
Less than 5%

WORLD DISTRIBUTION IN ORIGINAL NATIVE POPULATIONS
OF TYPE "B" IN THE A-B-O BLOOD GROUP SYSTEM

(Modified from Mourant and others)

Figure 8-4

feet 9 inches the average; the skin color might average "brown," but there might be variation from very light to very dark. But the blood type would be reported in hard figures 70 percent O, 20 percent B, 10 percent A.

The world distribution of blood types holds much interest, although it remains subject to different interpretations. The O type is strong, for example, among America's Indians (over 70, often 90 percent); in Northeast Asia it is still over 70 percent, and among Mongoloid peoples in East Asia it is 30 to 40 percent (Fig. 8-2). Does this mean that the affinity between American Indians and Asians is confirmed? Some researchers think so: they feel that the O type

was diluted in Asia by contact with other genes, but that the American Indians, by migrating into the Americas, retained their O type almost unchanged. This view holds that the "original" blood type was type O, and that first A, then B, and AB types evolved later and began to supplant the O type. And indeed, the O type remains strong in comparatively isolated areas of the world, such as central Africa and northern Australia. It might also explain the prevalence of the A type in Western Europe and the B type farther to the east, a later intrusion (Figs. 8-3 and 8-4). But the same theory raises questions. Although the O type dominates in large areas of Africa, the B type occurs there as well. Where did that B gene

come from? How did it also get to islands of the Pacific Ocean and even into the Americas? Many scholars now believe that people ranged far more widely over this earth in ancient times than was long believed, and that very early migrations are the answer. Few believe that parallel evolution in far-flung parts of the globe produced the situation. Whatever the eventual answers, the analysis of blood types has added enormously to the arsenal of evidence in the search for the origins and early dispersals of man.

165

Asian (Chinese)

African (Bantu)

Indian (India)

European

American (South America)

It would be pointless, as yet, to try to draw a map of the world showing the sources of man and arrows to suggest routes of initial migration. Scholars have changed their views several times and will again. One map that is frequently seen has three major areas of dispersal: in East Asia (the Mongoloids), in West Asia (the Caucasoids), and in Africa (the Negroids). The Negroid source area is usually placed in the vicinity of Nigeria/Cameroun, although the evidence is growing that African sources lie elsewhere. It was long assumed that Africa was populated from this source, first westward into West Africa and later, by the Bantu, southward into central and southern Africa. It is a convenient explanation, but the African source may well lie far to the west, in what is today Mauritania. And there may have been more than one source area: the Bantu may have emerged from quite another region of the continent. Again, as long as the uncertainties are of this scale, maps are premature, and this is the context in which you should view Figure 8-5.

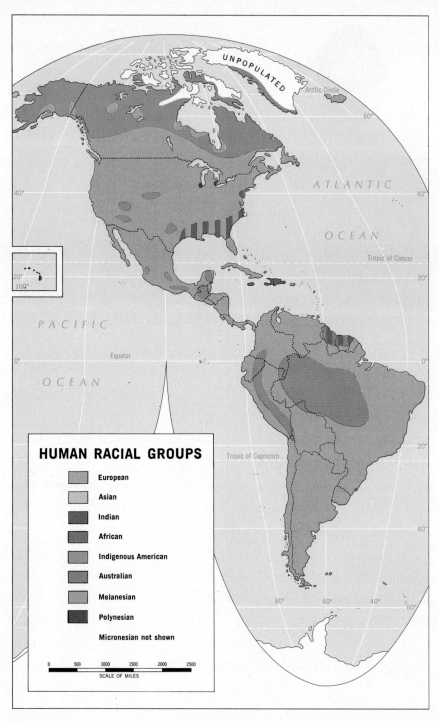

HUMAN RACIAL GROUPS

- European
- Asian
- Indian
- African
- Indigenous American
- Australian
- Melanesian
- Polynesian

Micronesian not shown

SCALE OF MILES
0   500   1000   1500   2000   2500

Figure 8-5

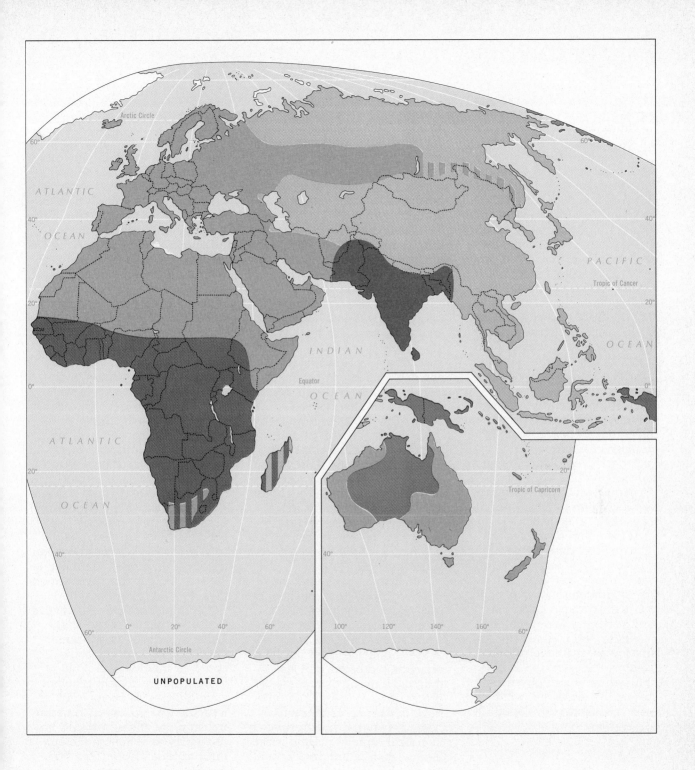

UNPOPULATED

169

Race and Culture

Culture, we stated earlier, is acquired and learned—not biologically inherited. And yet it is so easy to generalize about correlations between race and culture that this truth is all too easily forgotten. And from these correlations spring doctrines of racial superiority and inferiority, the roots of racism. When you postulate that Western society has advanced farther than other peoples because the white race is superior to other races, you assume that the cultural capacity of white people is greater than that of others—a proposition that has not been proved scientifically.

Certainly there have been scholars who have sought to prove that there are inherent qualities of superiority in certain races over others. Some are still working on the proposition. But there is no basis at present for concluding that the human races differ in their innate capacity for cultural development. True, peoples differ in their physical size, height, skin color, hair type, and in other ways. But these are not grounds for assuming that one racial group is better adapted for functioning under modern conditions than others. Nor, as anthropologists have proved, does the "closer to the ape" analysis of human physiology sustain the thesis that white peoples are more developed than

some of their contemporaries. All races have traits that resemble their distant ancestors —Europeans more than some others. Once again skin color pervades the argument more than it ought to.

These are sensitive topics, but this has not deterred scholars from searching in other directions for evidences of racial superiority, for example by calculating brain sizes and correlating these data with intelligence. There has been some evidence that larger brain size may be related to greater intellectual capacity, but larger brain size is connected with better nutrition and general physical well-being. The average brain size of several non-Western peoples (for instance, in Africa) is greater than that of whites. And there is evidence that Neanderthal man had a larger brain than modern man, or one at least as large. This may mean that it is not brain size, but the functional differentiation of the brain that has to do with intelligence.

And then, of course, there is the "evidence" from intelligence tests. How many times has it been reported that a group of white school children in Massachusetts or some other northeastern state did better in a test than did a group of minority children elsewhere? And how often have the wrong conclusions been drawn and popularized by uncritical reporting? Until racial inequities in plural (multiracial)

societies such as that of the United States are removed, intelligence tests will continue to reveal different levels of intellectual achievement between racially discrete groups. Those differences have to do *not* with the inherent ability of the children being examined but with the circumstances of their upbringing, their nutrition, education, access to stimulation, and cultural environment. And there is something else about those tests. They are practically always prepared by people of one cultural experience, to be applied to people with another cultural environment. Anthropologists have long warned against generalizations drawn from such cross-cultural testing when carried out, say, in Africa or Australia; but even within our own society there are tests that have cultural bias, applied every day. Even if it is impossible to prove the superiority of one race over another, it is also impossible to disprove the existence of differences between the races in terms of mental functioning and psychological capacities. Psychologists have reported that there are differences in the learning abilities of different breeds within the same species of animal; the same could be true for man. Still, there is no conclusive proof for such differences as yet (and difference does not mean superiority); to prove them, it would be necessary to eliminate the cultural experience variable from the test. No one has succeeded in doing that.

All this does not help us much in answering some of the questions posed by the map of cultures of the world. For example, some human races are culturally far more advanced than others. Why? And why have some of the cultures that once led the world fallen into disrepair? And again, why were some societies static for a long period of time, suddenly to blossom into major cultures? The answers may have eluded us so far, but at least we have an idea where *not* to search for solutions. Apparently they do not lie in predestination by environmental conditions, nor in race.

The fact is that we still do not know what generates, stimulates societies to achieve and accomplish in certain areas and at given times in their history. We, with our contemporary view of the world, find it all too natural that Western society is complex and "advanced," and that indigenous Australians and South American Indians have less advanced cultures. But in the context of human history it is only yesterday that Europeans were excelled by other cultures elsewhere in the world, in Asia, in Africa, and in the Americas. In another age, we would have had quite a different impression —and quite different explanations. Who, at the height of the power and splendor of Mesopotamia, would have predicted that barely a shadow of all that achievement would remain a few centuries later? Who, in the days of the Roman Empire,

would have imagined that Rome's distant, backward colony—Britain—would, before long, generate an empire to span the world? And who, 100 years ago, would have predicted for Japan, an isolated, poor island country off Asia, a meteoric rise and an explosion of cultural development? There are lots of explanations now, with the benefit of hindsight. But all those explanations do not seem to give us the confidence to predict where it will happen next. In Nigeria? In Brazil?

And so, when we speak of race and culture, we must do so with great care, for our knowledge is still very limited and incomplete. The racial composition of Japan did not change when the country experienced its enormous burst of cultural development (nor did the climate). When it comes to racial identifications, there may be greater differences *within* a racial group than *between* racial groups, in some categories. In this respect race shares with the concept of the region its primary quality as an intellectual construct, not reality.

Racial groups cannot exist in total isolation. A few communities, protected by distance and nearly impenetrable forest, remained beyond the reach of alien encroachment until the present day in such areas as the Amazon Basin and the mountains of the Philippines, but these are newsworthy exceptions. The rule in the modern world is contact and interaction, even where ethnocentrism militates against interracial mixing. A case in point is South Africa, where cultural distastes for interracial marriage led the ruling majority among the white population to enact legislation designed to eliminate sexual contact and "miscegenation" between racial groups, and specifically between white and African or Asian individuals. Nevertheless, South Africa's population of over 20 million counts some 2 million persons of mixed ancestry (and only 4 million whites), suggesting that even in that racially conscious society, racial interaction prevailed to a substantial degree.

When cultures of different strengths make contact, the stronger culture prevails. The culture of the weaker society may be somewhat changed, considerably modified, or even completely transformed, but in every case the stronger culture will contribute certain of its qualities to it. This process, whereby a culture is changed substantially through interaction with another culture, is *acculturation*.

Actually, the process of acculturation is not the one-way street our definition might suggest. Stronger cultures do impose many of their attributes on weaker ones, but they themselves may well adopt some of the weaker culture's properties. To take a case relating to the previous discussion of ancient culture hearths: when the Spanish invaders reached the Central American mainland, they soon were able to overthrow Aztec society (they were helped by enemies of the Aztecs who had long faced the threat of being carried off for purposes of human sacrifice to the sun god). Now the Spaniard's culture began to prevail: towns were transformed, a new religious order was introduced, economic realities changed drastically. Acculturation was in full swing. But Spanish culture underwent some changes too, subtle as they were. In their architecture, the Spaniards reflected some of the motifs of Indian buildings. Indian crops were taken back to Iberia; domesticated animals were acquired. The Spaniards began to wear clothing that revealed the influence of Indian color and cut. A few Indian words got into Spanish use. Indian cultures made their contributions too.

Some societies, such as the Southern African Bushmen, the Amazonian Indians, and other peoples isolated by desert, forest, mountains, or distance have experienced little acculturation. At the other end of the scale there are whole societies changed enormously by the process: Japan is the outstanding example. In the case of Japan, a national leadership arose that was bent on achieving power and equality for the nation, by purposefully adopting European technological innovations. In the process, the society was transformed, and a new Japan arose to emulate and surpass its Western competitors. This is not to suggest that nothing of the old Japan remains. On the contrary: the fabric of original Japanese culture has proved very durable, and it survives beside and interwoven with the new order.

Some societies have been fortunate enough to be able to select those elements of an alien culture to be adopted, but others have experienced acculturation through superimposition. To a greater or lesser degree the recent history of much of America, Africa, Asia, and Australia has been a history of Europeanization, as the beliefs, values, and practices of European cultures were imposed on indigenous societies. European-style cities arose, European languages became the "official" languages of distant countries, European religions were promoted, and European standards of law and justice were invoked. In spheres of life ranging from mode of dress to education, the image of Europe became a veneer over local cultures. African school children learned more about European history in their classrooms than about Africa's past. Asian families began to send their children to British and French schools and universities, for progress was now dictated by European rules. American Indians found their lands carved into huge estates, and if they were not lucky enough to be admitted as squatters, there were fences to keep them out. Changes in practices governing the possession and use of land were perhaps the most difficult of all elements in the acculturation process for the recipient society to accommodate.

Culture and Environment

The distribution of the old culture hearths we discussed in Chapter 7 inevitably leads to questions about the environment under which they thrived. Some ancient cultures lie revealed today by ruins in the desert and the tropical rainforest. Could the cities and other settlements have prospered under such conditions—or have climates changed so much that where there is desert today there may have been ample water supply thousands of years ago? And in any case, what are the optimum environmental conditions for the evolution and growth of civilizations? Present-day world culture hearths seem to lie in temperate climatic regions, not in the tropics or in the desert, nor in near-polar zones. Does this mean that we can generalize about "optimum" climatic conditions for the human success story?

Long ago, Aristotle thought so: he argued that the peoples of cold, distant Europe were "full of spirit but wanting in intelligence and skill; and therefore they retain comparative freedom, but have no political organization, and are incapable of ruling over others. Whereas the natives of Asia are intelligent and inventive, but they are wanting in spirit, and therefore they are always in a state of subjection and slavery. But the Hellenic race, which is situated between them, is likewise intermediate in character, being high-spirited and intelligent . . .," as he is quoted from a 1921 translation, The Works of Aristotle. And many geographers after Aristotle have held similar views. How easy it is to view people living in cold climates as "hardy, but not very intelligent," those of the warm tropics as "lazy and passive," and those in the intermediate zones as productive and progressive. Here is how Ellsworth Huntington, a twentieth-century geographer, stated it in a book entitled Principles of Human Geography, published in 1940: "The well-known contrast between the energetic people of the most progressive parts of the temperate zone and the inert inhabitants of the tropics and even of intermediate regions, such as Persia, is largely due to climate . . . the people of the cyclonic regions rank so far above those of other parts of the world that they are the natural leaders."

The doctrine expressed by these statements is environmentalism or, more specifically, environmental determinism. It holds that human behavior, individually and collectively, is strongly affected by and even controlled or determined by the natural environment under which society exists. It suggests that the climate is the critical factor in this determination: for progress and productiveness in culture, politics, and technology the "ideal" climate would be, say, that of Western Europe or the Northeastern United States. The people of hot, tropical areas or cold, near-polar zones might as well forget it. Their habitat decreed that they would never achieve anything even approaching the accomplishments of their midlatitude contemporaries.

And so, for a time, geographers set about their attempts to explain the distribution of present and past centers of culture in terms of the "dictating environment." In the early part of this century that was a major theme in the field—the manner in which the natural environment conditions human activities. Quite soon, however, there were geographers who doubted whether those sweeping generalizations about climate and character, environment and productiveness were really valid. They recognized exceptions to the environmentalists' postulations (e.g., the Maya empire may have arisen in tropical rain forest) and argued that human society was capable of much more than merely adapting to its natural environment. As for the supposed "efficiency" of the climate of Western Europe, this was an interesting idea but not scientifically proved. And surely it was best not to base laws of determinism on inadequate data and in the face of apparently contradictory evidence.

These arguments helped guide the search for answers to questions about the relationships between man and environment in different directions, but the unqualified environmentalist position was still held by some in the past several decades. For a more modern approach, it is interesting to read S. F. Markham's book entitled *Climate and the Energy of Nations*—still an environmentalist statement, but with the benefit of Huntington's massive writings and the works of several others behind it. Markham thought that he could detect, in the migration of the center of power in the Mediterranean (from Egypt to Greece to Rome and onward) the changing climates of that part of Europe during the most recent several thousand years of glacial retreat. He argued that Egypt was a good deal cooler when in its prime than it is now; Greece's climate, too, was more conducive to the generation of energy in people when the Greeks rose to prominence. Rome was so cool that public hot baths were a part of daily life. In all this, Markham saw the northward movement of isotherms. Like his predecessors, he tried to determine what is the "optimum" temperature for physical and for mental activity and he was sure that these temperatures prevailed in Egypt, Greece, and Rome (and later in Western Europe).

But geographers grew increasingly cautious about such speculative writings, and they began to ask their questions about humanity and environment in new ways. There still is the old interest in how man is affected by the natural environment, but if there are generalizations to be made, they ought to come from detailed, carefully designed research. Everyone agrees that human activities are in certain ways influenced by the environment, but man appears to be more the decision maker in this context than the subordinate the environmentalists believe us to be.

Out of these deliberations has come a whole new field of geography in which interest focuses *not* on the manner in which environment conditions human behavior but on the way people perceive the environment and act on the basis of these perceptions. We all have an image of the world around us, and we argue that our decisions and actions are based on this image rather than on reality. If this is the case, then our concern when we analyze behavior ought not to be with the objective realities of our environment but with these images we have in our heads. What goes into the formation of these images? Undoubtedly an Indian's view of the American Southwest would be quite different from most white Americans' image of that region. An urban ghetto is perceived quite differently by a black person living there than by white people who do not. Note that we have begun to involve not only the natural environment in our discussion, but also the social environment. Environmental determinists of the past mostly failed to recognize that the environment that interacts with man consists not only of landscapes and climates but also of attributes created by society itself—all elements of a cultural environment.

Now, when we want to study human activities in the context of environment, the magnitude of the problems involved begin to emerge. Experience, the accessibility of information, psychological state, physiological conditions, cultural traditions, social constraints—all these factors come into play. And this is only a short list; the longer it becomes, the less likely are we to engage in the business of sweeping generalizations about climate and behavior!

Out of this research, we may hope, it will be possible for us some day to know not only how we perceive a non-Western culture, but also how the people of that culture themselves view it. If Europeans had known more about the way Africans view their lands and herds, then the shock of the contact between the cultures might have been less. That land could lie unfenced, open to be used and exploited by all, was inconceivable to the white invaders. That land should be taken as personal property and parceled into private holdings was equally inconceivable to Africans. To the whites who urged the African cattleman to weed out the old and sick animals, so that the quality of the herd would improve and overgrazing would cease, an African replied: it is like suggesting that you take your billfold and throw out the dirty, worn money; your wallet will be much cleaner and less bulky. He could conceive of our money economy no more than Europeans could grasp the idea that in some parts of Africa, cattle numbers are all that matter to the owners, not how old, sick, or unproductive they are. It is all a question how such a resource is perceived.

9 Language and Culture

Language is a vital element of culture; no culture exists without it. In literate societies, written words serve to increase vastly the efficiency with which culture is transmitted from generation to generation. This is not to suggest that peoples who do not write (*preliterate* societies) cannot transmit their culture from one generation to another, but writing is an enormous asset and a necessity in complex, advanced cultures.

What is a language? The term has been defined in numerous different ways. Webster defines it as "a systematic means of communicating ideas or feelings by the use of conventionalized signs, gestures, marks, or especially articulate vocal sound." For our present purposes, the question of definition is not terribly important, as long as we remind ourselves that a language is a language, no matter how large or small the vocabulary or how large or small the number of people using the language. As we discuss language in the spatial context of culture we should also remember that languages are not static but constantly changing. That reminder should hardly be necessary, considering how our own use and vocabulary have changed over the past few years alone.

A language has several levels of variation. In complex cultures there may be an official, *standard* language, whose quality is a matter of national concern, sustained by official state examinations to be passed by teachers, civil servants, and others. Many speakers, nevertheless, will use some variation of this standard language, containing some incorrect words and phrasings ("he ain't seen nothin' yet"). One such variation is *slang*, with roots in the social structure of society, and it can be heard nearly everywhere the language is used. But there are also special uses and accents that have regional expression. These are *dialects*. A trained ear can tell much about the place or area of residence of a speaker. In the United States, it does not even take such a trained ear to recognize a Southerner, or a Bostonian.

177

Classification

In the context of culture, we are obviously interested in the way language is distributed in the world, what the forces creating this distribution are, and how the pattern is changing. But first, let us consider briefly the problem of language classification. Obviously, this relates to definition. Some scholars would classify Canadian French (the primary language spoken in Quebec Province) as a discrete language, others would view it as a dialect of European French. In that part of Africa where Bantu languages are spoken, many of those languages are closely related to each other and share major portions of vocabulary. Again, what is language and what is dialect is not always agreed on. So depending on these definitional problems and their disposition, between 2500 and 3500 languages are in use in the world today, over 1000 of them in Africa alone. Clearly we cannot begin to study the relative location of around 3000 items in the world without bringing some order to the mosaic.

In the classification of languages, we use terms also employed in biology, and for the same reasons: certain languages are related to each other, some are not. Languages grouped in a *family* are thought to have a shared origin; in the *subfamily* their commonality is more definite. These are divided into language *groups*, which consist of sets of *individual* languages.

Languages of Europe

The language map of Europe (Fig. 9-1) shows the Indo-European language family to prevail over the region, with pockets of the Ural-Altaic family occurring in Finland and Hungary and adjacent areas. Subfamilies include the Germanic languages (English, German, Swedish), the Romance languages (French, Spanish, Italian), the Slavic languages (Russian, Polish, Bulgarian), and others. Language groups in Europe are represented by such clusters as the Scandinavian languages (Swedish, Norwegian, Danish) and the Iberian languages (Spanish, Portuguese, Catalan). While the map shows a substantial coincidence between political and linguistic boundaries, significant exceptions do occur. The French linguistic region extends into Belgium, Switzerland, and Italy, but does not include the Western Bretagne (Brittany) Peninsula. The Celtic languages survive here (Breton), in Wales (Welsh), and in Western Scotland and Ireland (Gaelic), remnants of an early period of European history before the wave of more modern languages submerged them.

In an African village the storyteller is an important figure who not only entertains and teaches but who transmits folk history from one generation to the next. Here a storyteller in a village in the Ivory Coast has his young audience spellbound.

Figure 9-1

LANGUAGES OF EUROPE

ICELANDIC

0 100 200 300 400 500
MILES

FAROESE

SCOTS GAELIC
ENGLISH

IRISH GAELIC
ENGLISH

WELSH

ENGLISH
BRETON

FRENCH

GALICIAN
BASQUE
PORTUGUESE
SPANISH
CATALAN
CATALAN
CATALAN
SARDINIAN

ITALIAN
ITALIAN

MALTESE

NORWEGIAN
SWEDISH
SWEDISH
SWEDISH
SWEDISH
SWEDISH

DANISH
DANISH
DANISH

FRISIAN
DUTCH
FLEMISH
GERMAN
LUSATIAN
CZECH
SLOVAK
GERMAN
HUNGARIAN
GERMAN
SLOVENIAN
RHAETO-ROMANSCH
GERMAN
SERBO-CROATIAN
ALBANIAN
MACE-DONIAN
ROMANIAN
GREEK

LAPP
LAPP
LAPP
LAPP
FINNISH
KARELIAN
VEPSE
FINNISH
ESTONIAN
LATVIAN
LITHUANIAN
RUSSIAN
POLISH
POLISH
BYELORUSSIAN
POLISH

RUSSIAN
SAMOYED
KOMI
RUSSIAN
KARELIAN
UKRAINIAN
RUSSIAN
RUSSIAN

HUNGARIAN
ROMANIAN
BULGARIAN
BULGARIAN
TURKISH

INDO-EUROPEAN FAMILY

Germanic Subfamily   Baltic Subfamily

Romance Subfamily   Greek

Celtic Subfamily   Albanian

Slavic Subfamily

URAL-ALTAIC FAMILY

Finnic Subfamily   Turkic Subfamily   BASQUE

Ugric Subfamily   Samoyed   **AFRO-ASIATIC FAMILY**

179

Figure 9-2

As Figure 9-2 indicates, the Indo-European language family dominates not only in Europe but also in much of Asia (the Soviet Union and India, among other countries), North and South America, Australia, and in parts of Southern Africa. Indo-European languages are spoken by about half the world's peoples, and English is the most widely used Indo-European language today. Linguists theorize that a lost language they call Proto-Indo-European existed somewhere in East-Central Europe, and that the present languages of the Indo-European family evolved from this common heritage. In the process, as vocabularies grew and changed and peoples dispersed and migrated, differentiation took place. Latin arose out of this early period, to be disseminated over much of Europe during the rise of the Roman Empire; later Latin died out and was supplanted by Italian, French, and the other Romance languages.

The map of world language families tells us much about the story of human migration, which brought Indo-European languages to the Americas, Australia, South Africa, and other regions, and it also reveals something of the past in Eurasia itself. Note (Fig. 9-2) that Indo-European languages are spoken as far east as India; Hindi is one of the languages in this family. This reflects the Western source of the peopling of modern India, and the route through Southwest

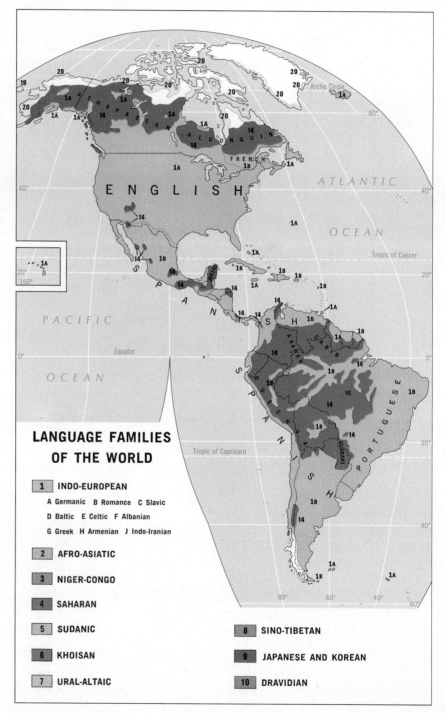

LANGUAGE FAMILIES OF THE WORLD

1 INDO-EUROPEAN
A Germanic B Romance C Slavic
D Baltic E Celtic F Albanian
G Greek H Armenian J Indo-Iranian

2 AFRO-ASIATIC

3 NIGER-CONGO

4 SAHARAN

5 SUDANIC

6 KHOISAN

7 URAL-ALTAIC

8 SINO-TIBETAN

9 JAPANESE AND KOREAN

10 DRAVIDIAN

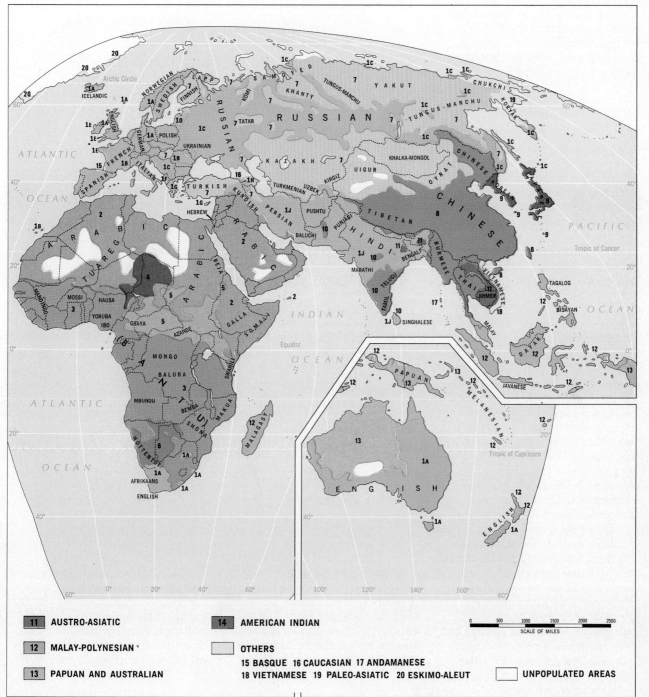

11 AUSTRO-ASIATIC　　　**14** AMERICAN INDIAN

12 MALAY-POLYNESIAN　　OTHERS
　　　　　　　　　　　　15 BASQUE　16 CAUCASIAN　17 ANDAMANESE
13 PAPUAN AND AUSTRALIAN　18 VIETNAMESE　19 PALEO-ASIATIC　20 ESKIMO-ALEUT　　　UNPOPULATED AREAS

Asia and Iran. The oldest inhabitants of the Indian subcontinent were driven into the tip of the peninsula by newcomers from the northwest, and the linguistic map is part of the proof.

Languages of Africa

The promise of the spatial study of languages and dialects in historical and cultural geography is especially evident in Africa. Perhaps as many as a thousand languages are spoken in Black Africa, and linguists have been working to record many of these; most of them were unwritten. From the resulting data, it has been possible to gain some significant insights into Africa's past.

The languages of Africa (Fig. 9-3) are mostly of the Niger-Congo family, which extends from West Africa all the way to the south. This Niger-Congo family can be subdivided into five subfamilies. One of these is the Bantu subfamily, whose languages are spoken by most of the people near and south of the equator. In West Africa, the languages are of the Atlantic, Voltaic, Guinea, and Hausa subfamilies. The oldest languages of Black Africa are the *Khoisan* languages, which share a "click" sound. These include the Bushman languages, spoken still by some tens of thousands of people in Southwestern Africa. Perhaps these Khoisan languages once were the main languages over much of Africa, but they have been reduced to comparative insignificance by the Bantu invasion, just as Europe's Celtic languages were.

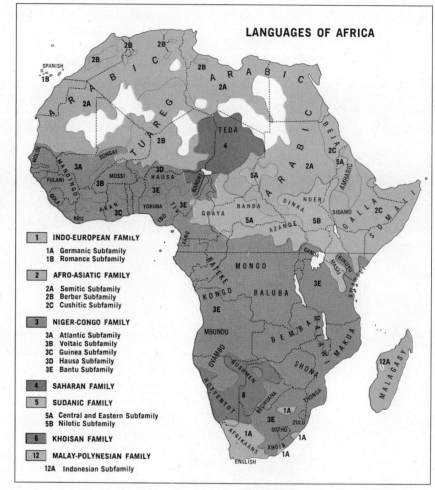

LANGUAGES OF AFRICA

	1	INDO-EUROPEAN FAMILY
1A	Germanic Subfamily
1B	Romance Subfamily

	2	AFRO-ASIATIC FAMILY
2A	Semitic Subfamily
2B	Berber Subfamily
2C	Cushitic Subfamily

	3	NIGER-CONGO FAMILY
3A	Atlantic Subfamily
3B	Voltaic Subfamily
3C	Guinea Subfamily
3D	Hausa Subfamily
3E	Bantu Subfamily

| | 4 | SAHARAN FAMILY |

	5	SUDANIC FAMILY
5A	Central and Eastern Subfamily
5B	Nilotic Subfamily

| | 6 | KHOISAN FAMILY |

| | 12 | MALAY-POLYNESIAN FAMILY |
| 12A | Indonesian Subfamily |

Figure 9-3

How can languages help us in reconstructing the cultural development of Africa? Consider what has happened in Europe, where the Romance language subfamily has differentiated into various languages including French, Italian, Spanish, and Portuguese. Even within these individual languages we can recognize differentiation, such as between Castilian and Catalan Spanish, and between Northern and Southern French and Walloon. Such differentiation develops over time, and it is reasonable to assume that the more time elapses, the greater will be the individuality of each language. If, therefore, the peoples of a large region speak languages that are somewhat different, but still closely related, it is reasonable to conclude that they have migrated into that region (or emerged there) relatively recently. On the other hand, languages that are of recognizably common roots yet strongly different must have undergone modification over a lengthy period of time.

Among the languages of the Niger-Congo family, those of the Bantu subfamily are much more closely related to each other than are those of other subfamilies. It may be deduced, then, that the Bantu peoples of Central and Southern Africa are of more recent origins than West Africans. Even a little general knowledge of African names can suggest the affinities. Thus the word Bantu should actually be written BaNtu (people), with the *Ba* a prefix. Sometimes the prefix is retained in common usage, sometimes not. The *Wa*tusi, for example, are sometimes called the Tusi or Tutsi. The people of Southeastern Uganda are the *Ba*Ganda or Ganda. The Zulu of South Africa are actually the *Ama*Zulu. In stories about Rhodesia you often read about the *Ma*Shona or Shona. Remember Basutoland, now called Lesotho? It was originally named after the Sotho, and *Ba*Sotholand was corrupted to Basutoland. The point

is becoming clear: *Ba*, *Ma*, *Wa*, and *Ama* are not very far removed from each other linguistically, and they reveal close associations between languages and peoples spread far and wide across Africa from Uganda to Zululand.

It is not just a matter of prefixes, of course. In terms of vocabularies and in numerous other respects Bantu languages reflect their close relationships as well. Linguists have traced the changes that occur over space in a single word, and thousands of miles away it often is quite close to the way it started. Take the familiar Swahili greeting, *jambo*, which you can use in coastal Kenya. In the Eastern Transvaal of South Africa and Swaziland, people will recognize *jabo!*

The situation in West Africa is quite different. Certainly there are languages that have close association, but the major languages of the West African subfamilies are much more discrete and individual. Of course, there are other pieces of evidence to support the conclusion that the peoples of Bantu Africa have a shorter history in that area than those of West Africa, but the linguistic evidence, and orally transmitted traditions, provide the basis. The linguistic evidence led to the conclusion that assumptions about a Cameroonian culture hearth for both West and Southern Africa were inaccurate, and it has even proved possible to reconstruct old migration routes from linguistic and oral data.

A *lingua franca* is a language used in trade, commerce, and general communication among peoples who mostly speak other languages of their own. In coastal West Africa, a lingua franca developed that is a mixture of English and West African languages, and you can hear it spoken from Freetown, Sierra Leone, to Port Harcourt, Nigeria, and beyond. This language is known appropriately as Wes Kos, and naturally it stands apart from the Guinea subfamily of languages. A more famous lingua franca is Swahili, spoken in Kenya, Tanzania, Uganda and even in Eastern Zaire and Northern Mozambique in modified forms. Swahili is essentially a Bantu language, but much modified by the tongue brought to East Africa by the traders— Arabic. Although various forms of Swahili are spoken in Eastern Africa, it serves effectively as a means of communication in a strongly multilingual area. Still another African lingua franca is Hausa. This language is spoken across much of West Africa's Sahel zone, from Eastern Senegal to Nigeria, where it serves in commerce and general contact.

In the Caribbean area, forms of pidgin based on English have come to serve as *linguae francae;* their use extends even to non-English-speaking territories such as Dutch-influenced Surinam. Elsewhere, lingua

183

Frankish Language

The time: the Middle Ages. The place: Southern Europe. The objectives: religious conversion and profitable trade.

The Europeans had pushed the Moslems from Iberia, and had asserted their strength during crusades to the heart of the powerful world of Islam. When the Mediterranean opened to the opportunities of trade and commerce, the traders of Southern Europe— Southern France and adjacent Italy—found themselves in favorable position to capitalize. And so the traders from France, the *Franks*, followed the routes of the crusaders and revitalized the ports of the Eastern Mediterranean, and brought there a tongue consisting of a mixture of French, Italian, Greek, Spanish, and the local Arabic. If you wanted to do business, you spoke the Frankish language . . . the *lingua franca*.

The days of the original lingua franca are over, but the term remains in use, applied to similar situations around the world.

In certain countries there is not only no effective lingua franca, but a linguistic fragmentation that may reflect a strong cultural pluralism and the existence of divisive forces. This is true in formerly colonial areas where peoples of diverse tongues were thrown together by the force of foreign interests, as happened in Africa and Asia. This also occurred in the Americas: as Figure 9-4 shows, Indian languages are spoken by more than half of the people in substantial areas of Guatemala and Mexico, although these countries tend to be viewed as Spanish speaking. Countries never colonized in comparable ways, but peopled from different cultural sources, may also display multilingualism. Canada's Quebec Province is the heart of that country's French-speaking sector, and Canada's multilingualism mirrors a cultural division of considerable intensity. In Belgium, a fairly sharp line divides

francas facilitate communication among hundreds of millions of people. Chinese serves as such for a region far beyond China itself in Eastern Asia, and "Bazaar Malay" functions as a lingua franca in much of Southeast Asia. Melanesian pidgin serves in the Western Pacific's numerous archipelagos and it resembles Caribbean pidgin, being based chiefly on English.

In India, Hindi and English are lingua francas for peoples who speak other languages in their daily lives. And through the former colonial world, European languages continue to serve as means of contact, as French does in West Africa and English in East Africa.

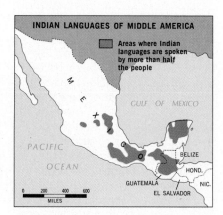

INDIAN LANGUAGES OF MIDDLE AMERICA

Areas where Indian languages are spoken by more than half the people

GULF OF MEXICO

MEXICO

PACIFIC OCEAN

BELIZE

HOND.

GUATEMALA

NIC.

EL SALVADOR

0 200 400 600
MILES

Figure 9-4

Manuela Rodriguez Hurtado

Where illiteracy is still widespread, professional letter-writers assist people wishing to communicate. This woman scribe and her client were photographed near Santo Domingo Square in Mexico City.

the northern, Flemish-speaking half of the country from the Walloon (French) speaking south (Fig. 9-1).

In the examples just given, the linguistic fragmentation is expressed regionally, but this is not always the case in multilingual countries. In multiracial South Africa, the white population of about four million speaks both Afrikaans and English, but both languages are spoken throughout the white-occupied areas of the country (although interior rural areas of the Orange Free State and the Transvaal are overwhelmingly Afrikaans speaking). The regionalism that does exist in the linguistic pattern of South Africa relates to the Bantu languages spoken there. As elsewhere in Africa, the black peoples of South Africa speak numerous discrete languages (about two dozen in that country). Thus Zulu is the major African language in Natal, Xhosa is important in the Transkei, and so forth. Certainly the (white) South African form of multilingualism is the exception rather than the rule: linguistic diversity normally means regional differentiation within the state.

Multilingual Problems

Countries in all parts of the world (India, Nigeria, and Switzerland, for example) are *multilingual* countries in which several languages are spoken. Multilingualism is far more common than you might believe: three or more languages are used by substantial population sectors not only in the countries we just identified, but also in the Soviet Union, Indonesia, Sudan, Zaire, and Guatemala—still a very incomplete list.

How large does a minority population sector using a separate language have to be in order for a country to be identified as multilingual? There is no specific rule for this. Take the case of Brazil. Most of us would consider Brazil a monolingual country, since 99 percent of its over 100 million people speak one common language, Portuguese. But literally dozens of indigenous Indian languages are spoken by Indian groups still living in Brazil's vast Amazonian interior. On the other hand, the numbers and fortunes of those Indian peoples are declining, and while Brazil may technically be a multilingual country, it effectively is a monolingual state.

Thus multilingualism is easily negated when the minorities are small and have little or no power or influence. That South Africa should be known to many people as a bilingual (two-language) country reflects the power position of the white minority more than it does linguistic reality there. Our impression of Guatemala as a Spanish-speaking area again mirrors the dominance of one sector of the population there; the Indian peoples, despite their numbers, do not yet have much of a say in the affairs of their country.

Multilingualism is far more evident, and presents greater problems, when the population sectors are more balanced in terms of power and influence as well as numbers. Despite 50 years of Russification, the Soviet Union is still marked by a complex linguistic pluralism. Lithuanian and Latvian are still used in the west, Armenian and Caucasian in the south, various Ural-Altaic languages in the

Moslem southeast. In Nigeria, there are three dominant linguistic regions and dozens of minor ones. The north speaks Hausa, the old lingua franca of the interior, the southwest uses Yoruba, and the southeast, where Biafra's ill-fated secessionist effort was made, is Ibo-speaking. In India, a dividing line across the lower part of the peninsula separates the Dravidian, older languages of the south from the Indo-European languages of the north, but there are further divisions on both sides of that line (Fig. 9-5). The Dravidian languages include Tamil, Telugu, Kannada, and Malayalam. Northern India speaks not only Hindi, but also Gujarati, Bengali, Punjabi, and Assamese, among other tongues.

People are sensitive about their language and its rights in a multilingual society, and they often resist efforts to introduce a "national" language for fear that, eventually, it may submerge their own. The Indian government's efforts to achieve linguistic uniformity through the promotion of Hindi as a lingua franca produced resistance and violent riots in some areas. Kenya's newspapers, at the time of the 1974 election, scoffed at the "archaic" rule whereby candidates must pass an English test. Welsh nationalists vigorously promote the language that is central to Welsh cultural identity. And there is no doubt about it: minorities are militantly pressing their causes in many countries of the world today, in Iraq, in Ethiopia, in the United Kingdom, in the Philippines, and in the United States. Multilingualism reflects cultural pluralism, and cultural pluralism is a complex problem everywhere.

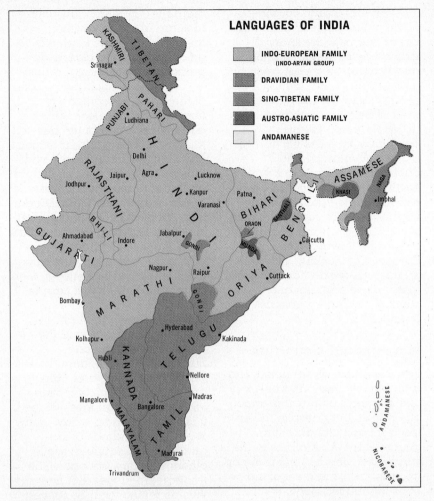

LANGUAGES OF INDIA

- INDO-EUROPEAN FAMILY
  (INDO-ARYAN GROUP)
- DRAVIDIAN FAMILY
- SINO-TIBETAN FAMILY
- AUSTRO-ASIATIC FAMILY
- ANDAMANESE

Figure 9-5 (above)

Bilingualism

Bilingual countries are those in which two languages are spoken to the practical exclusion of all others. It is necessary to qualify this definition, for even in the prototype of bilingual countries, Belgium, there is a tiny minority of German speakers—and so it is in Canada, in Czechoslovakia, in Guyana, all bilingual countries as well.

The participants in a recent O.P.E.C. Conference use the earphones to hear simultaneous translation of speeches given by representatives from Arab as well as non-Arab countries. (Below)

187

The case of Canada is of special interest. That Canada is perceived as an English-speaking country (and is still categorized as part of "Anglo" America) reflects the subordinate position of the French community there. But the population sector that is of British origins actually constitutes well under 50 percent of Canada's people; just over 30 percent are French-speaking, and some 20 percent are of other European stock. It was the British and other European people, however, who opened Canada's western interior, and as in the United States, these societies merged into a Canadian culture whose language was and remains English. The French, who were the earliest European immigrants to Canada, remained concentrated in their original region of Quebec even after the British took over the government of the country and the vast western hinterlands were opened. The French residents of Canada secured the right to retain their system of civil law, their language, and their (Roman Catholic) religion, and so their cultural identity—but part of this identity was a regional isolation, largely self-imposed. Quebec was "French Canada," but much of what made Canada a vigorous country lay beyond the confines of Quebec. By the time the French Canadians began to break their isolation and seek a share in the Canada that lay beyond, they found that they were at a disadvantage. The ensuing frustrations and their expression have become a prominent element of Canadian national life. Canada is divided regionally as well as culturally, and progress in the effort to forge a Canadian nation is difficult.

Other bilingual countries have found such efforts no easier. In Belgium, the sharp dividing line between Fleming and Walloon runs east-west, just about through the middle of the country, and the truly bilingual area of Belgium is very small indeed. Northern (Flemish) Belgium often looks northward, to the Netherlands, and Southern Belgium is oriented southward, to France. In Czechoslovakia, the boundary runs north-south. For centuries, Western, Czech-speaking Bohemia has looked toward Western Europe, and Eastern, Slovak-speaking Slovakia has been the more Slavic segment of a country marked by unstable boundaries.

Monolingual Countries

Few countries, as we noted, are truly monolingual, and use only one language. If Brazil is a monolingual country despite the existing mosaic of Indian languages, then Australia is in the same class, its small black minority (also speaking a set of indigenous languages) notwithstanding. Japan speaks overwhelmingly the same language, again with the minor exception of the Hokkaido-based Ainu minority. Several of the Arab states use Arabic and are monolingual, including Egypt and Libya, but others, such as Sudan and Algeria, have African minorities and are multilingual. In Middle and South America, monolingual countries are those with the smallest of Indian minorities (or, as in the case of Uruguay, no such minority at all). To identify Europe's monolingual countries, we need a careful look at

Figure 9-1; note that few countries are absolutely without linguistic diversity. Poland is among those most closely approaching monolingual status.

Why do political boundaries of the world not conform to linguistic boundaries? We have already seen part of the answer: this is a mobile world, in which people move and migrate and thus carry with them their cultural attributes to alien lands, there to preserve and foster them. In addition, conflicts between adjacent countries have caused boundary shifts that still separate people who speak essentially the same tongue: the border between Germany and France is a case in point. Still another factor involves the strength of an emerging language and the retreat of a declining one. Europe's old Celtic languages yielded to English and French, and this sort of fate has overtaken many languages—indeed, it is still happening today. Many of Africa's hundreds of languages will disappear, while others will grow stronger. The Khoisan languages that now survive as remnants in Southwestern Africa were supplanted by Bantu languages in the same manner that the Celtic languages were pushed back.

There is a counter to these factors that favor replacement, namely the determination of a minority group to retain its identity and to sustain its culture and especially its language. As we reported, the world is seeing more of this during the second half of the twentieth century as minority groups become conscious of their strength. Thus languages that might otherwise be doomed are retained and fostered, and the process of attrition, if not halted, is at least delayed.

Obviously the whole area of language in cultural geography affords innumerable opportunities for research and study. Language is a vital element in the reconstruction of past cultures; the transmittal of oral literature and its interpretation opens up whole new possibilities. The professional storyteller in an African village is not just a picturesque figure of incidental interest: he holds in his tales the history and psyche of the people of whom he speaks. The study of dialects and the spatial character of word modification can tell us much about peoples' movements, their external contacts or isolation, former distribution, and more. And then there is the relevant issue brought up by so many when it comes to debates about the value in learning a foreign language: language can reveal much about the way a people view reality, their own culture, as well as other cultures. In their structure and vocabulary and in their ability (or inability) to express certain concepts and ideas, languages reflect something of the way people think and perceive their world. There are African languages that have no word, no term for the concept of a god. Others (also in Asia) really have no system for the reporting of chronological events, no time scale, as it were. It would be difficult for us to understand those peoples' perception of the world about them, preoccupied as our culture is with the supernatural and dating and timing. Learning the language would be a first, timid step. But the rewards could be enormous.

Nonverbal Communication

Language is the chief means of communication, but it is not the only way we transmit our thoughts and emotions to others. By the look on someone's face, from the way she walks or sits, it is possible to interpret moods and feelings, even without a word being said. We communicate parts of our personality to others without even being aware that we are doing so. This is true in other cultures as well as our own, but nonverbal communication is culturally based as are other culture traits. It is the silent language of behavior.

This aspect of communication can lead to some serious intercultural misinterpretations. We, within our own culture, learn to interpret nonverbal signals (a frown, an embrace, turning one's back, leaning forward for emphasis, and so on); we acquire likes and dislikes (we do not like to be crowded, or breathed on; we mask body smells with unparalleled array of deodorants). When we exhibit such behavior in another culture, however, we may find that polite distance-keeping is viewed as rude aloofness, averting one's eyes during a conversation is seen as shameful disinterest, arriving punctually on time is considered pushy and aggressive. It is quite possible to offend one's hosts, quite unintentionally of course, without ever saying a word.

189

The faithful at the Friday service of the
Srinagar Mosque, Kashmir.

10 Religion and Culture

In many parts of the world, and especially in non-Western areas, religion is so vital a part of culture that it practically *constitutes* culture. Thus it is not surprising that we should have difficulty defining exactly what a religion is. The phenomenon manifests itself in so many different ways: in the worship of the souls of ancestors living in natural objects such as mountains, animals, or trees; in the belief that a certain living person or persons possess particular capacities granted by a supernatural power; in the belief in a deity or deities, as in the great world religions. In some societies, notably in the Western, industrialized, urbanized, commercialized world, religion has become a rather subordinate, ephemeral matter in the life of many people. But in societies in Africa or Asia religious doctrine may exert tight control over behavior, during the daytime through ritual and practice and even at night in prescribing the orientation of the sleeping body.

If we cannot define religion precisely, we can at least observe some of the properties of this element of human culture. There are, of course, sets of doctrines and beliefs relating to the god or gods central to the faiths. In each faith, there will also be a number of more or less complex rituals through which these beliefs are given expression. Such rituals may attend significant events in peoples' lives: birth and death, attainment of adulthood, marriage. They are also expressed at regular intervals in a routine manner, as is done on Sundays in most of the Western world. Prayer at mealtime, or at sunrise and sundown, at night when retiring or in the morning when arising, commonly attends religious ritual. Such ritual is likely to involve the use of the religion's literature, if a literature exists; we are most familiar with the Bible and the Koran.

Religions, especially the major, world-scale faiths such as Christianity and Islam, have produced vast and complex organizational structures. These bureaucracies have a hierarchy of officers and command a great deal of wealth; rank and status are confirmed by

191

costume and authority over people's lives. These religious officers police and maintain an approved set of standards and the code of ethics peculiar to each religion.

From this brief statement of properties it is evident how strongly a culture may be dominated by the precepts of the prevailing faith. Some scholars have argued that the idea that people depend ultimately on some supernatural power over which they have no control has led to apathy, even laziness in people, but obviously others have been inspired to compete and achieve. The idea that a "good" life has rewards and "bad" behavior risks punishment also must have enormous cumulative effect on cultures. Modes of dress, the kinds of food people should and should not eat, commercial practices, and even the location and structure of houses may be determined by the rules of religion. And it is hardly necessary to remind anyone of the daily influence of religious heritage when our calendar, our holidays, prominent architectural landmarks, many place names, even the slogan *In God We Trust* on money we spend comes directly from that source. Even in societies that are seeking to divest themselves of religion and religious influence, such as that of the Soviet Union, those very influences continue to mark living routines and cultural landscapes as a whole. Imagine, then, the role of religion in an almost totally Roman Catholic society such as Spain. In Islamic society, too, it is religion that sustains and perpetuates the culture. Religious doctrine has determined that much of India is vegetarian (and overrun by holy animals), that the eating of pork is taboo in Moslem countries (eliminating the profitable pig from domestic economies), and that eating meat on Fridays was inappropriate for Roman Catholics.

Organized religion has been discouraged by the government of the Soviet Union, and abandoned church buildings give silent evidence of religion's retreat. This one stands on the Leningrad-Novgorod highway.

If we can be subjective about such matters, organized religion has had powerful positive as well as deep negative effects on human societies. Religion has been a major force in the improvement of social ills, the sustenance and protection of the poor, in the furtherance of the arts, in education of the deprived, in medicine. But religion has also thwarted scientific work, encouraged oppression of dissidents, supported colonialism and exploitation, and condemned women to inferior status in society. In common with other bureaucracies and establishments, large-scale organized religion has all too often been unable to adjust to the needs of the times.

It is natural that our first questions should relate to the locational characteristics of the major religions: where lie the sources and what are present distributions? Let us begin by identifying the world's major religions in general terms. The religions of Christianity are presently the most widely distributed around the world, dominating in Europe and North and South America as well as Australia, the Philippines, and, residually, in the Soviet Union (Fig. 10-1). Christian religions today have an estimated 900 to 1000 million adherents, although such figures (for all faiths) must be viewed as guesses. Protestant Christian religions are in the majority in Northern and parts of Northwestern Europe, in Canada and the United States, in Australia, and in South Africa; Roman Catholicism prevails in Southern Europe, Middle and South America, and in the Philippines. The Eastern Orthodox churches, which were major faiths of the old Russia, are now diminished in the atheist U.S.S.R. Another Orthodox remnant is the Coptic Church of Ethiopia, isolated on the Ethiopian Plateau.

The faiths of Islam dominate Northern Africa and Southwestern Asia, extending into the Soviet Union and China and including outlying provinces in Indonesia, Bangladesh, and Southern Mindanao in the Philippines. Islam is strong along the East African coast, survives in Albania, has an outlier at South Africa's Cape of Good Hope, and has adherents in the United States. Islam has perhaps 500 million faithful, more than half of them outside the culture realm often called the Islamic World; a substantial Islamic minority still resides in India.

The Hindu faith, as Figure 10-1 shows, is the religion primarily of India. The vast majority of Hinduism's 450 million adherents are Indians, although the faith also extends into Nepal, Bangladesh, Burma, and Sri Lanka. Another religion that had its source in India, Buddhism, is now a minority faith in that country but still strong in Southeast Asia, China, and Japan. Buddhism's various faiths are estimated to have about 230 million adherents today, and Shintoism, the Japanese religion closely related to Buddhism, some 70 million.

The Chinese religions, too, have elements of Buddhism mixed with local Chinese belief systems. As we note later, the Chinese traditional religions never involved concepts of supernatural omnipotence. Confucianism was mainly a philosophy of (earthly) life, and Taoism held that human happiness lies in one's proper relationship with nature. Chinese Buddhism was a pragmatic version of what the Buddha had originally preached, and it related well to Chinese religious styles. The faiths survive in China today, but we do not know in what strength.

193

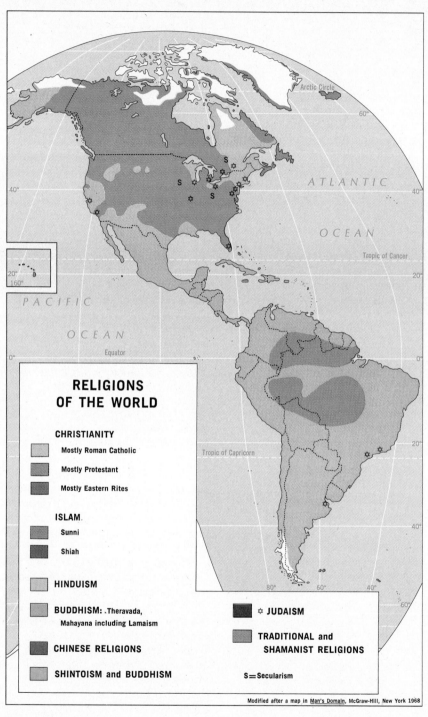

Figure 10-1

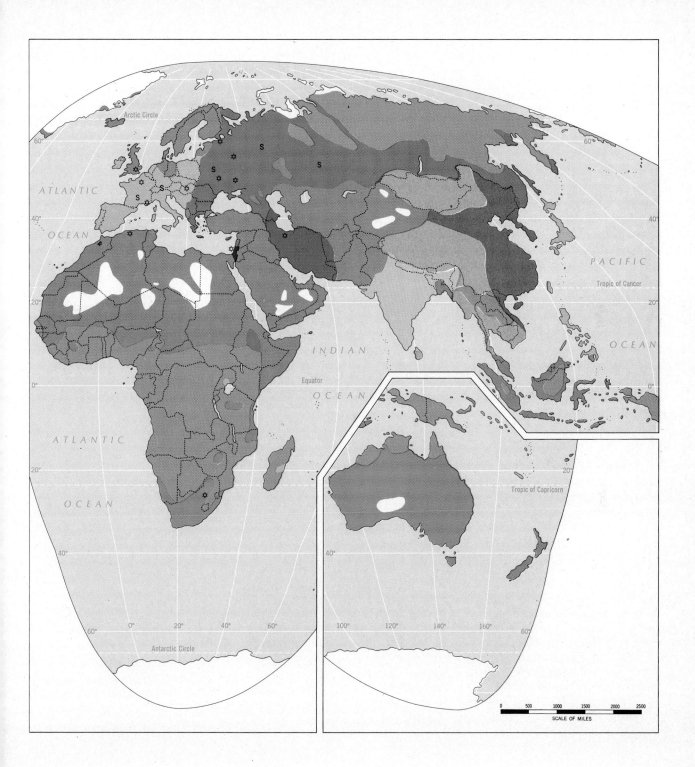

195

Our map shows Judaism to be distributed through parts of the Middle East and North Africa, the Soviet Union and Europe, and parts of North and South America. Judaism is one of the world's great religions, but apart from the state of Israel it is now scattered and dispersed across much of the world. Judaism today has about 14 million faithful.

Finally, Figure 10-1 shows large areas in Africa and several other parts of the world as "Traditional and Shamanist." Shamanism has origins in Eastern Siberia, where tribal peoples worshipped the *shaman*, a religious leader, teacher, healer, visionary—but, in the Chinese tradition, a man of *this* world, not of another. A shaman appeared to various peoples in many different parts of the world, in Africa, in Indian America, in Southeast Asia. Scholars of religion have noted that there have been similar effects of such an appearance on the cultures of peoples scattered far and wide across the world, and they employ the term *shamanism* to identify such faiths. We might guess that if these shamanist religions had developed elaborate bureaucracies (which they did not) and had sent representatives to international congresses (as do the Christian faiths) then they would have negotiated away their differences and created still another world religion. But unlike Christianity or Islam, the shamanist faiths are small in scale and comparatively isolated.

Shamanist religion, then, is traditional religion, an intimate part of a local culture and society. But not all traditional religions are shamanist. African traditional religions involve beliefs in god as creator and invisible provider, in divinities both superhuman and human, in spirits, and in life hereafter. Christianity and Islam made inroads into traditional religions, but as the map indicates they failed to convert the African peoples except in particular areas. Where Figure 10-1 shows traditional religions to exist, they remain in the majority today.

The major religions originated in a remarkably small area of the world. Judaism and Christianity began in what is today the Israel-Jordan area. Islam arose through the teachings of Mohammed, a resident of Mecca in Western Arabia. The Hindu religion, which has no central figure and is a complex, multifaceted faith, originated in the Indus region of what is today Pakistan, long before Christianity or Islam. Buddhism emerged from the teachings of Prince Siddharta, a man who renounced his claims to power and wealth in his kingdom, located in Northeast India, to seek salvation and enlightenment in religious meditation.

These source areas coincide quite strongly with the culture hearths shown on Figure 10-1, and there can be no doubt that while developments in other spheres were occurring in these regions—urbanization, irrigated agriculture, political growth, increasingly complex social orders, and legal systems—religious systems also became more sophisticated.

The World Religions

The world's religions can be grouped or classified according to several different sets of criteria, but we would serve little purpose in debating the merits of each system. The true *universal* religions of today are Christianity, Islam, and the various forms of Buddhism. We might call the *cultural* religions those faiths that dominate primarily one national culture, as Hinduism does in India, Confucianism and Taoism in China, and Shintoism in Japan. Judaism is a special case because of its dispersal. The *traditional* religions of Africa form the focus of a third group of religions, represented also in Indian South America, in interior areas of Southeast Asia, and in New Guinea and Northern Australia. We consider the major faiths chronologically in the segment that follows.

Reverence for life, and the belief that cattle are holy animals, produce scenes such as this in Benares, India.

Hinduism

Chronologically, the Hindu religion is the oldest of the major religions and one of the oldest extant religions in the world. It emerged, without a prophet or a book of scriptures, and without evolving a bureaucratic structure comparable to those of the Christian religions. Hinduism appears to have begun in the region of the Indus valley, perhaps as long as 4000 years ago. The fundamental doctrine of the faith is the *karma*, which involves the concept of the transferability of the soul. All beings are in a hierarchy; all have souls. The ideal is to move upward in the hierarchy and

then to escape from the eternal cycle through union with the *Brahman*, the top of the ladder. A soul moves upward or downward according to one's behavior in the present life. Good deeds and adherence to the faith lead to a higher level in the next life. Bad behavior leads to demotion. All souls, those of animals as well as humans, participate in this process, and the principle of reincarnation is a cornerstone of the faith: mistreat animals in this life, and chances

are that you will *be* that animal in a future life.

Hinduism's doctrines are closely related to the caste system, for castes themselves are steps on the universal ladder. But the caste system locks people in social classes, reducing mobility —an undesirable feature manifested especially in the lowest of the castes, the untouchables. The untouchables until a generation ago could not enter temples, were excluded from certain schools, and were restricted to

197

Bathing in the holy river Ganges is a ritual of great spiritual importance in Hindu India.

performing the most unpleasant of tasks. The coming of other religions to India, the effects of modernization during the colonial period, and especially the work of Gandhi, India's famous leader, loosened the social barriers of the caste system and bettered the lot of the 70 million untouchables.

Hinduism, born on the Indian subcontinent's western flank, spread eastward across India and, even before the advent of Christianity, into Southeastern Asia. It would penetrate by first attaching itself to prevailing traditional faiths and then slowly supplanting them. Later, when Islam and Christianity appeared and were vigorously promulgated in Hindu areas, Hindu thinkers sought to assimilate certain of the new teachings into their own religion. For example, elements of the Sermon on the Mount now form part of Hindu preaching, and Christian beliefs led in some measure to the softening of caste barriers. In other instances, the confrontation between Hinduism and other faiths led to the formulation of a compromise religion. Thus the monotheism of Islam stimulated the rise of the *Sikhs*, who disapproved of the worship of all sorts of idols and who disliked the caste system, but who nevertheless retained concepts of reincarnation and the *karma*.

The Hindu faith remains primarily India's religion, but remnants still exist in Southeast Asia (where Islam later replaced much of Hinduism). During the colonial period, many hundreds of thousands of Indians were taken to other parts of the world, such as East and South Africa, the Caribbean, and Northern South America. In those locations, the Hindu faith still thrives and cultural landscapes are embellished by the numerous and colorful temples and shrines that are part of Hindu religion.

The Hindu religion is more than a faith: it is a way of life. Meals are religious rites; commands and prohibitions multiply as the ladder of caste is ascended. Pilgrimages follow prescribed routes and rituals and are attended by millions; festivals and feasts are frequent, colorful, and noisy. With 200 million holy animals wandering the streets, and with a huge variety of religious structures marking almost every urban and village scene in India, the faith is a visual as well as an emotional experience.

Buddhism

Buddhism appeared in India during the sixth century B.C. as a reaction to the less desirable features of Hinduism. It was by no means the only protest of its kind (*Jainism* was another) but it was the strongest and most effective. The faith was founded by Prince Siddharta, heir to a wealthy kingdom in what is now Nepal. The Prince, known as Gautama to his followers, renounced his fortunes and sought salvation through meditation and teaching. He was profoundly shaken by the misery he saw about him, which contrasted so sharply against the splendor and wealth that had been his own experience. The Buddha (enlightened one) was perhaps the first prominent Indian religious leader to speak out against Hinduism's caste system. Salvation, he preached, could be attained by anyone, no matter what his or her caste. Enlightenment would come to a person through knowledge, especially self-knowledge: the elimination of covetousness, craving, and desire, the principle of complete honesty, and the determination not to hurt another person or animal. Thus part of the tradition of the *karma* still prevailed.

Following the death of the Buddha in 489 B.C. at the age of 80, the faith grew rather slowly until, during the middle of the third century B.C., the Emperor Asoka became a convert. Asoka was leader of a large and powerful state that covered India from

Buddhism retains strength in countries of Southeast Asia, including Thailand, where this photograph of a house-blessing ceremony was taken.

the Punjab to Bengal, and from the Himalayan foothills to Mysore. Asoka not only ruled his country in accordance with the teachings of the Buddha but he also sent missionaries to the outside world to carry the Buddha's teachings to distant peoples. Buddhism now spread as far south as Sri Lanka, and later west toward the Mediterranean, north into Tibet, and east into China, Korea, Japan, Vietnam, and Indonesia, all over a span of some

10 centuries. But while Buddhism spread to distant lands, it began to decline in its region of origin. During Asoka's rule there may have been more Buddhists in India than Hindu adherents, but after that period of success the strength of Hinduism again began to assert itself. Today, Buddhism is practically extinct in India, though it still thrives in Sri Lanka, in Southeast Asia, in Nepal and Tibet, and in Korea. Along with other faiths it also exist in Japan.

Buddhism is fragmented into two sectarian groups, Mahayana Buddhism and Theravada Buddhism. Theravada Buddhism is the faith of the source, Gautama's teachings, and it survives in Sri Lanka, Burma, Thailand, Laos, and Cambodia. It holds that salvation is a personal matter, achieved by worldly good behavior and religious activities including periods of service as monks or nuns. Mahayana Buddhism, practiced mainly in Vietnam, Korea, Japan, and for centuries in

200

China, holds that superhuman, holy sources of merit do exist and that salvation can be aided by appeals to these sources. Mahayana Buddhists do not serve periods as monks, as the Theravadans do, but spend much time in personal meditation and worship.

Buddhism is experiencing a period of revival that started two centuries ago and has recently intensified. It has become a universal religion.

Chinese Religions

While the Buddha's teachings drew converts in India and the issue of the transmigration of souls was debated there, a religious revolution of quite another kind was taking place in China. Confucius (551–479 B.C.) and his followers constructed a blueprint for Chinese civilization in almost every field—philosophy, government, education, and more. In religion, Confucius addressed the traditional Chinese cults that included beliefs in heaven and the existence of the soul, ancestor worship, sacrificial rites, and shamanism. He postulated that the real meaning of life lay in the present, not in some future abstract existence, and that service to one's fellows should supersede service to spirits.

Chinese philosophy was, at the same time, being influenced by another school. The beginnings of Taoism are unclear, but many scholars believe that an older contemporary of Confucius, Lao-Tsu, slightly preceded Confucius' works by publishing a volume entitled *Tao-te-ching,* or "Way and Its Virtue." In his teachings, Lao-Tsu focused on the oneness of man and nature: people, he said, should learn to live in harmony with nature, viewing themselves as but an insignificant element in the great universal order. Taoist virtues were simplicity and spontaneity, tenderness, tranquility. It advocated against competition, possession, the pursuit of knowledge. Taoist transgressions were war, punishment, taxation, and ceremonial ostentation. The best government, according to Lao-Tsu, was the least government (!)

Taoism suffered much falsification as time went on, and it became a cult of the masses. Lao-Tsu himself was worshipped as a god (among many), something he would have disapproved. People, animals, even dragons became objects of worship as well, and a sort of Taoist witchcraft emerged. In the face of this situation, Confucius' emphasis on the present, on good relationships between people (parents and children, rulers and subjects) proved its practicality. During the Han Dynasty (second century B.C.) Confucianism became the state ethic. Worship of and obedience to the emperor constituted central elements of Confucianism, and as a national creed it prevailed until the twentieth century. Reactions against Confucianist philosophy set in during the Republican period after 1912, and especially during the reexaminations of the communist period.

Into this complex Confucianist-Taoist contest, Buddhism was introduced during the Han Dynasty as well. The Buddhist faith blended easily with domestic belief systems with their reverence for departed souls and appreciation for nature. Thus China developed a quite discrete religious posture, taking elements from several teachings to create, if not a distinct single faith, certainly a Chinese religious way of life.

Emperor worship, a reverence for nature, and a strong feeling for land and nation are elements that forged the *Shinto* religion of Japan. Early Shinto arose from ancient forms of shamanism and other traditional religious faiths and developed into a national religion that unified state and faith; religion and government were indivisible. Then Buddhism made substantial inroads, and Shinto was much modified. But the events of the nineteenth century in East Asia, and Japanese determination to reject external influences, brought Shinto back as a religious-political force. In the early period following the Meiji Restoration, Buddhists were persecuted, Buddhism attacked, and Buddhist statues removed. Later these campaigns became less intense, but Shinto remained the state religion. Following Japan's defeat in World War II, Shinto's role as the official state religion was terminated and the doctrine relating to the emperor's divine descent also was rejected.

201

Judaism

The oldest major religion to emerge west of the Indus region, Judaism grew from the belief system of the Jews, one of several Semitic, nomadic tribes that traversed Southwest Asia about 2000 B.C. The Jews led an existence filled with upheavals. Moses led them from Egypt, where they had suffered oppression, to Canaan—where an internal conflict arose and the nation split into two, Israel and Judah. Israel was subsequently wiped out by enemies, but Judah survived longer, only to be conquered by the Babylonians. Regrouping to rebuild Jerusalem, the Jews fell victim to a sequence of alien powers and saw their holy city destroyed again in 70 A.D. Now the Jews were driven away and scattered all over the region, and eventually into Europe and much of the rest of the world. For many centuries, indeed until the late eighteenth century, they were persecuted, denied citizenship, driven into ghettos, and massacred. And as the twentieth century has proved, the world has not been a safe place for Jewish people even in modern times.

In the face of such constant threats to their existence, it has been the faith that has sustained the Jews, the certainty that the Messiah would come to deliver them from their enemies. The roots of Jewish religious tradition lie in the teachings of Abraham, who united his people and during whose time the faith began to take shape. Among the religions adhered to by the ancient Semitic tribes, that of the Jews was unique in that it involved the worship of only one god who, the Jews believed, had selected them to bear witness to his existence and his works. But the Jewish faith also evinced the many contacts with other beliefs and other peoples. From *Zoroastrianism*, which arose in Persia during the sixth century B.C., Judaism acquired its concepts of paradise and hell, angels and devils, judgment day, and resurrection.

Modern times have seen a division of Judaism into several branches. During the nineteenth century, when Jewish people began to enjoy greater freedom, a Reform movement developed whose objective was to adjust the faith and its practices to current times. But there were many who feared that this would cause a loss of identity and cohesion, and the Orthodox movement sought to retain the old precepts as effectively as possible. Between these two extremes is a sector that is less strictly orthodox but not as liberal as the reformers: the Conservative movement. We observe here the stresses of an acculturation process of Jewish society in America.

The objective of a homeland for the Jewish people, an idea that gained currency during the nineteenth century, produced the ideology of Zionism. The Zionist ideals were rooted in a determination that Jews should not be absorbed in and assimilated by other societies. Zionism's goal of a Jewish state became reality in 1948, when Israel was created under U.N. auspices on the shores of the Mediterranean.

Christianity

The Christian religions had their beginnings in the Jews' search for deliverance from Roman oppression and the appearance of Jesus. Many saw in Jesus a manifestation of God, but probably even more hoped that he would be a temporal as well as a spiritual leader and secure freedom as well as salvation. Among the Apostles was Paul, a Jew who had a Greek education and who, after the crucifixion, began offering the teachings of Jesus to non-Jews. It was Paul who played a central role in organizing the Christian church and in disseminating Jesus' teachings to the European Mediterranean world. After Paul's death the church continued to grow, but at the cost of many lives as Roman authority resisted the intrusion. A crucial event in the development of the Christian faith was the conversion of the Emperor Constantine, and from the fourth century A.D. onward it was the state religion. The Roman Empire soon was to decline and break up, and while the sector centered on Rome fell on hard times, the eastern half, with Constantinople at its heart, became

The focus of the Catholic faith: St. Peter, Rome.

the focus. It was there, in the eastern realm, that Christianity thrived and from where it radiated into other areas including the Balkan Peninsula. Today the Eastern or Orthodox Churches still form one of the three major branches of the faith (Fig. 10-1), despite the blows it sustained when Constantinople fell to the Turks and Islam invaded Eastern Europe (in the fifteenth century) and again when the church was threatened in Russia by the rise of communism (in the twentieth century).

In Rome, the papacy was established and there came to lie the center of the second branch of the faith, Roman Catholicism. In the Middle Ages the power of the church was at its zenith, with all the excesses this involved; a reaction was inevitable. It came during the fifteenth and sixteenth centuries with the teaching of Luther, Calvin, and others. Widespread friction and open warfare marked the deteriorating relationships among Christians of different views on the continent. But the Protestant movement —the third major branch— could not be denied.

The worldwide dispersal of Christianity was accomplished by the era of colonial acquisition on which Europe embarked at about the same time. Spain invaded Middle and South America, bringing the Catholic faith to those areas. Protestant refugees, tired of conflict and oppression and in search of new hope and freedom, came in large numbers to North America. A patchwork of missionary efforts produced mixed conversions in much of black Africa; Catholicism made inroads in Zaire (Congo),

Angola, and Mozambique. A very small percentage of the people in formerly British India were converted to Christianity; Catholicism scored heavily in the Philippines during the period of Spanish control.

Today, Christianity is the most widespread and largest of the universal religions, and it is still gaining adherents in many areas. The faith has always been characterized by the aggressive and persistent proselytism of its proponents, and Christian missionaries created an almost worldwide network of conversion during the colonial period (Fig. 10-2).

Buildings of the Russian Orthodox Church in Novgorod, U.S.S.R., are today maintained as a museum; services are no longer held here.

Figure 10-2

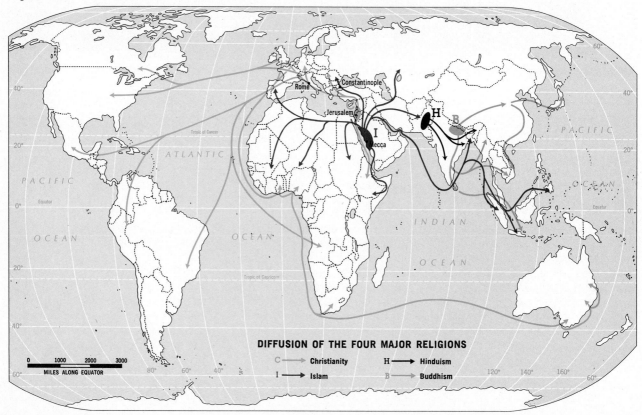

DIFFUSION OF THE FOUR MAJOR RELIGIONS

C → Christianity   H → Hinduism
I → Islam   B → Buddhism

MILES ALONG EQUATOR
0 1000 2000 3000

Islam

The faith of the Moslems is the youngest of the major religions, having been born of the teachings of Mohammed (Muhammad), born in 571 A.D. According to Moslem belief, Mohammed received the truth directly from Allah in a series of revelations that began when the prophet was about 42 years of age. During these revelations Mohammed involuntarily spoke the verses of the Koran (Qur'ān), the Moslems' holy book. Mohammed, a student of religion even before this event, admired the monotheism of Christianity and Judaism; he believed that Allah had already manifested himself through other prophets (including Jesus). But he, Mohammed, was the real and ultimate of prophets.

Mohammed became a towering figure in Arabia during the seventh century A.D. Born and soon orphaned, he grew up under the tutelage of his grandfather, then leader of Mecca (Makkah); after his grandfather's death an uncle continued his upbringing. After his visions, Mohammed at first had doubts that he could have been chosen to be a prophet, but once convinced by continued revelations, he committed his life to the fulfillment of the divine commands. In those days, the Arab world was in religious and social disarray, with various gods and goddesses admired by peoples whose political adjustments were, at best, feudal. Soon Mohammed's opponents sensed his strength and purpose, and they began to combat his efforts. The prophet was forced to flee Mecca for the safer haven of Medina (al Madīnah), and from this new base he continued his work.

The precepts of Islam constituted, in many ways, a revision and embellishment of Judaic and Christian beliefs and traditions. There is but one god, who occasionally reveals himself to prophets; Islam acknowledges that Jesus was such a prophet. What is earthly and worldly is profane; only Allah is pure. Allah's will is absolute; he is omnipotent and omniscient. All humans live in a world created for their use, but only to await a final judgment day.

Islam brought to the Arab world not only a unifying religious faith, but also a whole new set of values, a new way of life, a new individual and collective dignity. Apart from dictating observance of the "five pillars" of Islam (repeated expressions of the basic creed, frequent prayer, a month of daytime fasting, almsgiving, and at least one pilgrimage to Mecca), the faith prescribed and proscribed in other spheres of life as well. Alcohol, smoking, and gambling were forbidden. Polygamy was tolerated, although the virtues of monogamy were acknowledged. Mosques made their appearance in Arab settlements, not only for the Friday prayer but also to serve as social gathering places to bring communities closer together. Mecca became the spiritual center for a divided, far-flung people for whom a joint focus was something new.

Islam's impact in Sahara Africa was profound and lasting. Worshippers at the Mopti Mosque in Mali bow in Friday prayer.

The Black Muslims: Nation of Islam

The faith of Islam has a foothold in the United States on the strength of an Afro-American religious and nationalist movement commonly called the Black Muslims but officially known as the Nation of Islam. The movement was born in the 1930s, although it traces its antecedents to Ali's Moorish Science Temple of America, established as early as 1913. In 1930 a split developed in the Temple movement, and one of the fragments was to become the Nation of Islam, under the initial leadership of W. D. Fard.

The Nation of Islam was founded on American blacks' desire to be delivered of white oppression. Believing themselves to be members of a lost Islamic tribe, the Black Muslims await messianic deliverance; they often compare themselves to the children of Israel when in Egyptian bondage. W. D. Fard preached this message in the Nation's first temple in Detroit. In 1933 the Chicago Temple of Elijah Muhammad was founded, and upon Fard's sudden disappearance Muhammad became the Nation's leader. Fard has become a *Mahdi*, a prophet to the Black Muslims, but it was Elijah Muhammad who brought the Nation of Islam unprecedented strength. In 1935 membership in the Nation was just a few hundred; by 1960 it was probably in excess of 10,000, and when Elijah died in 1975 there were perhaps a half million members and active sympathizers. The largest temples (now called Mosques) now are No. 7 in New York and No. 27 in Los Angeles.

The ideology of the Nation of Islam has been a mixture of nationalism (including a separate homeland as a primary objective) and much-modified Islam (although the "five pillars" are prescribed). Tight discipline, substantial contributions from members, business enterprises, educational programs, a newspaper (*Muhammad Speaks*), and an annual convention on February 26 and 27 all contribute to the Nation's cohesion and appeal. In the late 1950s and early 1960s a young member named Malcolm X rose to prominence in the movement, bringing it unprecedented national visibility. A clash with orthodox leadership followed, and Malcolm X was assassinated in February, 1965—a low point for the Nation.

Elijah Muhammad's death in 1975 was the end of an era, but his son, Wallace Muhammad, immediately began a modernization that promises to bring the Nation greater power. He ended the Black Muslims' aloofness from politics in America (Elijah had condemned participation as sinful), strengthened the movement's ties with African and Caribbean countries by creating mosques there, permitted the first white person to join the movement, and began to bring ritual and practice back toward orthodox Islam. Several of these reforms were first advocated by Malcolm X, and in recognition of Malcolm's efforts the Harlem Mosque was renamed after him. Like Malcolm X before him, Wallace Muhammad appeared to be determined to bring the Nation of Islam out of its long-term isolation and seclusion. If his reforms succeed, Islam's strength in America will increase.

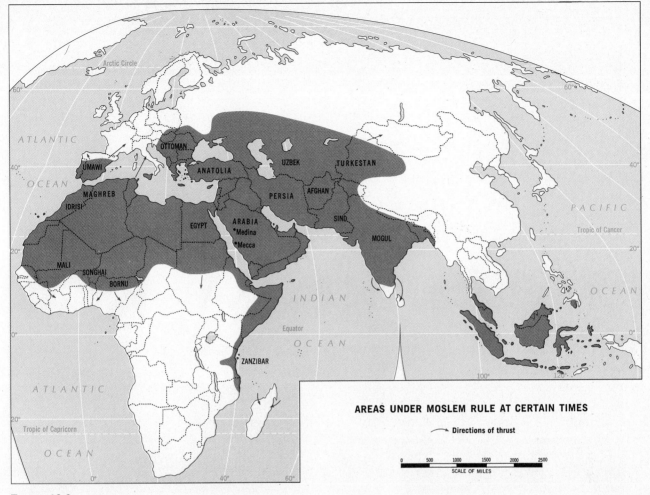

Figure 10-3

AREAS UNDER MOSLEM RULE AT CERTAIN TIMES

Directions of thrust

The stimulus given by Mohammed, spiritual as well as political, was such that the Arab world was mobilized overnight. The prophet died in 632, but his faith and fame continued to spread like wildfire. Arab armies formed, they invaded and conquered, and Islam was carried throughout North Africa. By the early ninth century A.D., the Moslem world included emirates extending from Egypt to Morocco, a caliphate occupying most of Spain and Portugal, and a unified realm encompassing Arabia, the Middle East, Iran, and most of what is today Pakistan (Fig. 10-3). Moslem influences had penetrated France, attacked Italy, and invaded what is today Soviet Asia as far as the Aral Sea. Ultimately the Arab empire extended from Morocco to India and from Turkey to Ethiopia. The original capital was at Medina in Arabia, but in response to these strategic successes it was moved, first to Damascus and then to Baghdad. In the fields of architecture, mathematics, and science the Arabs far overshadowed their European contemporaries, and they established institutions of higher learning in many cities, including Baghdad, Cairo, and Toledo (Spain). The faith had spawned a culture; it is still at the heart of that culture today.

207

Sidney Opera House: images of sea and sail on the waterfront of an island continent.

11 Architecture, Art, and Music in the Cultural Landscape

Culture is expressed in countless ways. When the Moslems invaded the Iberian Peninsula, and later the Balkan Peninsula, they introduced not only their faith to these regions but also something more tangible and visible in the cultural landscape: their architecture. We know it today as "Spanish" or "Mediterranean" architecture, but its arches and pillars and elaborate decorative features are rooted in the Moorish period. And when the Greeks and Romans built their great public buildings they embellished them with thousands of statues and monuments that gave art a new prominence in society, and visibility in the landscape. And again, how many times have you heard the expression "the sights and sounds of . . ." to describe some distant place? Yes, even the sounds, the music of a region can contribute to our overall impression of the culture. The jazz and blues of black America are unmistakable in source and cultural association, and in a way describe a whole culture.

Architecture

In the cultural landscape, architecture is expressed in two salient ways. First, every society that is able to build permanent structures creates buildings that are exceptional in terms of their functions (religious, governmental), their durability (far beyond that of a house, for example), and their form and configuration (thus expressing ideas and aspirations of the culture). Architecture in most cultures is closely associated with religion, for societies poured their resources into the creation of temples and shrines appropriate to the significance of the faith and the importance of worship; in towns and villages from the United States to Iran and from Sweden to Sri Lanka the most imposing building remains the church, mosque, or temple. Second, there is what we might call utilitarian architecture, the styles that mark ordinary houses and public build-

209

An example of the ornamentation for which Mediterranean townscapes are known: Rossio Square, Lisbon, Portugal.

St. Basil's Cathedral, Moscow: built between 1554 and 1560, it reflects the resources that were poured into religious structures. A supreme example of Russian national art, St. Basil's was built not only as a church but also as a monument to the defeat of Kazan.

ings of lesser importance. Such styles extensively mark the cultural landscape, but they involve buildings of lesser permanence and structures that are also less expressive of the culture as a whole.

Religion has stimulated and influenced architecture in several ways. Ancient cultures in several parts of the world built impressive pyramidal structures, on top of which would be situated the temple, accessible only to the holiest of religious men. The Aztec pyramids, and those of the Maya built even earlier, are examples of such dominant religious structures in a society where other buildings were modest and temporary. The thrust upward displayed by the pyramids finds expression in other ways in the mosques of Islam and the churches of the various Christian faiths, where towers and spires rise over the landscape. Unlike the pyramids, however, the mosques and churches were to be entered by as many of the community's faithful as they could contain, and from the earliest times they were built large, spacious, and splendidly embellished. And the faith required more than places of worship: it also needed buildings to accommodate schools, hospitals, and other church-related institutions. Many of these were built in the image of the church, on a large scale and with decorations to underscore the religious affiliation. Catholic convents, monasteries, and abbeys formed focal points in Europe's cultural landscape, as did Buddhist structures of similar function in Asia.

Wherever cathedrals, churches, or other religious structures were built, the ultimate in architectural know-how was invested. Magnificent towers, soaring roofs, beautiful glasswork, and the finest artwork inside and out would combine to

The capitol building in Madison, Wisconsin. As do many other government buildings, the capitol occupies large grounds and rises prominently above the surrounding townscape.

create more than merely a place of worship: here was a tribute to the divine power through a manifestation of what the society could accomplish. Architectural miracles, wonders of construction, were first achieved for the faith.

Many more modest buildings reflected the images of the culture's great churches and temples, and religious architecture always had a strong impact on utilitarian or domestic architecture. Doorways, window shapes, facades, even towers and spires were imitated to become part of residential homes.

In recent centuries this association has been loosened, as religion has begun to lose its importance in several of the world's major culture realms and religious architecture lost much of its individuality and primacy.

A second influence on architecture has been that of government and authority. Just as religious buildings were created to express the importance and significance of the faith, so governments have used architecture to lend emphasis to their power and authority. In some totalitarian societies the power of the government is expressed in the dimensions and monumentality of

the buildings that house the administration, and in such cases the structures are larger and more ornamental than seems justified by the offices they contain. In other societies, where government and religion are closely associated, government buildings display aspects of religious architecture. The wealth of European royal houses produced several of the world's most magnificent palaces, dominating urban landscapes and surrounded by magnificently landscaped grounds; the Palace of Versailles, built in France during the second half of the seventeenth century, is a prominent example.

211

In modern times a number of countries have chosen new sites for their capitals and have created not merely a group of buildings, but whole new cities to accommodate the government and its tentacles. Washington, D.C. is an example of such new capitals, where impressive buildings with powerful domes and columned facades accommodate congresses and parliaments, law courts, and all the various administrative, legislative, and judicial functions of government. Here, too, are the monuments to leaders of the past, museums that house the products of national achievements, libraries. In this collection of buildings, their surroundings, their contents, and most of all their architectural qualities, the nation seeks to express its historic associations, its aspirations, its accomplishments. Washington was an early example (in modern times) of such a newly built capital, but it has been done repeatedly in the present century as well. Brasilia, the new capital of Brazil, is a prominent example, built in the image of a new, modern, progressive Brazil looking toward its vast and potentially productive interior. Canberra, Australia, is another new capital. Islamabad, Pakistan's newly constructed capital, evinces in its architecture the religious associations of government. Several recently independent countries preferred to create new capitals, symbolizing their freedom and their determination to leave behind the troubles of a colonial past. In Africa, Malawi is building a capital at Lilongwe, Botswana at Gaberone, Mauritania at Nouakchott. In Central America, Belize is doing the same at Belmopan.

What the architectures of these new capitals (and many modernized older headquarters) have in common is their comtemporary, often avant-garde styling, contrasting sharply against the character of the country as a whole. Architecture is being used here to symbolize the new era, to express the goal of modernization.

The architecture of government dominates many cities, from London and its famed Houses of Parliament to the small American state capital whose capitol building is its focal point. Fly into Washington, Paris, or Moscow, and you will observe the extent to which governmental buildings dominate the urban landscape, and the use to which architecture was put to convey particular impressions—from the Pentagon and the Washington Monument to the walls and towers of the Kremlin.

U.S. cities these days are adding a new element to their urban landscapes: huge domed stadiums capable of seating as many as 60,000 people attending sports events under controlled climatic conditions. These enormous structures reflect the importance of competitive sports in this culture, and they underscore the impact recreation has had on architecture. Actually, the modern domed stadium is more an engineering feat than an achievement in architecture, but in the past many recreational facilities were built that provided architects with opportunities similar to those associated with religious and governmental building. The ancestors of those

domed stadiums are the open-air theaters built by the ancient Greeks and first modernized by the Romans; our football stadiums have much in common with them even today. No Roman who frequented the Coliseum would have trouble recognizing for what purposes the University of Michigan football stadium was built.

Other kinds of recreational buildings did undergo a great deal of modification, however. The early Greeks and Romans built libraries and museums, but not on the scale of the British Museum, London, or the Guggenheim Museum, New York. National theater buildings in many countries symbolize the significance that is attached to the arts, and many such buildings, such as the Sydney, Australia, Opera House, are true architectural innovations.

Art

Architecture is an art form. It is one of the ways artists communicate ideas, concepts, and feelings. Unlike paintings or volumes of literature, however, architecture's products have a direct, visible impact on the cultural landscape. This impact varies from culture to culture and from one time period to another ("Victorian" architecture in England represents such a period). Thus architecture reveals the outlook, the atmosphere of a culture and impresses those abstracts tangibly in the landscape. In Europe, the church spire remains the tallest structure in many towns; in the United States, it may be the bank or the insurance company's office building.

A new architectural landmark: the domed stadium. This is Houston's Astrodome.

In many American cities and towns the most prominent building is the office tower. In European towns the church spire still tends to rise highest. This is the cathedral of Chartres, France.

Architecture is inseparable from other art forms also visibly imprinted in the landscape. We took note earlier of the statues and sculptures created in huge numbers by Greek and Roman artists to adorn and embellish temples, public buildings, and other structures. Triumphal arches through which paraded victorious armies were in themselves achievements in stonework. These traditions of ornamentation survived for centuries—indeed, they began to wane effectively only during the emergence of the more functional, abstract-form architecture of the twentieth century.

213

In cultures other than those spawned by Greece and Rome, art also took a prominent role in association with architecture. Hindu temples often are elaborate sculptures in themselves. The walls of palaces and houses in the Islamic realm were (and in certain areas still are) elaborate, raised-relief mosaics of vibrant color and spectacular contrast, not simply embellishments of architecture but integral parts of it.

In the Western world, contemporary architecture has undone those persistent ties with ornamental arts, and it is now far more difficult to gauge the "outlook" of our culture from a study of modern buildings. The old symbolism is largely gone, as it is from painting, sculpture, and serious music. But something new has appeared: expressive public art works given pride of place in urban areas, in parks, town squares, even shopping center malls. Following the end of World War II, there was a veritable wave of art works in Europe expressing the agonies of that disaster. One of the continent's hard-hit cities was Rotterdam, whose center was devastated by German bombing in May, 1940. After the war, the central city was rebuilt in modern style, and at the point of maximum pedestrain traffic there was placed a sculpture by the Russian-French sculptor Ossip Zadkine to serve as a reminder of what had once been there. Entitled "Destroyed City," the sculpture's abstract-form figure, resembling a person, has a gaping hole where the heart would be.

Two views of Picasso's steel sculpture, Chicago.

Freestanding sculpture works such as can be seen in cities and towns in many parts of the world today are a far cry from the statues of war heroes and political leaders, explorers and philosophers that used to dominate the scene. One of Chicago's major attractions is a 60-foot high "Steel Sculpture" by Picasso, a controversial work placed in the Civic Center Plaza in 1967. A gift from the artist to the city, the sculpture has been a topic for debate from the day it was unveiled. From the side, the profile resembles a woman's head, but from the front, it produces quite a different impression. When the wind blows through the steel structure it whistles softly in many tones. Chicago's Picasso is a dramatic example of the changing form and role of the art.

Art also plays a strong role in cultures less complex or technological than our own. No one

today as they did hundreds of years ago. This is not to suggest that all such traditional art is precocious, of course. As with artistic expression in our own culture, there is a wide range of quality, and much "primitive" art is crude and childlike. But even among the art relics of the late Paleolithic, for example the cave drawings of Lascaux, France and Altamira, Spain there are products evincing great skill, marvelous powers of observation, and the capacity to instill vitality and drama. Those cave drawings of hunters and animals continue to this day to inspire artists—14,000 years later. A more recent example of the power of artists of "primitive" societies are the Bushman painters of Africa, who adorned exposed rock surfaces and cave walls with beautiful, brightly colored images of ceremonies and dress modes, hunters and hunted. A good deal of what we know about those ancient Bushmen peoples is gleaned from the surviving work of their artists, revealing Bushman migrations through Africa during the past two millenia. As Bushman society disintegrated under the pressure of Bantu expansion and European invasion the capacity for artistry was largely lost, but Africa's Bushman paintings remind us that the art of "primitive" society is not necessarily primitive in terms of caliber.

When it comes to the impact of artists on the cultural landscape, however, the sculptors and carvers of stone clearly have the upper hand. The monumental buildings and statues of ancient Egypt continue still to dominate vistas along the Nile. From the decorated pottery and murals of Crete and the columns and sculptures of Greece and

is certain, but it has been suggested that Picasso was saying something quite uncomplimentary to Chicago with his gesture; many contemporary artists feel that our modern, technological civilization is so empty, ungenuine, and dishonest that art can only be truthful if it ridicules. The artists of less complex, more traditional societies have no such problems. Theirs is sometimes labeled "primitive" art, but much "primitive" art is highly sophisticated. Magnificent

paintings, sculptures, carvings, and other art works are done in the workshops of artists in villages far removed from our frenetic world. They are done in traditions and with objectives that seem to have changed little over centuries, and their place in the culture is secure. There are artistic traditions in Africa (West African sculpture, for example) and Asia (such as Japanese dance) that manifest themselves

Stone sculptures along the road to the Ming Tombs, near Peking, China.

The stained-glass artistry of the thirteenth century is preserved in the Sainte-Chapelle, Paris.

Rome to the Byzantine mosaics and Moorish arches of later centuries, the artists who worked in the most durable media achieved the greatest transformation of the visible cultural scene. Still there were others who also contributed: the carvers of magnificently detailed wooden doors that centuries ago adorned Nigerian homes (many of which are now valuable museum pieces), the glassmakers whose stained-glass artistry in France, Germany, and England reached its apogee during the twelfth and thirteenth centuries and who gave new dimensions of beauty to religious structures, the creators of magnificent gardens that covered whole countrysides from Kyoto to Versailles and from China to England.

Art that is visible in the cultural landscape manifests itself in many ways. The Maori of New Zealand developed tatooing into a veritable art form. Clothing in many societies has become more than a matter of custom and comfort: fashion design is an art form and the latest designs from Paris can be seen on the streets of most major cities. (Some novel fashions are not quite so permanent. Remember the Mao suits that were briefly and expensively the rage?). Even headgear contributes to the cultural impress: the straw hat of East Africa, turban and fez of Moslem and eastern Mediterranean countries, bowler hats of England.

Less obviously, but importantly nevertheless, forms of dance and theater make their marks on the cultural landscape. Certain areas of the world, notably East Asia (Japan, Korea, China) have a combined tradition of dance and theater, but in the Western world ballet, spoken drama, and concert music have developed individually. In Japan, dance-theater (*kabuki*) and other expressions of the art have religious roots, which accounts for their central position in the culture. Performances that depict the protection given by Buddha are ubiquitous, and theater often involves various gods (represented by colorful costumes and masks) who are implored to provide longevity, good harvests, happiness, and good health.

Chinese traditional drama tends to be ethical (based on Confucian precepts of morality) rather than religious, and during the nineteenth century there were opera houses in almost all sizable Chinese cities and towns—perhaps as many as 400. When the Communist administration took over, dance and theater were given strong support, but there contents became matters of official policy. At first, the old Chinese operas continued to be performed, with some passages offensive to the new regime deleted. Then, beginning in the early 1960s, new themes were introduced, featuring workers and soldiers as "revolutionary heroes" and requiring modern dress rather than costumes. Acrobatic dancing and great expenditures of energy mark the new operas. But they do have one thing in common with their traditional predecessors, now almost completely phased out: unlike Western opera, there is no doubt about virtue or villain, or about the eventual triumph of justice.

Dance in the Western world has a number of individual forms of expression, including folk dancing (Eastern Europe has especially well-developed folk dances), ballroom dance, "social" dance (twist, rock), and theatrical dancing (ballet). Ballet, which began in Western Europe, took root in Russia where, before the Revolution, the *Ballet Russe* achieved international acclaim as perhaps the best ballet company ever to perform. After the Revolution the tradition continued, and the Moscow Ballet and the Kirov (Leningrad) still rank among the world's leading groups.

After centuries of success in its headquarters, London, and a long period of growth in New York, it appears that theater is facing a period of decline. The impact of the theater on London (and other English cities and towns) and New York is reflected by any map of the theater districts of these places: they occupied prime, central locations and competed for and drew loyal audiences. Now theaters are closing or struggling, and there is talk of a crisis in British theater, threatening a tradition that lies at the very heart of British culture.

Western theater, with its ancient Greek origins, has suffered degeneration repeatedly. The theater rose to great heights of virtuosity and specialization during the heyday of ancient Athens, when large audiences in outdoor theaters saw tragedies by Aeschylus, Sophocles, and Euripides and comedies by Aristophanes and, later, Menander. Those Athenians witnessed the birth of a tradition, a tradition that was to survive even when Athens' power and glory—and with it its great theater—declined. It is noteworthy that truly great, enduring theater seems to prosper when national energies are at their height, and that theater proves to be a most fragile art form when society's fortunes take a downturn. The theatrical traditions born in ancient Greece and temporarily sustained in Rome went into a long dormancy that did not end until the rebirth of theater in Elizabethan England and the resurrection of Greek tragedy in France during the seventeenth century. The modern decline of theater in England and the United States may signal more than the effects of excessive materialism or damaging inflation.

Movie theaters dominate the entertainment districts of American cities.

Tradition and formality: the New York Philharmonic on concert at Avery Fisher Hall, New York City.

There are those who point to the rise of a new art form, cinema, as contributing to the latest decline of live theater. And certainly the film has had its impact on the townscapes of countless places, large and small. In "The Last Picture Show" the movie theater is a focal point in a small, dying town; in cities the world over the brightly lit marquees of dozens of film theaters dominate the entertainment districts. From small-town main streets to city shopping centers, movie theaters are prominent landmarks. They outdraw live theater by a huge margin, and film has become an industry as well as an art form.

Music

The culture of a people, we have noted, is substantially a description of their way of life. Music is an important ingredient of this description. In preliterate societies, the role of music is vital because songs and plays describe and transmit the history of the people. Elsewhere, too, music tells of the way people worship their god or gods, and it describes the emotions of life as perhaps no other art form can. Music can express happiness and sorrow, hope and despair. It does not take very much musical knowledge to recognize a Viennese waltz, a Polish polka, or Spanish or Latin American rhythms. African drums and Japanese songs are similarly distinctive; note that we have already begun to attach regional identities to the musical terms. And certainly there is regionalism to music. French music such as that of Debussy or Ravel has unmistakable qualities that are essential elements in the whole of French culture. The music of India, of Japan, of the Arab world conjures up the sights and smells of those places unfailingly.

Music as a cultural phenomenon should be of great interest to cultural geographers. Numerous opportunities present themselves for research and study into the processes of diffusion, for example. Musical instruments are invented, then often borrowed by other people when contact between peoples occurs. Musical ideas—melodic, structural, rhythmic, stylistic—are generated and dispersed. Music also changes as culture changes. In Europe, the baroque, classical, romantic, and modern periods in music parallel phases of cultural expression in other fields. In architecture, for example, there was also a "baroque" period. It would not be difficult to select a piece of modern music with enigmatic qualities similar to those of Picasso's "Steel Sculpture."

Music is also a force in a culture, a force that can be put to use in the attainment of goals. Revolutionary songs, war marches, and anthems are only a few of the musical expressions that have political overtones. Who has not seen that famous, moving segment in *Casablanca* in which Germans in Sam's bar begin to sing their national anthem, to be drowned out by an emotional outpouring of the Marseillaise, sung by a growing number of Frenchmen rising to their feet? During World War II, the German administrations in occupied European countries forbade the playing of music written by Jewish composers, and the singing of the national anthems of occupied and enemy countries.

Music frequently is a matter of national pride, and its preservation and promotion have priority. In the Soviet Union, a major effort has long been under way to gear music composed by major composers to "folk culture." Beethoven, although a beloved composer in the U.S.S.R., has been officially criticized for his "bourgeois" music. Even the famous Soviet composer Shostakovitch temporarily fell from official grace because his music was allegedly beyond the grasp of the masses and somehow "not representative" of the nation's life and aspirations. Such attempts to straightjacket musical expression also affect other areas of artistic work, as in 1974 when Soviet authorities closed, with the aid of fire hoses, an outdoor exhibition of modern painting. In countries where ideological fervor is strong, the importance of music's role is reflected by attempts to suppress certain kinds of music and to support and foster other music. Americans saw on their television screens the strident music and ballet that have become part of the new culture in China when the 1972 presidential visit to Peking took place. Several African countries have ordered their national radio services to play a minimum number of hours of national music. Foreign visitors to the United States are invariably surprised by the frequency with which the national anthem is played and sung, for example at baseball games and other sports events where no international competition is involved.

A jazz group plays before a room-size audience in New Orleans.

Indeed, the United States itself affords some of the most interesting examples of the relationships between music and cultural geography. Much interaction has occurred between the European schools of music and American composers such as, for example, Aaron Copland, whose marvelous musical descriptions of American life and countryside are quite comparable to, say, those of Britten and Delius in England. But there is another major tradition in this country, and it stems from quite another source, Afro-America.

Black people during the period of slavery needed their music to survive their ordeal, and their traditions in this context were African. But they also made contact with European folk music, church hymns, popular songs, military marches, and so on. The African traditions of strong rhythm and powerful singing were welded to the melodic qualities of European music, and a distinct Afro-American musical tradition began to emerge, including blues and dance music.

It was from this dance music that jazz, the most distinctive type, evolved.

Improvisation, of course, is the hallmark of jazz. At first such improvisation was essentially embellishment, the addition of brief new phrases to an existing melodic line. But the practice developed into a unique and complex form whose practitioners, such as Ella Fitzgerald, spin variations as intricate as the rhythmic underpinnings of West African music. And these rhythmic qualities, too, were transferred to the Afro-American scene. In general, European ears were accustomed to rather complex harmonics but fairly simple beats. African and Afro-American rhythms are more complicated and, when subjected to syncopation, give jazz another distinctive quality.

Jazz, and the music of black America in general, are more than just one facet of Afro-American cultural expression. In a sense the music of black America *is* black America, with its roots in Africa, its qualities of release born of the desperation of the era of slavery, its chromaticism a virtue of black musicians wherever in the world they make music, and its performers' virtuosity a universal standard.

How is all this related to cultural geography? Consider the birth of a popular musical phenomenon that occurred in the United States in the 1950s, rock and roll. This music evolved from a union of (white) country and western music and (black) rhythm and blues, to become a form attractive to followers of both styles. But the process was not simple: it involved various forms of diffusion, acculturation, regional acceptance and rejection. The emergence of rock and roll (and later, rock music) also was attended by racial discrimination and various efforts of suppression, and factors of significance in the process included "talent pools," levels of urbanization, degrees of racial integration in various areas, and economic patterns. All this is detailed in a significant article by Professor Larry Ford (1971), on which the following commentary is largely based.

The music of Appalachia has its roots in the songs and ballads of the Scottish and Irish settlers who migrated into that region. In the early days, the fiddle was the most popular instrument, and the melodies the settlers played changed but slowly, for Appalachia always was an area of comparative isolation. As time went on and outside influences penetrated the region, the banjo, electric guitar, and other instruments came into use, and country music emerged. Tunes and songs now changed more rapidly, and new compositions gave additional distinction to country music. And, of course, people migrated to the cities, as they did everywhere during the twentieth century, carrying their musical tastes with them. Nearby Nashville became the country music center, and "The Grand Old Opry" radio program was the major point of dissemination in the decades following 1925, the year of its opening.

Musicians came from all over Appalachia, from the Tennessee hills (hence "hillbilly" music) and from the South and Southwest to perform in Nashville. Texas cowboy songs mixed with the country styles and country and western music was born.

In the meantime, black musical traditions were also going through their formative period in the South. One major lineage was gospel music, derived from the spirituals sung during the era of slavery on the plantations. After the Civil War, black composers and choirs sustained a style of church music, characterized by intensity and fervor, abandoned by whites. Black gospel choirs performed all over the country. A second major tradition came from the chants and songs of the people who worked the fields, such as the cotton

Rock music festivals have begun to attract thousands (often tens of thousands) of fans. This is Woodstock.

221

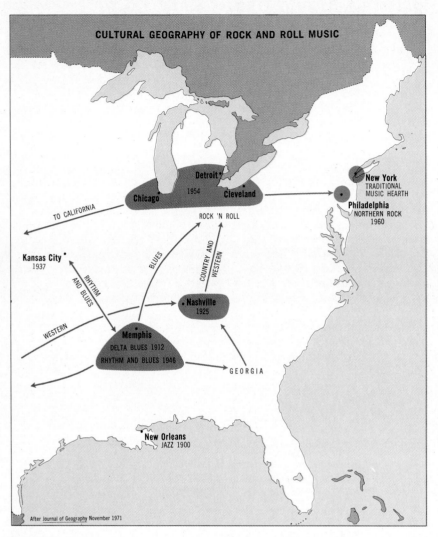

CULTURAL GEOGRAPHY OF ROCK AND ROLL MUSIC

Detroit 1954

Cleveland

Chicago

New York
TRADITIONAL
MUSIC HEARTH

Philadelphia
NORTHERN ROCK
1960

TO CALIFORNIA

ROCK 'N ROLL

Kansas City
1937

RHYTHM AND BLUES

BLUES

COUNTRY AND WESTERN

WESTERN

Nashville
1925

Memphis
DELTA BLUES 1912
RHYTHM AND BLUES 1946

GEORGIA

New Orleans
JAZZ 1900

After Journal of Geography November 1971

Figure 11-1

pickers. This tradition has strong African overtones, not only in its rhythms but also by its structure, involving a statement by an individual and a response by a chorus. Such songs contained a unique "blue" note, a flattened third and seventh note (in any key). In the early 1900s these blue-note work songs were first written down by the black American composer Handy, who used a characteristic 12-bar style that

became the standard blues form. Since Memphis was the South's cotton center, that city became to blues what Nashville was to country music (Fig. 11-1).

Neither country and western music nor blues attained national popularity for a long time, in part because the musical, Eastern-based establishment looked down on "hillbilly" music and also because black compos-

ers and musicians faced the usual barriers to progress and participation. But again the forces of migration and urbanization broke these barriers. Many black as well as white Southerners moved to northern cities, and there created an unprecedented demand for their respective musical preferences. Blues developed into a more sophisticated rhythm and blues in the new urban environments of Cleveland, Detroit, and Chicago; country and western bands were playing in other parts of town.

And then, in the early 1950s, rhythm and blues music got on the air at a major Cleveland radio station, and its popularity with white as well as black audiences was confirmed as thousands came to hear live performances. Country and western bands took note of this popularity and began to play this form—and "rock and roll" was born. It happened in the large cities of the Midwest, and the new style was to become popular in many parts of the world, indeed, wherever it was tolerated or could penetrate. Even the Eastern musical establishment was persuaded.

Later, rock and roll evolved into American rock music, with infusions from the new Motown blues, British rock (the Beatles and the Rolling Stones), and contributions from California, where the style had also been modified. But the most vital phase of its development surely was that dramatic merging of styles in Cleveland in the early 1950s—styles that began as Celtic ballads and African songs and ultimately fused in twentieth-century urban America. And the entire process touches on just about every ingredient of cultural geography.

Reading

The definition of culture by A. Kroeber and C. Kluckhohn comes from "Culture: a Critical Review of Concepts and Definition" in the *Papers of the Peabody Museum of American Archeology and Ethnology*, Vol. 47, 1952. The article by J. Spencer and R. Horvath, "How does an Agricultural Region Originate," was published in the *Annals of the Association of American Geographers*, Vol. 53, March, 1963. D. W. Meinig's "American Wests: Preface to a Geographical Introduction" also appeared in the *Annals*, Vol. 62, June, 1972. For further discussions of the culture concept, you will want to consult some anthropology literature, for example the book by M. Swartz and D. Jordan, *Anthropology: Perspective on Humanity* (Wiley, New York, 1976) and E. A. Hoebel's *Anthropology: the Study of Man* (McGraw-Hill, New York, 1974). A paperback by E. L. Schusky and T. P. Culbert, *Introducing Culture* (Prentice-Hall, Englewood Cliffs, 1967) is also useful.

A number of books deal with world regions in detail, including R. Murphey's *Introduction to Geography* (Rand McNally, Chicago, 1971) and J. Wheeler, Jr., J. T. Kostbade, and R. Thoman, *Regional Geography of the World* (Holt, Rinehart and Winston, New York, 1974). Also see H. J. de Blij, *Geography: Regions and Concepts* (Wiley, New York, 1971). For an excellent example of geographic coverage of a single world region, see R. West and J. Augelli, *Middle America: Its Lands and Peoples* (Prentice-Hall, Englewood Cliffs, 1976).

On questions of race, see F. Hulse, *The Human Species* (Random House, New York), and B. Campbell, editor of *Sexual Selection and the Descent of Man* (Aldine, Chicago, 1972). Many questions are covered in *Cultural Geography* by J. E. Spencer and W. L. Thomas, Jr. (Wiley, New York, 1969) and in *Introduction to Cultural Geography* (Ginn, Waltham, 1970) by S. N. Dicken and F. R. Pitts. The environmentalist position as stated by E. Huntington himself can be found in his *Civilization and Climate* (reissued by Archon, 1971, from the 1925 version), and in a textbook you may want to compare to this one: *Principles of Human Geography* (Wiley, New York, 1940).

An early article on geography and language was written by P. Wagner, "Remarks on the Geography of Language," *The Geographical Review*, Vol. 48, January, 1958. On Africa, see J. H. Greenberg, *The Languages of Africa* (Indiana, Bloomington, 1963). On religion, an excellent place to start is the *Historical Atlas of the Religions of the World*, edited by I. R. al Fārūqi and D. E. Sopher (Macmillan, New York, 1974). Also see D. E. Sopher, *The Geography of Religions*, Prentice-Hall, Englewood Cliffs, 1967. A detailed work on a specific region is J. D. Gay's *Geography of Religion in England* (Duckworth, London, 1971). Also see E. Isaac, "The Pilgrimage to Mecca," *The Geographical Review*, Vol. 63, July, 1973.

Literature on art and music in the context of cultural landscape is not easy to find. A seminal work is *The Anthropology of Music* (Northwestern, Evanston, 1964) by A. Merriam. Also see J. L. Fischer, "Art Styles as Cultural Cognitive Maps," in the *American Anthropologist*, Vol. 63, 1961, and E. Wellesz, editor, *Ancient and Oriental Music* (Oxford, London, 1957). The article by L. Ford entitled "Geographic Factors in the Origin, Evolution, and Diffusion of Rock and Roll Music" appeared in the *Journal of Geography*, Vol. 70, November, 1971. Also see G. O. Carney, "Bluegrass Grows All Around: the Spatial Dimensions of a Country Music Style," *Journal of Geography*, Vol. 73, April, 1974.

PART THREE
settlements

African village: on the Niger in Mali.

12 Dwellings and Villages

Shelter ranks high on the list of human needs. Throughout the world, in the coldest regions but also in the warmest, in the rainiest areas but also in deserts, people build dwellings that are the focal places of their daily lives. These dwellings have several functions, and protection against cold, wind, and rain is only one of them. In our living places we find privacy, a certain degree of comfort, a place to store accumulated belongings, even an opportunity to display our values and achievements.

We geographers have many reasons to be interested in the housing of the world's human population. A house reveals much about regions and cultures: the building materials that are available, the social and economic needs and the cultural traditions of the occupants, the natural (physical) environment whose forces the house must withstand. In the *form* of houses we can sometimes see one culture give way to another. If you were to take a trip southward on a Nile riverboat, you could observe the square, flat-roofed Arab houses of Egypt and the Northern Sudan yield to the round, steeproofed African houses of the Southern Sudan and Uganda. House types can be valuable indicators of cultural transitions. In the *function* of houses we get an impression of traditions and needs: in areas of Eastern Europe, for example, the people and some of their livestock live under the same roof, so that the structure is part house and part barn. Consider the contrast with our elaborate suburban home, in which different rooms serve different purposes such as cooking, bathing, eating, and sleeping. The *materials* used in the construction of dwellings reflect local availability and purpose. In the cold, forested areas of Europe the log cabin developed, with its thick walls and its pitched roof to withstand extreme cold and heavy snowfalls. In tropical areas, cold weather is not normally a problem, and you will find leaves, branches, and matting used in the construction of dwellings. And, of course, we are interested in the *spacing* of houses in various parts of the world. There is a rela-

African house under construction in Kenya, East Africa (top); occupied house and outbuildings on farm in Senegal, West Africa (bottom).

tionship between the density of houses and the intensity of crop cultivation, but it is necessary to generalize carefully. In the U.S. Midwest, for example, individual farmhouses lie quite far apart in what we would call *dispersed* settlement. Still, the land is intensively cultivated, but by machine rather than by hand. In Java, the populous Indonesian island, you run into a village every half mile to one mile along a rural road, and settlement is *nucleated*. Land use is just as intense, but the work is done by animals and human hands. So when we consider the density of human settlement as it relates to the intensity of land use, we should keep in mind the way in which the land is cultivated.

When houses are grouped together in small clusters or *hamlets*, or in larger clusters we call *villages*, their arrangement also has significance. Sometimes it is possible to identify the culture sphere just by looking at the ground plan of a village. In parts of Africa where cattle form the main means of existence, the houses in a village are arranged in a circle (that of the chief or headman will be larger and somewhat separated), surrounding a central corral where the livestock are kept at night. In the low-lying areas of Western Europe, the houses of a village often are situated on a strip of higher ground (a dike or a levee), and when you look at the map of such a village it is simply a row of evenly spaced units, perhaps on two sides of a road but often on only one side. In Eastern Europe, Nigeria, and other parts of the world the houses of the old villages are not regularly arranged, but closely clustered together, a defensive measure that included the construction of an outer wall. While the need for such defenses has disappeared, the traditional village still remains on the landscape and people continue to build compact villages reminiscent of bygone centuries. The arrangement of houses in villages thus occurs in many different forms. Tradition, political imposition, physiographic limitation, protection, and many other factors lie behind the development of the villages we see today.

Dispersed settlement (east of Cedar Rapids, Iowa, above) and nucleated settlement (West Germany near Coblentz, below).

229

Dwelling Types

In recent centuries of human history, the fundamental functioning group has been the family, and when we discuss houses and villages, we tend to think of these in terms of the single-family unit. There is some evidence that the family is breaking down in some cultures, including our own; it is also likely that the family was not yet the basic human group when people first began to build shelters. Thus we may assume that our distant ancestors lived in groups the size of *bands*—from a dozen to 50 or 60 individuals—which moved from place to place, setting up campsites for temporary residence when the opportunity seemed good. We can only speculate on the appearance of these campsites, because nothing very permanent was built there. Perhaps holes were dug into the ground, and covered with branches and leaves. Later these burrows may have been improved and enlarged, with posts to support rafters across the roof. In any case, it is unlikely that the cave was man's earliest or early man's sole dwelling, as we might be led to believe. Our ancestors lived in many areas of the world, including those where no such convenient natural housing was available.

Such communal living (of which there are now several modern versions) gave way to family structures as human society developed, and dwellings came to accommodate single families rather than groups. As our capacity to domesticate animals, grow crops, and store

Bushman dwellings, Botswana.

Chinese village houses made of mud walls and thatched roofs, Shantung Province.

food increased, so did the size and complexity of human groups. Tribes emerged, larger and more highly organized than those early bands, and among adopted rules were those of marriage, inheritance, food allocation, domestic duties, and many more. It also became necessary to build structures other than those used for living: the tribe had a chief or headman, whose residence must appear more imposing than others; facilities were needed for the storage of food and implements, for guest quarters, and for the housing of livestock. Thus we begin to see some functional differentiation in the buildings. Even today, we can observe human groups whose life-styles and dwellings must resemble those of many

thousands of years ago. In the Kalahari Desert of Southern Africa, the Bushmen live in bands probably similar to those of the distant past; their shelters often are mere windbreaks made of a few branches across which an animal skin is stretched. Campsites are occupied only temporarily, for the people must pursue wandering animals in their constant hunt for survival. Elsewhere in Africa, tribal peoples build the kind of central places that give evidence of the differentiation and increasing complexity of society, as in the case of the cattle-raising peoples of East Africa.

Although, 10,000 to 5,000 years ago, humanity was not

nearly as numerous as today, there is much evidence that people were scattered widely across the globe, occupying warm as well as cold regions, tropical forests, and deserts. Obviously this was not always a matter of choice: from the very beginning, peoples fought over territorial space. The losers would be forced to withdraw into less desirable areas, there to do as well as they could. From very early on, the dwellings and other structures built by tribal groups differed in form, appearance, func-

Stilt houses of village in Benin, West Africa.

Igloo in the Canadian Arctic.

231

tion, and in other ways. We still associate some peoples most directly with their buildings: who but the Eskimo would build the igloo? Where but among nomadic desert peoples would you expect to find portable tents to be the chief shelter? Where but in flood-prone areas do we find stilthouses?

Notwithstanding this regional and structural variety, it has not proved to be a simple problem to regionalize, categorize, or classify the world's dwelling types. If you read the geographic literature, you will find that scholars have tended to focus on particular cases, such as log houses in Mexico or the houses of China. Some studies even focus on barns and fences! But in all-encompassing view of human abodes is still missing. In a way this should not surprise us, for the complications are many. Here are some to consider:

Historical Aspects

Although cultural traditions promote continuity and permanence in building types and styles, time does bring change. In parts of the world—areas of the Arab realm, for example—dwellings appear much as they did centuries ago. In parts of Africa, too, dwellings in rural areas and even in some cities are still built according to centuries-old principles. You can walk some of the streets of Kano, Nigeria, and imagine that you are in another age. On the other hand, the effects of modernization can be seen even in the African bush, where many a house builder now substitutes corrugated metal sheeting for the thatch formerly used on the roof. Now the floor

The use of mud as a building material in the Arab world: Syria (top) and Egypt (bottom).

Tent dwellings are erected and taken down as their nomadic occupants travel. The photograph shows the Kuchi nomads in Afghanistan's mountains.

plan of the house may remain the same, but the building materials are no longer those of the region. Perhaps we should recognize four groups of houses: unchanged traditional, modified traditional, modernized (where both building materials and floor plan show changes), and modern.

Periods of Occupance

By no means all the dwellings people build are intended for permanent occupance. The Bushmen and other wandering, food-gathering peoples build windbreaks that are simply abandoned when the band must move. The nomadic peoples of African and Asian deserts carry with them the tents they erect when a temporary settlement is established. Such settlements may be occupied for days, weeks, sometimes months, and occasionally even longer, but eventually they are abandoned, all portable materials are loaded on camels, horses, or other animals of burden, and the search for a new site begins. There are groups of Masai people in East Africa who build dwellings that stand permanently but are not occupied year round. Where those dwellings stand, the group may spend a half year, raising some crops nearby but mainly attending to the cattle herd, which can obtain enough food and water in the vicinity. Then, when the dry season arrives at the settlement, the people pack their belongings on their animals and start to move, following the rains. Later they return to their temporarily abandoned settlement and occupy it for another season. Finally, there are the dwellings built to be occupied all year, as are the houses of the Andean Indians of South America, the cocoa farmers of West Africa, the wheat farmers of Northern China. So even when it comes to the duration of occupance, we are confronted with several contrasting circumstances.

Structure

Could we approach the problem from the viewpoint of the structure of dwellings, the degree of their intricacy and complexity? Cultural geographers interested in house types differentiate between dwelling types on some very obvious bases. At one end of the scale, there is the cave dwelling (today, people still live in caves in several areas of the world), the windbreak of the remaining wandering, food-gathering peoples, the pit dwelling built and modified perhaps as long as human societies have existed, and the simplest of "huts," little more than stacked-up sticks, branches, grass, and leaves. At the other end, we have the complex and imposing villas and mansions in suburban areas of Western cities, as well as millions of single-family homes of simpler character that are, nonetheless, a world away from those rudimentary dwellings mentioned above. Between these ends of the continuum there are countless millions of dwellings ranging from the beehive-shaped Zulu house, an elaboration of "hut" construction, to the quite substantial and complex houses of several of the peoples of South, Southeast, and East Asia.

Materials

Another way to approach the study of world housing involves the materials from which they are constructed. Houses made principally of *wood* still show some regional association with

The beehive-shaped Zulu house.

234

the world distribution of forests, although wood as a building material is, of course, transported to all world areas today. The log house, which probably originated in the cold forest zones of Northern Europe, became a haven for the early European settlers in Northern North America, where the forests were plentiful and the cold at least as severe. Comparatively few log houses are still built today; log cabins are built in remote areas as recreational rather than residential structures these days. You could build a log house or cabin with an axe, but modern sawmills now produce cut lumber that makes building with wood even easier. Thus the frame house became a commonplace in and near forested areas. Walls and ceilings are attached to a frame of cut lumber. The walls may be constructed of wooden planks or board, the ceilings of paper; both products are derived from trees. The roof is normally made of wood as well, with a protective layer of tarpaper, shingles, or tiles. The frame house occurs in large numbers in North America and in Western Europe.

Where wood is not so readily available, houses are likely to be built of *bricks*. We tend to define a brick by what is familiar to us—a hard, cement- and oven-baked block of various standard sizes. But bricks elsewhere in the world are made of the earth itself. In the Middle East (and, nearer home, in the Southwestern United States and Mexico) wet mud is poured into wooden frames, allowed to dry briefly, and then placed in the sun to harden. Then these bricks are used in wall construction, more

moist mud forming the mortar, and after the structure dries out the walls are smeared with mud as well. For the roof, a frame of sticks, branches, and straw is covered with mud. In arid areas of the world, such dwellings are adequate protection against heat and cold; when infrequent heavy rain does occur, it causes havoc, for the sun-baked mud bricks never become as hard as the oven-baked bricks and tiles used in the Western world. Variations of the method just described occur in many parts of the world. The mud-brick house is a common form in timber-poor, fairly dry Northern China, and it is thought by some scholars that the house building method used there may have come from the Middle East.

Wood as a building material in a typical house on Norway's tundra.

Dried mud-brick houses in the Taos Pueblo, New Mexico.

Houses are also built of *stone*. In the high Andes of Peru, Indian house builders pile rough stones on top of each other, without mortar, caulk the remaining openings with mud, and make a roof of thatch. Some European homes, for example, English cottages, also are made of natural stone and cement mortar, and with a thatch roof. In Southern and interior Egypt, where natural building stone is also plentiful, stone houses are also built. On the world map, however, stone houses would be mere patches: wood and mud-brick are far more common building materials. In the United States and other Western countries, natural stone is sometimes used as a decorative building material on homes already constructed mainly of wood and brick.

For want of a better term, we identify as *wattle* those numerous houses built from poles and sticks, woven into a tight network, and then plastered with mud. In fact these dwellings are built of a combination of wood (the poles and sticks) and the same material from which mud bricks are made. Many African houses are constructed this way, with a thick thatch roof against the occasionally heavy rains.

Our list of building materials is by no means comprehensive. The Zulu's beehive-shaped dwellings are made almost exclusively of tall African grass. The tents of nomadic peoples are made of cloth or skins. Even blocks of ice, we know, are used as building materials. Bamboo serves in parts of Southeast Asia. In extreme Northern Europe sod may be piled on the roof to enhance insulation, and in summer

The use of stone as building material in Southern Africa (top) and Andean South America (bottom).

236

you can see goats grazing the new grass growing up there. People live permanently on boats and in trailers. Again the variations are almost infinite, and regionalization nearly impossible.

Form

The houses of the world's many cultures display a great variety of form and layout. We in North America are accustomed to houses that have corners and rooms that are square or rectangular, but many of the peoples of Africa and other parts of the world live in dwellings that are round, not angular. Much variation occurs within each of these major categories, as we can observe in our own region in the case of the square or rectangular house. The log house, a simple form, was brought to this continent from Northern Europe; the flat-roofed Spanish house with its covered and often enclosed patio was first built by European immigrants in Mexico and later in what is today the southwestern part of the United States, especially Arizona and California. Along the Atlantic coast, the European settlers built several kinds of houses. Professor F. Kniffen, who has researched house types in the United States, identified (a) the New England type, a two-story frame house often with a central chimney, (b) the Middle Atlantic type, with a wing extending from the main section, and (c) the Lower Chesapeake type, extending from Chesapeake Bay southward and marked by chimneys at both sides and a covered patio along the front.

L-shaped and T-shaped houses in a residential development near Miami, Florida.

We have only to look around us to see how things have changed. In the Midwest and in the South and elsewhere we still encounter many single-family houses that are variations of the Atlantic coast models described by Professor Kniffen, but we also find L-shaped ranch houses, T-shaped homes with the bedrooms clustered in the two wings of the T, and U-shaped houses with a patio and perhaps a pool in the enclosed area. The condominium and town house have contributed to the suburban transformation as well. The two-car garage has become a component of the suburban house; the fireplace, once a necessity for heat and cooking, has become a luxury since central heating now prevails.

There is more to studying the shape and form of the world's dwellings than first meets the eye. Take the case of Africa, where peoples have moved and migrated in recent centuries, but where no written record remains of these events.

237

If the people built distinctive houses, it is sometimes possible to reconstruct their migrations from remnants of these dwellings. For example, some African builders, after constructing the skeleton of their houses, raise the floor by a foot or so to keep out moisture that might otherwise seep in. This slightly raised platform now is compressed over prolonged use, and long after the house is abandoned and the structure has collapsed, evidence for that raised floor can still be observed. This can be a key to the reconstruction of old occupance patterns in a region.

Even when all surface evidence has disappeared, dwellings can reveal the past. In Rhodesia there are a number of stone structures of which the most famous is Zimbabwe. So impressive is the stonework there, with walls over 30 feet high and up to 12 feet thick, that it appears that the builders may not actually have occupied their buildings. Some scholars described Zimbabwe as an ancient, abandoned city, but it was not clear exactly where the occupants lived. Then a technique we know today as remote sensing solved the problem. Infrared photography from airplanes was used over Zimbabwe, and the evidence came clear: thousands of people did live here, but not in the stone structures we see today. The photography showed a large number of circles, invisible to the naked eye, etched in the soil. Even the vegetation, where the soil could not be seen, showed circular tinges. The circles, it was obvious, represent the location of long-destroyed African houses. While they stood, the walls made of wattle and mud, rainwater

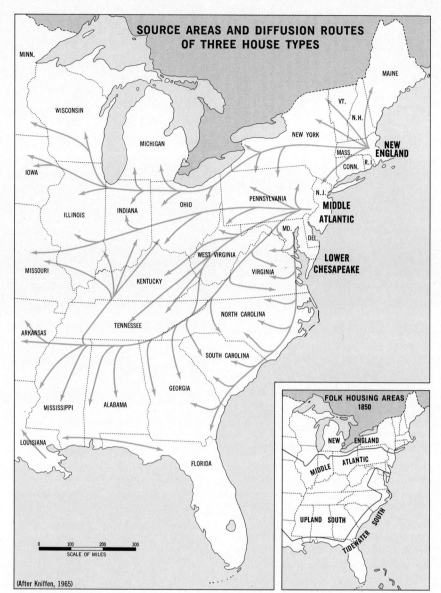

Figure 12-1

would run down their sides, dissolving bits of material in the mud walls and depositing it along the foot of the wall, in the soil. In this way the normal soil content (say of iron and aluminum, common soil ingredients there) was slightly changed—slightly, but

permanently. Eventually the houses were abandoned and they decayed away, but the soil continued to contain its additives. Finally the infrared film caught it and printed the map of village patterns of hundreds of years ago.

The trailer park has become commonplace in American settlements. These mobile homes are part of such a park near Los Angeles, California.

ranch-style house is now seen from California to Florida.

In Chapter 11 we considered another aspect of buildings and structures: their aesthetics. Suffice it to remind ourselves here that we build houses not only to accommodate us but also, in Western as well as other cultures, to reflect our status and position in society. This is evinced by the size of homes and the land surrounding them and also by the decorations with which they are often adorned. Sometimes it is possible to identify the culture area in which you would expect to find a particular house *not* by its form but by its aesthetic qualities—the way shutters are hung and painted, the ornateness of exterior doors, the use of decorative stonework, the shape and framing of windows, and so on. When they have the resources, individuals and families try to tell the world something about their capacities and objectives, just as cultures build monuments and government buildings that will appear impressive and imposing.

Purpose

Many people—and their number is growing—are not able to lavish adornments on their homes. This is because they do not live in the kind of dwelling we have discussed in this chapter, the single-family house. More and more, and notably in our own culture, the single-family home is becoming a luxury and people are moving to apartment buildings or other multiple-family structures such as townhouses and duplexes. When we discuss dwelling types, therefore, we should take note of the purpose of the building, whether it accommodates one family or several.

Professor Kniffen has argued persuasively that the study of house types can be productive in modern society as well. This is true not only in Europe, where the mobility of many population groups and the relative durability of houses produce fertile fields for research into migration and diffusion, but also in the United States. As Figure 12-1 shows, the coastal source areas of the three major east-coast building styles generated several routes of diffusion into the interior. The New England type was carried into the Northern Midwest, the Middle Atlantic type diffused into the midsection of the Eastern United States from Southern Indiana and Ohio to Northern Georgia and Alabama, and the Lower Chesapeake type spread along the Southern Atlantic coastal plain. As this process continued, the house types were modified according to the availability of materials and perceived environmental demands. Thus they reveal aspects of the sources, traditions, and changes of the culture they represent. The process of diffusion had eastward as well as westward directions. The western,

Villages

Dwellings housing more than one family are not unique to Western culture. Communal dwellings are used in Southeast Asia, New Guinea, and Eastern Ecuador in South America, among other areas. The "long house" form of multiple-family dwelling, characteristic of these areas, also was built by North American Indian peoples such as the Iroquois. The long house tends to look a bit like a quonset hut, with doors at both ends and a passageway down the middle; the space on either side of this hallway is divided into living units. Usually, the long house residents would be members of an extended family, and not totally unrelated nuclear families. More modern versions of the system have been built in China during the commune experiment and in Israel as part of *kibbutzim* settlements.

Multiple-family buildings have reached their ultimate development, however, in Western cities. Apartment buildings dozens of stories high contain 10, 20, or more single-family units on each floor, imposing a sameness and anonymity on their clustered occupants that lead to stresses with which not everyone can cope. The advantages of such apartments—lower costs than individual houses, less land occupied, greater proximity to work—may be outweighed by the social stresses caused by overcrowding and inadequate design.

We now turn our attention from individual dwellings to *settlements*, which are clusters of houses and other buildings. These clusters may consist of only a few (say a half dozen) units called *hamlets*, or they may be as large as towns or cities. The smaller settlements, hamlets and villages, are identified as *rural* settlements. The larger clusters, including towns and cities, are referred to as *urban* settlements. Unfortunately, this does not mean that there is a generally applicable classification into which we can fit settlements on the basis of size. In Canada, all settlements with more than 1000 people are classified as urban, but in the United States, incorporated settlements with over 2500 inhabitants are given urban status. In India a rural village can have up to 5000 residents; larger places are urban settlements. In Japan, a settlement must have as many as 30,000 residents to be classified as an urban place! So when you see statistics comparing the degree of urbanization in various countries, you should be sure that some standard criterion has been adopted.

There is another complication. In certain countries the difference between rural and urban settlements is not primarily a matter of size, but rather of status or function. In the United Kingdom, for example, "urban" is not a matter of dimension or population numbers; communities are given urban status after they apply for it and government approval is given. In Italy, "urban" is considered a matter of employment. More than 50 percent of the economically productive population must be engaged in nonagricultural pursuits for a settlement to be classified as an urban place.

Rural settlements, in any case, are at the lower end of the scale: they tend to be small. They are most closely and directly connected to the land, and most of their inhabitants' livelihood depends on the cultivation of nearby farmland. As such, they tend to reflect historical circumstances or prevailing necessity. Japanese farming villages, for example, are tightly packed together, so that only the narrowest passageways remain between the houses. This reflects the need to allocate every possible square foot of land to farming; villages must not sprawl where crops could grow. In the hilly regions of Europe you will see villages clustered on hillslopes, leaving the level land for farming. Often an old castle sits atop the hill, and so the site had two advantages: protection as well as land conservation. In the low-lying areas of Western Europe villages are often positioned on dikes and levees, so that they take on *linear* characteristics (Fig. 12-2A). Where there is space, the house and outbuildings may be surrounded by a small garden; the farms and pasturelands lie beyond. Where no such physiographic limitations exist, the village may attain *cluster* characteristics. It may have

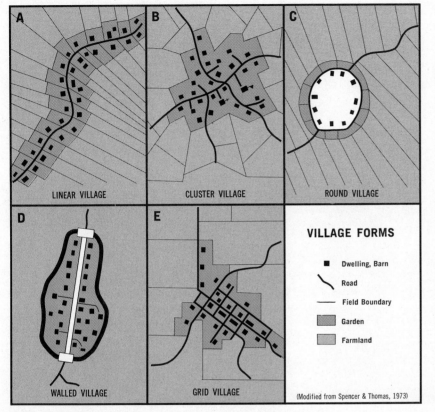

A LINEAR VILLAGE

B CLUSTER VILLAGE

C ROUND VILLAGE

D WALLED VILLAGE

E GRID VILLAGE

VILLAGE FORMS

■ Dwelling, Barn

╱ Road

— Field Boundary

▨ Garden

▦ Farmland

(Modified from Spencer & Thomas, 1973)

Figure 12-2

begun as a small hamlet at the intersection of two roads, and then developed by accretion. The European version of the East African circular village, with its central cattle corral, is the *round* village or *Rundling* (Fig. 12-2C). This layout was first used by Slavic farmer-herdsmen in Eastern Europe, and later modified by German settlers.

In many parts of the world, farm villages were fortified to afford protection against marauders. Ten thousand years ago the first farmers in the Middle East's Fertile Crescent faced the attacks from the horsemen of Asia's steppes, and clustered together to ward off the danger. In Nigeria's Yorubaland the farmers would go out into the surrounding fields by day, but retreat to the protection of walled villages at night. Villages as well as larger towns and cities in Europe were walled and moated; when the population became so large that people had to build houses outside the original wall, a new wall would be built to protect them as well. *Walled* villages (Fig. 12-2D) still exist on the landscape of many countries, reminders of a turbulent past. More modern villages, notably planned rural settlements, may display their origins by a *grid* pattern. This is not, however, a twentieth-century novelty. The Spanish invaders of Middle America laid out grid villages and towns centuries ago, as did other colonial powers elsewhere in the world as they organized their acquired possessions. In urban Africa, as we will see in Chapter 20, this is a pervasive colonial imprint.

Villages, thus, display an enormous variety of sizes and forms. Their unifying quality is their agricultural orientation. The great majority of residents make their living by farming; the houses are farmhouses, and additional buildings are barns, sheds, and other structures of similar purpose. Villages are likely to include a place a worship, perhaps a medical clinic, a school, and a public gathering place; larger villages may accommodate professional people such as teachers, doctors, and ministers, as well as shopkeepers and repair mechanics. But all these people serve a population whose major tie is to the land.

13 Towns and Cities

The modern age is an age of urbanization. Throughout the world, in India, in the Netherlands, in Brazil, and here in North America, people are moving to the cities. Villages are growing into towns, towns into cities, and cities coalesce into megacities—of which the megalopolis that extends from Boston to Washington is a prime example.

The rise of the megacity is a pervasive phenomenon attending the explosive growth of world population during the twentieth century. It is a condition of industrialization: 4 of 5 Britons and Germans live in urban centers, 3 of 4 Japanese, 7 of 10 Americans. Tokyo, New York City, London—their populations, in the 10 to 20 million range, are larger than those of many countries. Consider it: there are more people in New York City than in Sweden. There are more people in Tokyo than in Portugal. There are more people in London than in Austria.

But huge cities have emerged in the less industrialized world as well. Calcutta and Cairo, Karachi and Canton contain many millions of residents, their numbers growing with each passing month. While many of these huge urban places stand singly in the midst of large agricultural regions, cities elsewhere are spaced so close that they are growing toward each other and coalescing into huge megalopolitan complexes. This is happening not only in eastern North America, but also in Europe, in South Africa, and in Japan among other areas.

In large cities, people often are crowded closely together, in apartment buildings, in tenements, and in teeming slums. People continuously arrive from outside the city to add to the natural increase of the already resident population; no housing expansion could keep up with the flow, and acres of shacks are thrown up overnight, without even the barest of facilities. From Lima to Lagos, from Mombasa to Madras hundreds of thousands of people live in substandard housing. And urban poverty is by no means a monopoly of the developing world. Inadequate housing exists in every

243

major city of the United States, too.

Over the past 15 years or so, a number of social scientists, including psychologists, sociologists, and geographers, have begun to prove that there is more to excessively high urban density than the physical limitations imposed by housing and facilities. When circumstances force people to live closely packed together in an urban environment, they are placed under an emotional stress many of them cannot bear. Noisy streets cause loss of sleep. Congested stores irritate. Traffic jams have tempers flaring. It is a vicious circle: as the city grows, so do the stress-producing conditions.

In the Middle Ages, a city could be a dangerous place to live because famine and epidemics took their heaviest tolls there (as we noted in Chapter 4). Today a new sort of epidemic threatens urban dwellers, and it is a double-barreled one. The stresses of urban life can generate hypertension, ulcers, sexual failure, and glandular malfunctions, and they appear to be related to the incidence of suicide attempts and withdrawal symptoms. In aggregate these are related to a breakdown of the social order, a high frequence of aggressive behavior, and violence. The urban dweller who manages to adjust to the stresses of urban life may fall victim to the behavior of others less able to absorb them.

It has proved difficult to measure the stressful effects of urban life on city residents. Psychologists have experimented with animal populations of rats, cats, and monkeys, placing them under the sort of crowded circumstances humans in cities often face: too many individuals in a living space, no escape from confined surroundings, no privacy. Dramatic results were recorded: in some individuals, aggressiveness became a dominant trait, while others, unable to find a sanctuary from the constant threat imposed by their violent neighbors, died—not from any attacks they suffered, but from psychological trauma arising from the ever-present threats, harassment, and defeat. Mothers failed in their maternal functions and the young died in large numbers. Males either withdrew from sexual activity or developed deviant behavior. In one experiment, a researcher actually built a simulated tenement building complete with rooms, hallways, and stairs. He then populated the structure with a comparatively small number of mice. In the beginning, the individuals distributed themselves through the building with ample space for all. But then the colony began to multiply. For a while the structure could accommodate the increase, but eventually it began to become overcrowded. As it did, troubles arose in the community. Fights broke out. Older individuals even cannibalized the young. Stillbirths increased in number. Mothers abandoned babies. All the orderliness that had marked the community prior to this phase disappeared.

We cannot conclude, of course, that these experiments produced results that can be applied to human populations. After all, we could argue, humans have the capacity of choice and they could leave circumstances such as those described above. But is this always so? What are the options of people driven or born into poverty, trapped in slums, deprived of adequate education, mired in debt, without marketable skills? The word "trapped" we just used is a cultural reality in many parts of the world; the trap is as effective as the cages in those experiments.

And there is some evidence that the consequences of such entrapment are not altogether unlike what we might expect after study of the psychologists' experiments. There are correlations between overcrowding and mental health problems; for example, urban congestion is related to a comparatively high incidence of attempted suicide. The cramped living and depersonalization of life in large cities have much to do with alcoholism, drug addiction, and delinquency. Crimes of violence, steadily rising in practically all large urban areas, multiply in part because increasing numbers of individuals feel that they have no stake in the social order, no accountability, no commitment. Alienation and despair can lead individuals to acts of transgression; whole communities can explode into destruction and revolt. Then it does not mat-

The cramped, bleak, frequently insecure life of tenement dwellers is often too much
for them, resulting in severe social dislocation.

ter that many if not most of the victims are their own, that the dwellings that are burned are in the slums they themselves occupy, and not in the roomier, more comfortable areas of the city. High urban densities coupled with deficient living conditions may not have the same effects on humans that crowding has on test animals, but the effects are deeply destructive, beyond doubt.

Urbanization is not an entirely modern phenomenon, of course. There were cities and towns thousands of years ago, long before the Industrial Revolution and its side effects began to have their impact on urban conditions. Those old cities, too, had their problems. What *is new*, though, is the greater and still growing *proportion* of populations living in cities. The ratio of urban to rural inhabitants changed rather little for many centuries; although there were towns and cities, societies remained primarily rural and agricultural. But then the onslaught of the Industrial Revolution occurred. As we recounted in Part I, the rate of population growth increased, and the image of the city as a place of jobs and opportunities, combined with the often grinding poverty of rural areas, led to a mushrooming of urban populations that is unprecedented in the history of the world—and continues unabated today. The people continue to come to the cities, and the cities

are unable to accommodate them. So they trade one set of miseries for another, these urban-bound migrants, and for many of them the move ends disastrously.

In various parts of the world, national governments as well as local administrations have tried to stem the tide of in-migration and growing congestion by introducing growth-control legislation. The consequences have not been uniformly positive, for growth control raised the values (and hence the cost to buyers) of homes in local areas, pushing new growth to greater distances from the business centers. Low-income home buyers found themselves disadvantaged on all fronts: they could not afford the higher prices of even modest homes in the controlled areas, nor could they bear the cost of either the far-away homes or the long-distance commuting there. Thus poorer people were victims of the very policies designed to alleviate the crowding that prevails in their urban areas.

Since cities existed long before the Industrial Revolution began, we should examine urbanization in its historical-geographical context. The first substantial urban centers (as opposed to early farming villages) may have appeared as long as 6000 years ago, probably in Mesopotamia. Sustained agricultural surpluses probably were the key, just as sedentary agriculture generated the first rural settlements: when farming no longer required the constant, daily work of every able person in a society, there was time for other activities. These activities no doubt included early efforts at writing and record-keeping, arithmetic, calendrics, politics, the arts, and religion. It was also possible now to consider and plan better ways of defending the community against enemies, to make better tools and weapons, and to store and distribute food. Such developments required the building of structures other than those intended for shelter alone. They were accompanied also by political and social changes—society was beginning to become more complex. The first stage of the urban revolution had begun.

The earliest towns probably experienced the same growth conditions that later sustained the modern rise of such cities as Paris and London: as the principal centers, crossroads, markets, places of authority, and religious headquarters they drew the talents, the trade, the travelers from far around. Where should the beginnings of metallurgy have been based but

Overview of one of West Africa's most important preindustrial cities: Kano, Nigeria.

in these incipient cities? Where would a traveler, a tradesman, a priest, or a pilgrim rest before continuing the journey? And so the town had to have facilities, the kinds of facilities you would not find in farm villages: buildings to house the visitors, to store the food, to treat raw materials, to worship, to accommodate those charged with the protection and defense of the place. The cities grew—and drew attention at a price. Their contents of food and wealth, and their status and regional influence, spread their reputations far and wide, and soon there were enemies who realized that the takeover of a city would mean power, prestige, and riches. So the early cities built defenses—walls, moats, and the like—and maintained armed forces. Those forces also came in handy when it was necessary to exact tribute and taxes from the surrounding rural region and to subdue rebellious elements within the city's own sphere.

How large were the ancient cities? We have only estimates, for it is impossible to conclude from excavated ruins the total dimensions of a city at its height or the number of people that might have occupied each unit. But it seems that, by modern standards, the ancient cities were not large. The cities of Mesopotamia, and those of the Nile Valley, may have had between 10,000 and 15,000 inhabitants after nearly 2000 years of growth and development. That, scholars conclude, is about the maximum size that could have been sustained by existing systems of food gathering and distribution, and of social organization. So these urban places were but islands, exceptions in an overwhelmingly rural society. Urbanized societies such as we know did not emerge until several thousand years later.

Cities did grow larger, of course, as time went on and societies became more complex. Each advance, every additional element in the culture was reflected in some way in the city. Greece's city-states had capitals that were much larger than the old Egyptian towns, and Rome was larger still—ancient Rome may have had more than 300,000 residents at its zenith as the capital of the Roman Empire. Later Constantinople, heir to the Roman Empire, probably reached the same size. The second stage in the urban revolution began approximately 600 B.C., about the time of the rise of ancient Greece, and continued until the fall of the Roman Empire. Following the collapse of Rome, Europe's trade connections were destroyed, Moslem power gained footholds in Mediterranean areas, and Europe was forced to survive mainly on its own agricultural merits—which were not enough to sustain the urban vitality Roman power had generated. Cities survived, but they stopped growing; some even declined in size.

Rome on the Tiber River, ancient headquarters and modern capital. The Coliseum lies in the left background.

The walled city of Avila, Spain, a European preindustrial center.

In what way did Greece and Rome bring stimuli to city growth? The answer lies in trade and transportation, in intensified exchanges of commodities, and in improved agricultural methods and yields. Farming was better organized now, tools were improved, crops had been developed for particular environments. It was feasible to import foodstuffs from across the Mediterranean to sustain Greek and Roman cities. Rome benefited from its government's tight control over the empire of which it was the focus, and from the pro-

248

duce it requisitioned. Rome's manufacturers (of metalware, jewelry, pottery, and the like) sent their wares by ship to distant colonies in North Africa, and the ships came back carrying grains and other foodstuffs.

We should not assume, however, that the Middle East and Europe had a monopoly on early urbanization. Cities emerged in other parts of the world as well. Approximately contemporaneous to the Mesopotamian-Egyptian urbanization, cities arose in the core area of ancient China, the valleys of the Hwang and Wei Rivers. Cities arose also in the Indus valley (now Pakistan), where Mohenjo Daro and Harappa emerged; in Persia, where Persepolis was the center of a major culture, and in West Africa's savanna belt. Between the tropical forests of Africa's west coast and the drier interior where today the Sahara Desert lies, there developed a zone of cities and towns that grew in response to the active trade routes between forest and desert. Timbuktu, about 1350 A.D., was a city of major consequence, a seat of government, a university town, a market, and a religious focus. Farther to the east in Africa, in the upper valley of the Nile, Meroe had become the "Pittsburgh of Africa," the place where metallurgy, especially the smelting of iron and the making of weapons, was a major industry. And in the Americas, too, urban growth took place. In Yucatan sizable ceremonial centers developed; on the Mexican plateau much larger urban centers emerged.

Mexico's largest pre-Columbian city, Teotihuacan, may have had over 100,000 inhabitants nearly a thousand years ago. Like Rome, Teotihuacan (near present-day Mexico City) benefited from tight control over a substantial, tribute-producing empire, and water transportation. Though not on the scale of the Romans, the Aztecs moved their goods on the lakes and connecting canals of their heartland, by boat.

While some of these far-flung urban places flourished, Europe's urbanization in post-Roman times came virtually to a stop. Damascus, Bagdad, Cairo, and Constantinople were the cities of vitality and growing technology. In Europe's cities there often was stagnation, poverty, and disease. But then came the Christian counterthrust to the Moslem successes: first the invaders were halted, and then the Crusades commenced. The colonial, imperial era of Europe was about to begin, and old trade routes were reopened. In the dormant cities, the effects had quick expression. The pulse of commerce picked up again, there was work to be had, and population numbers resumed their growth. Paris, Amsterdam, Antwerp, Lisbon, Venice, Naples and many other cities and towns were revived. It is important to keep a perspective on the magnitude we are talking about here—London by the middle of the fifteenth century had perhaps 80,000 inhabitants, Paris 120,000. And while colonies were secured and riches poured into the continent, London around the beginning of the nineteenth century still had fewer than one million residents, and Paris only 670,000.

What were the preindustrial cities like as places to live and work? Well, the adage of the "good old days" hardly applies. If today's cities are no bargain for many of their residents, neither were preindustrial Ghent, Manchester, or Warsaw. With more efficient weaponry and the invention of gunpowder, cities faced threats not confronted before: walls and moats could no longer withstand armies. So cities developed into veritable fortifications just at a time when they must also accommodate growing numbers of people. Those fortifications could not simply be moved outward; once built, they more or less marked the confines of the place. Thus the only way people could be contained in greater numbers was by building not outward, but upward, and so four- and five-story tenements began to appear. By the seventeenth century the European cities were generally slum-ridden, unsanitary, and depressing. Epidemics, disastrous fires, much crime, and social dislocation prevailed. Yes, the picturesque, four-story merchants' homes overlooked the canals of Amsterdam and the parks of London. But their residents were the fortunate few, who were in a position to manipulate the labor force in the city and to control the lucrative overseas commerce. For the ordinary people, the overcrowded cities more often than not were no place to be. Many decided just that when the chance came to leave for America, Australia, and other parts of the world.

Non-Western Cities

The changes that have come to urban life throughout much of the world as a result of the forces of European dominance and industrialization sometimes lead us to forget that the urban "norm" we are used to—represented perhaps by our hometown, or by our image of New York, San Francisco, or London—has its exceptions. As we note in Chapter 14, we can recognize certain recurrent features in the layout and structure of American and other Western cities, and we make generalizations about these features, sometimes believing that we have discovered some universally operative rules of urban development. After all, we take it for granted that cities have "downtown" areas, suburbs, and parks. Surely all cities everywhere have these characteristics, right? The answer is—no.

Despite the nearly 200 years that have passed since the Industrial Revolution began to change the British Midland towns, and the globe-circling imprint of Europe on the non-European world, and the worldwide adoption of modern technologies, there still are cities that remain essentially preindustrial in character, and many more in which the impact of the industrial era is but limited as yet. Here most of the people still travel on foot (although the bicycle has made inroads), or by horse and cart. Houses, hostels, workshops, and other special-function buildings

In the central business district of an American city: Fifth Avenue, New York.

are all mixed up, so that a downtown area is hard to find. There is little vertical development in these urban places, and from a vantage point overlooking the city you see a sea of roofs, all looking much the same, crowded together and separated by narrow, winding paths and lanes suitable for walking, but not for vehicular traffic. Perhaps a roadway has penetrated the city, as has occurred almost everywhere, but preindustrial cities and traditional urban areas display a marked lack of internal interconnections for vehicular traffic.

We call our downtown area the central business district (or CBD for short), and none of us would have difficulty finding it or listing the kinds of services (banks, movies, and department stores) we would expect to find there. As you approach a town or city you can often navigate on the tall buildings that mark the heart of the CBD, and find your way downtown. Once there, you find lots of pedestrians on the sidewalks, congested street traffic, and land that is more expensive per square foot than anywhere else in the city. Such CBDs exist in non-Western cities too, but when you find them (as in Nairobi, Kenya) you can be sure that those are colonial cities, laid out and developed by Europeans. In the true non-Western city, such a CBD is still hard to locate. You may find that one of the traditional business areas of the city (usually non-Western cities have several)

has begun to show the effects of modernization; many non-Western cities have two business districts today, one traditional and the other modern. In India's smaller cities and towns, the CBD is generally still traditional in character, with a religious shrine, the civil court, the moneylender, and the clothing retailer competing with the houses of the wealthy for space near the busiest part of town, thereby breaking all kinds of "rules" we derive from studying our Western downtown areas. In the traditional towns of West Africa, the old market center with its economic, political, and social functions still survives some distance away from a newer, more modern CBD. Other non-Western cities, such as Kumasi (Ghana), Ibadan (Nigeria), and Colombo (Sri Lanka), have central business districts that show the yet-incomplete transition from traditional to modern.

As every observer of the American city knows, the CBD here is surrounded by an urban zone consisting of light manufacturing plants, automobile sales, and other establishments that need too much space to locate within the CBD itself. This zone is missing in the traditional non-Western city, where the zone surrounding the market or business center (and even the modernized CBD, if there is one) is densely populated. Many people go to work on foot or by bicycle, and

proximity to the market or the business district is an advantage. Again, the traditional character of the non-Western urban population comes through: these areas on the doorstep of the market or CBD are often still laid out not as city blocks, but in groupings of dwellings clustering around the house of a local chief, headman, or religious leader. Many non-Western cities contain a great variety of ethnic clusters, and these tend to be associated with particular areas of the urban region. New immigrants to the city will look for the settlement of their own kind, and will seek to stay there, no matter how severe the shortage of space or how poor the facilities. Thus many of these areas near the CBD have become some of the world's worst slums. However, the problems they present are not simply eradicated by clearing the slums and building high-rise apartments. As many urban administrations have found out, the facilities can be improved, but high-rise life tears at the fabric of society, already frayed by urban environments.

While the residents of areas near downtown in American cities have fled to the suburbs, the reverse has been true in most non-Western cities. Thus the very heart of the non-Western city differs fundamentally from that of the Western city, and the question is: will the non-Western city eventually begin to respond to the forces of urban development we recognize as operative here in America? The way those incipient CBDs are emerging in non-Western cities would suggest an affirmative answer, but we should be careful with our generalizations. In the first place, Western cities have a different heritage. They inherited their land-value structure, the high-cost CBD, from preindustrial cities that were quite unlike non-Western preindustrial cities. Second, the Western city has emerged and has differentiated regionally and specialized functionally on the basis of the distribution and circulation of considerable wealth—wealth that is simply not available in non-Western cities and is not likely to be for a very long time. And third, there are deeply rooted differences in attitude—toward ownership and property, toward the family and schooling, toward older people, for example—between Western and non-Western societies. Those, too, will be reflected in the urban scene. The non-Western city will be different for a very long time to come, and perhaps forever. We should remember this as we resume our study of the urban development of Europe and the rest of the Western world.

The impact of the Industrial Revolution and its associated effects upon Europe's cities came full force during the first half of the nineteenth century. As we noted earlier, European cities about 1800 were not especially large by modern standards; London still had well under a million residents, and Paris somewhat more than a half million. Large cities were not especially numerous either; there were perhaps 20 cities in Europe with more than 100,000 inhabitants, and together they contained less than 4 percent of the continent's population. Urbanization ratios in those days compare with those of the underdeveloped countries of today.

Even so, the cities of Europe were no longer dormant; they were productive, crowded, and growing. The rules by which cities thrived (or failed) were the rules of commerce and finance. Now the permanent advantages of each really came to play their role. Could the city expand and accommodate new industries and businesses? Where was the city positioned relative to resources and competition? Among the most basic qualities of a city are its *site* and its *situation*, and these are crucial in the new, modern age.

Site

The site of a town or city can be a major factor in its development. The term refers to the actual, physical qualities of the place the city occupies: whether it lies in a confining valley, on a section of a coastal plain, on the edge of a plateau, or perhaps on an island. In Europe, a site's defensibility often was an important factor in the development of cities. A good example is that of Venice, which was a small coastal settlement at the head of the Adriatic Sea that grew into a city of wealth and splendor. The city could have continued to develop on the mainland, but there was little natural protection to be found on that site. So the rich merchants built their warehouses, their mansions, and their monuments to the accumulated wealth on a group of islands offshore, thereby deterring attackers from land. Today the site of Venice is causing some unforeseen problems: it is sinking, and many of the old, historic buildings are endangered by rising water.

Another example of the role of site in the emergence of a major city is Paris. The capital of France was founded on an island in the middle of the Seine River, again a place where security and defense were enhanced—and also a place where the Seine could be crossed and the cross traffic controlled. Exactly when settlement on this *Ile de la Cité* began is not known, but it probably happened even in pre-Roman times. Paris functioned as a Roman outpost for several centuries, and later the Roman regional administration there was replaced by

Paris and the Ile de la Cité.

were hoarding wealth, when pirates from the sea and marauders from land preyed on them, defensibility was of prime concern.

Situation

More important still than the city's site is its situation. By situation is meant the position of the city with reference to nearby and surrounding areas of productive capacity, the extent of its *hinterland*, the location of competing towns, its accessibility—in short, the greater regional framework in which the city finds itself, its *relative location*. Our previous example, Paris, combines advantages of site with a most fortuitous situation. The city lies near the center of a large and prosperous farming region, and as a growing market and distribution point its focality increased continuously (Fig. 13-1). The Seine River, a navigable waterway, is joined near Paris by several tributaries, all of them navigable as well, which thus connect Paris to various parts of the Paris Basin, and to areas beyond. To the west, the Seine River runs into the English Channel, and although today's oceangoing ships cannot reach Paris, the smaller vessels of the past could—and today only one transshipment, at Le Havre or Rouen, is necessary. Paris thus had good connections to

other authority—always making use of the defensible qualities of the island city. Eventually the rather small island proved too restrictive for Paris' growth, and the city sprawled onto the nearby riverbanks. But authority remained centered on the island, and potential adversaries knew that there was no point in challenging the outskirts if there were no prospects of conquering the *Ile de la Cité*.

Today, we tend to look at city sites from other viewpoints. The site of a city may hamper urban expansion and interconnection; marshes, swampy, areas, valleys, escarpments, shallow or silting harbor waters, limited dockage, and numerous other problems can confront the growing urban center. Cities positioned in valleys may suffer from pollution problems because air circulation is inhibited. But in the days when European cities

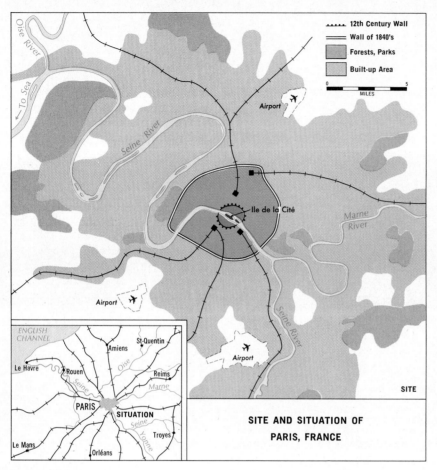

Figure 13-1

Map labels (within Figure 13-1):

12th Century Wall
Wall of 1840's
Forests, Parks
Built-up Area

0 ... 5
MILES

Oise River
To Sea
Seine River
Airport
Ile de la Cité
Marne River
Airport
Seine River
Airport
SITE

ENGLISH CHANNEL
St-Quentin
Amiens
Oise
Le Havre
Rouen
Reims
Seine
Marne
PARIS
SITUATION
Le Mans
Troyes
Orléans
Yonne

SITE AND SITUATION OF
PARIS, FRANCE

overseas spheres when the time came, but in the city's longevity and steady growth its internal connections were perhaps even more important. The rivers that join the Seine (the Marne, Oise, and Yonne) from the northeast, east, and southeast, and the canals that extend them even farther, connect Paris to the regions of the Loire, the Rhône-Saône, the Lorraine industrial area, and the industrial complex on the French-Belgian border (Fig. 13-1). And, of course, Paris always lay at the focus of land transport routes as well. As the authority based on the *Ile de la Cité* gained greater political influence in surrounding regions, Paris found itself near the very center of one of Europe's largest and most lasting nation-states. Subsequent governments did everything possible to improve the city's connections with the country generally. Under Napoleon's regime, for example, a whole network of roads was laid out specifically designed to intensify the interaction between

Paris and the nation. Thus Paris situation proved time and again to be its most valuable asset, its guarantee of continued primacy (Fig. 13-2).

The situational qualities of a city can improve and change for the better, but they can also change for the worse. Changes in transport systems, resource production, agricultural productivity, or other regional transformations can put a city at a disadvantage. We can see the effect of this on the formerly busy commercial center of a medium-sized town that has suddenly been bypassed as a result of the construction of a new superhighway. Restaurants, gasoline stations, and other establishments feel the effects as connectivity patterns are changed and traffic declines. That same superhighway may improve the situational qualities of other towns it does connect.

The effect of the Industrial Revolution on the cities and towns of Europe was varied. New resource needs arose; some cities found themselves positioned very near coalfields, their situational assets enhanced. Other towns were more remote from the foci of industrial activity and lagged. The need for intensified circulation and the construction of railroad networks, new roads, and additional waterways completely modified the competitive circumstances of many European urban centers. Some cities, such as Manchester, England, experienced truly explosive growth. Manchester in 1800 had about 70,000 residents; in 1850 there were 300,000 inhabitants. Everywhere —in Britain first, then in mainland Europe—the proportion of urban to rural residents began to change so drastically that it was clear that a new stage of urbanization had begun. By the middle of the nineteenth century, more than half of the entire population of England and Wales was classified as living in urban areas, the first time that had happened anywhere in the world. Even if towns shared only marginally in the changing economic order, they could not escape the impact of the population explosion. Whole new industrial towns emerged. As the European mainland began to sustain the impact of the Industrial Revolution, the urbanizing phenomenon, occurred there, too. Germany was the first mainland country to record a larger urban-based than rural population (Fig. 13-3).

If you could have taken an airplane flight, at low level, over those mushrooming European industrial towns, you would have seen three prominent sights: acres of factories, with a forest of smoke stacks belching an enormous amount of pollution into the air; miles of gray, dirty, endlessly monotonous slums; and huge railway installations and yards carrying raw materials and finished products in great quantity.

Worldwide Impact

The urbanizing stimulus provided during the nineteenth century still continues today. London, the United Kingdom's capital and leading city, now houses, in its metropolitan area, about 20 percent of the total British population; again, such cities as Paris, Rome, Moscow, Berlin, and Madrid, and other places that not long ago counted their populations in hundreds of thousands, have become multimillion-aire cities. And cities outside Europe have overtaken their European counterparts in size: Tokyo is generally acknowledged to be the world's largest, with 8.87 million people according to the 1970 census but with 22 million residents in the conurbation of which Tokyo is the heart. That, again, accounts for more than one fifth of Japan's population. Shanghai, China, also is larger than any mainland European city, with over 10 million people in the city proper and its immediate environs. New York had 7.85 million inhabitants according to the 1970 census, but more than 16 million people live in the urban region of which New York City is the focus, and thus New York, too, is larger than any European city today. In the underdeveloped countries of South Asia, Latin America, and Africa there are cities today of dimensions that would have

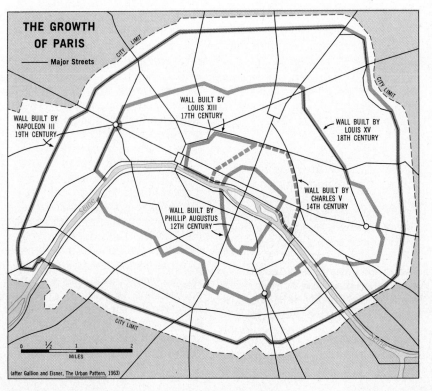

THE GROWTH OF PARIS

—— Major Streets

WALL BUILT BY NAPOLEON III 19TH CENTURY

WALL BUILT BY LOUIS XIII 17TH CENTURY

WALL BUILT BY LOUIS XV 18TH CENTURY

WALL BUILT BY CHARLES V 14TH CENTURY

WALL BUILT BY PHILLIP AUGUSTUS 12TH CENTURY

CITY LIMIT

Seine

0 ½ 1 2
MILES

(after Gallion and Eisner, The Urban Pattern, 1963)

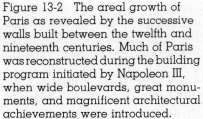

Figure 13-2 The areal growth of Paris as revealed by the successive walls built between the twelfth and nineteenth centuries. Much of Paris was reconstructed during the building program initiated by Napoleon III, when wide boulevards, great monuments, and magnificent architectural achievements were introduced.

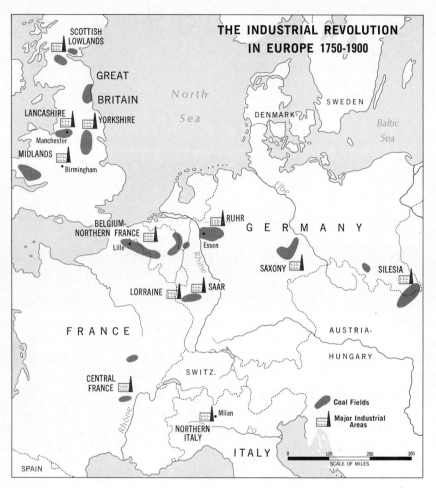

THE INDUSTRIAL REVOLUTION IN EUROPE 1750-1900

SCOTTISH LOWLANDS

GREAT BRITAIN

North Sea

SWEDEN

DENMARK

Baltic Sea

LANCASHIRE YORKSHIRE

Manchester

MIDLANDS

Birmingham

Elbe

BELGIUM-NORTHERN FRANCE

Lille

RUHR

Essen

G E R M A N Y

Rhine

SAXONY

SILESIA

LORRAINE

SAAR

F R A N C E

AUSTRIA-HUNGARY

SWITZ.

CENTRAL FRANCE

Rhône

Milan

Po

Coal Fields

Major Industrial Areas

NORTHERN ITALY

ITALY

0   100   200   300
SCALE OF MILES

SPAIN

Figure 13-3

seemed absolutely unimaginable just a century ago. Calcutta's urban area counts over 7 million people, and Bombay has 6 million residents. Of Brazil's 100 million inhabitants, no less than 16 million live in the urban areas of the country's two largest cities, São Paulo and Rio de Janeiro. Cairo, whose nearly 7 million inhabitants (immediate environs included) constitute one fifth of the country's population, ranks among the world's 20 largest cities.

Many of these large world cities—Cairo, Bombay, and Calcutta—developed for reasons different from those that stimulated the fast growth of such places as Manchester and Liverpool, Glasgow and Stuttgart. Most of them are not major industrial centers on the scale of their European and other Western counterparts. Their emergence is testimony to the explosive population growth made possible by the technological advances made in

those grimy European cities of the nineteenth century, including those in public hygiene and sanitation. It was possible now to construct multistory apartment houses with built-in sewerage systems and pipes to bring fresh water to every floor. Cities planned and laid out disposal systems and water treatment plants, and urban life became somewhat more tolerable, and safer. Those innovations were exported to the outside world, and we can read the results on any map of urban places.

The large and populous non-Western cities should not lead us to assume, however, that the *ratio* of urban to rural residents has changed significantly in their regions. The urban-rural ratio, the true measure of urbanization, has in fact changed comparatively little in non-Western areas, with a few exceptions. India's cities have mushroomed, true—but the country's total population (and therefore its rural component) has skyrocketed too. When it comes to the urban-rural ratio, things are only slightly different from what they were before world population began to grow so rapidly. The most significant change in the non-Western world occurred in Japan, but Japan already had an urban tradition even before the European cities began their nineteenth-century growth: in 1800, Tokyo already was larger than London and probably was the largest urban center in the world. It is difficult to secure comparable statistics for urban populations even today, as we noted earlier, and we can only estimate for the nineteenth century. It is believed that under 3 percent of the people of the world in 1800 were living in cities and towns over 20,000; in 1900 it may have been around 9 percent; in 1970, perhaps 35 percent. Most of the increase reflects changing conditions in the Western world and Japan. In Britain, for example, the urbanized population in 1800 was 9 percent of the total; in 1900 it was 62 percent, and in 1970, 85 percent!

In our discussion of urbanization we have referred to industrialization as a leading stimulus for the growth of cities. But have you noticed that, when you go to a big city these days, to New York, to London, or Paris, that there seem to be huge numbers of people around who are very obviously not industrial workers. And indeed, the employment picture in these cities is changing. The European city on the eve of the Industrial Revolution was a place of commerce and what we would call light manufacturing. Many of the inhabitants of the cities and towns, even children, were engaged in these activities. Then, with the advent of the Industrial Revolution, cities became factory complexes, with even larger industrial labor forces. But as industry evolved, it required fewer hands: machines were invented that could do the work quickly and in larger volume. In the meantime, people were earning more than they had in the past, more than would cover the bare essentials of life. So when the numbers of people employed in the industries began to decline, there was other work to be done: service. Transportation, retailing, banking, entertainment, government services, health services, and other industries quite different from those of factories and foundries now became a major and growing source of employment, and for some these formed viable alternatives. But for others, the decline of the industrial labor market spelled trouble. In the United States today, the service industries employ not much less than two-thirds of the entire labor force. Many cities and towns have become principally service centers, though others retain their primarily industrial base.

Consequences of Decentralization

Undoubtedly you have seen those rather attractive-looking industrial parks that, in recent years, have begun to mark the outlying areas of major urban centers. These well-designed, spacious industrial parks are manifestations of the decentralization process now affecting American cities, a process that has major implications for the millions of workers who are employed in urban areas.

The reasons for the decentralization process are obvious enough. Urban transport systems have improved. The central city has lost much of its centrality and it no longer offers amenities that are critical to many manufacturers' operations. Indeed, the crowded heart of the city and the high prices of land there militate against the location of modern, extensive, single-floor plants of the technological age. If it is important to have administrative offices in the CBD, any plant in an outlying industrial park can be connected by computer to such facilities. The old city center no longer has its former primacy.

But it was that old city center, with its factories and railroad terminals, its flow of raw materials and products, that attracted and employed the countless thousands of unskilled and semiskilled workers who still reside there, and who now see their opportunities diminish. Already modern technology continues to eliminate their jobs, but worse: when a central-city plant closes and relocates 20 miles away in a suburban industrial park, it is the skilled, white-collar worker who benefits, the same white-collar worker who dominates employment in the service industries. The poorer, unskilled worker cannot follow, cannot afford to live there in the suburbs, even if his or her job survived the transfer. The situation is not always this stark, of course. But decentralization and the emergence of the new urban structure has had a powerfully negative impact on job opportunities for those workers living in the inner cities. It is a major element in our growing urban dilemma.

Port city, capital, historic focus: Lisbon,
Portugal.

14 Urban Patterns

Geographers are naturally interested in the patterns and forms that
have emerged as urbanization progressed. The spacing of cities
and towns, the character of urban regions, and the special functions of cities all are topics for research and study.

One problem that confronts urban geographers lies in the com-
pleteness and accuracy of available data. As we noted earlier,
census taking in underdeveloped countries still involves much guesswork and estimating; but even in the United States with its modern
techniques of data gathering there are still difficulties. For example, the municipal boundaries of a fast-growing city may lose
their meaning as suburbs sprawl far beyond, but those boundaries
may still remain as the framework for the census count. Imagine
this: in 1960 a certain city's population within those municipal boundaries was perhaps 250,000, and the 1960 census shows that figure
as the city's population. Then in 1970 the population within those
same boundaries was 259,000. But in fact, the whole urban agglomeration was much larger by 1970, exceeding 360,000. Most of the
growth occurred outside the municipal boundaries—all but 9000 of
it. Still the census takers had no alternative: they had to use the
same boundary framework, or successive census figures could not
be compared.

In any case, many "cities" consist in fact of a group of municipalities, not a single one. San Francisco is only one municipality
among a contiguous grouping that also includes, among others,
Daly City, South San Francisco, San Mateo, and, across the Bay,
Berkeley, Oakland, Alameda, and others. If you were to go on vacation to Miami, you would find that there is more to Miami than
Miami and Miami Beach: there is also Coral Gables, South Miami,
West Miami, Hialeah, North Miami Beach, and a number of other
places. Indeed, Miami's conurbation sprawls from Dade County
northward into Broward County. Thus the concept of the *urbanized
area* is used now to count all the people living not only within all

Hierarchy

the cities of an urban region, but also in all contiguous built-up areas. In the case of New York, the difference between city proper and urbanized area is shown by the 1970 census figures: city, 7,847,100; urbanized area: 16,206,841.

Another unit of measurement employed to help define urban populations is the *standard metropolitan statistical area* (SMSA), which is county-based and includes the central city or a set of coalescing cities counting at least 50,000 inhabitants. But counties must satisfy certain criteria to be included in SMSAs, and when an urban agglomeration fills two counties and just edges into a third, that third county may not yet qualify. So the SMSA population statistic is often less useful for comparative purposes than the urbanized area.

Comparisons between cities, therefore, must be based on standardized frameworks. There is little point in comparing conditions in San Francisco and Miami, for example, without employing data that cover all of the Bay Area and all of the Dade-Broward County urbanized areas. Miami is merely a sector of the South Florida urban agglomeration, and San Francisco lies at the heart of a much larger conurbation.

In Chapter 13 we used the terms hamlet, village, town, and city to imply a hierarchy, a ranking of settlements according to certain criteria we did not specifically define. The term originally had religious use (*hierarch*, religious leader) to denote the organization of a ruling body of clergy into ranks. Today we use it to identify an order or gradation of phenomena, each grade being superior to the one below it and subordinate to the one above. Thus a hierarchy is like the steps of a ladder. The question is: can criteria really be employed to confirm the hierarchy implied by such terms as village and town, or is the continuity too tight to allot these words any real utility?

Obviously, population size alone will get us nowhere. If we put all the settlements in the United States on a piece of graph paper, from the smallest to the largest, there would be a near-continuous string of sizes, with real breaks showing up only in the largest categories. You would not be able to discern a gap between "villages" and "towns." But we could look at those settlements in another way—not in terms of size, but in terms of the *functions* they perform and make available to their respective surrounding areas, their service areas.

Thus a *hamlet*, a settlement (in the United States) of less than 100 people usually, has the smallest number of services, probably less than 10. There might be

a general store, a gas station, perhaps a coffee shop. But you would not find a post office, a church, a grocery—for those more specialized services you would have to go to a *village*. In a village in, say, the Wisconsin dairy region, you could expect perhaps 60 or 70 establishments, including a couple of gas stations, a restaurant and one or two bars, a farm elevator, a grocery or two. Obviously such a village would draw customers from a much wider area than the hamlet; in fact, people from the nearby hamlets have to come to the village for certain services. Again, a *town* of about 2500 inhabitants has a still greater variety of functions and services. Here we find a greater degree of specialization, and people would come for a particular kind of doctor, a dentist, stores such as hardware, furniture, appliance stores, and a bank. Certain of the town's services are not available in either villages or hamlets, and so the towns have greater service areas still. Thus, rather than counting heads, we might define a town as a place where a certain assemblage of services is available, and whose *hinterland* includes the service areas of surrounding hamlets and villages.

This approach can be extended to include cities, metropolises, and still larger conurbations. The advantage is that we do not rank settlements merely according to their population, but rather as a reflection of their strength as places of trade and commerce. This approach to the determination of a hierarchy of urban places takes into account something that mere population numbers do not reveal—the interaction between the urban center and its trade area. We might look at the whole problem the other way: instead of measuring the available goods and services in the urban centers themselves, we could identify the surrounding service areas, and thus determine the *economic reach* of each settlement. Our ranking can then be based on this economic reach, which generates a measure of *centrality*. It would, then, be quite possible for a somewhat smaller urban center to have greater centrality than a larger one.

When someone asks you a question about your hometown, you are likely to identify it by name, and then add: "it's a university town" (or a port city, or a mining town, or a farm village). In doing so you try to summarize the nature of your home town, to define what *kind* of an urban place it is. You are, in effect, classifying it with other places of the same type, disregarding size. There are mining towns large and small, industrial centers ranging from a few thousand to several million inhabitants. What these places share is not the same rank in the hierarchy we just discussed, but the same assemblage of dominant functions. So this is one of the bases geographers use to classify urban places.

At first, classifying cities seem quite easy. You could jot down a list rather quickly: there are resort towns, retirement centers, ports, fishing towns, and so forth. But when we look deeper into the matter, we find that port cities also have stores (and thus retail functions), factories (and thus industrial functions), universities, and other facilities. This means that many port cities must be *multifunctional*, that is, they possess more than one sphere of economic activity, among which the transportation function (of the port) is the chief one. But what about a city that does not have such a dominant function as a port city has, or as you might find in a resort town or in a mining town? There are many cities, such as Denver, Kansas City, and Memphis, where no single function stands out to typify the place. On what basis can such cities be included in a generally applicable system of classification?

One approach lies in the activities of the labor force in cities. Where do people find employment? The census gathers such information; it determines the place of employment of the labor force in major cities, and reports the number of workers engaged in each economic activity. In 1943, Professor C. D. Harris published an article in the *Geographical Review* entitled "A Functional Classification of Cities in the United States," in which he used these data to develop a system according to which all U.S. cities could be classified. Thus he recognized two types of *manufacturing* cities: the M' type, in which the total employment in manufacturing is at least 74 percent of the total employment in retailing, wholesaling, and manufacturing combined, and the M type, in which that figure is reduced to 60 percent. In addition to these two classes of manufacturing cities, Harris recognized eight other classes of cities: (1) *retail* centers, in which employment in retailing is at least half of the total number of people employed in retailing, wholesaling, and manufacturing combined, and (2) *wholesale* cities in which employment in wholesaling is unusually strong. Others in the classification are (3) *transportation* centers, in which transportation

Manufacturing Cities

- M' Cities
- M Cities

Retail Centers

Diversified Cities

Wholesale Centers

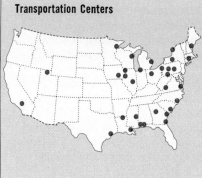

Transportation Centers

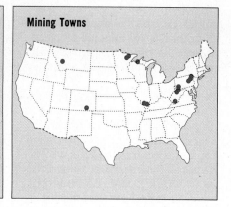

Mining Towns

Educational Centers

Education Secondary

Resort and Retirement Centers

State Capitals

- Clearly Dominant
- Probably Dominant
- Secondary

FUNCTIONAL CLASSIFICATION OF CITIES IN THE UNITED STATES

(After a map in C. D. Harris, "A Functional Classification of Cities in the United States," <u>The Geographical Review</u>, 33 (1943), p. 88.)

Figure 14-1

262

and communication industries employ at least 11 percent of the labor force, (4) *diversified* cities, where the census data yield no clear-cut, paramount function, (5) *mining* towns, where more than 15 percent of the workers are employed by mining industries, (6) *university* cities, whose chief industry is constituted by the campus of a large educational institution, (7) *resort-retirement* towns, where the majority of the gainfully employed are in the service of recreational or retirement oriented establishments, and (8) *political* centers, including not only Washington, D.C., but also a number of state capitals.

It is not surprising that many geographers have tried to modify the Harris classification. This can easily be done by adding new classes of cities, or by suggesting changes in the quantitative boundaries used by Harris to establish his system—which were admittedly somewhat arbitrary. But despite these reconsiderations, the pattern shown on Figure 14-1 stayed much the same, and is still quite current. Manufacturing cities of both classes (M' and M) are heavily concentrated in the Northeastern United States, and in the North American heartland generally. Retailing centers, on the other hand, tend to lie outside this manufacturing zone and, with wholesale cities, are concentrated in a wide belt that extends from north to south across the country from North Dakota to Texas. Diversified cities show a stronger concentration in the eastern half of the country; transportation centers lie both along the coast and along major rivers, and in places where railroads converge. University towns, as the map shows, are especially preva-

New York City: wholesaling, manufacturing, and transportation center.

lent in the midsection of the country, where many small towns are dominated by large universities. Resort-retirement towns, predictably, concentrate in the southern, warmer sections of the United States. And finally, mining towns are associated (of course) with mineral deposits—mainly the coalfields.

Since the Harris classification was proposed, a number of other systems have been suggested, all seeking to improve on that effort. This has not proved to be an easy task: the Harris article of 1943 has become something of a classic in the literature of urban geography. In 1955, Professor H. J. Nelson published an article entitled "A Ser-

vice Classification of American Cities," in which he made an effort to overcome a problem with the Harris classification: its lack of accommodation for multifunctional cities. In the Harris classification, cities would specialize in only one economic sphere (except in the Diversified category), when it was very evident that other functions were also important. For example, there is more wholesaling in New York or Chicago than in many of those cities classified as Wholesale Cities—but you will not find New York or Chicago mapped as wholesale cities in Figure 14-1. That is because other functions of these two great cities are similarly so important that the only feasible class to put them in was—diversified cities. Nelson, trying to overcome that difficulty, developed a more complex statistical formula based, like that of Harris, on employment figures expressed as percentages of the labor force. Essentially, Nelson calculated how far cities exceeded the average derived from all available data for all cities. This gave a more objective measure of specialization than Harris had achieved: Chicago, for example, could score high as a wholesale city, a manufacturing city, *and* as a transportation center.

Is this search for a satisfactory classification system really worth the effort? Urban geographers feel it is. Apart from their effect in stimulating a continuing debate over specifics, the Harris and Nelson systems have thrown light on the nature (and changing character) of functional specialization of cities, their interaction with hinterlands, and the directions of their growth.

In the foregoing discussion we have referred several times to the hinterlands of cities, their service areas. To such regions, the cities are *central places;* even a village is a central place to a small area. How, then, do these service areas relate to each other? Do they overlap? Do towns of approximately the same size lie about the same distance away from each other? What rules govern the arrangement of urban places on the landscape?

In 1933 a geographer named W. Christaller published a book entitled *The Central Places of Southern Germany.* In this volume, which was not translated into English until the mid-1950s, Christaller laid groundwork for central place theory. Addressing himself to questions such as those we just raised, he attempted to develop a model that would show just where central places in the hierarchy (hamlets, villages, towns, and cities) would lie with respect to one another. In his effort to discover the laws that govern this distribution, Christaller began with a set of assumptions. The surface of the region would be flat, without physical barriers. Soils would have equal, unvarying fertility. He also assumed an even population distribution and purchasing power, and a uniform transport system permitting direct travel from each settlement to the other. Finally, Christaller assumed that a constant maximum distance or range for the sale of any item produced in a town would prevail in all directions from that town.

Christaller's idea was to cal-culate the nature of the central place system that would develop under such idealized circumstances, and then to compare that "model" to the real world situation, explaining variations and exceptions. Some places, he realized, would be more "central" than others. The central functions of larger towns will cover regions *within* which smaller places with lesser central functions nevertheless exist. What was needed, Christaller reasoned, was a means to calculate the degree of centrality of various places. In order to do this, Christaller identified *central goods and services* as those provided only at a central place. These would be the goods and services a central place would make available to the consumers in a surrounding region, as opposed to services that might be available anywhere, without focus, and unlike those that are produced for distant and even foreign markets and are thus of no relevance to the local consumers. Next came the question of the *range of sale* of such central goods and services: the distance people would be willing to travel to acquire them. The limit would lie halfway between one central place and the next place where the same product is manufactured and sold at the same price—for under the assumptions Christaller used, a person would not be expected to go 51 kilometers to one place to buy an item if it were possible to go only 49 kilometers to another.

Figure 14-2

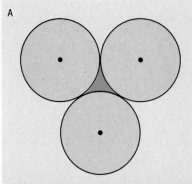

A

The unserved areas are shown in orange

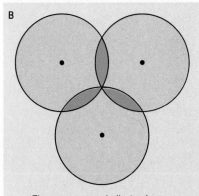

B

The orange areas indicate places where the conditions of monopoly would not be fulfilled

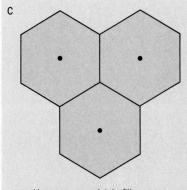

C

Hexagons completely fill an area without overlap

Each central place, therefore, has a complementary region, within which the town has a monopoly on the sale of certain goods, since it alone can provide such goods at a given price and within a certain range of travel. From what we have just said, it would seem that such complementary regions would be circular in shape. But when we construct the model on that basis, problems arise: either the circles adjoin and leave "unserved" areas, or they overlap, and when they do there is no longer a condition of monopoly. These two problems, and the solution (a system of hexagonal regions) are sketched on Figure 14-2.

Now Christaller proceeded to derive his model for the spatial arrangement of central places. To illustrate the result, let us take a specific case. Assume that a certain central place provides 100 different kinds of goods and services. We rank these in order of importance from 1 to 100. Thus the product ranked number 1 will draw consumers from the widest area and thus have the largest "limit," while that ranked number 100 has the latest importance and the smallest service area. If we now placed five central places, each producing 100 central goods and services (Christaller called these G places) 100 kilometers away from each other, the following would happen. The hexagonal region shown in black on Figure 14-3 surrounding the centrally positioned city marks the limit of the product ranked number 1. The product ranked number 2 has a limit marked by a circle just inside the hexagon, and number 3 (not shown) has a limit again slightly smaller than that. Now when we draw circles for each of the 100 products, we begin to leave an area outside of, say, circle 20 or 21 where there would be no service (in theory, of course). By the time we draw the circle for item ranked number 30, this "unserviced" area is large enough to accommodate its own hexagon and central place, and so a new network of places (the red-lined set surrounding the towns on Figure 14-3) is born. Christaller called these secondary centers B places. Now both G places (our cities) and B places (our towns) provide goods ranked 31 and lower and as we proceed and reach circles for products ranked somewhere between 55 and 60, we find that the situation we just described repeats itself, and once more there is room for a system of central places of still lower order, in this case the system centered on the villages, called K places by Christaller. On Figure 14-3, the ultimate projection of the model also includes hamlets, so that a fourth set of complementary regions emerges.

Christaller was aware that many factors in the real world would operate to distort his model. But his book brought on a storm of discussion and debate—and the debate is still

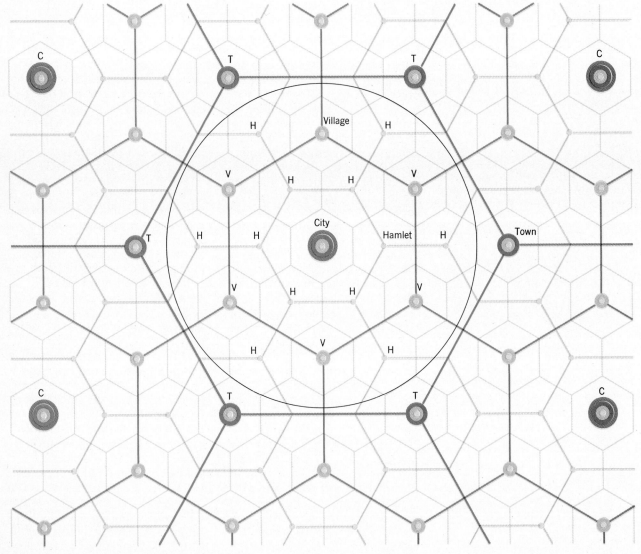

Figure 14-3 Christaller's model of a central place hierarchy. The *cities* represent Christaller's G places, the *towns* (T) are what he called B places, the *villages* (V) are his K places.

going on today, after numerous modifications of the system. Immediately, there were geographers who saw hexagonal systems everywhere; others saw none at all. Soon there were attempts to alter the Christaller model, and to relate it to various areas of the world. Christaller himself joined the debate; in 1950 he published a new volume entitled *The Foundations of Spatial Organization in Europe.* He insisted that he had been correct all along: "When we connect the metropolitan areas with each other through lines, and draw such a network of systems on the map of Europe, it indeed becomes eminently clear how the metropolitan areas everywhere lie in hexagonal arrangements" (pp. 17–18).

Christaller may have been overly optimistic about the validity of his model, but he set the pattern for future research on central places. Such research has focused on the nature and impact of city size on the model (since a large city dominates smaller urban places, even for the same product or service), the effects of physical barriers and cultural differences, the cumulative, agglomerative effect of time, the failure of people to make rational decisions (some people *will* travel those 51 kilometers instead of 49), and other matters. After all, the hexagons need not be perfectly regular; they could be dis-

torted, having some short and some longer sides, and maybe the distorted model comes closer to reality than the regular one. Changes in transportation, consumers' ability to travel ever longer distances, advertising and image making for places and products, and changing demands of the market have loosened the bonds between central places and their immediate hinterlands. Earlier we referred to the impact a superhighway-bypass can have on the service center whose main street formerly carried all that traffic. The town declined, but competition can also stifle a small settlement and render it virtually dormant. On the other hand, a small town may find itself increasingly in the orbit of a nearby large city, and may become a satellite—resulting in the opposite kind of change. Obviously, then, Christaller's model should be viewed as a beginning—but it was an important one. If you look at the periodical literature in geography these days, you will see numerous articles in which geographers are trying to unravel the complexities which Christaller, through his assumptions, circumvented. In the process, our understanding of the forces that influence the distribution of urban places and their growth and decline is strengthened.

A look at the world distribution of major urban centers (Fig. 14-4) quickly suggests that Christaller's proposed regularity is more the exception than the rule. Although many large cities do lie well apart, many others have developed so close together that they are coalescing. In North America, that process is making a vast urban complex of the eastern seaboard from Boston to Washington (the name Bosnywash has been applied to this urban region). This enormous megalopolis, the greatest of its kind in the world, includes also New York, Newark, Philadelphia, Baltimore, and a host of smaller cities; it counts more than 40 million inhabitants and continues to grow, pushing suburbs into the countryside and absorbing towns and villages. Another such a megalopolis, in a less advanced stage of development, extends from Detroit and environs to Pittsburgh, and includes Cleveland, Toledo, Akron, and Youngstown. Farther to the west, a Chicago-Milwaukee conurbation is emerging. And on the West Coast, two urban clusters of megacity proportions are evolving: the largest, centered on Los Angeles, counts nearly 15 million residents and the other, of which San Francisco is the focus, about half that number.

In Europe, England's conurbations are approaching megalopolitan unification: London and immediate environs count over

267

13 million residents, and London lies at the center of a population cluster approaching 20 million. The cities of South Wales and the Midlands lie but a short distance away. On the European mainland, a major urban complex is emerging in Western West Germany, in the Ruhr-Rhine zone, including cities such as Düsseldorf, Essen, Frankfurt, and Stuttgart. In the Netherlands, planning for a triangular megalopolis (Amsterdam-Rotterdam-The Hague) is a matter of national priority; an attempt is being made to guide this megalopolis, already being called *Randstad*, into a twenty-first-century megacity model, with parks, spacious housing, good communications and public transportation, and optimal social services. Belgium, too, is experiencing the development of a coalescing urban complex, with Brussels and Antwerp the twin foci.

Other major urban agglomerations in Europe include the region centered on Paris, the less advanced but developing Northern Italian region, and the complex that extends from East Germany's Saxony to Poland's Silesia. Elsewhere there are major individual cities, such as Moscow, Leningrad, and Madrid, but not yet a true multicity, urban region. Of course, we should keep the scale of things in Europe in perspective, and Figure 14-4 is worth another look

Figure 14-4

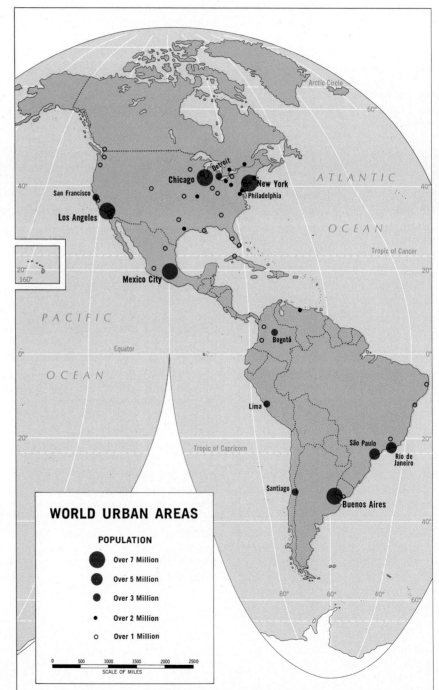

WORLD URBAN AREAS

POPULATION

- Over 7 Million
- Over 5 Million
- Over 3 Million
- Over 2 Million
- Over 1 Million

SCALE OF MILES
0 500 1000 1500 2000 2500

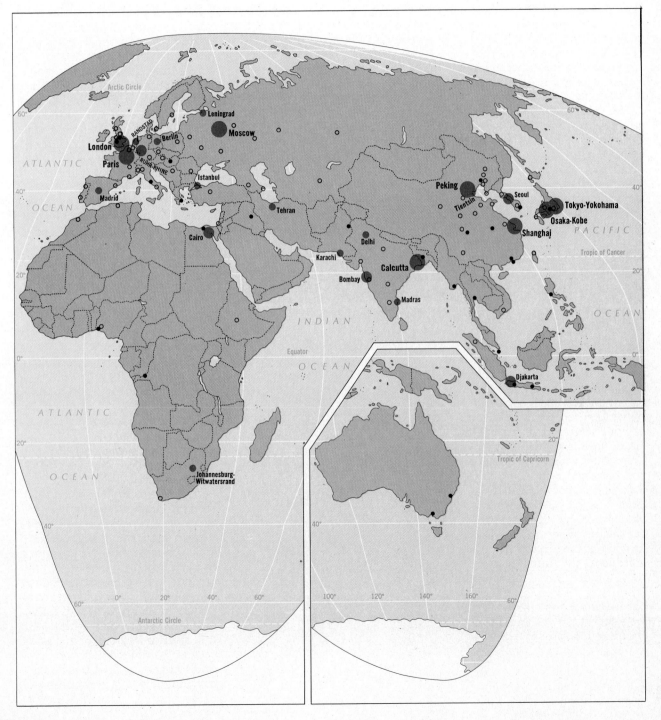

Arctic Circle

60°

Leningrad

Moscow

RANDSTAD

Berlin

London

Paris

RUHR-RHINE

ATLANTIC

40°

OCEAN

Madrid

Istanbul

Tehran

Peking

Tientsin

Seoul

Tokyo-Yokohama

Osaka-Kobe

Shanghai

40°

PACIFIC

Cairo

Delhi

Tropic of Cancer

Karachi

20°

Calcutta

OCEAN

Bombay

Madras

INDIAN

Equator

OCEAN

0°

Djakarta

ATLANTIC

20°

Tropic of Capricorn

40°

OCEAN

Johannesburg-Witwatersrand

0°   20°   40°   60°   100°   120°   140°   160°

Antarctic Circle

269

from this point of view. The whole urbanized area, from Britain's Midlands to West Germany's Ruhr-Rhine region, extends over an area not much larger than North America's megalopolis. Yet Europe's political fragmentation and cultural diversity lead us to identify discrete units within its huge urban core.

The only other area where true megalopolitan development is occurring is Japan. The Tokyo-Yokohama and Osaka-Kobe conurbations rival those of Europe and the United States, and they continue to grow by accretion and absorption.

This is not to suggest that the urbanizing trend that has generated Bosnywash and Randstad is not being experienced in other areas of the world. Johannesburg (South Africa) lies at the center of a smaller-scale megalopolis that includes several medium-sized cities along the Witwatersrand and that eventually will incorporate Pretoria to the north and the Northern Orange Free State to the south. But, in general, urbanization outside Europe, the United States, and Japan has not reached comparable proportions. Even where a high percentage of the population is urbanized, the numbers are not large enough to create huge urban complexes: Australia has several large cities, but no megalopolis as yet. In Argentina, Buenos Aires is a city

of world proportions, but its nearest substantial neighbor, Rosario, lies 200 miles (320 kilometers) away. The area between São Paulo and Rio de Janeiro (Brazil) does not have the urban development to support the emergence, in the near future, of a coalescing supercity. That mirrors the situation in the UDCs: large cities tend to stand alone, islands in a rural-dominated scene.

Cities are not simply disorganized, random accumulations of buildings and people. Instead, they have *functional structure*—they are spatially organized to perform their functions as places of commerce, production, education, residence, and much more. Just as Christaller raised questions about the spacing of cities and towns, we could prepare a model of the internal layout of the "ideal" city. How and where are the various sectors of the city positioned with respect to each other? If there are forces that govern the distribution of central places on the landscape, then surely there are forces that affect the way cities are internally organized? It is not difficult to think of one of these forces: the price of land. This tends to be highest in the central city, and then declines irregularly outward. So you would not look for a spacious residential area near the heart of a city, nor for the downtown area on a city's periphery!

Just by using these terms—residential area, downtown—we reveal our awareness of the existence of a regional structure in cities. Yes, cities have regions. When you refer to downtown, or to "the suburbs," or to the municipal zoo, you are in fact referring to urban regions, where certain functions are predominantly performed (retailing, residing, and recreation, in the three just mentioned). All these urban regions or zones, of course, lie adjacent to another and together make up the total city. But *how* are they arranged?

Is there any regularity, any recurrent pattern to the alignment of the various zones of the city, perhaps reflecting certain prevailing processes of urban growth? In other words, do the city's regions constitute the elements of an urban structure that can be recognized to exist in every urban center, perhaps with modifications related to such features as the city's particular site, its size, functional class, and so forth?

One way to go about this problem is to study the layout of a large number of cities, to compare resulting maps, and to determine recurrent features. In very general terms, we would soon conclude that cities have *central* zones, consisting mainly of the central business district, and *outer* zones, where the sprawling suburbs and shopping centers lie. between the central and outer zones it is often possible to discern a *middle* zone, an ill-defined, often rather mixed and disorganized region. In the middle zone, change is frequently evidenced, as in the deterioration of housing and the development of slums.

This suggests that cities have a certain concentricity in their structures, and that impression was first formalized by Professor E. W. Burgess nearly 50 years ago when he studied the layout of Chicago. Although

Central and middle zones of Los Angeles, California.

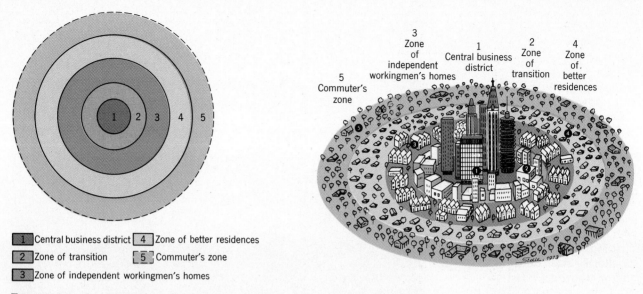

Central business district   4 Zone of better residences

2 Zone of transition   5 Commuter's zone

3 Zone of independent workingmen's homes

Figure 14-5 A schematic and oblique view of Burgess' concentric structural model of urban morphology.

downtown Chicago lies near Lake Michigan, and the whole urban area is therefore semicircular in shape, Burgess nevertheless suggested that his *concentric zone theory* applied here as in most American cities. Burgess recognized five concentric zones in the city rather than three, counting the central business district as the innermost zone. This, the heart of the city, contains shops, offices, banks, theaters, and hotels; the larger the city, the more likely is the CBD to be divided into several districts of specialization, such as a theater district, a financial district, and perhaps even an area of warehousing and wholesaling, near the edge of the CBD. The CBD (region 1, Fig. 14-5) is the zone marked by high land values and by maximation of floor space through the building of skyscrapers. Transport lines converge on

this central zone, disgorging tens of thousands of workers into streets that bustle with traffic during peak hours . . . but may be nearly deserted late at night, after the theaters are closed.

Surrounding the CBD, Burgess pointed out, lies a transitional area, a zone of residential deterioration (and the scene of urban renewal programs), marked also by the encroachment of business and light manufacturing. This is region 2 (Fig. 14-5), a zone of persistent urban blight these days, of tenements and slums, inadequate services, and deepening dislocation. Still farther out from the CBD lies what Burgess called the "zone of working men's homes," region (3), a ring of closely built but adequate residences of the urban

labor force. The next zone consists of middle-class residences (4), suburban areas that are characterized by greater affluence and spaciousness. At this distance from the CBD, local business districts (shopping centers) make their appearance. Now we reach what we might call the "urban fringe," the commuters' zone (5) consisting of communities that are, in effect, dormitories for the CBD, where most of the economically active residents go to work. Here lie some of the urban area's highest-priced residential areas. Here, too, urban and rural areas interdigitate, and here lies the leading edge of the advancing city. Small rural towns may be engulfed by the rising tide of urbanization.

Burgess suggested that the zones he identified are not static, but are mobile and encroach on each other. As a city grows, he argued, the whole system expends outward, so that CBD functions invade region (2), and the characteristics of zone (2) begin to affect zone (3), and so forth. Zone (5), thus, will lie even farther from the center of the city. This, certainly, is something we can see occurring in many cities—but the Burgess theory also has its shortcomings when put to the test of real situations. It does not account adequately for heavier industries in cities; these certainly do not form a ring around the whole city center, but tend to be concentrated in one or two transportrelated areas. Certain urban facilities cannot move outward, as the Burgess concept of outward mobility would require: railroad yards, port facilities, and large industries tend to remain entrenched. In fact, as Chicago itself has shown, this is true even of certain residential areas, especially when they have a strong cultural-national flavor. On the other hand, the experiences with airports tend to confirm Burgess' idea. Chicago's Midway Airport was an edge-of-town field when he did his study, and it grew into one of the nation's busiest. Then urban sprawl overtook Midway, and more distant O'Hare Airport was built. Next time you fly into Chicago, note what is happening to all that open space there used to be around O'Hare. Some decisions will soon have to be made: an airport still farther away, to be added to existing facilities, or perhaps an airport out in Lake Michigan, on an artificial island.

Urban residential and business encroachment on a major airport: the case of Midway, Chicago.

274

A more specific objection to the Burgess concept casts doubt on its central theme: its concentric framework. Do cities really have concentric structures? When you travel into a city via a major roadway, you will note that certain functions tend to cluster along that major artery. Rarely do you see expensive homes along truck-congested, four-lane highways; rather you see factories, auto sales, and the like. This means that arterial routes tend to interrupt Burgess' concentric scheme—so much so that it is possible to argue that the major structural features of a city are pie-shaped rather than concentric. And this is precisely what economist H. Hoyt concluded in his study of urban layout (*The Structure and Growth of Residential Neighborhoods in American Cities*, 1939). He proposed a *sector theory* of urban structure, based on data specifically related to residential land use. Hoyt showed that much could be learned from an analysis of one aspect of urban life: the rent that people in residential areas pay. Following Burgess' theory, we would conclude that rent consistently increases with distance from the CBD, since the quality of housing is lowest in zone (2) and highest in zones (4) and (5).

Hoyt, however, argued that a low-rent area could extend all the way from the center of a city to its outer edge. Similarly, high-rent "sectors" could be recognized in cities he studied, flanked by intermediate-rent areas. For example, a high-rent sector might extend along a very fast, convenient, uncluttered route into the city center (rapid transit or highway), but where communications were somewhat less efficient this would be reflected by intermediate-quality residential areas.

When we view the whole urban structure of any city we may know fairly well, we can probably discern a pie-shaped arrangement of urban zones. Industrial plants may be concentrated along one or several arteries that connect the city to raw material supplies and hinterland markets. A low-rent residential sector may adjoin this industrial complex; a high-quality residential sector may fan outward from the central city in another part of town. Major transport lines may be bunched so closely together that a transport sector can be recognized (Fig. 14-6). A major university and several schools can also form a discrete sector, as our map suggests. As is so often the case when conflicting theories exist, it is perhaps possible to discern elements of both concentricity and sectorial development in the city you know well.

Still another kind of urban structure may be recognized. In 1945, Professors C. D. Harris and E. L. Ullman, having concluded that both the concentric and sector theories left unsolved problems, proposed a theory that holds that cities consist of a number of discrete areas that form and evolve around separate nuclei. Once again, the idea arose from something we can see every day as we live in or visit cities: the CBD is losing its dominant position as the undisputed nucleus of the city, and it is getting competition from other, vigorously growing business centers that are, in effect, secondary nuclei. Thus the *multiple nuclei theory* proposes that a city, especially a large city, may

Transport sector of Seattle, Washington. Note the penetration of this transport-dominated zone, all the way to the central city.

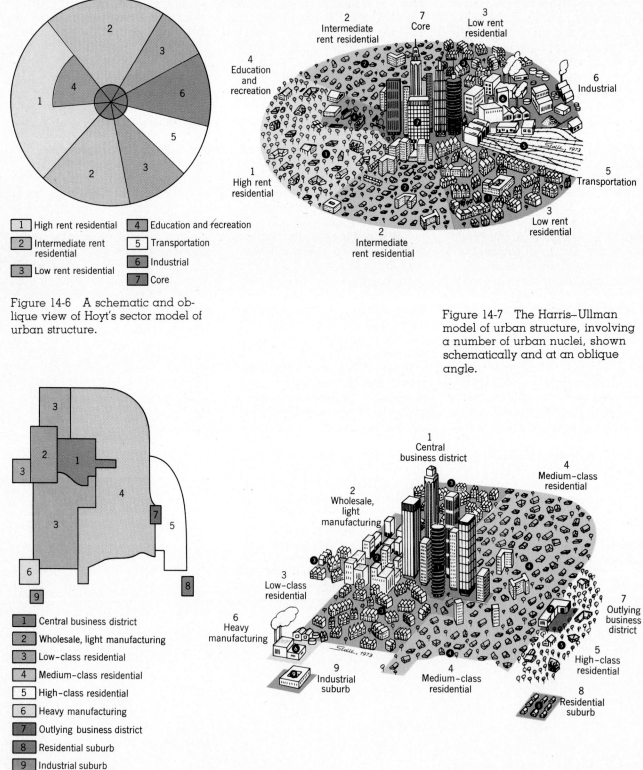

Figure 14-6 A schematic and oblique view of Hoyt's sector model of urban structure.

1 High rent residential
2 Intermediate rent residential
3 Low rent residential
4 Education and recreation
5 Transportation
6 Industrial
7 Core

Figure 14-7 The Harris–Ullman model of urban structure, involving a number of urban nuclei, shown schematically and at an oblique angle.

1 Central business district
2 Wholesale, light manufacturing
3 Low-class residential
4 Medium-class residential
5 High-class residential
6 Heavy manufacturing
7 Outlying business district
8 Residential suburb
9 Industrial suburb

grow and develop not around just one focus, but several. These several foci include not only the CBD itself and subsidiary business centers, such as large shopping malls, but any other element—a university, a port, or a government complex—that can stimulate urban growth and attract other functions. In their diagram (Fig. 14-7), Harris and Ullman suggest schematically what such a city might look like; note that there is none of the regularity of the Burgess and Hoyt models. A city that comes to mind immediately in this context is Los Angeles, but nucleated development of this sort is occurring in most of the world's larger cities today.

Even the multiple nuclei theory fails, however, to account for all the spatial properties of the modern city, and it shares with its two predecessors the problem that it is perhaps an excessive oversimplification of the situation in today's huge conurbations. Still, the next time you spend time in a large urban area—perhaps the place where your university or college is located—try to discern the elements of urban structure and relate them to the models we have just discussed (perhaps using a foldout street map available at gasoline stations as your base for recording observations). You are likely to find the exercise quite interesting, and perhaps you can produce your own theory of urban structure, integrating the theories already proposed. At the very least, you will get to know the layout of your urban environment a great deal better!

Essay: Crisis in the Inner City

The inner city in America has become a place of crisis, of tenements, dirty air, polluted waterways, violence, and decay. New York typifies the situation: here nearly three million black Americans are crowded into apartment buildings, averaging six stories high, that were built as walkups during the late nineteenth and early twentieth century. Most of those buildings are old, unsanitary, and worn out. Many are rat infested. Yet the apartments here are overfilled with people who must live with this discomfort and who cannot escape the vicious cycle that put them there. And still Harlem becomes more, not less crowded as the years pass, as population growth and immigration continue unabated. Nor is urban renewal, tried in so many places these days, always the answer. In the poverty of ghetto and slum life, the neighborhood, social structure, and life-style are nevertheless something of value. The construction of high rises and the relocation of the people may so disrupt that sense of community that the liabilities ultimately outweigh the assets, and people feel themselves to be no better off than they were before.

Spend a night in the downtown area of an American city, and compare your experience with a similar one in Europe—in Paris, Amsterdam, or Hamburg. In those European cities, the streets are busy late at night, lights are on in windows above shopping streets, in apartment buildings. In the American city, the streets are quiet and dark. Except for some activity in theater districts, and in such areas as Atlanta's Underground or Chicago's near North Side, the streets are dormant, buildings dark. Why the difference? One major contrast lies in the continuing residential function of the downtown area in many European cities. The skyscraper has made its appearance, and some European cities are taking on American aspects architecturally (central Rotterdam, for example), but where the war did not destroy the inner city, old patterns of mixed retailing and residential living still prevail. Thus downtown stays alive, and its continuity is reflected by old establishments, always dependent on local, neighborhood patronage that still survives. Thus what is happening in the American city may not be symptomatic of Western cities in general, but a regional phenomenon born of the special circumstances of American society. By building exclusive, expensive high-rise apartments near the central city (Chicago's Marina Towers, for instance), attempts are now being made to lure the better-off residents back into the downtown area. But the rising prices of land have driven the bulk of those who might have remained—the broad population base the heart of the city needs—away. So the downtown region lies surrounded by the sickest sector of the urban complex, whose diseases spill over into the unsafe, deserted concrete canyons.

If this seems an overly pessimistic appraisal, it may be because you have not experienced the circumstances of life in the cities' inner areas. The most positive, optimistic descriptions of the condition of the inner cities are written in the libraries of comfortable suburban homes, and in some government offices. The kind of furor that was unleashed in America's cities during the 1960s did not come about accidentally—nor have the causes been eliminated.

Three prominent problems beset the American city as it struggles to combat its ills: government, environment, and communication. Declining revenues and increasing dissatisfaction among the Black population combine to render city administrations impotent; schools are overcrowded, services get worse instead of better, housing projects lag, law and order break down. Not only do Black urban residents face residential and occupational discrimination; they find that poverty also means political weakness as they are unable to stop their living space from being torn apart for the construction of expressways—along which the suburban white worker travels back and forth to his downtown job every day. Despite all efforts to reverse the prevailing trend, the crisis in which the large cities find themselves is deepening still. Government is enmeshed in endless complications; it is divided and duplicated, and coordination is lacking. Planning on an integrated, overall basis, with long-range objectives such as those of Holland's Randstad, is practically impossible, for there is little cooperation in multigovernmental urban regions.

In the process, it is not just the city's buildings that degenerate. Urban areas where industries and other plants (power generators, for example) cluster suffer from environmental deterioration. The natural climate is modified, the air is less pure, atmospheric circulation fails, noise and smell and ugliness assail the senses. The city's waterways are fouled by minicipal, industrial, and even recreational wastes. Water shortages and power failures occur. Land for recreation, parks, waterfronts, playgrounds is being taken over for business and financial gain. Zoning boards yield to pressure and the urban scene become a patchwork of inconsistencies.

Inevitably all this has an impact on the city's accessibility, its internal circulation. To function adequately, to be a reasonable place to live and work, a city must have good accessibility. The city provides advantages to various functions by permitting them to cluster closely together. But that advantage disappears when the system of contact and communication breaks down. We have seen this happen: larger numbers of people in faraway suburbs need over wider, multilane ex-

Sunday street scenes in busy Madrid (top) and almost empty Atlanta (bottom).

pressways. The expressways are built, but somehow the volume of automobiles seems to increase faster than the carrying capacity of the roads. A four-lane expressway is so congested that six lanes become necessary; no sooner are the six lanes put in service than they become just as congested as the four lanes were a short time ago. In America's widely sprawling cities, mass transit systems cannot be expected to solve such problems altogether either. In such places as New York and Chicago the subways and trains carry thousands of commuters, but the highways are terribly overcrowded nevertheless.

The mushrooming use of the automobile, and the resultant personal mobility of large numbers of the population, has contributed greatly to the problems now confronted by the cities. Some cities have already experimented with schemes that would ban cars from certain downtown areas (the Mayor of New York closed Fifth Avenue to traffic some years ago, just for one day, and made that bustling street a shopping mall for pedestrians only); parking problems have led to drastic tow-away measures. These measures, however, are mere stopgap answers when much more comprehensive action is needed. In the northeastern megalopolis, the outer fringes of cities are beginning to meet, and traffic congestion focused on outlying "nuclei" is approaching that of the central city itself. No one could forsee the impact the increased use of the personal automobile would have on the spatial characteristics of our cities, and the implementation of potential solutions is difficult for reasons we noted earlier—principal integrated planning being the one.

Our cities are the foci of our culture, still the centers of production, innovation, administration, and the arts. But our cities also mirror our society's major problems. People who can afford it need to work in the cities but want to live as far away from them as they can. People who cannot afford to live away from the city must face the realities of a deteriorating environment. The cities assimilated East and West Europeans into the American life-style, but they failed to achieve the same with their latest immigrants—black Americans. They fragmented spatially, and thus came to reflect society as a whole. Ours at present remains a broken society, whose healing must start where the problem is most acute: in the great urban areas of America.

Reading

Much reading on settlement and house forms is scattered throughout the geographical literature. A good place to start is the section entitled "The American House" in W. Zelinsky's *Cultural Geography of the United States* (Prentice-Hall, Englewood Cliffs, N.J., 1973). F. Kniffen's article "Folk Housing: Key to Diffusion," appeared in the *Annals of the Association of American Geographers*, Vol. 55, December, 1965. Another useful source is A. Rapoport, *House Form and Culture* (Prentice-Hall, Englewood Cliffs, N.J., 1969). Among additional articles and books, see W. Zelinsky, "The Log House in Georgia," *The Geographical Review*, Vol. 43, April, 1953; J. E. Rickert, "House Facades: a Tool of Geographic Analysis," *Annals of the Association of American Geographers*, Vol. 57, June, 1967; J. J. Winberry, "The Log House in Mexico," *Annals of the Association of American Geographers*, Vol. 64, March, 1974; and parts of *Colonial New England* (Oxford, New York, 1975) by Douglas R. McManis.

The problems of urban-industrial decentralization and its complicated side effects are discussed by A. Pred in a number of articles including "Industrialization, Initial Advantage, and American Metropolitan Growth" in *The Geographical Review*, Vol. 55, April, 1965, and *Major Job-Providing Organizations and Systems of Cities*, Association of American Geographers, Washington, 1974. For a discussion of the urban complex on the northeastern seaboard of the United States, see Jean Gottmann's *Megalopolis* (M.I.T., Cambridge, 1961), still a fascinating account. An introduction to urban geography is *The North American City* (Harper & Row, New York, 1971) by M. Yeates and B. Garner; you may also want to consult a book by R. E. Murphy, *The American City* (McGraw-Hill, New York, 1974). D. Herbert's *Urban Geography: a Social Perspective* (Praeger, New York, 1972) also contains much that is of interest, and your library will prove that a host of readers have been published in recent years, all dealing with urban issues in some particular context M. Levin's *Exploring Urban Problems* (Urban, Boston, 1971) contains some worthwhile segments.

C. Harris' seminal article on the "Functional Classification of Cities in the United States" appeared in *The Geographical Review*, Vol. 33, January, 1943. H. J. Nelson's discussion of a "Service Classification of American Cities" was published in *Economic Geography*, Vol. 31, July, 1955. On models of urban structure, see L. S. Bourne, *Internal Structure of the City* (Oxford, New York, 1971). Also see L. A. Swatridge, *Problems in the Bosnywash Megalopolis* (McGraw-Hill, Toronto, 1972). Arthur E. Smailes' *The Geography of Towns* (Hutchinson, London, 1965) remains something of a classic, and *Suburbia in Transition* (a New York Times assemblage, 1974) chronicles the exodus to the outskirts. An article by C. Harris and E. Ullman, "The Nature of Cities," appeared in the *Annals of the American Academy of Political and Social Science*, Vol. 242, 1945. If you want to go deeply into urban geography, you will find a mass of material in B. Berry and F. Horton, *Geographical Perspectives on Urban Systems*, Prentice-Hall, Englewood Cliffs, N.J., 1970.

PART FOUR
livelihoods

Fishermen of the Niger in Mali drag their nets ashore.

15 Ancient Livelihoods on Land and Sea

We are beyond the Industrial Age, entering a period that may become known as the age of technology—and yet there are societies on this earth who live and work as people generally did thousands of years ago. The revolutionary changes so commonplace to our lives have barely touched the existence of millions of our contemporaries. *We* may be experiencing the postindustrial age, but many Asian farmers, African pastoralists, and South American Indian hunters and food gatherers are not. In this chapter we focus on the ways these peoples made, and continued to make, their living.

The processes whereby food is produced, distributed, and consumed form a fundamental part of every culture. The way land is allocated to individuals or families and the manner in which it is used, the functions of livestock, food preferences and taboos all are elements of culture. Food consumption is often bound up with religion: religious dogma prohibits adherents of Islam from eating pork, Hindu believers from consuming meat. Various forms of partial or total abstinence occur among human cultures, including periodic fasts. Such prescriptions, like the religions that generated them, tend to be old and persistent, and change comes slowly, even when change would seem to be beneficial. The Islamic prohibition against pork deprives millions of people of a useful source of nutrients. India's huge population of holy cattle puts a drain on already inadequate food supplies (Fig. 15-1).

Most of the food we consume comes, directly or indirectly, from the soil. It may be that an age of synthetic foods is approaching, and that the technological age will bring a declining dependence on the soil; but for the time being, practically everything we consume is the product of a process or a sequence of processes that begins in the earth itself. Farming has become the basis of existence all over the world.

Before Farming

There was a time, before the invention of agriculture, when human communities existed by means other than farming. Viewed in the perspective of all human history, farming is actually a rather recent innovation—its beginnings date back a mere 12,000 years and perhaps even less. Even today some societies survive much as they did before agriculture was developed: by hunting and by gathering what food nature has to offer, and sometimes by fishing. Peoples who still subsist this way have been pushed into difficult environments by more powerful competitors (as the Bushmen were by the Bantu and the white man), and their survival seems to involve the weathering of one crisis after another. Drought is the worst enemy. It withers the vegetation, kills or drives off the wildlife, cuts off natural water supplies such as springs.

Still the Bushmen of Southern Africa, the black peoples of Australia, the Indians of Brazil, and several other groups in the Americas, Africa, and Asia manage to sustain themselves in the face of great odds. They do so by knowing and exploiting their environment exhaustively. Every seed, root, fruit, berry, and beetle is sought out and consumed. Hunting is done with poisoned spears, bows and arrows, clubs, and sticks. When the people do not depend on a particular water hole for their own water supply, they may poison it and follow the animals that have drunk there. Thus the community must be on the move much of the time; the group cannot become too large, nor can settlements normally be permanent. But without agriculture and without the practice of storing food in preparation for future periods of shortage (very few hunting-gathering peoples do this), life is difficult. It was easier where the land was more productive, but most of the remaining hunting-gathering peoples have been driven from better-endowed areas into dry, cold, less hospitable environments.

We should, therefore, not be misled into the assumption that the human groups that survive today as hunters and gatherers are entirely representative of early human communities that lived by the same means. While Europe's plainlands opened up following the most recent glacial retreat, our distant ancestors hunted the mammoth and other, plentiful wildlife. They set elaborate traps and cooperated in driving wildlife to areas where it would be vulnerable; communities were much larger than the present-day Bushman clan. And

Figure 15-1

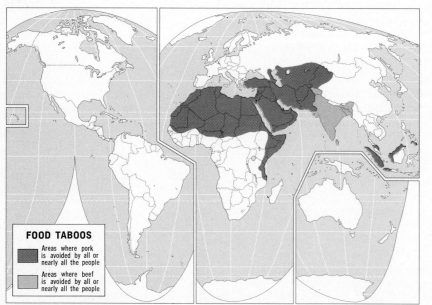

FOOD TABOOS

Areas where pork is avoided by all or nearly all the people

Areas where beef is avoided by all or nearly all the people

very early on there were peoples who subsisted on hunting and gathering and fishing who had learned to specialize to some extent in some area of production. The oak forests of parts of North America provided an abundant harvest of nuts, sometimes enough to last more than a full year, and so Indian communities collected and stored this food source. Other Indians near the Pacific Ocean coast became adept salmon fishers. The buffalo herds of North America also provided sustenance for centuries before being virtually wiped out. In more northern regions, people followed the migrations of the caribou herds. The Eskimo and the Ainu (now confined to Northern Japan) developed specialized fishing techniques.

Members of a Bushman clan in search of food in the Kalahari country of Botswana.

Fishing

It is quite likely that our distant ancestors learned to fish, and added dried fish to their diets, during the warming period that attended the retreat of the last of the Pleistocene glaciers. Perhaps 15,000 to 20,000 years ago, the glaciers melted, sea level began to rise, and coastal flatlands were inundated as the water encroached on what we today call the continental shelves. We may surmise that until this time, coastal waters over most of the earth had been cold and rough, and shorelines marked by steeply dropping relief. Coastal areas were not the most hospitable parts of the human habitat, and marine life was not nearly as plentiful as it was to become.

When glacial melting began and water levels rose, the continental shelves became shallow seas, full of lagoons and patches of standing water. The sun warmed these thin layers of water very quickly, and soon an abundance of marine fauna flourished. Coastal regions became warmer, more habitable places to establish settlements, and numerous communities moved to the water's edge.

Bushman hunters of the Kalahari take their catch back to camp.

Thus we can deduce to some extent the means by which our distant predecessors survived. Undoubtedly certain of the hunting-gathering communities found themselves in more favorable locations than others; for example, it may be that forest margins provided such advantages. There, people could gather food in the forest when hunting yielded poor results, to return to hunting when the opportunities improved again. Possibly those communities could become semisedentary and stay in one place for a length of time, perhaps to create a more or less permanent settlement. That is one of the contributions the development of agriculture made: it permitted people to settle permanently in one location, with assurance that food would be available in seasons and years to come.

There, they were able to harvest all kinds of shellfish, and they learned to cut small patches of standing water off from the open sea, trapping the fish. Equipment was invented to aid in catching fish: harpoons, with which larger fish could be speared, and baskets, suspended in streams where fish were known to run.

In several areas of the world human communities were able to achieve a degree of permanence by combining hunting and fishing with some gathering, and by making use of the migration cycles of fish and animal life set up during the changing climatic regimes. Indian peoples along the North American Pacific coast, Eskimo peoples on Arctic shores, the Ainu of Japan and coastal East Asia, and communities in coastal Western Europe caught the salmon as they swam up rivers and negotiated rapids and falls; huge accumulations of fish bones have been found at prehistoric sites near such locations. When the salmon runs ended they stalked the deer on their annual movements of the spring and fall, trapping them where they would habitually cross the river, in narrow

Fishing village in Senegal, West Africa.

valleys they would traverse each season, or in some other favorable place. The summer salmon runs and the wildlife migrations of fall and spring would leave only the winter to endanger the permanence of the settlement. It had been learned that dried meat could remain edible for

months, and undoubtedly the coldness of winter provided natural refrigeration that delayed spoilage. But the early fishermen and hunters had their bad years too, and sometimes the months of winter brought hunger and death. Such winters forced the riverside dwellers to abandon their settlements in pursuit of the distant herds.

Agricultural Origins

It is likely that human groups began to domesticate plants simultaneously in several different parts of the world. Scholars are still not certain about the sequence of events, but independent invention in areas as widely separated as the Middle East, Central and South America, and Southeast Asia seems plausible. The process itself, which happened between 10,000 and 20,000 years ago, was not a clear-cut "agricultural revolution," as it is sometimes called. It is more likely that people slowly came to realize that it was possible to do more than simply gather wild crops. Perhaps rotten fruit, thrown away of refuse heaps near settlements, began to grow, the plants eventually bearing new crops. Possibly this suggested that roots and plants from the forest could be transplanted to a site near the settlement; roots and tubers could be stuck in the ground and they would "take," adding to the food secured by gathering. Some scholars have suggested that the first cultivation probably occurred in association with some other means of survival, and it has been theorized that the fishing villages of ancient times, which afforded a measure of permanence of settlement, may have been the places where the first agriculture was tried.

It is one thing to plant a root or tuber and leave it to grow, but seeding is quite another. Again, we may assume that seeding and harvesting were learned after the planting of root crops. Seeding involves the gathering of grains from plants, the preparation of a piece of land (and the invention of the tools necessary), then the sowing, followed perhaps by some weeding and general attention to the crop.

Where could agriculture have developed, more than 10,000 years ago? Again, we are compelled to speculate to some extent. In a book entitled *Agricultural Origins and Dispersals* (1952), Carl O. Sauer suggests that Southeast Asia may have been the place where the first farmers lived. He points out that the conditions of natural vegetation, climate, and soils must have been favorable for such a development, and believes that the knowledge about cultivation gained there spread out into China, India, even Africa. Other scholars have described the region of agricultural invention that existed in Middle and South America, where the first cultivation of roots and cuttings also was followed by the more sophisticated practice of seeding. The Middle East, both in North Africa and in Southwest Asia, was another leading region of plant domestication; here lies the famous Fertile Crescent, to which we will refer again later. China's source area (the Hwang-Wei region) also may have been the site of independent agricultural invention. And although it took a long time for scholars to recognize it, Africa, too, shared in the process. Significant areas of plant domestication lay in West Africa and in the East African Great Lakes region (Fig. 15-2).

From these areas of agricultural invention and early development, the new techniques of cultivation diffused to other parts of the world. It is thought that millet, a small-seed grain, was introduced to India from West Africa, and sorgum, another grain crop, from West Africa to China. The watermelon spread from West Africa, first to nearby regions but eventually all over the world. Corn (maize) spread from Middle America into North America; later, after the Portuguese brought it across the Atlantic, it became a staple in much of Africa. The banana came from Southeast Asia, as did a variety of yams. The process of dispersal went slowly for many thousands of years, but the worldwide communications set up with the expansion of Europe during the past 500 years accelerated it greatly.

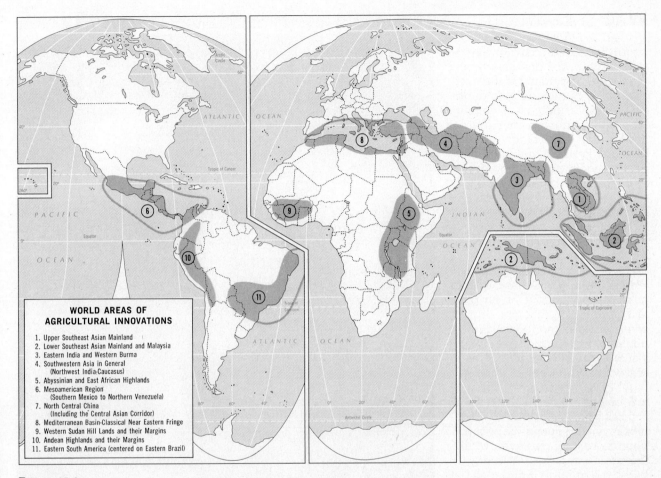

Figure 15-2

291

Animal Domestication

While our distant ancestors learned to plant crops, they also began to keep animals as livestock. Again, we are unsure of the nature and timing of the transition from hunting to animal domestication. Hunting was a mainstay of early human communities for many tens of thousands of years. Perhaps animal domestication came about when communities grew larger and better organized, and more sedentary. Animals became part of the local scene, and were kept as pets or for some other (for example, ceremonial) purpose. Quite possibly animals attached themselves to human settlements as scavengers and even for protection against predators, thus contributing to the idea that they might be tamed and kept. Any visitor to an African wildlife reserve can observe that when night falls, a permanent camp will be approached by certain species (gazelle, zebra, monkeys) that spend the night near and sometimes even within the camp's confines. With daybreak the animals wander off, but the dangers of the next nightfall bring them back. Similar behavior probably brought animals to the settlements of the ancient forest farmers. Hunters might bring back the young offspring of an animal killed in the field and raise it. Such events probably contributed to the emergence of the concept of animal domestication.

Masai herdsmen draw blood from the neck of one of their cattle.

Just when this happened is still a matter for debate. Some scholars believe that animal domestication came earlier than the conscious cultivation of the first plants, but others think that animal domestication began as recently as 8000 years ago—well after the practice of farming had started. In any case, the goat, pig, and sheep became part of a rapidly growing array of domestic animals, and in captivity they changed considerably from the wild state. Archeological research indicates that when such animals as wild cattle are penned in a corral, they develop types different from the original as time goes on. Protection from predators led to the survival of animals that would have been eliminated in the wild, and then inbreeding entrenched the modifications that nature would have wiped out. Our domestic versions of the pig, the cow, and the horse differ considerably from those first kept by our ancestors.

How did the ancient communities select their livestock, and for what purposes was livestock kept? It is thought that wild cattle may have been domesticated first for religious purposes, perhaps because the shape of

their horns looked like the moon's crescent. Apparently cattle were strongly associated with religious ritual from the earliest times, and, as we have noted, there remain societies today where cattle continue to hold a special position as holy animals. But those religious functions may also have led to their use as draft animals and as suppliers of milk. If cattle could pull sledlike platforms used in religious ceremonies, they could also pull plows. If cattle whose calves were taken away continued to produce milk and needed to be milked to provide relief, cattle could be kept for that specific purpose.

The domestication of animals provided early human communities with another new source of food. Whether animal domestication or plant domestication stated first in various parts of the world, soon societies were combining the two and thus lessening their dependence on a single food source.

Shifting Cultivation

The ancient farmers learned to plant crops, but they knew little about soils, fertilizing, or irrigation. It is likely that they had to abandon areas in tropical and subtropical zones after the soils became infertile and the crops stopped growing. Then the farmers would move to another parcel of land, clear the natural vegetation, turn the soil, and try again. This practice of *shifting cultivation*, like hunting and gathering, still goes on. In tropical areas, where the redness of the soil signifies heavy leaching but where luxuriant natural vegetation thrives, a plot of cleared soil will carry a good crop at least one time, perhaps two or three. But then the area is best left alone, to regenerate its natural vegetative cover and to replenish the nutrients lost during cultivation. Several years later the plot may yield a good harvest once again.

Shifting cultivation is a way of life for many more people than is hunting and gathering. Between 150 and 200 million people sustain themselves this way in Africa, Middle America, tropical South America, and in places even in Southeast Asia. At one time in human history this was the chief form of agriculture in the inhabited world, just as hunting and gathering were previously the prevailing modes of existence. It goes by various names: *milpa* agriculture, "patch" agriculture, and so on. As a system of cultivation, it has changed but little over thousands of years of practice.

The process of shifting agriculture involves a kind of natural rotation system in which areas of forest are used without being permanently destroyed. It does not require a nomadic existence by the farmers, because usually there is a central village and parcels of land in several directions, which are worked successively. When the village grows too large and the distances to workable areas become too great, a part of the village's population may move to establish a new settlement some distance away. This implies, of course, that population densities in areas of shifting agriculture cannot be very high; there has to be room. But high population densities were rare in ancient times, and today, shifting agriculture continues in areas where population densities are far lower than, say, in regions such as the Nile delta or the Ganges valley.

Shifting agriculture appears destructive, wasteful, and disorganized to people who are accustomed to more intensive forms of farming. There are not the neat rows of plants, carefully turned soil, precisely laid-out fields. But in fact shifting agriculture conserves both forest and soil, its harvest yields are substantial given the environmental limitations, and it requires better organization than uninitiated observers might imagine. Patch agriculture is a complex adjustment to a fairly delicately balanced set of environmental conditions, and

many an outsider has learned this lesson expensively. European farmers in Africa sometimes cleared the land, seemingly underutilized and so freely available, plowed the soil, and planted their crops. Soon the plants would die, often after only one apparently promising season, and no amount of fertilizer seemingly could restore them. And, of course, there was no way to quickly get the original vegetation back. So the land lay abandoned, barren, unusable to shifting cultivator nor white farmer. The methods of the shifting cultivators have many merits, ancient as they may be.

Subsistence Farming

We tend to think of agricultural geography in terms of cash cropping (that is, farming for sale and profit), plantations, ranches, mechanization, irrigation, and the movement of farm products, marketing, exports and imports, and so on. When we associate certain crops with particular countries, these are usually cash crops: Brazilian coffee, Colombian tobacco, Egyptian cotton, Australian wool, and Argentine beef, for example. But the fact is that a great number of the world's farmers are not involved in corporate agriculture at all. Hundreds of millions of farmers use their plots of land in the first instance to grow enough food to survive, sometimes with only marginal success. Their chief objective is subsistence, not profit. The shifting cultivators are subsistence farmers, as are the nomadic pastoralists who follow their life-sustaining herds of livestock. But the subsistence farmers in many other areas of the world (Fig. 15-3) cannot migrate, nor do they practice patch agriculture. They are confined to a small field of soil, from which they must wrest the means to survive, year after year. And very likely they do not own the soil they tend.

Scholars customarily divide agricultural societies into groups, including "subsistence," "intermediate," and "developed" or, using different terms to express the same idea, "primitive," "traditional," and "modern." Actually, the world's many hundreds of societies lie along a continuum, and these divisions are for purposes of simplification and discussion and are not absolute. Neither is the definition of the term *subsistence* beyond debate. It is sometimes used in the strictest sense of the word, that is, to refer to farmers who grow food only to sustain themselves and their families or communities, who use their natural habitat to find building materials and firewood, and who do not enter into the cash economy of their country at all. Those remaining societies where shifting agriculture is practiced, in remote areas of South and Middle America, Africa, and South and Southeast Asia, would qualify under this definition. On the other hand, farm families living at the subsistence level, but who sometimes sell a small quantity of produce (perhaps to pay taxes imposed by some authority) would not. Yet the term subsistence ought surely to be appropriate to societies where small-plot farmers may be able sometimes to sell a few pounds of grain on the market, but where poor years threaten hunger, where poverty, indebtedness, stagnation, and sometimes tenancy are ways of life. The Indian peoples in the Amazon Basin, the sedentary farmers of Africa's savanna areas, villagers in much of

Figure 15-3

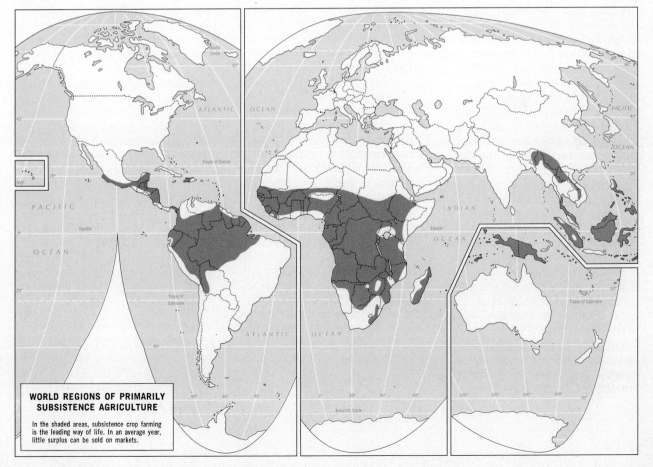

WORLD REGIONS OF PRIMARILY SUBSISTENCE AGRICULTURE

In the shaded areas, subsistence crop farming is the leading way of life. In an average year, little surplus can be sold on markets.

India, and peasants in Indonesia all share subsistence not only as a way of life but also as a state of mind. Experience has taught the farmer and his father and grandfather before him that moments of comparative plenty will be paid for in times of scarcity, and that there is no point in expecting fertilizer to become cheaper and improved seed strains to solve age-old problems.

It is tempting to try to think of ways the subsistence agriculturalist might be helped to escape this situation, when the rewards might be not only higher productivity but also better nutrition, healthier children, and longer life spans. European colonial powers put such thinking into practice in a variety of ways, by demanding taxes that compelled the farmers to raise some funds, by genuine assistance in the form of land-consolidation schemes, soil surveys and crop research, social incentives, and by initiating forced cropping schemes. The colonial powers were in the business to make profit, and it was often frustrating to them that subsistence farming areas could not be made to produce some gain. The forced cropping schemes were designed to solve this problem. If a farming population in a subsistence area cultivated a certain acreage of, say, corn, it was compelled to grow a stipulated acreage of some cash crop—cotton, for example—as well. Whether this cotton would be grown on old land formerly used for grain, or on newly opened land, was the farmers' decision. If no new land was available, the subsistence farmers would simply have to give up food crops for the compulsory cash crops. In many instances severe local famines resulted, and indigenous economies were disrupted and damaged. The colonial powers, however, enforced their cropping schemes regardless. Among the most notorious projects of this kind was the large-scale forced cropping project involving cotton in formerly Portuguese Mozambique.

If you read some of the literature relating to subsistence agriculture, you will find many a scholar wondering, with less profit motive than the colonialists, how "to tempt (subsistence farmers) into wanting cash by the availability of suitable consumer goods," as A. N. Duckworth and G. B. Masefield said in their book *Farming Systems of the World* (1970). We seem to have this compulsion to bring "progress" and "modernization," and one way to do so is to help subsistence farmers to escape their cycle of stagnation. But there are some aspects of subsistence farming we should not lose sight of. Changing those farmers' attitudes could have destructive effects on the society's cohesion. Subsistence brings with it the communal holding of land, and society is of need quite equal: surpluses are shared by all in the community, the accumulation of personal wealth is restricted, and individual advancement at the cost of the group as a whole is limited. As A. H. Bunting wrote in *Change in Agriculture* (1970):

To allocate the land or manage the seasonal migrations, and to survive through hardship and calamity, these societies have to be cohesive, communal and relatively little differentiated socially and economically: the chiefs, elders or elected headmen may be little richer than their fellows—to many of whom they are in addition linked by ties of relationship within the extended family. Mutual dependence, imposed by the environment and the state of the agricultural art, is maintained and reinforced by genetic relationships. The community is enclosed socially and may even tend to be isolated culturally. Landlords and feudal rulers are unknown; the cultivators are poor but free.

Perhaps this describes to some extent the ancient human communities that first developed agriculture as a way of life, and which have shown such amazing durability. Change the economic system, and there will be unpredictable and incalculable modifications in the society, which, indeed, may break apart under the stresses of "progress."

But, of course, it *is* happening. Subsistence land use is changing to more intensive farming, cash cropping, even to the kind of mechanized, almost automated kind of farming in which huge pieces of equipment, not people, do the work and actually touch the soil. In the process, societies from South America to Southeast Asia are profoundly affected. Land once held communally is parceled out to individuals when cash cropping becomes a major element in life. The system that ensured an equitable distribution of resources breaks down. The distribution of wealth becomes stratified, with poor and nearly destitute people at the bottom and rich landowners at the top. It is thought by some scholars that the innovation of irrigation may have contributed to the first differentiation of subsistence society, but there is no doubt that the greatest number of societies that are today "intermediate" find themselves in their present situation as a result of the changes brought to their part of the world by expanding, imperializing Europe. In the aftermath, it is a bit ironic to call these the "traditional" societies, as is often done: they are caught between traditions destroyed when the European invasion came and traditions found inadequate when the Europeans sought to introduce their own.

And so, in our industrializing, modernizing world there are still millions of farmers whose methods of cultivation, whose communities and lifestyles relate quite directly to those prevailing thousands of years ago, when the blessings of agriculture first made life somewhat more secure.

Harvesting wheat in Washington State.

16 Farming in the Modern World

In our changing world we sometimes tend to look on the Industrial Revolution as the beginning of a new era, thereby losing sight of another revolution that began even earlier and had enormous impact on Europe and the world: the agricultural revolution. This was perhaps a less dramatic development than the revolutionary changes that came to Europe's industries, but it had far-reaching consequences nevertheless. After centuries of comparative stagnation and a lack of innovations, farming in Western Europe underwent some major changes. The tools and equipment of agriculture were modified to do their job better. Methods of soil preparation, fertilizing, crop care, and harvesting improved. The general organization of agriculture, storage, and distribution were made more efficient. Productivity increased to meet rising demands; Europe's cities were growing and their growth posed new problems of supply. And then, of course, the products of the Industrial Revolution stimulated the revolution in agriculture. The harnessing of power made mechanization possible, and eventually tractors and other machines did the work done for so long by animals and human hands.

Farming, we know, is by no means possible everywhere on this earth. Vast deserts, steep mountains, frigid polar areas, and other environmental obstacles prevent agriculture over much of our globe. Where farming *is* possible, the land and the soil are not everywhere put to the same use. The huge cattle ranches of Texas represent a very different sort of land use than the dairy farms of Wisconsin—or the rice paddies of Taiwan. Within a few miles of the subsistence life-styles of forested Middle America lie rich plantations whose products travel by boat to North American markets. We can see the differences around out own cities: travel by car or train from Chicago or Cincinnati or St. Louis into the countryside and you can see the land use change. Close to the city, the soil is used most intensively, perhaps for vegetable gardens whose crops can'

299

be sent quickly to the nearby markets. Farther away, the fields are larger and time becomes a lesser factor. The corn fields of Iowa are dotted by grain elevators for storage and shipment, and some of the corn may be consumed not in Chicago or St. Louis but in India or Bangladesh. Still more distant from the cities we enter the pasturelands of the Great Plains, almost an opposite extreme from those vegetable gardens: the land is allocated by the thousands of square miles rather than by the acre.

What factors and forces have combined to produce the spatial distribution of farming systems existing today? This is a very complicated question, to which no complete answer may be possible. It involves not only the effect of different conditions of climate and soil, variations in farming methods and technology, market distributions, and transportation costs, but it also has to do with the domination of the world by an economic structure that favors the developed, Western world: the United States and Canada, Europe, and the Soviet Union. Decisions made by colonial powers in Europe led to the establishment of plantations from Middle America to Malaya, plantations whose products were grown not for local markets but for the consumers in Europe; U.S. companies similarly founded huge plantations in the Americas. The European and Western impact transformed the map of world agriculture just as the pattern of European farming was changed by the agricultural revolution.

The first geographer who tried to identify the factors governing the development of agriculture's spatial patterns was J. H. Von Thünen (1783–1850). Europe during Von Thünen's time was changing quite dramatically: population growth was unprecedented, towns and cities were expanding, and the demand for food increased proportionately. Von Thünen was himself a farmer. In 1810 he acquired a fairly large estate not far from the town of Rostock in the German state of Mecklenburg. As he farmed his lands, Von Thünen became interested in a subject that still concerns economic geographers today: the effects of distance and transportation costs on the location of productive activity. For four decades, he kept meticulous records of all the transactions of his estate, and while doing so he began to publish books on the spatial structure of agriculture. His series, under the title *Der Isolierte Staat* (The Isolated State) in some ways constitutes the foundations of spatial theory. Von Thünen's conclusions are still being discussed and debated today.

Von Thünen called his work *The Isolated State* because he wanted to establish, for purposes of analysis, a self-contained country, devoid of outside influences that would disturb the internal workings of the economy. Thus he created a sort of regional laboratory within which he could identify the factors that influence the location of farms around a central urban area. In order to do this, he made a number of assumptions. First, he stipulated that the soil and climate would be uniform throughout the region. Second, there would be no river valleys or mountains to interrupt a completely flat land surface. Third, there would be a single, centrally positioned city in the "isolated state," which was surrounded by an empty, unoccupied wasteland. Fourth, Von Thünen postulated that the farmers in the "isolated state" would transport their own products to market (no transport companies here), and that they would do so by oxcart, directly overland, straight to the central city. This, as you can imagine, is the same as assuming a system of radially converging roads of equal and constant quality, and, with such a system, transport costs would be directly proportional to distance.

Von Thünen combined these assumptions with what he had learned from the actual data collected while running his estate, and he now asked himself: what would the spatial arrangement of agricultural activities be in his "isolated state?" He concluded that farm products would be grown in a series of concentric zones outward from the market center (i.e., the central city). Nearest to the city those crops would be grown that yielded the highest returns, for example, vegetables; dairying would also be carried on in this innermost zone. Farther away, you would find more durable goods such as potatoes and grains. And eventually, since transport costs to the

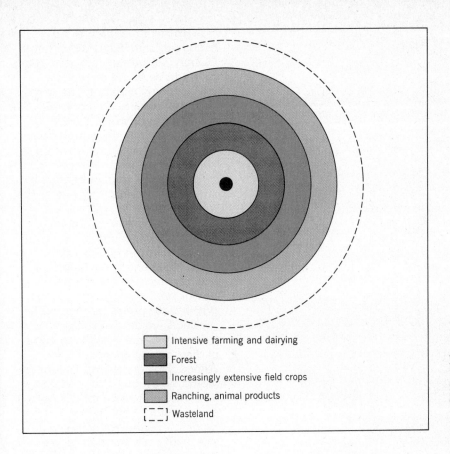

Intensive farming and dairying

Forest

Increasingly extensive field crops

Ranching, animal products

Wasteland

Figure 16-1   Von Thünen's idealized "isolated state." In the center lies the region's focal point, the town that is also the market place for the products grown in the surrounding land–use zones.

city increased with distance, there would come a line beyond which it would be uneconomical to produce crops. There the wasteland would begin.

Von Thünen's model, then, incorporated five zones surrounding the market center (Fig. 16-1). The first and innermost belt would be a zone of intensive agriculture and dairying. The second zone, Von Thünen said, was an area of forest, used for timber and firewood. Next, there would be a third belt of increasingly extensive field crops. A fourth zone was occupied by ranching and animal products. The fifth and outermost zone was the unproductive wasteland. If the location of the second zone, the forest, surprises you, remember that the forest was still of great importance during Von Thünen's time as a source of building materials and fuel. All that was about to change with the onslaught of the Industrial Revolution, but there are lots of towns and cities left in the world that are still essentially preindustrial, as we noted in Chapter 13. When Professor R. J. Horvath went to study Addis Ababa, the capital of Ethiopia, in this context he found a wide and continuous belt of eucalyptus forest surrounding that city, positioned more or less where Von Thünen would have predicted it to be and serving functions similar to

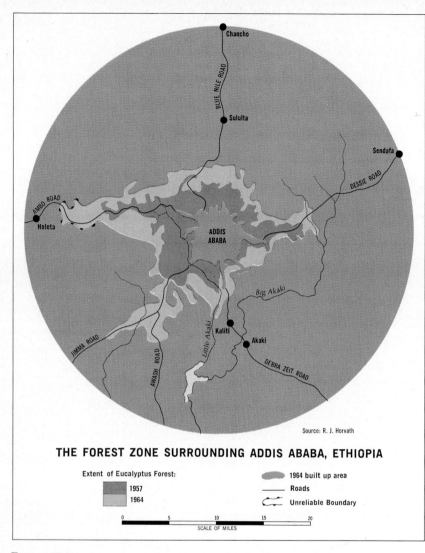

Source: R. J. Horvath

THE FOREST ZONE SURROUNDING ADDIS ABABA, ETHIOPIA

Extent of Eucalyptus Forest:
- 1957
- 1964

- 1964 built up area
- Roads
- Unreliable Boundary

0   5   10   15   20
SCALE OF MILES

Figure 16-2

those attributed to the forest belt of the "isolated state" (Fig. 16-2).

Still, the real world does not present situations comparable to those postulated by Von Thünen. Transport routes serve certain areas better than others. Physical barriers impede the most direct communications. Rivers and mountains disrupt the surface. External economic influences invade every area. Each

of these (and many more) complications serve to distort and modify Von Thünen's conclusions—and yet Von Thünen had a point. We can see modern cities still ringed by recognizable agricultural zones, even though modern transport networks, urban sprawl and suburbanization, and numerous other developments have disrupted older

patterns so much that those zones are sometimes difficult to identify. Some decades ago you might have found economic geographers willing to discern Thünian patterns in the farmlands around, say, Chicago; these days they might talk about remnants of such patterns. But a concentric zonation still prevails around many smaller centers in America, and in many places in the rest of the world.

Let us carry Von Thünen's concept of concentricity some steps farther. In his "isolated state," the consumers in that central city, by their purchasing power and their willingness to pay certain prices for particular products, could determine to a great extent the spatial structure of the farming economy. Although the real-world situation would be greatly changed as Von Thünen's assumptions are swept away, Von Thünen's model nevertheless points to a significant relationship between consumers and producers. By the size and quality of its demands for certain products, an urban market strongly influences the behavior and decisions of farmers in its hinterland. The city is more than a market: it also is a center of political power and a source of economic influence. Farmers who have taxes to pay derive their incomes from the sale of their products on urban markets, but it is not the farmers who decide how high those taxes shall be or what prices their products will command. When regions of the world are struck by food shortages and famines, note that the areas worst affected are *not* the cities, but the rural areas—

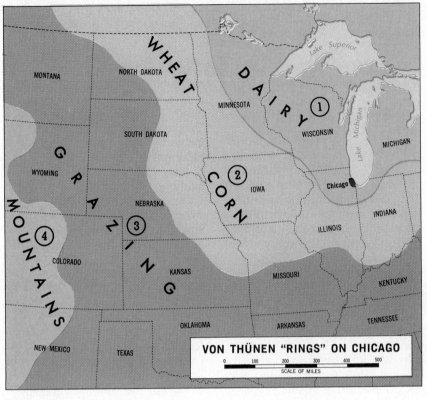

Figure 16-3

The "rings" are not smooth and regular as Von Thünen saw them in theory in his Isolated State, of course. Climatic variations, soil differences, terrain irregularities, river systems, an intensive transport network, and local interruptions such as irrigation projects are but a few of the distorting factors. Still, we can record a certain concentric zonation, with dairying concentrated in the eastern heartland, mixed farming and feed grain production in an adjacent zone, wheat cultivation beyond, and beef cattle and sheep raising still farther away (Fig. 16-3). The cultivation of specialty crops around urban centers and in particularly favored and suitable areas from Florida to California further disrupts an already distorted Thünian pattern, but the fact remains that Von Thünen's fundamental geographic theory is sustained by what we observe in the field.

where, one would imagine, such problems could be staved off by local production. This reflects the power of cities the world over, and it is one of the reasons for the urban inmigration in countries from Brazil to India. When we discussed the transportation and distribution of relief supplies of grain from the United States to India (Chapter 3) we noted that the lion's share went to the largest cities, and that smaller places and rural areas were comparatively deprived. Urban centers dominate rural areas in many ways, and even though the farmers produce the sustenance of city people, it is the city

folk who in large measure control the lives of farmers. Thus Von Thünen's agricultural zones represent decisions by farmers about the use of their land, but those decisions were impelled by requirements and demands made by the urban inhabitants.

If a single urban center can generate certain patterns of land use, a group of cities—a megalopolis—or a large urbanized region has an even wider impact. In North America, we can observe nearly an entire continent oriented toward the population core centered on the great eastern cities (see Chapter 2).

World Patterns

If Thünian patterns of agricultural land use can be discerned around individual cities, urban regions, and even on a whole continent, can world agriculture be interpreted in this context? We know that Argentinian beef is consumed in U.S. homes, as well as Brazilian coffee, Colombian tobacco, and sugar from Caribbean countries. Europeans import tea from Asia, cotton from Africa, wheat from Australia. Cuban sugar goes to the Soviet Union. While Von Thünen was studying his isolated state as a closed system totally unaffected by outside influences, the Europe of Von Thünen's time was in the process of mobilizing much of the world to its own sustenance and comfort. Europe's cluster of colonializing powers functioned much as Von Thünen's central city did, as a market for agricultural products from all around, but with an added dimension: Europe manufactured and sold in its colonies the finished products made from imported raw materials. Thus the cotton grown in Egypt, the Sudan, India, and other countries colonized by Europe was cheaply bought, imported to European factories, made into clothes, which were them exported and sold, often in the very colonies where the cotton had been grown in the first place.

Obviously we should not view world agriculture in the kind of isolation assigned by Von Thünen to his experimental model. The evolution of a world-wide transport network, of ever growing capacity and efficiency, continually changed the competitive position of various activities. The beef industry of Argentina, for example, secured a world market when the invention of refrigerator ships made long-distance transportation possible for what was previously a highly perishable commodity. European colonial powers did not simply permit farmers in their dependencies to decide on the crops they would grow for export to Europe: they frequently imposed the cultivation of specific crops on traditional farmers. American economic power made itself felt in Middle and South America, creating an empire of plantations and orienting production to U.S. markets. Thus the forces tending to distort any world Thünian zonation are many.

And yet we can observe in this world pattern of agriculture, represented by Figures 16-4 to 16-10, elements of the same sort of order Von Thünen recognized in his Isolated State. We have already noted that the Industrial Revolution had a major impact on agriculture, and when we attempt to describe the relationships between the urbanized core areas of the world and agricultural patterns, we should view the urban centers as urban-industrial cores, not merely as markets. To these urban-industrial cores, in Europe, in North America, and in the Soviet Union, flow agricultural (and industrial) raw materials and resources from virtually all parts of the inhabited world. Superimposed on the regional zones and on the continental-scale zonation we saw in North America, therefore, is a world system that also has elements of concentric zonation.

It is important to recognize, as we examine world agriculture in the following pages, that the pattern we observe has come about only in part through the decision-making processes envisaged by Von Thünen. In the Third World, much of the farming (other than for local subsistence) is a leftover from colonial times, but it cannot simply be abandoned, for it continues to provide a source of revenues that are badly needed, even if the conditions of sale to the urban-industrial world are not often favorable. In the Caribbean region, whole national economies depend on sugar exports (the sugar having been introduced by the European invaders centuries ago). Selling the harvest at the highest possible price is an annual concern for these countries, but they are not in an awfully good position to dictate: sugar is produced by many countries in various

An economic legacy lingers.

parts of the world, and by farmers in the technologically developed countries themselves as well (Fig. 16-4). Thus it is the importing countries that fix tariffs and quotas, not the exporters. In the ideological conflict with Cuba, the United States cut off its imports of Cuban sugar. While the Cuban export trade was cushioned by alternative buyers in Canada and the Soviet sphere, it was a staggering blow. The wealthy, industrialized importing countries can threaten the very survival of the economies of the producers—much as the farmers in Von Thünen's isolated state were at the mercy of decisions made by the buyers in the central city.

There are signs that the producing countries are seeking to unite, to present a common front to the rich, importing nations (as the OPEC countries did in the energy arena). But what was possible in the petroleum field will not prove as easy in other areas. Countries that share world market problems in one particular commodity do not face the same difficulties in another, and so the importing countries are in a position to divide and rule. Also, a general withholding of the harvest not only endangers economies: it also stimulated domestic production in the importing countries. While sugarcane accounts for more than 70 percent of the commercial world sugar crop each year, farmers in the United States, Europe, and the Soviet Union produce sugar from sugar beets. Already in

Figure 16-4

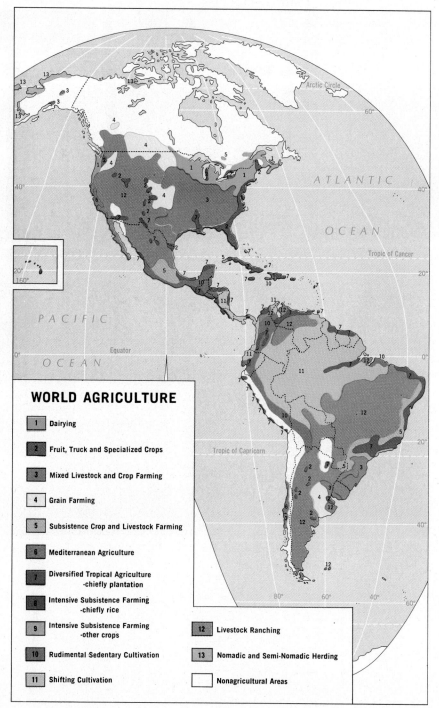

WORLD AGRICULTURE

1 Dairying

2 Fruit, Truck and Specialized Crops

3 Mixed Livestock and Crop Farming

4 Grain Farming

5 Subsistence Crop and Livestock Farming

6 Mediterranean Agriculture

7 Diversified Tropical Agriculture -chiefly plantation

8 Intensive Subsistence Farming -chiefly rice

9 Intensive Subsistence Farming -other crops

10 Rudimental Sedentary Cultivation

11 Shifting Cultivation

12 Livestock Ranching

13 Nomadic and Semi-Nomadic Herding

Nonagricultural Areas

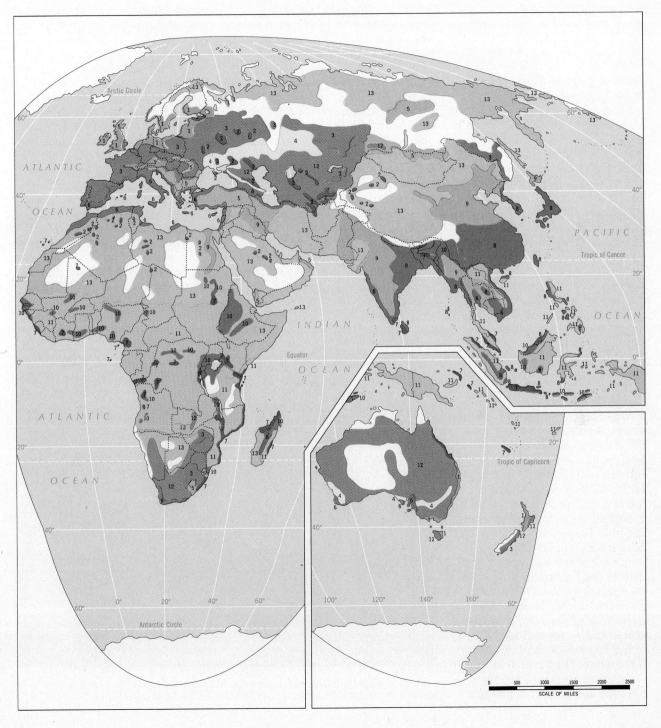

Europe and the Soviet Union, these beets produce 25 percent of the annual world sugar harvest. Collective action by countries producing sugarcane could serve to raise that percentage.

Farming in many former colonial countries, then, was stimulated and promoted by the colonial powers, representing imperial interests. Cotton and rubber, two industrial crops, are good examples. Today, cotton is grown in the United States, in Northeast China, and in Soviet Central Asia; a fourth large producer, India, owes its cotton fields to colonial Britain. But cotton cultivation was promoted on a smaller scale in numerous other countries: in Egypt's Nile Delta, in the Punjab region shared by Pakistan and India, in the Sudan, in Uganda, in Mozambique, in Mexico and Brazil. Cotton cultivation expanded greatly during the nineteenth century, when the Industrial Revolution produced machines for cotton ginning, spinning, and weaving that multiplied productive capacity, brought prices down, and put cotton goods in reach of mass buyers. As they did with sugar, the colonial powers laid out large-scale cotton plantations, sometimes under irrigation (for example, the famed Gezira Scheme, in the triangle between the White and the Blue Nile in the Sudan). The colonial producers would receive low prices for their cotton; the European industries prospered as cheap raw materials were converted into large quantities of items for sale at home and abroad. Today, many of the former colonial countries have established their own factories producing goods for the home markets, and synthetics such as nylon and rayon are giving cotton industries increasing competition. Still, the developed countries have not stopped buying cotton, and for some developing countries cotton sales remain important in the external economy. Japan, the United Kingdom, and Western European countries continue to import cotton fiber, but the developing countries have a formidable competitor for those markets in the United States, whose cotton exports also go there.

The case of rubber is rather more complicated. Initially, rubber was a substance not cultivated but gathered, collected from rubber-producing trees that stood (among many other tree species) in equatorial rain forests, mainly the forests of the Amazon Basin in South America. Those were the days, around 1900, when the town of Manaus on the Amazon River experienced an incredible rubber boom; a similar if less spectacular period of prosperity was experienced by the rubber companies exploiting the (then) Congo Basin in Africa.

The boom in wild rubber was short lived, however. Ways were sought to create rubber-tree plantations, where every tree, not just some among many, would produce rubber, where the trees could be given attention, and where collecting the rubber would be more efficient and easier. Seedlings of Brazilian rubber trees were planted elsewhere, and they did especially well in Southeast Asia. Within two decades after the Amazonian rubber boom, nearly

Rubber plantation in Sumatra, Indonesia. Southeast Asia proved to have several areas suitable for rubber plantations, notably on the Malaysian Peninsula.

90 percent of the world's rubber production came from new plantations in colonial territories in Malaya, the (then) Netherlands East Indies, and neighboring countries.

As time went on, more and more uses for rubber were found, and the demand grew continuously. The advent of the automobile was an enormous boost for the industry, and still today most of the rubber produced is used up in vehicle tires. Then World War II forcefully brought the need for alternative sources for rubber to U.S. attention, since Japan had occupied much of Southeast Asia. This stimulated the production of synthetic rubber, and although plantation-produced rubber came back to some extent after the war, synthetic rubber has remained in the lead. In 1975, world production was some eight million metric tons, five million of it synthetic; of the remaining three million tons, 90 percent continued to be produced on the plantations of Southeast Asia.

The location of the rubber plantations in Southeast Asia rather than in sections of the Amazon Basin or the Congo Basin relates less to environment than to the availability of labor. The colonial powers were aware that Southeast Asia combined conditions of tropical environment and labor availability that neither Amazon South America nor equatorial Africa could match. Eventually a large-scale African rubber industry developed in Liberia, and lately efforts have been made to introduce the plantation system along the Amazon River in the heart of Brazil.

Brazil is among the world's leading coffee exporters. The photograph shows a coffee plantation in Parana, the country's largest coffee-growing state. (top).

South Asia's tea exports go mainly to the United Kingdom and other European countries. This is a tea plantation in Sri Lanka. (left).

Similar considerations—a combination of suitable environment and available labor—led the European colonial powers to establish huge plantations for the cultivation of luxury crops such as tea, cacao, and coffee.

Coffee was first domesticated in Northeast Africa (in the region of present-day Ethiopia), but today it thrives in Middle and South America, where 70 percent of the world's annual production is harvested; The United States buys more than half of all the coffee sold on the world markets annually, and Western Europe imports most of the remainder. Compared to coffee, tea is consumed in lesser quantities by weight and in greater amounts in the areas where it is grown: India, China, Sri Lanka, and Japan. Whereas coffee is the beverage cultivated and consumed dominantly in the Americas, tea is the Eurasian equivalent: it goes from the Asian producing areas to the United Kingdom and Europe. Tea is a rather recent addition to Western diets. It was grown in China perhaps 2000 years ago, but became popular in Europe only during the nineteenth century. The colonial powers—chiefly the British—established enormous tea plantations in Asia, and the full-scale flow to the European markets began. It has continued after the decolonization period.

Orientation to the Western World

Thus the wealth and power of Europe and the Western World could reorganize economies half a world away, and land and labor from Southeast Asia to South America were placed in the service of European and North American consumers. Europe's plantations in the colonial world transformed huge areas from subsistence to cash cropping; they caused large reaches of land to be taken from their indigenous users (a process termed land *alienation*); they generated enforced migrations involving millions of people for labor purposes; and they produced enormous wealth for some of their owners (companies as well as individuals). Some of the plantations established in South America cover more than 250,000 acres, or 400 square miles. While many plantations are smaller, the average plantation is much larger than the average farm in the United States. And even though the colonial era is nearly at an end, the plantation still survives. The character of plantations is changing, but the institution remains.

Plantations are owned by private individuals or by corporations (such as the United Fruit Company, which has large banana plantations in Middle American countries). In recent years, plantations formerly owned by whites have been bought or taken over by the governments of newly independent states. But those governments have had to acknowledge the continuing relationships with the markets of the richer nations and have sometimes set up corporations to run the plantations, simply substituting for the white owners, as has been done in Kenya. In a few cases the plantations, once taken over, have been divided among peasants. This was a great experiment in Mexico, part of the revolution that began in 1910 and stipulated by the constitution of 1917. As of that year, landowners with more than 750 acres had their lands taken over for redistribution to Indian farming families. In other cases, large estates were expropriated and incorporated in collectives and communes, as in the Soviet Union and China. But all these are changes of the twentieth century. Originally the plantation was an individual or a corporate enterprise.

Whether a United Fruit Company plantation, a Venezuelan *hacienda*, a Brazilian coffee *fazenda*, or a Liberian rubber plantation, today's remaining plantations still are predominantly in the hands of people of European extraction. Large estates were plentiful in Europe during the days of colonial expansion (Von Thünen's time!), and the possession of land was a matter of great prestige. Slaves, indentured laborers, tenants, or hired labor did the work (tenancy still survives), and millions of acres around the world that lie under sugar, cotton, coffee, tea, bananas, and tobacco were first laid out as plantations. The map showing the distribution of present and past plantations (Fig. 16-5) suggests a Thünian zone of plantations ringing the world far from the Western markets that demand their products.

Distant Livestock

Nothing evokes a world Thünian scheme quite as much as does the world distribution of livestock whose products are destined for Western markets (Fig. 16-6). In a zone lying beyond the plantations, in the southernmost countries of the Southern Hemisphere, ranchers raise great herds of cattle and sheep whose products, while also sold on local markets in Argentina, South Africa, Australia, and New Zealand, are sent thousands of miles to be sold in the cities of Europe, the Soviet Union, and North America.

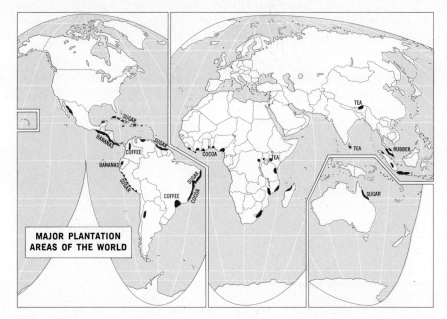

Figure 16-5

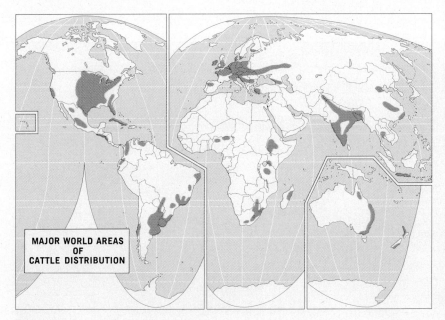

Figure 16-6

The map might give the misleading impression that India is part of this process. India does have millions of cattle, but the religious prohibition on eating meat prevents the use of this big herd for consumption—local or external. Thus it is important, in considering Figure 16-6, to differentiate between production and export of livestock products. In terms of beef and veal production (veal is the meat of a calf normally not more than 12 weeks old), the United States leads all countries with about one third of the world total, virtually all of it consumed at home. When it comes to exports, Argentina is in the lead, with about one third by weight of all the meat traded internationally each year. Argentina's cattle herd is concentrated in the Pampa, where climatic conditions are favorable and where alfalfa can be grown as a fodder crop much as corn is grown in the United States to fatten livestock. Argentina's beef goes primarily to the United Kingdom and several European countries, and some comes to U.S. markets. Behind Argentina, Australia ranks as the next most productive beef-exporting country, followed by New Zealand. It is important to remember the high cost, in terms of grain consumed, of beef: Europe's markets can command such use of the soil thousands of miles away, when those same areas could produce enormous tonnages of grain to support the hungry populations of the poorer countries.

This is less true of sheep, raised not only for wool, but also for their meat, mutton. Sheep are able to live off land that could not sustain cattle, and subsistence farmers raise them not only for their meat and fiber but also for milk (and the cheese made from it), and even for the skin, used for the production of leather garments and other items. The world distribution of sheep (Fig. 16-7) should, as in the case of cattle, be seen in this context. The dense sheep population in the United Kingdom, Eastern Europe, and Southwest and South Asia constitutes herds kept for local production; the South

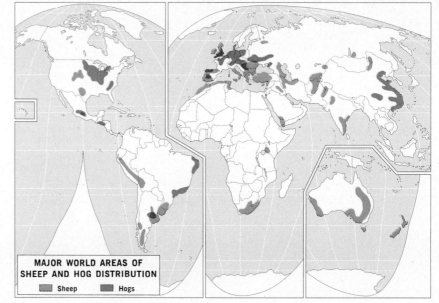

MAJOR WORLD AREAS OF SHEEP AND HOG DISTRIBUTION

◻ Sheep   ◼ Hogs

Figure 16-7

A small part of Argentina's huge sheep herd. The photograph was taken in Patagonia.

American, South African, Australian, and New Zealand sheep herds are maintained largely for external (European) markets. The valuable export item, of course, is their wool: textile makers in the United Kingdom, Western Europe, Japan, the United States, and the Soviet Union use wool imported from Southern Hemisphere countries.

When we first viewed the model developed by Von Thünen, we noted that high-priced, perishable items such as dairy products were produced nearest to the central market. And still today, in cities around the world, the production of milk, butter, cheese and similar items comes from the immediate environs. On our map of North America a "Dairy Belt" is discernible, showing a marked orientation and proximity to the population core of the East. Europe has a similar concentration. But when we check an atlas map showing the world distribution of the dairy industry, it seems at first to contradict what we have just reported. Far away from the European and North American markets, New Zealand and Australia generate dairy products and export them in quantity. Again it is a matter of the primacy of the European market: Europe produces a large volume of milk and other dairy items, but its consumers demand and can afford more. And just as refrigerator ships made long-distance beef exports possible, refrigeration eliminated time as a factor in the export of cheese, butter, and other dairy products from Southern Hemisphere countries.

This should not suggest that the consumption of dairy products is a monopoly of the wealthy midlatitude countries. The dairy industry is nowhere as well developed as it is there, but in other parts of the world people also consume milk when they can obtain it, and dairy belts have sprung up around major urban centers from Santiago to Seoul. Milk is a prominent item in Masai diets; in India, where there are so many cattle, milk is about the only substantial benefit from that overpopulation. Milk is a vital dietary ingredient, especially for young children, and hundreds of millions of people do not consume nearly enough of it because it is too expensive to obtain. Goat's milk serves as a substitute in some areas, and condensed and powdered milk stands on the shelves of village stores from Bolivia to Burma. But the ample supply of dairy products that is commonplace in the wealthy Western countries is an exception and a privilege in this world.

Goats, hogs, and poultry are among livestock that contribute importantly to the diets of people in many parts of the world. Hogs, the source of pork, bacon, and lard, are a most useful alternative where meat sources are hard to come by. Hogs (or pigs, or swine) can survive in widely different environments. In the United States and Europe they are raised commercially, and fed corn- and potato-derived feed. But in many other parts of the world they are simply scavengers, surviving on leftovers and garbage. Thousands of Chinese villages would be imcomplete without their hog population (China is probably the world's leading hog producer), and hogs abound also in Brazil, Mexico, and other South and Middle American countries. Hogs could serve even more effectively to diversify diets if religious taboos (chiefly Moslem) did not exclude them from large areas of the world. There are no hogs in any great number in North Africa and Southwest Asia, or in Southeast Asia, and very few in India and Africa. Almost anomalously, the major production (other than China's) is in the already meat-rich Western countries, which trade among themselves, in ham, pork, bacon, and lard.

If hogs can survive under difficult circumstances, goats can thrive on even poorer land. They manage to climb the steepest slopes after the smallest tuft of vegetation, and they live in large numbers in even the most arid of populated countrysides. From Africa to Southern Europe to the Middle East to Southern Asia, the goat provides milk, meat, skin, even hair to its owners. Goats require little care, and multiply rapidly; one negative aspect of their large numbers is that in their persistent search for food they contribute to soil erosion and land denudation.

Poultry, perhaps the oldest of all domesticated livestock, also provides its owners with a set of valuable commodities in return for little attention or land. Chickens live as scavengers, but can also be fed systematically. In terms of weight, they generate the best return per pound of feed expended. They produce meat and eggs, crucial in diets where proteins are badly lacking. In the technologically advanced countries, the poultry industry is as thoroughly organized as that of cattle or hogs, and the local markets consume enormous quantities of poultry products. Breeding has created specialized strains, some noted for their eggs, others for their meat. The poultry industry has not been immune from efforts to establish plantationlike production systems in colonial countries: a prominent (and disastrous) experiment was aimed at the creation of a huge poultry scheme in Gambia, West Africa.

Crucial Grains

People in the wealthy countries as well as the poor, the well-fed nations as well as the hungry, are sustained chiefly by the major grain crops, the *cereals.* Along with two root crops, the potato and the cassava, the three leading cereals (rice, wheat, and corn) account for more than three quarters of the food supply produced on this earth each year. Grain crops of lesser, local importance, such as sorghum, millet, barley, oats, and rye (among others); fruits (the banana is a staple in a few areas); vegetables; meats; and dairy products make up the remainder.

Probably as many as half the people of the world depend upon rice for their daily sustenance. The map showing present areas of substantial rice cultivation (Fig. 16-8) indicates that rice continues to be grown predominantly in and near the region where it was first domesticated. Compared to the areas where wheat and corn are cultivated (Figs. 16-9 and 16-10) the extent of the rice-producing areas seems rather limited. But the map should be viewed in the light of per-acre yields, which for rice are much higher than for wheat—nearly twice as high, in fact. Fast-maturing rice strains have been developed, and now two crops can be harvested on the same acre of land during a single growing season, with time left over for some vegetable growing. There are even places where three rice crops are harvested in a single year.

A comparison of Figures 16-8 and 2-1 suggests how large a percentage of the world's population is concentrated in the rice-producing region and how important rice is as food. Nearly 90 percent of the rice is grown in East, Southeast, and South Asia, and most of the people there, more than three quarters of them, are busy producing it. This regionalism of production and

Hillside terracing and rice cultivation in the Philippines. Rice is the world's great staple grain.

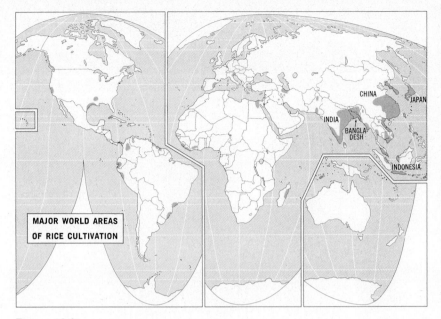

MAJOR WORLD AREAS
OF RICE CULTIVATION

Figure 16-8

consumption also occurs with the other grains, although it is strongest in the case of rice. The rice-producing countries consume rice and trade with each other in rice, but there are no large-scale exports of rice to, say, Europe or North America.

Whereas rice is the subsistence crop of the developing countries of Asia, wheat is the staple of the developed world. This generalization should be qualified, for wheat is cultivated and consumed in India and China as well as in Europe and the U.S.S.R., the United States, Argentina, and Australia. But our map of world wheat-producing areas (Fig. 16-9) reflects this cereal's association with the richer countries. First domesticated in Southwest Asia, wheat still grows on the shores of the Mediterranean from Syria to Morocco. But today the bulk of

the world's wheat stands in the (Soviet) Ukraine, in the American Great Plains, in Argentina's Pampa, in Australia, and in Northern China. It is a distribution very different from that of rice.

While rice is the crop of small paddies and individual attention, wheat is the crop of huge fields and mechanized production. True, wheat is grown in India and China as rice is, on small plots and with much individual attention, but in the Soviet Union (the world's leading producer), in the United States, in Canada, Australia, and Argentina wheat is grown on a large scale, with machines doing the seeding and harvesting. And here we have a situation that distorts our Thünian view of the world, for the wealthy, developed countries are not the importers of wheat (except the U.S.S.R. in recent decades), but exporters of this

staple. As providers of sustenance for the hungry world, the wealthy countries thus are able to perpetuate their considerable control over the fortunes of the poor nations. While rice is largely consumed in the country where it is produced—only about 5 percent of all the rice produced annually enters international trade—wheat moves in giant cargo ships across oceans to distant consumers. Tonnages vary with harvests in successive years, but between 15 and 20 per cent of the world's annual wheat production is exported to hungry buyers.

If rice is Asia's grain crop, corn (or maize, as it is called in other parts of the world) is the cereal of the Americas. First domesticated by American Indians and not known to other peoples until the sixteenth century, corn today grows in practically all parts of the world and is a subsistence crop in Africa and Asia as well as in America. But the world's leading area of corn production still lies in America: the U.S. Corn Belt (Fig. 16-10).

Corn is a versatile crop capable of growing in moist as well as comparatively dry climes, in valleys and on high mountain slopes, and under growing seasons of less than three months. It has become a primary subsistence crop in Africa, where yields per acre are naturally far lower than those of the favored U.S. Corn Belt. In the United States, however, most of the corn produced is not consumed directly but used to feed livestock. Only about 10 percent of the U.S. corn production (which amounts to more than half of that of the entire world) is made into cornbread, breakfast

315

cereals, cornmeal, margarine, and related products. A small quantity is consumed as a vegetable. Corn is also exported in comparatively small quantity to Western Europe and Japan, and of course there is some local, regional trade in certain areas. But very little corn enters international trade, nor is corn nearly as significant in the combat of world hunger as wheat or rice.

Although not a cereal, we should take note of the growing role of soybeans in the provision of much-needed vegetable protein in hungry countries. The soybean plant shares with corn its ability to grow under quite unfavorable conditions. It is able to withstand drought because of its deep root system, which helps improve the soil. First domesticated in East Asia, the soybean now grows in most areas of the world, and the United States has become the leading producer, surpassing even China. In Asia, the soybean serves as a staple as corn does in Africa, and is consumed fresh, fermented into beverages, ground into meal, and dried for storage. In the United States, most of the soybean harvest is either ground into meal and used for animal feed, or the oil is squeezed out of the beans and used for food (the soybean oil also has industrial uses). The versatility of the soybean and its nutritional qualities are reflected by the growing consumption in the United States as food. If you have seen those "meat substitutes" in supermarkets, products made to look and taste like meat but much cheaper, their base is likely to be the soybean. Not surprisingly, the international trade in soybeans and soybean products is also growing substantially.

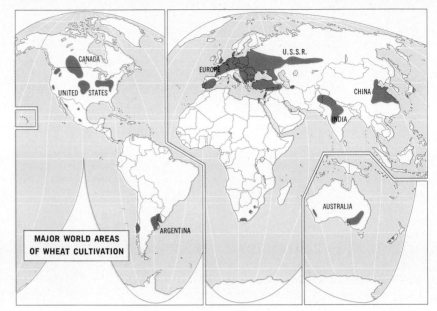

Figure 16-9

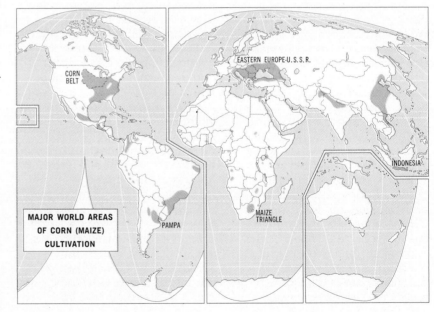

Figure 16-10

The United States is now the world's leading exporter as well as producer, selling more than two thirds of all the oil, three quarters of the meal, and about 90 percent of all the beans bought on international markets.

It would be unproductive for us to enumerate all the other cereals and bean crops grown in various parts of the world, for although there are many, none compares in world importance to rice, wheat, corn, or soybeans. Barley, for example, has a distribution pattern not unlike that of corn and is used both as food and animal feed, and in the production of liquors and beer as well. Millet and sorghum are hardy grains that sustain subsistence farmers in localized areas from Africa to China. Rye is an important bread grain in Europe; oats ranks behind corn as a feed crop. In some areas of the world (notably West Africa) the peanut is a staple.

Neither are the root crops a match for the cereals in the sustenance of the world's billions. The potato (the *white* potato, to distinguish it from other varieties) was grown by American Indian peoples before the European invasion, and the Europeans took it back to Europe—where it became a staple from Ireland to Russia, sustaining the great seventeenth and eighteenth century population explosion. The potato provides starches, proteins, iron, and some vitamins; it is used both as a food staple and as animal feed. In terms of nutrient value, the potato is the only crop that can match rice, but although it is spreading in many areas the great bulk of the world's potato crop is still produced and consumed in Europe and the Soviet Union. Still less significant in the world perspective, but locally the basis for survival, are such root crops as the yam and the cassava (also called manioc), whose plants can grow with comparatively little attention and under conditions of heat and humidity that preclude the maturing of a grain crop.

If it appears strange that, in a world as hungry as ours, enormous tonnages of corn and potatoes can be fed to animals, huge tracts of land can be set aside for unessential luxury crops, and large numbers of people labor on the soil to produce frills rather than food, we should remind ourselves one final time of the Thünian model and its implications. What Von Thünen saw locally (and what we noted on regional and even continental scales) now has worldwide expression. The range and variety of products familiar to us on the shelves of supermarkets is an anomaly in this world of simple, ill-balanced, often inadequate diets. A global network of farm products is oriented to that one fifth of the world's population, highly urbanized, powerful, and wealthy, living in the United States and Canada, Europe, and the U.S.S.R. The farmers in distant lands may be even less able to make decisions on the use of their land than those in Von Thünen's isolated state, for it is the Western world that decides what will be bought at what price, and the wealthy countries that have the choices, not the poor. From the proceeds gained through the cultivation of tobacco, coffee, and sugar the hungry countries must buy staples for survival—staples often grown by the farmers of the wealthy world. The colonial age may have come to an end, but the age of dependence has not.

Essay: Land and Culture

To us, here in the capitalist world of free enterprise, land is, quite simply, a commodity that can be bought, owned, and sold. The structure of urban regions, the pattern of land use in agricultural areas, the layout of those huge Western ranches all are bound inextricably to the value of land. Parcels of land are carefully surveyed and demarcated; fences, hedgelines, and other markers produce a pattern of fragmentation that, from the air, resembles a giant jigsaw. Some lands are owned by the federal government, by states, by municipalities, and by other agencies for allocation to public use (as parks, for example), and there are areas whose natural beauty is protected by law. But you can find beaches, forests, entire lakes, and every other kind of land under private ownership in the United States.

Ours is the *freehold* form of land ownership, in which the farmer has possession by deed of the land he cultivates. It was introduced from Europe by the white man's invasion of North America, and became the major source of conflict between American Indian peoples and the European immigrants: fences and gates were alien concepts to American Indians, who viewed land as open for general exploitation and competition. Land alienation also was a leading source of conflict between Europeans and Africans from Senegal to South Africa, and between the colonialists and Asians in India and elsewhere. But the concept of private ownership was adopted as a desirable objective even where it had not been part of traditional culture—and even after the European colonizers had departed.

Although large farms and ranches are quite numerous in the United States and Canada, the great majority of freehold farms are small—under 50 acres in most of Europe and under 10 acres in Asia. Even a small farm gives the owner-farmer an advantage, however, because it permits him to borrow money for fertilizer and other necessities, an opportunity denied, mostly, to farmers who cultivate on land that is not their own.

What the Europeans found in India, in tropical Africa, and in America were various forms of *communal* tenure, whereby the land is owned by the community, not by individuals. Families may be awarded certain plots for their private use (and they may consume and trade what they grow there), but by using it they do not acquire it. So long as the societies did not use money, this system worked well. But with the European invasion came the money economy, and as products acquired monetary value, so did the land on which they could be grown. Now those who had the power to allocate land to individuals and families found themselves in powerful positions, able to secure personal gain; in Africa many chiefs and headmen readily sold communally owned land to prospective white farmers.

The concept of communal ownership has been revived in modern forms during the present century, and in several cultures. Among the earliest was the Mexican *ejido* program, an adaptation of the old Indian village farming communities. This was a product of the Mexican Revolution, in which huge *haciendas*, taken by the Spanish invaders many generations ago, were taken over by the government and parcelled out to peasant communities generally consisting of 20 families or more. The land is owned by the group, and plots are assigned to each member for cultivation. No plots can be sold by those cultivating them. Another modern example of communal land tenure is the *kibbutz* system of Israel, and the vast agricultural reform program in China also has its roots in communal forms of land use. The Soviet Union's *kolkhoz* collective farms combine communal effort with a remnant of private enterprise, for the farmers on the collectives are permitted to retain a small plot (about an acre or a little more) for their own use.

The Europeans brought to the world of communal land tenure their large *estates* and plantations (we have already discussed the latter in Chapter 16). This does not suggest that large estates or large-scale land ownership did not exist at all in other cultures; in India, for example, the aristocracies held huge possessions. But the European estate was something different. It was laid out specifically to produce such commodities as sugar, cotton, and tea and organized for maximum profit. Countless numbers of African slaves found themselves working on those estates (*latifundia* in Latin America); when slavery was abolished, indentured labor was imported. Or the estate owners kept workers in a state of serfdom through debt; the use of wage labor on the remaining estates is a relatively recent phenomenon.

The estate has proved to be remarkably durable, surviving through the emancipation of the slave labor on which it first depended, through revolutions and land reforms. In Europe itself the worst features of estate practice persisted in Italy into the 1930s and in Spain and Portugal to the present day (true reform may now be at hand in Portugal); in Latin America the system also survives. In some places, as in the Philippines and in Kenya, estates that were subdivided actually reappeared. Kenya's large European estates have in some cases been divided into individual farms and in other cases their European family-owners have been replaced by a larger group of communal owners. But other estates have simply been taken over by African individual proprietors.

What of the peasant who does not own land but must feed a family? His (and her) lot is that of *tenancy*, another form of servitude found not only in European culture but also in Asian and African societies. The Indian aristocracies who held large estates were (unlike the European estate owners) mainly collectors of rent from tenants whose lands they owned but did not themselves organize for cultivation. Several forms of tenancy occur. *Labor* tenancy pays the worker for his work by permitting him to cultivate a small plot on the estate owner's lands. This form of tenancy was infrequent in Asia, fairly common in parts of Africa, and prevalent in Latin America. Today it survives only in Latin America, if you choose to view the Soviet *kolkhoz* system in a different light. *Share* tenancy is the predominant form of tenancy in Latin America and Asia, and sharecropping occurs still in the United States, in Australia, and in Europe. Under this system the tenant gives the owner of the estate a part of the crop he has cultivated. It is not a progressive system at all, for the tenant does not receive credit for investments he may have made in his effort to increase production; sharecropping is another form of rent collection.

Perhaps the most satisfactory system is *cash* tenancy, whereby the tenant pays the land owner in cash, not in work or crops. This money is paid by contract and remains the same whatever the production of the land the tenant has purchased the right to farm. Thus the tenant has every reason to improve the soil and care for the land: the benefits will be his, for he cannot be summarily ousted. The tenant's contract stipulates not only the amount that must be paid to the land owner, but also the length of time the tenant may remain on the property. This form of tenure is very common in Britain, where nearly two thirds of all farmers are tenants. If it is surprising to find tenancy so common in a developed country, it is proof that, under proper governmental scrutiny, the system can be made to work satisfactorily, without the fearful exploitation that marks it in so many other areas of the world.

17 The Industrializing World

Two centuries of industrial intensification have transformed human societies in ways unprecedented in world history. At one end of the scale, several of the "developed" countries have become huge manufacturing complexes, whose factories consume raw materials at enormous rates and pour products by the millions onto domestic and world markets. But even at the other end, in the most isolated village of the most "underdeveloped" country, the industrial age has its impact. Bottles, cans, some textiles, a bar of soap, a bicycle, perhaps even a transistor radio are nothing new to people who otherwise still are remote from the push of industry.

It is proper to describe our modern age as one of industrial *intensification*, for industrial development did not begin with the Industrial Revolution; instead, it accelerated and diffused from certain areas of innovation to other parts of the world. Long before the momentous events of the second half of the eighteenth century, when the foundations for mass production were laid, industries already existed in many parts of the world, and trade in their products was widespread. In the towns and villages of India, workshops produced metal goods of iron, gold, silver, and brass; India's carpenters were artists as well as craftsmen and their work was in demand wherever it could be bought; India's textiles, made on individual spinning wheels and handlooms, were acknowledged to be the best in the world. These industries were sustained not only by the patronage of local Indian aristocracies, but also by trade on international markets. So good were the Indian textiles that British textile makers rioted in 1721, demanding legislative protection against the Indian competition that was dominating local British markets.

China, too, possessed a substantial industrial base long before the Industrial Revolution, and so did Japan. European industries, from the textile makers of Flanders and Britain to the iron smelters of Thuringen, had also developed considerably, but in terms of price and quality European products could not match those of

321

other parts of the world. But what European manufacturing products lacked in finesse, Europe's merchants and their representatives made up in aggressiveness and power. Europe's commercial companies (such as the Dutch and British East India Companies) laid the groundwork for the colonial expansion of Europe: they gained control over local industries in India, Indonesia, and elsewhere, profited from the political chaos they precipitated, and played off allies against enemies. British merchants could import about as many tons of raw fiber for the textile industries as they wanted, and all they needed to do, they knew, was to find ways to mass produce these raw materials into finished products. Then they would bury the remaining local industries in Asia and Africa under growing volumes and declining prices. Even China—where local manufactures long prevailed over inferior and more expensive European goods—would succumb.

During the eighteenth century, European domestic markets were growing, and there was not enough labor to keep pace with either the local trade or the overseas potentials. Machines capable of greater production were urgently needed, especially improved spinning and weaving equipment. The first steps in the Industrial Revolution were not so revolutionary, for the larger spinning and weaving machines that were built were driven by the old source of power: water running downslope. But then

Watt and others who were working on a steam-driven engine succeeded (1765-1788), and this new invention was adapted for various uses. At about the same time, it was realized that coal could be transformed into coke, and that coke was a superior substitute for charcoal in the smelting of iron.

These momentous innovations had rapid effect. The power loom revolutionized the weaving industry. Freed from their dependence on dwindling wood supplies from the remaining forests, iron smelters could now be concentrated near the British coal fields—the same fields that supplied fuel for the new textile mills. And one invention led to another, each innovation made to serve some particular industry also serving other industries. Pumps could now keep water out of flood-prone mines. Engines could move power looms as well as locomotives and ships. As for the capital required, there was plenty available for investment. British industrialists had been getting rich from the overseas empire for many years.

Thus the Industrial Revolution had its effects also on transportation and communications. The first railroad in England was opened in 1825. In 1830 the city of Manchester was connected to the port of Liverpool, and in the next several decades thousands of miles of rail were laid. Ocean shipping likewise entered a new age as the first steam-powered vessel crossed the Atlantic in 1819. Now England enjoyed

even greater advantages than those with which it entered the period of the Industrial Revolution. Not only did England hold a monopoly over products that were in world demand, but Britain alone possessed the skills necessary to make the machines that manufactured them. Europe and America wanted railroads and locomotives; England had the know-how, the experience, and the capital. Soon the fruits of the Industrial Revolution were being exported, and British influence around the world reached a peak.

Meanwhile, the spatial pattern of modern, industrial Europe began to take shape. In Britain, industrial regions, densely populated and heavily urbanized, developed in the "Black Belt"—near the coalfields. The largest complex was (and remains) positioned in north-central England. In mainland Europe, a belt of major coalfields extends from west to east, roughly along the southern margins of the North European Lowland, due eastward from Southern England across Northern France and Southern Belgium, the Netherlands, Germany (the Ruhr), Western Bohemia in Czechoslovakia, and Silesia in Poland. Iron ore exists in a broadly similar belt, and the industrial map of Europe reflects the resulting concentrations of economic activity (Fig. 17-1). But nowhere in the mainland are the coalfields, the iron ores, and the coastal ports located in such close proximity as they are in Britain.

322

EUROPEAN MANUFACTURING REGIONS

Legend:
- Focused on Major Urban Concentrations
- Situated on and near Major Raw Materials
- Based on Long-term Regional Growth
- Railroad
- Canal

SCALE OF MILES

0   100   200   400   600

Arctic Circle

Norwegian Sea

NORWAY

SWEDEN

FINLAND

Stockholm
Eastern Sweden

Baltic Sea

DENMARK

North Sea

Scotland

Glasgow

Edinburgh-Glasgow Corridor

UNITED

Northeast England

IRELAND

KINGDOM

Liverpool   Leeds

Manchester   Midlands

Wales   England

South Wales   Birmingham

London

NETHERLANDS

Benelux-Ruhr

BELGIUM   Cologne

Bonn

WEST   EAST

GERMANY   Berlin

GERMANY

Leipzig
Saxony   Dresden

Warsaw

POLAND

Silesia

LUX.

Paris Basin   Paris

Saar-Stuttgart-Frankfurt Triangle

Lorraine

Ostrava

Moravia

CZECHOSLOVAKIA

Carpathians

U.S.S.R.

FRANCE

SWITZERLAND

AUSTRIA

HUNGARY

ROMANIA

Lyons

Bilbao

PORTUGAL

SPAIN

Turin   Milan

Northern Italy

ITALY

Rome

Adriatic Sea

YUGOSLAVIA

BULGARIA

Barcelona

ALBANIA

GREECE

TURKEY

ATLANTIC OCEAN

Mediterranean Sea

Longitude West 0° East of Greenwich

Figure 17-1

Location Factors

Industrial activity takes place in certain locations; it does not occur in others. What determines where industries develop? We observed that the Industrial Revolution itself centered in a particular region, and then diffused to other areas, and noted some of the factors involved in these processes. Today, several discrete areas of the world are outstanding industrial regions. Where do they lie—and can their evolution be accounted for in terms similar to those that stimulated the original Revolution?

Industries differ in kind. The making of steel is an industry, but so is fishing. The fishing industry is Iceland's very means of survival, more important even to that nation than our steel industry is to us. But somehow fishing, the extraction of fish from the sea, is not the same kind of industry as the manufacture of a product such as steel rails. Fishermen catch what exists in nature. Steel makers mix raw materials and come up with something artificial, new. And what about the transportation industry? It produces no product at all, but moves people and goods from place to place. Still it is also an industry!

Thus three classes of industry can be established. The *primary* industries are extractive, as fishing is. Other primary industries include forestry, mining, quarrying, and hunting. Though in a different subgroup, the various forms of agriculture discussed in Chapter 16 are also

primary industries. The *secondary* industries are the manufacturing industries. Raw materials are transformed into products ranging from plastic toys to railroad cars. When we speak of "industrial" nations, we really mean the manufacturing nations. Finally, there are the *tertiary* industries, involving the production not of goods, but of services. Teaching is such an industry, as is transportation. There is such a thing as the medical industry. Dentists, bankers, bus drivers, and postmen all operate in this sector.

Decisions

In the primary industries, production has to take place where the resources are. The timber, the fish, and the ores and fuels leave no choice—it is necessary to come and get them where they are. But we noted just a moment ago that textile industries and other industrial plants began to position themselves in clusters as Europe's Industrial Revolution gained momentum, and that iron smelters, among these others, were positioned near the coalfields of the "Black Belt." This means that the iron ores had to be brought to the coalfields, and that reality illustrates

Logging is a primary, extractive industry. Here, logs are consumed by a paper-pulp mill at Vicksburg, Mississippi.

an important aspect of the secondary industries, the manufacturing industries: decisions have to be made about where to locate them. Weight and bulk have a lot to do with such decisions. Is it not more sensible to refine an ore or to saw off useless waste from tree trunks practically at the site of production and *then* to ship the raw material for final processing into finished products than to ship them long distances first? In the case of iron ore and coal, both needed in large quantities to make steel, the alternatives are (1) to take the iron ore to the coalfields, (2) to take the coal to the iron ore deposits, and (3) to transport both to an intermediate location. Most frequently, the ore is transported to the coalfields, sometimes after the partial elimination of waste and impurities. There are exceptions: for example, coal is transported in large quantities to the French Lorraine industrial region, where coal is scarce. When an industrial complex develops near coalfields and the coal supplies become exhausted, it may be less expensive to start importing coal from elsewhere than to move the factories. Even when both coal and iron ore are shipped over large distances to some intermediate location, the iron ore usually travels the farthest.

Raw Materials

Numerous considerations enter into such decisions, and these questions are of prime interest to economic geographers who want to know what the processes are whereby economic activity organizes and adjusts spatially. Obviously the resources involved—the raw materials—play a major role. One example is the coastal steel industry of the United States along the eastern seaboard. Those industries are there in large measure because they use iron ore shipped in from Venezuela, Liberia, and other overseas mines. Instead of transferring them from the arriving ships into trains and railing them inland, the ores are used right where they arrive—practically at the point of unloading. So in this case faraway ore deposits had much to do with the location of industry in the United States.

Labor

A second factor of industrial location is the availability of labor. Even in this day of automated assembly lines and computerized processing, the available skills of a substantial labor force remain important criteria in the location of manufacturing plants. Over decades and generations a certain cumulative effect has manifested itself, whereby the people in certain areas become known for their particular talents. The Swiss make fine instruments, specialized textiles are made (still) in Britain, cameras in Japan. The book publishing industry in the United States is concentrated in New York, with a secondary center in San Francisco. Here the several skills needed to transform a manuscript into an attractively designed book are available. A new industry would be likely to consider strongly availing itself of the available capacities, and locate in or near these centers.

The Primary Industries

The primary industries are the extractive industries, including cultivation and pastoralism (see Chapters 15 and 16) as well as mining and quarrying, fishing and hunting, and forest-product industries.

Mining. Mining must, quite obviously, take place where the resources are located. An ancient industry (we refer to the Stone Age and the Iron Age of human history), mining today is strongly mechanized and employs only about 1 percent of the world's labor force.

No country in the world, no matter how large, possesses a complete range and adequate volume of all mineral resources, and so there is an active trade in minerals and mineral fuels. A constant search for new reserves goes on, and new industries establish themselves when discoveries are made. At the same time, the exhaustion of the highest-quality reserves brings lower-grade resources into production.

Fishing. Fishing is another ancient human occupation that has been made more efficient through mechanization. Improved technologies and the concentration of fish catches on continental shelf areas now threaten the oceans' fish resources. Japan, the Soviet Union, the United States, Peru, and China harvest the bulk of what may be a declining resource through the use of fleets of fishing boats and floating canning factories.

Forestry. Forests, ancient allies of human communities, provided shelter, food, building materials, firewood, even clothing. Still today, the forests—heavily depleted through centuries of exploitation but supplemented now by reforestation—provide building materials (lumber), paper (pulpwood), and many less important products such as cork, bamboo, resin, gums, tannin, and quinine.

It may not be skills, but the cheapness of labor that will attract some industries. In the United States, there are areas where prevailing wages are lower than they are elsewhere, and unless other factors of industrial location are of overriding importance, a manufacturing concern may locate where it can pay labor less.

Market

Another, very obvious influence in the location of industry is the market. Obvious though the influence may be, it is not so easy to understand. In the developed countries, much depends on the transport networks as well as the location of large population concentrations. A company is likely to establish itself in or near the largest city, where it has the largest market nearby, knowing that good communications radiate outward into the rest of the country, so that distribution there will be very efficient. Industries that produce perishable goods (e.g., dairies) will locate as near to their markets as they can. Some industries make products specifically designed to be used by other industries, certain equipment for automobiles, for instance. It would not be sensible for a factory making speedometers for cars to position itself very far from Detroit. But there is still more to the issue. When a commodity is very heavy and bulky, the proximity of the market is far more significant than when it is smaller and lighter and, as is likely, more valuable per unit of weight. Even if the Swiss sell more watches in the United States and Canada than in Europe, it is unlikely that they will move their factories to New York. On the other hand, an American automobile manufacturer planning to sell a small car on the European market may decide to build the factory in Europe, rather than to build the cars here.

Energy

Another factor in the location of industry is the availability of an energy supply. This used to be much more important than it is now; those British textile mills, while they depended on water rushing down hillsides to drive the looms, had little alternative in the context of location. But these days power comes from different sources, and can be transmitted via power lines over long distances without much loss. Industries are thus able to locate primarily on the basis of considerations other than power, except when the industry needs really exceptionally large amounts of energy—for example, aluminum-refining plants. Those industries are positioned near sites where abundant energy is created, as is the case at hydroelectric plants.

The role of power supply should not be understated, however. In the developed countries, dense transmission networks bring power to most areas, but in the underdeveloped countries, electrification still is an elusive goal for whole regions. The electrification program undertaken in the Soviet Union during the present century has been one of the prideful accomplishments there. Elsewhere, hydroelectric projects and power lines have

the same aura of modernization and progress that causes underdeveloped countries to pour huge investments into the face-lifting of capital cities and the maintenance of a money-losing national airline. The hope always is that the cheap electricity, once available, will attract industries. Those anticipations do not always materialize.

Transportation

We have referred to the role of transport and communications several times in discussing other location factors, and it is difficult to isolate the role of transport facilities in the location of industries. There may be a huge market for a product, but if that market is not served by good transport networks its influence is lessened. When you compare the maps of manufacturing regions in this chapter with maps of transport systems (railroads, roads, ocean routes, and air routes) you observe immediately that these highly developed industrial areas are also those served most effectively by transport facilities. Industrialization and the development of transport systems go hand in hand, and in a sense the Industrial Revolution *was* a transport revolution—a revolution that is still going on. Every year, more freight is carried by air; in the United States, trucks haul goods formerly carried on trains.

In the location of industry, wide transport systems permit the acquisition of raw materials from far away and the dissemination of finished products to a far-flung market. Manufacturers want maximum efficiency, the lowest possible costs, and the availability of alternatives in the

event of emergencies (e.g., trucks when train traffic is for some reason unavailable).

When decisions are made relating to the location of industries, numerous aspects of transportation must be taken into account, and no generalization can do justice to the complexities of the problem. For example, when goods are hauled, costs are incurred when the carriers are at the terminal (i.e., at the loading dock, in port, in the rail yard). These costs vary; they are much higher for ships than for trucks. Another cost involves the handling of the freight, moving it from loading platform to carrier. Then, of course, there is the actual cost of transportation, which increases with distance, but at a decreasing rate, making long-distance transport cheaper per mile. Such longhaul economy makes it possible for a manufacturer to reach out to distant suppliers of raw materials and to sell to far-away customers. Still another factor has to do with the weight and volume of the freight. The goods may be of light weight, but they may occupy a lot of space in the railroad cars or ships' holds, and still be expensive to transport. Consider all these aspects of transportation—and remember that transport is only one factor affecting industrial location among a number of others!

Other Factors

Factors other than those we have identified may also be at work in industrial location. If several plants have already located in a certain area, others might be influenced to do the

Water transport played a major role in the unfolding of the Industrial Revolution. Some of Europe's rivers became highways for the transport of raw materials and finished products. Traffic on the Thames River at Tower Bridge, London.

same—not only because of the advantages of that site but because of a certain clustering effect that comes into play. Had those already-established plants not been there, the other industries might have been positioned elsewhere. There is also a factor of political stability and receptiveness to investment: industries are frightened away if there are signs of uncertainty in the political future of a country, or when a government gives indications that it intends to nationalize industries owned by foreigners. Policies of taxation also play a role, and some countries try to attract industries by offering huge tax exemptions over long time periods. Sometimes influential industrialists can simply decide to locate a major plant in some area and can afford to ignore theories of industrial location. The directors of global (so-called multinational) corporations can affect the course of regional industrial development in many countries almost at will. And some industries are located where they are because of environmental conditions; the film industry has been so strongly concentrated in Southern California because of the large number of clear, cloudless days there. Industrial location, we can see, is no simple matter, and there are no easy explanations to account for the maps we are about to see.

Day-care centers, and nursery schools like this one, form an industry—one of the many people-oriented tertiary industries.

The Tertiary Industries

The tertiary industries do not (as the primary and secondary industries do) generate an actual, tangible product. Tertiary industries include services such as transportation and communications, financial services (banking is such an industry), retailing, recreation, teaching, even government. Here the measure is not the quantity of a commodity produced, but the effectiveness with which the particular service has been performed.

Although the tertiary industries do not produce tangible commodities, they do employ large numbers of people. In the United States, for example, the tertiary service industries employ *more* people than the primary and secondary industries combined. This should not surprise us: primary industries such as fishing and mining do not employ large numbers of people, and the secondary industries are becoming increasingly mechanized. So the big job is to bring the producer and the consumer together—through advertising, transporting, selling, installing, servicing, lending money, and so on.

Tertiary industries are often quite small, so that in number they outrank both secondary and primary establishments. In terms of location, these are the most directly people-oriented of the industries, so that a map showing population clusters (Fig. 2-1, for example) is quite a good indicator of the world distribution of tertiary activities. Tertiary industries quite naturally tend to concentrate in cities and towns; unlike the primary industries they are not tied to the location of raw materials, nor are they as closely governed by locational factors as are the secondary industries. Indeed, certain tertiary industries are sometimes called the *footloose* industries!

329

Planning

We have discussed the factors of industrial location as they affect decision making in a capitalist system, but in many noncapitalist countries the crucial decisions are made by professional planners who may ultimately base their decisions on quite different grounds. Certainly these planners take account of the distribution and availability of resources, energy, transport facilities, and other factors, but more important may be the security of the state (dispersal of industries rather than their concentration could result) or the need for stimulation and national expansion in a particular region that needs an infusion of economic activity. In the U.S.S.R. some industries were built to produce goods that could have been bought more cheaply than they could be made at home; in the 1930s plants were located far from the potential military threat (Germany to the west), so that they could continue to function even in the event of invasion and war.

Whatever the underlying causes, and they are many and complex, a small number of major industrial regions exist today whose factories produce a large proportion of the entire world's industrial output. Take note that we are now considering the *secondary* industries, the industries that manufacture goods from raw materials made available in the primary industries. It is hardly necessary to enumerate these industries, for when we view the major regions we will frequently have occasion to refer to specific manufactures. There are four such regions: (1) Western and Central Europe, (2) the United States and Canada, (3) the core area and eastward extension of the Soviet Union, and (4) the Japan-China industrial concentration.

European Manufacturing Region

It is appropriate to begin with Europe, for here the Industrial Revolution commenced. The industrial regions of Europe largely *constitute* the European heartland. Europe's industrial region consists of a number of districts, from the British Midlands in the west to Silesia in the east.

Nowhere is the principle of functional specialization better illustrated than in the industries of Britain. Wool-garment producing cities lie east of the Pennines, the mountain backbone of the island, centered on Leeds and Bradford. The textile industries of Manchester, on the other side of the range, produce cotton goods. Birmingham, now with 2.5 million inhabitants, and its neighbors concentrate on the manufacture of steel and metal products, including automobiles, motorcycles, and airplanes. The Nottingham area specializes in hosiery; Leicester adds boots and shoes to that field. In Northeast England, shipbuilding and the manufacture of chemicals are the major large-scale industries, alone with iron and steel production and, of course, coal mining. Early on coal became an important British export, and with this resource's seaside locations in Northeast England, Scotland, and Wales it could be shipped directly to almost any part of the world. In Wales coal mining is supplemented by shipbuilding and the production of iron and steel. The same complex of industries is based on the coalfields of Scotland, where Glasgow (2 million) has become one of Britain's major industrial cities. It is a measure of the impact of the Industrial Revolution that today four-fifths of the population of Scotland is concentrated in the area identified on Figure 17-1 as the Edinburgh-Glasgow Corridor.

Britain, at the vanguard of the Industrial Revolution, has not always kept up with modern developments. Plants which at one time were the epitome of industrial modernization still operate today—comparatively inefficient, expensive to run, slow, and wasteful. With the relative decline of the industrial cities of the Midlands and Northern England, there is a tendency for industrial enterprises that can afford and are able to do so, to relocate near the old focal point of Britain: London. Here, still, is the greatest domestic market of the British Isles, and increasingly that market is of importance to local manufacturers as the competition for markets from elsewhere intensifies. All this reflects the decreasing importance of coal in the energy-supply picture (which is changing toward nuclear power), the desire to start afresh with up-to-date machinery, and a realization that London, in addition to forming a huge domestic market, is also a good port through which to import raw materials. And so London, too, shows up on Figure 17-1 as an industrial district within the European region.

Paris does also. When the Industrial Revolution came to the mainland, Paris was already continental Europe's greatest city—but Paris did not (as London did not) have coal or iron deposits in its immediate vicinity. Nevertheless, Paris was the largest local market for manufactures produced for hundreds of miles around, and when a railroad system was added to the existing road and waterway connections, the city's centrality was strengthened still further. As in the case of London, Paris itself began to attract major industries, and the city, long a center for the manufacture of luxury items (jewelry, perfumes, fashions) experienced great industrial expansion in such areas as automobile manufacturing and assembly, the metal industries, and the production of chemicals. With a ready labor force, an ideal position for the distribution of finished products, the presence of governmental agencies, a nearby ocean port (Le Havre or Rouen can serve), and France's largest domestic market, the development of Paris as a major industrial center is no accident.

But Europe's coal deposits lie in a belt across northern France, Belgium, and Western Germany to Southern Poland—and along this zone developed mainland Europe's real concentrations of heavy industry. Before its fragmentation into an East and a West Germany, three such industrial districts lay in the German state: the Ruhr, based on the Westphalia coalfield, the Saxony area near the boundary with Czechoslovakia (now in East Germany), and Silesia (now in Poland). Among these, the Ruhr has become the greatest industrial complex of Europe. After Britain, Germany is Europe's top coal producer; it is Europe's first iron and steel producer bar none.

The Ruhr, named after a small tributary of the Rhine River, provides us with an illustration of the advantages of a combination of high-quality resources, good accessibility, and a position near large markets of high purchasing power. The coal of the Ruhr is of excellent quality for steelmaking

European countries continue to produce a large volume of automobiles. This is part of the BMW plant in Munich, West Germany.

purposes. Although the iron ore locally available was soon exhausted, ores can be shipped in from overseas with only a single transshipment. Long before the Ruhr emerged as Germany's major complex of heavy industries, cities had been growing nearby along the Rhine, including Köln (Cologne) and the present capital of West Germany, Bonn. The surrounding agricultural area was productive and densely populated. After the early 1870s the Ruhr expanded rapidly and increasingly received the benefit of government support in the form of subsidies and tariff protection. The chief manufactures made here are iron and steel (and products forged from these, such as railroad equipment, vehicles, machinery, and the like), textiles, and chemicals, with an almost endless variety of associated products.

While the Ruhr region specializes in heavy industries, Saxony (now in the German Democratic Republic, or East Germany) is skill and quality oriented. Today this region, which includes such famous cities as Leipzig (printing and publishing), Dresden (ceramics), and Karl-Marx-Stadt (textiles), benefits from nearby coalfields, but even before the Industrial Revolution made its impact here these places were substantial manufacturing centers.

Farther eastward, the industrial district of Silesia also was first developed by the Germans, although it now lies in Poland and extends into Czechoslovakia. A major industrial district is developing here in Southern and Southwestern Poland, based upon local, high-quality

coal resources and lesser iron ores that are, however, supplemented by imports from the Soviet Ukraine. Czechoslovakia shares the raw materials with Poland; they lie astride the gap between the Erzgebirge (the Ore Mountains) and the Carpathians. In Czechoslovakia this particular industrial district is called Moravia, and the city of Ostrava, with its metallurgical and chemical industries, lies at the center.

Our map shows other industrial districts in Europe, notably those focused large cities such as Berlin and Warsaw, and the rapidly emerging Northern Italian district. Even so, the map is but a generalization of Europe's total industrial strength: we have highlighted only the really outstanding areas. Other noteworthy concentrations of industry exist in Eastern Sweden, around Stockholm (noted for paper, wood products, textiles, and precision instruments), in Northern and Eastern Spain, and in East-Central France, where the focus is on the Lyon textile complex. These industrial areas, just districts in Europe's massive industrial structure, would stand out as major concentrations in other parts of the world.

North American Manufacturing Region

Notwithstanding Europe's industrial prowess, the North American industrial complex has no rival in the world today. Served by a wide array of natural resources and spurred by networks of natural as well as manmade transport networks, remote from the devastation wrought by wars in other industrial regions, on the doorstep of the world's richest market, North American manufacturing developed rapidly and successfully. Ample capital, mass production, specialization, and diversification mark the growth of this region

The bulk of American manufacturing (in the United States and Canada) is concentrated in the region delimited on Figure 17-2, a region that extends from the eastern seaboard to Minneapolis and from Montreal to St. Louis. Manufacturing in North America began in *New England* as early as colonial times, but New England is not especially rich in mineral resources. Still, the oldest manufacturing district continues to produce quality, light manufactures. This is one of those manufacturing districts where skills are generated, the kinds of skills that contribute importantly to balance in industry. But, as we know, other areas have overtaken New England in terms of productivity and diversity. As white settlement in North America marched westward, manufacturing spread as well. And farther west is where some great mineral deposits, fuels as well as ores, were discovered.

Another district of rather early importance centers on metropolitan *New York*, at the very heart of megalopolis and the

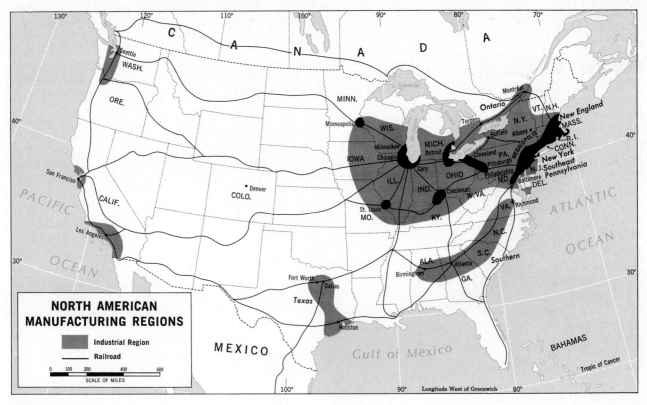

NORTH AMERICAN
MANUFACTURING REGIONS

Industrial Region
Railroad

0   100   200   400   600
SCALE OF MILES

Figure 17-2

locus today of tens of thousands of industrial establishments. Again, New York and its immediate environs are not especially well endowed with mineral resources, but we have here a situation not altogether different from the one we encountered in the cases of London and Paris. The agglomeration process plays a major role, New York being the country's largest, most concentrated market (and lying at the heart of a larger market still), the place where a huge skilled and semiskilled labor force exists, the focus of an intensive transport network, one of the

world's greatest ports and break-of-bulk locations. New York is also a center for business and finance; numerous companies with nationwide tenacles have their head offices, their management here in the city. As for the character of its manufacturing, the New York district, like New England but on a more massive scale, is an area of predominantly light industries. Clothing is made here, as are books, metal goods, various kinds of food; there is some treatment of incoming commodities from overseas, for example the refining of petroleum and sugar.

Still farther south along the eastern seaboard, the southern end of Megalopolis stands out as

a district of heavier manufacturing. This district centers on *Southeast Pennsylvania*, specifically Philadelphia, but it extends on to Baltimore. As we noted earlier, iron ores shipped all the way from South America and Canada are smelted right on the waterfront in "tidewater" mills; in the past the district's raw materials came from local sources. In addition to steel mills there are chemical industries, textile factories, and lighter manufacturing plants. A large market is clustered here, and a substantial labor force, some of the major ports on the eastern seaboard, and an excellent transport network serves the district.

333

Farther west we can discern a rather well-defined industrial district in interior *New York State*, extending approximately from Albany, on the Hudson River, and Buffalo, on the shore of Lake Erie. As in England, much local specialization occurs in this district, and a wide variety of manufactures is produced. Some familiar city names and products here: Rochester for its cameras and optical products, Albany for textiles, Syracuse for shoes, Buffalo for its flour mills and steel-making plants. The old Erie Canal, dug early in the nineteenth century to connect the east coast to the (then) far interior, used to serve this district.

On the other side of Lake Erie (that is, on the northern and western side) lies Canada's *Ontario* district, really a continuation of the Albany-Buffalo industrial belt. Toronto is the focus of this district, which is Canada's industrial heartland and extends all the way to Windsor, opposite Detroit. Toronto and Hamilton manufacture steel, and various locales in the region manufacture products ranging from heavy machinery to clothing to canned foods. Figure 17-2 also shows Montreal to lie in an area of manufacturing. The Montreal-Ottawa area, along the St. Lawrence River, is no match for the Ontario district, but it has one big advantage: cheap hydroelectric power. This, we know, attracts such industries as aluminum refining and paper making; other industries have followed suit and now flour mills, sugar refineries, and textile plants have located there.

Returning to the United States, Figure 17-2 shows several major industrial districts to lie west of New York State, including those we might identify

as Pittsburgh-Cleveland, Detroit-Southeast Michigan, Chicago-Gary-Milwaukee and, on a lesser scale, those focused on Minneapolis, St. Louis, Cincinnati, and a large number of still smaller but yet substantial urban centers. Collectively we might identify these as the U.S. *interior* industrial districts, but to try to identify the really huge variety of products created here would be pointless. Many of them are common knowledge—who thinks of Pittsburgh without thinking at the same time of its huge steel mills, or of Detroit without the image of automobiles, or of Gary (Indiana) and Chicago without miles of furnaces and mills, Lake Michigan barges bringing loads of iron ore from Lake Superior shores? This is where U.S. industrial power really transforms the landscape, where Appalachian coal and Mesabi iron ore are converted and autos, bulldozers, harvesters, armored cars, and tanks roll off the assembly lines. Computers, refrigerators, record players, toys, cornflakes, and pills—these and thousands of other products pour from the factories of the Midwest.

Figure 17-2 reminds us, however, that this industrial heartland we have been discussing is not the only region of significant development in the United States. A region we might call the *Southern* district extends from the vicinity of Birmingham, Alabama to Richmond, Virginia. Birmingham is a name associated with iron and steel in this country as well as Britain, and local raw materials have sustained this industry here for

many years. Atlanta, rapidly rising as the South's urban focus, has a growing industrial base. Cotton and tobacco rank high in this district's array of manufactures, and as we noted, timber is an important product also. On the Gulf of Mexico, the *Texas* district is emerging, centered on major urban areas of Houston and Dallas-Fort Worth. The oil fields generate a major petrochemical industry here, and meat-packing and flour-milling industries are also substantial. We know Houston from our space-flight reports emanating from there (". . . this is mission control . . .") and the new aerospace industry employs thousands of people in this industrial district as well. Denver, also outside the major industrial region of the United States, shares substantially in the growth of this industry. And finally, our map shows three manufacturing areas lying on the West coast—in the Los Angeles, San Francisco, and Seattle environs. These *West Coast* districts respond to the West's growing markets; the particular physical environments have boosted food-processing industries (citrus products in Southern California, wines in the vicinity of San Francisco). Many of the aircraft you may have traveled on are built in the Seattle area: the aerospace industry here is of major proportions. Nevertheless, these large cities with their substantial industrial complexes are but outliers of the North American industrial region, still the most productive world region of its kind.

The ultimate in the technology of mass-production: assembly line of the DC-10 passenger aircraft at the Douglas plant, Long Beach, California.

Soviet Manufacturing Region

As one would expect in so vast a country, the Soviet Union's manufacturing districts lie widely dispersed. Two of them, the districts around Novosibirsk and Karaganda in Soviet Asia, do not appear on our map (Fig. 17-3), which focuses on the western part of the U.S.S.R. Although those distant districts show signs of developing into important centers, they are so far dwarfed by the districts shown on our map: the area around Moscow, the Ukraine industrial district, the Volga district, and the district that lies astride the Urals. These lie in what some

geographers would term "European Russia," still the most populous region of the country and demarcated to the east by the Ural Mountains.

The Moscow district, often called the *Central Industrial Region*, is the Soviet Union's oldest industrial district. It is not especially well endowed with natural resources, but it has other advantages. With the present distribution of population, Moscow has great centrality: roads and railroads radiate in all directions, to the Ukraine in the south, to Minsk, Belorussia, and Europe in the west, to Leningrad and the Baltic coast in the northwest, to Gorky and the Ural district in the east, and to the cities and waterways of the Volga in the southeast. A canal links the

city to this, the U.S.S.R.'s most-used navigable river. Moscow is the focus of an area that includes some 50 million people (more than one fifth of the country's total population), many of them concentrated in such major cities as Gorky, the automobile-producing "Soviet Detroit" (over one million), Yaroslavl (one-half million), the tire-producing center, Ivanovo, the "Soviet Manchester" with its textile industries, and Tula, the mining and metallurgical center of the south.

The comparative paucity of natural resources within the Central Industrial Region is counterbalanced by the excellent transport system that facilitates the

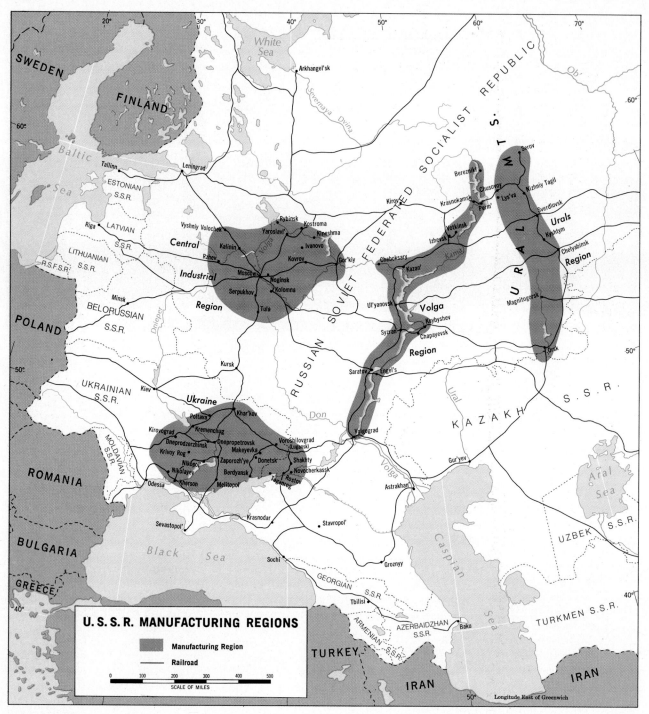

U.S.S.R. MANUFACTURING REGIONS

▨ Manufacturing Region

— Railroad

| 0 | 100 | 200 | 300 | 400 | 500 |

SCALE OF MILES

Figure 17-3

inflow of a wide range of commodities—gas from Stavropol, petroleum from the Volga fields, and electricity from Volga River dams for energy, and metals, wood, wool, cotton, flax, and leather (among many other items) for processing. The major flow, other than that of food, is of these materials into the C.I.R. and of finished products being distributed to the consumers. Thus the manufactures of the district are marked, as are those of the London and Paris areas, by high values in relation to bulk. Moscow has always been the leading center of skilled labor in the Soviet Union, and the available skills are those which—as Russia found out after Western Europe had—do not develop quickly and cannot be imparted overnight to peasant labor freed of farm work. Primacy, time and place have favored Moscow and the Central Industrial Region.

In the *Ukraine* the Soviet Union has one of those regions where major deposits of industrial resources—fuels and ores—lie fairly close together. The Ukraine began to emerge as a major region of heavy industry toward the end of the nineteenth century, and one major reason for this was the Donets Basin, one of the world's most productive coalfields. This area, known as *Donbas* for short, lies north of the city of Rostov (Fig 17-3). In the early decades this Donbas field produced over 90 percent of all the coal mined in the country. Other fields have since been opened up, but even today, three quarters of a century later, the Donets Basin alone still accounts for between one quarter and one third of the total Soviet coal output. And the

In the Soviet industrial heartland: the Togliatti Auto Factory, near Kuybyshev on the Volga.

coal is of high grade, some of it is even anthracite, and most of it is suitable for coking purposes.

What makes the Ukraine unique in the Soviet Union is the location, less than 200 miles from all this Donbas coal, of the Krivoy Rog iron ores. The quality of this ore is very high, and although the best ores have been worked out the field still produces. Major metallurgical industries arose on both the Donets coalfield and near the Krivoy Rog iron ores: Donetsk and its satellite, Makeyevka, dominate on the Donets side of the district (this is the "Soviet Pittsburgh"), while Dnepopetrovsk is the chief center in the cluster of cities on the Krivoy Rog side. In one way or another all the major cities located nearby have benefited from the fortuitous juxtaposition

of minerals in the southern Ukraine: Rostov, Volgograd, and Kharkov, and even Odessa and Kiev farther away. Like the Ruhr, the Ukraine industrial district lies in an area of dense population (and hence, available labor), adequate transportation, good agricultural productivity, and large local markets. And when the better ores were exhausted, somewhat lower-grade ores proved to be available on the basis of which production could be maintained. The biggest development in this context is the discovery of the so-called Kursk Magnetic Anomaly, positioned north of the Ukraine district and south of the Central Industrial Region (Fig.17-3), and thus able to serve both districts.

The Kursk Magnetic Anomaly is a large iron ore deposit whose exploitation had been delayed by technical problems. Mining began in 1959 and the ores have given the metallurgical industries from Tula to Rostov a new lease on life

Two other, elongated industrial districts appear on Figure 17-3. Their elongation relates to their uniting physiographic feature: the Volga River and the Ural Mountains. The *Volga* region has witnessed major development in the decades starting during the Second World War. With the Ukraine and the Moscow area threatened by the German armies, whole industrial plants were dismantled and reassembled in Volga cities, protected from the war by distance. Kuybyshev was even the Soviet capital for a time. Then, after the war, the progress set in motion continued. A series of dams were constructed on the Volga, and electric power became plentiful. Oil and natural gas proved to exist in quantities larger than anywhere else in the U.S.S.R. Canals linked the Volga to Moscow and the Don River, making the importing of raw materials easy. The cities along the river Volga, spaced at remarkably regular intervals, developed specializations: Kazan is known for its leathers and furs, Volgograd for its metallurgy, Saratov for chemicals, Kirov for wood products, and Kuybyshev for its huge oil refineries. This district's contribution to the Soviet economy is still rising rapidly.

The last major industrial district on our map is the *Urals* region—the easternmost district

of major importance. This area also developed rapidly during World War II. But there has been nothing artificial in its growth: the Urals yield an enormous variety of metallic ores including iron, copper, nickel, chromite, bauxite, and many more. The only serious problem is coal, of which there is not enough and what there is does not have the required quality. So coal is railed in all the way from the Kuznetsk Basin, a thousand miles to the east. In the cities of the Urals

district, metals, metal goods, and machinery are produced in great quantities. With the Siberian centers, the Urals district now produces as much as half of all the iron and steel made in the entire Soviet Union. It is a sign of the eastward march of the country's center of gravity, and a part of the national planners' grand design.

Among Japan's most successful industries is shipbuilding. Here a huge oil tanker is under construction at the Kure Shipyard.

Japan-China Industrial Region

Japan is presently the world's third industrial power, and, if current rates of growth continue to prevail, Japan will be in second place (after the United States but surpassing the U.S.S.R.) within a few years. This is all the more remarkable when it is realized that Japan has a very limited domestic natural resource base. Much of what Japan manufactures is made out of raw materials bought all over the world, and shipped to that small archipelago off the East Asian coast.

Japan rose from comparative obscurity, from an underdeveloped country to a modern industrial power, in just one century. But we should not forget that Japan, prior to its modernization era, did have a domestic manufacturing industry. During the first half of the nineteenth century, manufacturing in Japan, especially the handcraft variety, was widespread. In home industries and community workshops the Japanese produced silk and cotton-textile manufactures, porcelain, wood products, and metal goods. During those days the small domestic resources were enough (Japan does have some ores) to supply the local industries. Power came from human arms and legs and from wheels driven—as in England—by water. The chief source of fuel was charcoal.

Figure 17-4

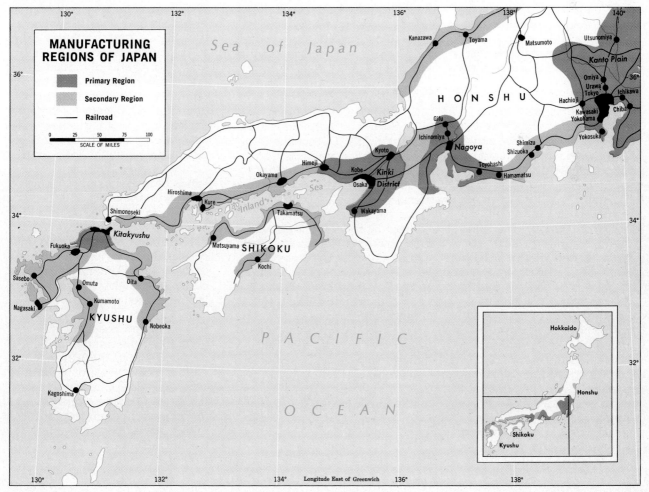

339

Thus there was an industry, there was a manufacturing-oriented labor force, and there were known manufacturing skills.

Japan's push toward industrial modernization began with the integration and enlargement of these community and home workshops, the export to world markets of light manufactures, and the adoption of the techniques generated by the Industrial Revolution. There was some coal, and Japan's topography produced numerous sites for hydroelectric power development. As industry grew and the Kyushu coalfields became worked out, it was realized that raw materials would have to come from overseas. The age of the factory had arrived: the coastal cities were in the best position to receive the raw materials and to convert them to finished products. Now the regional industrial pattern shown in Figure 17-4 took shape.

Figure 17-4 reveals that the largest district of manufacturing in Japan is the Kanto Plain, which contains not only Tokyo (the capital and largest city) and Yokohama, its major port, but also several smaller but substantial industrial towns such as Kawasaki and Chiba. The Kanto Plain and its giant conurbation produces between one fourth and one fifth of the country's industrial output. Tokyo is the leading steel producer, with ores coming from as far away as the Philippines, Malaya, India, and even Africa. Although hydroelectric power is brought in from the interior mountain sites, coal is shipped to Tokyo from a new field in Hokkaido (the northernmost major island of Japan) and from Australia and America.

Petroleum comes from Southwest Asia and Indonesia. The Japanese are able to pay for all this by selling enormous quantities of their manufactures on the world's markets.

The second-ranking manufacturing district in Japan is the Kobe-Osaka area, with Kyoto as an outlier (Kyoto is the ancient Japanese capital, still a significant light manufacturing center). This district, long an area of diversified manufacturing, has been developing heavier industries in recent decades and now produces not only textiles and chemicals but also iron and steel, machinery, ships, and airplanes. The Kobe-Osaka district, as Figure 17-4 shows, lies at the eastern end of the Inland Sea. The Inland Sea in many ways is the heart of Japan; overlooking its waters are dozens of large and small cities, and criss-cross traffic is as busy as one any of the world's major rivers.

Between the Kanto Plain and the Kinki District (the general name for the Kobe-Osaka-Kyoto triangle) lies the *Nagoya* district, where a wide variety of textiles are made, and where heavy industries are also developing. Many of the Japanese automobiles you see on the world's roads are built at Nagoya.

At the opposite end of the Inland Sea from Kobe-Osaka lies a fourth major industrial district, called *Kitakyushu*—a conurbation of five North Kyushu cities. Here were Japan's first coal mines, and here the first steel mills of modernizing Japan were built, which for many years remained the largest the country

had. Look for this district to develop even faster than it has, should the trade normalization with China continue: no place in Japan is located in a better position to do business with mainland Asia. Presently, heavy industries dominate here, with shipbuilding and iron and steel making in the lead, supplemented by a major chemical industry and numerous lighter manufacturing plants.

Only one manufacturing district in Japan, in the area depicted by our map, lies outside the belt extending from Tokyo in the east to Kitakyushu in the west. This is the district centered on *Toyama*, on the Sea of Japan. The advantage here is cheap electricity from nearby hydroelectric stations, and the cluster of industries reflects it: paper manufacturing, chemical industries, and textile plants have located here. Of course, our map gives an inadequate picture of the variety and range of industries that exist throughout Japan, many of them oriented to the local (and not insignificant) market. Thousands of manufacturing plants operate in the cities and towns other than those on the map, even in the cold, northern island of Hokkaido. As we did in the case of Europe, North America, and the Soviet Union, we have focused here on the really outstanding manufacturing regions of Japan.

China. China has more than eight times the number of people of Japan, but its industries cannot match those of its island neighbor. Still, China too is on the move, and we ought to look at the places where its progress in industry is most evident. In the past, China's industries were

The Anshan iron and steel works in China—a complex of more than 60 factories. Here, people on their way to work.

established and maintained by foreigners—first the Europeans, who built factories in the coastal cities to process goods to be sold at home, and then the Japanese, who invaded Korea and established a sphere of influence in Manchuria, China's northern province (Fig. 17-5). As in the case of the Soviet Union but on a smaller scale, some dispersal of industries into the interior was occasioned by World War II (Chungkiang and Chengtu, for example, grew substantially during this period). But the major industrial development of China has occurred during the modern, communist period. When the communist planners took over in Peking, one of their priorities was to develop as rapidly as possible China's own resources and industries.

China is a very large country, and it is likely that some of its natural resources have yet to be discovered. Even so, China has already proved to possess a substantial domestic resource base—one that is far superior to Japan's, for example. In terms of coal, there is hardly a limit on industrialization in China: the quality is good, the quantity enormous, and many of the deposits are near the surface and easily mined. China's iron ores are not so productive, and are generally of rather low grade—but new finds are frequently made and the picture has improved steadily.

China's industrial heartland extends from Manchuria to the Lower Yangtze, from the vicinity of Shenyang to the environs of Shanghai. As Figure 17-5 shows, this industrial region is not contiguous, but consists of three

Figure 17-5

major and several minor districts. *Southern Manchuria* has become China's industrial heartland, and the northeast's largest city, Shenyang (formerly Mukden), with a population of over 5 million, has emerged as a Chinese Pittsburgh. This is based on Manchuria's coal and iron deposits, which lie in the basin of the Liao River. There is coal within 100 miles to the west of Shenyang and about 30 miles to the east, at Fushun, as well; to the southwest, just 60 miles away, there is iron ore at An-shan. Since the iron ore is of rather low grade, the coal is hauled from Fushun to the iron

reserves. Under the circumstances this is the cheapest way to make iron and steel here. An-shan has become China's leading iron and steel producing center, but Shenyang has the largest, most diverse overall industrial complex, with metallurgy, machine making, and other large engineering works. Before long the city of Harbin will become part of a contiguous Manchurian industrial region. Already, Harbin with 2.5 million residents has plants making farm machinery, textile factories, food processing, and light manufacturing.

The *North China* district, including the capital, Peking, the port of Tientsin, and the city of Tanghsien (among others), also benefit from nearby coalfields. As one might expect, here in the productive basin of the Hwang River, food processing and textile making rank next to the heavy industries. Still farther to the south lies the third district in China's industrial heartland, the *Yangtze* district. On our map the Yangtze district divides into two areas, one centered on Shanghai, China's largest industrial city, and the other focused on Wuhan, astride the Yangtze several hundred miles upstream. In fact, still farther upstream along

342

Concrete canalboats being manufactured at Hangchow, China. As wood has become more scarce and expensive in China and elsewhere, these concrete boats are replacing the older wooden types.

the Yangtze River lies Chungkiang, the city that grew so strongly during wartime. Whether we view this Yangtze district as one region or as three, this too is a Chinese industrial heartland, if not in terms of iron and steel production alone then in terms of its diversification of production and its local specializations. Railroad cars, ships, books, foods, chemicals—an endless variety of products comes from the Yangtze district.

Industrial growth by agglomeration and in response to the expansion of urban markets has generated manufacturing centers in and near the Canton-Hong Kong area and in China's larger interior cities. The fortuitous, wide dispersal of the country's raw materials places many such cities near natural resources, stimulating industrial development and broadening China's industrial base.

Industrialization Elsewhere

Compared to the regions we have discussed so far, industrial development in other parts of the world is but minor. Industrialization in *India* is yet in an initial phase of development. India's industrial core area lies on the margins of the Chota Nagpur upland (Fig. 17-6). There is good coking coal in West Bengal (though not as much as India would wish), and high-grade iron ore in the same general area. Jamshedpur has become the center of this manufacturing district, positioned fortuitously on the doorstep of the great Ganges population cluster and not far from Calcutta, the great urban focus here. Unlike its Southwest Asian neighbors, India does not have large oil fields (some oil is being produced in Assam), and while there are good hydroelectric sites in many parts of India, their development is expensive and

343

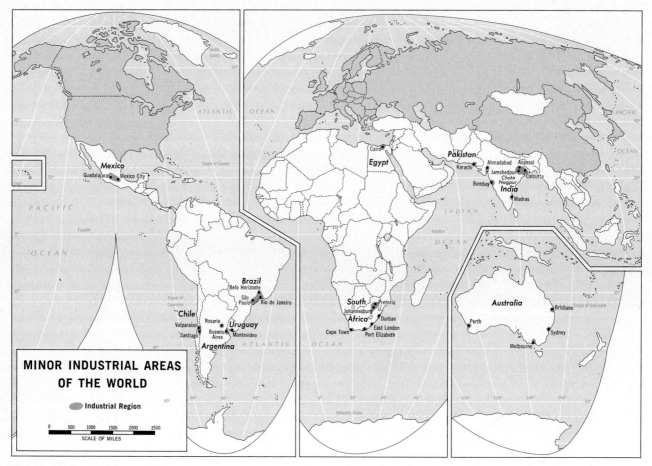

MINOR INDUSTRIAL AREAS
OF THE WORLD

Industrial Region

0   500 1000 1500 2000 2500
SCALE OF MILES

Figure 17-6

the rate at which they can be developed is necessarily slow. Still, with the coal situation deteriorating to the point that India must consider importing this commodity, and the expense of moving locally available coal over great distances to India's widely dispersed cities, the Indian government is investing quite heavily in hydroelectric projects, especially those near major cities (Bombay and Madras, for instance, are served by hydroelectric power) and those where dam construction leads not only to improved power supply but also to new irrigation areas and improved flood control.

In addition to iron and steel industries in Jamshedpur, India has a major cotton manufacturing industry, centered on Bombay and Ahmadabad (India is the world's second ranking textile exporter, after Japan), and has, in Calcutta, a major center of diversified manufacturing. Calcutta has railway assembly plants, food processing factories, jute mills, chemical industries, printing plants, and a host of other industries mainly oriented toward the domestic market.

This last factor—orientation and response to local markets—is an important one to consider in any discussion of world manufacturing. In developed countries such as *Australia* and New Zealand and in developing countries such as *Brazil* and *Nigeria*, manufacturing is encouraged primarily *not* because it is hoped that the products of the factories will immediately sell well on the world market. The hope is to reduce the country's dependence on foreign manufactures, which are expensive to buy. Light manufacturing, then, dominates in those areas, and tends to concentrate in and near the largest local markets, the urban centers. In Australia, manufacturing centers on Sydney, Melbourne, Brisbane, and Perth; production for the domestic market includes the making of clothing, shoes, foods and beverages, and similar industries. Australia, of course, does have a substantial export trade in certain foodstuffs (dairy products, meats) and wool, and some of the country's manufacturing involves the processing and packing of these goods.

In *Africa*, a growing industrial complex lies in the Southern African interior, in the Southern Transvaal and the Northern Orange Free State. Johannesburg lies at the center of this industrial district of some four million people, which includes the iron and steel works near Pretoria and steel mills in the Orange Free State. This complex had its origins in the Witwatersrand gold fields and subsequently benefited from the presence of other, industrial resources nearby. Lesser industrial districts have developed around Cape Town and Durban, and at Port Elizabeth, all on the South African coast. South Africa is blessed with a wide range of mineral resources, and its industrial strength is considerable—far ahead of any other African country. In second place might be Egypt, which boasts a steel mill built about 20 miles south of Cairo where iron ore

from the country's southern reserve is smelted with coking coal imported via the Nile. Egypt has also developed a rather substantial textile industry, based on its agricultural output principally of cotton.

In *South America*, substantial industrial development is taking place in few areas, and the pattern of light manufactures for local markets, concentrated in the major cities, prevails. The exceptions, as Figure 17-6 indicates, are concentrated in just four South American countries. Brazil, which can count coking coal and iron ore among its resources, has a developing industrial region in the Rio de Janeiro-São Paulo district that includes steel making and other heavy industires. Light manufacturing dominates in the core area of Argentina and neighboring Uruguay. Central Chile's industries also serve principally the local market, although some Chilean plants process mineral ores prior to export.

Throughout this discussion of the world's leading industrial regions, we have been using the names of urban centers as our points of reference. And there is

no doubt about it: the urbanized world is also the industrialized world, and the same regions we identified in Chapter 16 as having oriented an agricultural world to their comfort and convenience are also the regions of major, world-scale industrialization. The "developed" world is, in fact, the urban-industrial world, and the landscape of urban agglomeration and industrial concentration, skyscrapers and smokestacks is, in a very real sense, the landscape of power.

Essay: Three Worlds

Ours is a divided world, not only politically but also economically. We express those divisions in a number of ways. For example, we see a *capitalist* world (including such countries as the United States, Australia, and Japan), a *socialist* world (the Soviet Union, China, Cuba, Eastern Europe), and a *third* world (Brazil, Nigeria, India, and other South and Central American, African, and Asian countries that are neither capitalist nor socialist). About half the people of the world live in Third World countries, about one third in socialist-communist countries and somewhat under one fifth find themselves in capitalist countries. This breakdown depends, of course, on sometimes arguable decisions as to what constitutes a socialist country and what does not. In the socialist and Third World countries, there is much variety. Yugoslavia and China are both in the socialist world, but Yugoslav socialism is something very different from Chinese communism. Mexico and Tanzania are both Third World countries, but they, too, have strongly different systems. We in the capitalist world are sometimes belabored with the singularity and inflexibility of communism. Actually, there is considerably more variety in the socialist world than in the capitalist system.

We have also become accustomed to identifying countries as "developed" and "underdeveloped," the developed countries being the industrialized, rich, well-fed minority and the underdeveloped countries the raw material supplying, generally poorer, often hungry majority. Between these categories lies a group of "emerging" countries that have begun to throw off the most pervasive symptoms of underdevelopment and are showing signs of what is sometimes called "takeoff."

As always, the criteria on which we base such a classification are subject to debate; they are not absolute, and that is the spirit in which we must view any map showing the distribution of the developed, intermediate, and underdeveloped countries. Some economic geographers classify Argentina and Venezuela as developed countries rather than intermediate; some view Nigeria and India as intermediate rather than underdeveloped. And many argue that South Africa is indeed a developed country, despite the regional and social separations between its developed (mostly white) and underdeveloped (mainly black) sectors.

What are these criteria that determine the level of a country's development? With so many people in the subsistence sector, an underdeveloped economy is marked by a low level of output per worker and, at the same time, a low level of consumption of goods and services per capita. When economists measure development, they consider not only the incomes of a country's population (converted to a per-person figure that exceeds $2000 in developed countries, falls below $ 100 per year in underdeveloped economies), but also the occupational structure of the labor force (how many people must work to produce food?), the consumption of various forms of energy, the availability of transport and communication facilities, the use of metals, and such data as literacy rates, calorie intake, percentage of family income spent on food, personal savings, and similar information.

It is difficult to escape the conclusion that the developed countries are also the industrialized countries, and that the route to "take-off" and development lies in rapid industrialization. Small wonder, then, that some countries whose governments seek to accelerate their economic development have tried to go the route of factory building; underdeveloped countries from Indonesia to Egypt want their own steel mills and national airlines as symbols of progress. But not all countries have made this decision. The governments of some underdeveloped countries realize that the criteria by which development is measured reflect not only those particular features of the economy but also the degree of transformation of the whole society. A domestic steel mill or some other major industrial plant will do little to speed that transformation, and it remains little more than a foreign anomaly, a costly producer of misleading statistics. A good example of a different approach is the case of Tanzania where, after independence, the *first* national order of business was to change the country's agriculture, to help farmers living a life of shortage and hunger gain toward adequate production, to disseminate improved farming techniques, fertilizers, and tools, and to encourage and support farm cooperatives. This program, which involved also the relocation of farmers away from overcrowded areas, did not proceed without problems, and there was sometimes militant opposition in the countryside. Still there was progress and success—although

The stock market: epitome of capitalist enterprise. Shown here is the Paris Bourse.

few of the results would appear on the list of development criteria. Unhappily the great droughts of the 1970s severely damaged Tanzania's courageous self-help efforts.

The developed countries, obviously, are the advantaged countries—but why cannot the underdeveloped and "takeoff" countries catch up? It is not, as is sometimes suggested, simply a matter of environment, resource distribution, or cultural heritage (a resistance to innovation, for example). The sequence of events that led to the present division of our world began long before the Industrial Revolution occurred. Europe even by the middle of the eighteenth century had laid the foundations for its colonial expansion; the Industrial Revolution magnified Europe's demands for raw materials while its products increased the efficiency of its imperial control. While Western countries gained an enormous headstart, colonial dependencies remained suppliers of resources and consumers of the products of the Western industries. Thus was born a system of international exchange and capital flow that really changed but little when the colonial period came to an end. Underdeveloped countries, well aware of their predicament, accused the developed world of perpetuating its advantage through neocolonialism—the entrenchment of the old system under a new guise.

There can be no doubt that the world economic system works to the disadvantage of the underdeveloped countries, but sadly it is not the only obstacle the poorer countries face. Political instability, corruptible leaderships and elites, misdirected priorities, misuse of aid, and traditionalism are among circumstances that inhibit development. External interference by interests representing powerful developed countries have also had negative impact on the economic as well as the political progress of underdeveloped countries. Underdeveloped countries even get caught in the squeeze when other developing countries try to assert their limited strength: when the OPEC countries, mostly underdeveloped themselves, raise the price of oil, energy and fertilizers slip still farther from the reach of the poorer underdeveloped countries not fortunate enough to belong to this favored group. As the developed countries get stronger and wealthier, they leave the underdeveloped world ever farther behind: the gap is widening, and the prospects for the underdeveloped countries are not bright.

Reading

The book by A. N. Duckham and G. B. Masefield, *Farming Systems of the World* (Praeger, New York, 1970) contains a wealth of information and opinion. The quotation on p. 294 is from A. H. Bunting, editor, *Change in Agriculture*, another Praeger publication of 1970. A standard work in geography is H. F. Gregor's *Environment and Economic Life* (Van Nostrand, New York, 1963). The same author also wrote an overview entitled *Geography of Agriculture: Themes in Research* (Prentice-Hall, Englewood Cliffs, N.J., 1970), an excellent place to start a bibliography search for any paper. Also see E. Isaac, *Geography of Domestication* (Prentice-Hall, Englewood Cliffs, N.J., 1970) for much detail on questions only touched on in our chapter. You will also find J. R. Tarrant's *Agricultural Geography* (Halsted-Wiley, New York, 1974) quite useful. C. K. Eicher and L. W. Witt edited a volume on *Agriculture in Economic Development* (McGraw-Hill, New York, 1964) that still contains worthwhile essays. A volume that covers other topics as well as agriculture, *Economies and Societies in Latin America: a Geographical Interpretation* (Wiley, New York, 1973) by P. R. Odell and D. A. Preston, is worth your attention as well. And R. K. Nelson's *Hunters of the Northern Forest* (University of Chicago, 1973) describes the mode of survival of the Kutchin Indians of Alaska.

C. O. Sauer's *Agricultural Origins and Dispersals*, first published by the American Geographical Society, New York, in 1952, remains a classic in the field. The second edition, published by M.I.T. in 1969, contains three additional papers and a new introduction. Also see P. P. Courtenay, *Plantation Agriculture* (Bell, London, 1965), and a volume edited by J. A. Taylor, *Weather and Agriculture* (Pergamon, Elmsford, 1967). A volume by D. B. Grigg, *The Agricultural Systems of the World* (Cambridge, New York, 1974) is a useful source as well.

Industrial geography is discussed from many viewpoints in R. S. Thoman, E. C. Conkling and M. H. Yeates, *The Geography of Economic Activity* (McGraw-Hill, New York, 1968) and by R. M. Highsmith and R. M. Northam in *World Economic Activities: a Geographical Analysis* (Harcourt, Brace, New York, 1969). Another useful volume is R. S. Thoman and P. B. Corbin, *The Geography of Economic Activity* (McGraw-Hill, New York, 1974). A. Weber's classic, *Theory of the Location of Industries*, was translated by C. J. Friedrich and published by the University of Chicago Press, 1929. A technical but readable volume is D. M. Smith, *Industrial Location: An Economic Geographical Analysis* (Wiley, New York, 1971)).

For a recent application of principles of industrial location to a real-world situation see A. Rodgers, "The Locational Dynamics of Soviet Industry," *Annals of the Association of American Geographers*, Vol. 64, June, 1974.

PART FIVE
politics

Ancient Greece: theater and experiment.

18 Roots of the State System

Gone are the days when a family could load its possessions on a wagon or two, buy a span of horses, and trek away from the law-abiding, settled world into an open, unclaimed, often lawless frontier. Open spaces still exist, to be sure, but they are no longer free and unclaimed. A family that decides to leave crowded coastal Brazil to try its luck in the farthest interior of the Amazon Basin will still find itself under Brazilian jurisdiction and subject to the laws of Brazil. So it is in Australia, in the Soviet Union, in Argentina. Our world is divided today into the territories of some 150 separate states, and even deserts and other uninhabited areas (the ice fields of Antarctica, for example) have been claimed by national governments. To this number must be added the dwindling (but in 1977 still substantial) number of non-independent areas, some of which will also become sovereign states.[1] Ours is a fragmented world.

Viewed in the context of the whole of human history, the tight political jigsaw with which we are familiar today is a very recent development. Even one century ago the world map still contained large regions that were not controlled by any established state. Africa was the scene of colonial rivalries and ill-defined "spheres of influence," and the elements of the African political map we know today were not established until the colonial powers assembled in Berlin in the mid-1880s to sort matters out and draw boundary lines between their empires. In the Middle East, in Asia, even in Middle and South America large areas remained, just 100 years ago, that were not under any national jurisdiction. The modern political map is substantially a twentieth-century manifestation of human spatial accommodation. And now we are in the final chapter of the allocation of the earth's surface to national states, for we have begun to claim large regions of the last free frontier: the oceans. Before long you will begin to see maps showing boundaries between states not only on land, but at sea as well.

Although the "complete" political world map of today is a re-

[1] The United Nations on August 1, 1976 had 144 member states, but several countries (including Switzerland, the two Koreas, Angola, Taiwan) were not members. Mozambique and Angola, two former Portuguese dependencies, became self-governing in 1975. Sikkim was absorbed by India. In 1976 approximately 60 territories (many of them islands or groups of islands) remained dependencies.

353

Early States

cent creation, the idea that states should have clearly defined national territories is not new at all. Nearly 2000 years ago the leaders of the Roman Empire built walls across the northern part of a Roman colony called Britannia to mark the territorial limit of Roman jurisdiction and to defend Roman Britain against attacks by tribal peoples. At the other end of Eurasia, the rulers of feudal states in what is today Northern China also constructed walls to mark territorial boundaries—walls that were consolidated into a major system of national defense during China's Han Dynasty (202 B.C.–220 A.D.), when the famous Great Wall was built. The ancient Romans and Chinese were not the only peoples of their time to seek ways to demarcate national boundaries. Rivers often served as trespass lines, as did mountain ridges. Some of the boundaries we see on the modern world map have very ancient origins.

We tend sometimes to regard the state as a European invention, exported to the peoples of Africa, Asia, and America on the wings of colonialism, confirmed during Europe's era of industrial supremacy, and finally authenticated during the past 30 years by the emerging statehood of many former dependencies. After all, we still argue the merits of Greek and Roman political innovations, and measure our U.S. federal experiment against the pronouncements of European philosophers. And was it not Europe that brought the whole idea of the state to the tribal peoples of Africa, the Indians of America, the villages of Asia?

The answer is no. While it is true that European states achieved perhaps unprecedented political sophistication, complex organization, and national power during the past two centuries, Europe's accomplishments in this sphere came quite late. Even ancient Greece and the Roman Empire, more than 2000 years ago, did not stand alone as political achievements —nor were they without forerunners. Concepts of statehood took root in Asia, Africa, and America long before the Europeans came to introduce their versions of it during the colonial and postcolonial period. Europe transformed the political world, but Europe did not create it.

In Chapter 7 we considered humanity's early *culture hearths*, regions of cultural growth and development. In those areas of comparative success and progress, clusters of population developed; natural increase was supplemented by the inmigration of those attracted from afar. New ways were found to exploit local resources, and power was established over resources located farther away. Farming techniques improved, and so did yields. Settlements could expand, and began to acquire urban characteristics. The circulation of goods and ideas intensified. Traditions emerged in various spheres of life, and these traditions, along with inventions and innovations, radiated outward into the realm beyond. Among the ideas that took hold and developed were political ideas: the theory and practice of the political orgnization necessary to cope with society's growing complexity.

Such developments occurred on several continents. The Middle East was a prominent source area, where culture hearths lay in the area between the Tigris and Euphrates Rivers

(Mesopotamia), in the Nile Valley (Egypt), and in the Indus River Basin (in what is now Pakistan). A major culture hearth was centered on the confluence of the Wei and Hwang Rivers, there forming the roots of Chinese culture. In Middle America, the Yucatan Peninsula and later the Mexican Plateau were significant culture hearths. In South America the Central Andes Mountains witnessed the rise of a major human civilization. And in West Africa's savannalands a culture hearth also emerged.

Did these culture hearths and political developments occur spontaneously in all these areas, or was there interaction? This question is still under study. There is no doubt that there was indeed substantial contact between the three Middle Eastern culture hearths. But was there contact between Egypt and Middle America? Some scholars think so, pointing to the similarities between the Egyptian pyramids and the stone structures built by the inhabitants of the Yucatan Peninsula centuries later. One researcher even went so far as to build a boat similar to those known and used by the Mediterranean peoples of ancient Egypt's time and trying to sail it across the Atlantic, to prove that contact *was* possible. It is also believed that the ancient culture hearth of Northern China received innovations from Southwest Asia, but now there is a question as to the direction of this contact. Was it the Chinese who influenced the Indus and Mesopotamia rather than the

other way around? And again, there are questions about the statecraft practiced in savanna West Africa during the first millenium A. D. How much of West Africa's political tradition came from the Nile Valley?

To crucial questions such as these we do not yet have incontrovertible answers, proving again that time is no barrier when it comes to exciting and intriguing research. Scholars are saying now that it seems that we have underestimated the range of movement of ancient peoples (and therefore, surely, the range of ideas and innovations). Some surprises are undoubtedly in store.

Nevertheless, we can be certain of the Middle East's primacy as one of the earliest (if not the first) hearths of human culture. Mesopotamia, the land "between the rivers," flanked the Fertile Crescent, one of the places where people first learned to domesticate plants and gather harvests in an organized way (Fig. 18-1). Mesopotamia was a crossroads for a whole network of routes of trade and movement across Southwest Asia, the recipient of numerous new ideas and inventions, and many innovations originated in Mesopotamia itself, to be diffused to other regions of development. In addition to the organized and planned cultivation of grain crops such as wheat and barley, the Mesopotamians knew how to make tools and implements from bronze, they had learned to use draft animals to

pull vehicles (including plows designed to prepare the fields), and they employed the wheel, a revolutionary invention, and built carts, wagons, and chariots.

The ancient Mesopotamians also built some of the world's earliest cities. This development was made possible by their accomplishments in many spheres, especially agriculture, whose surpluses could be stored and distributed to the city dwellers. Essential to such a system of allocation, of course, was a body of decision makers and organizers, people who controlled the lives of others—an elite. Such an urban-based elite could afford itself the luxury of leisure, and could devote time to religion and philosophy. Out of such pursuits came the concept of writing and record keeping, an essential ingredient in the rise of urbanization. Writing made possible the codification of laws and the confirmation of traditions. It was a crucial element in the development of systematic administration in urbanizing Mesopotamia, and in the evolution of its religious-political ideology. The rulers in the cities were both priests and kings, and the harvest the peasants brought to be stored in the urban granaries was a tribute as well as a tax.

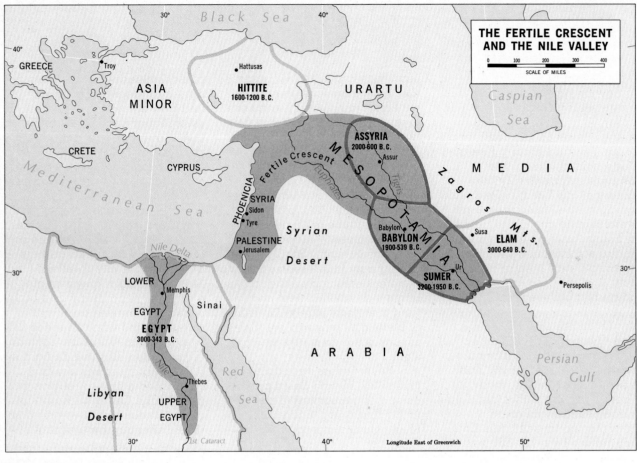

Figure 18-1

Mesopotamia's cities emerged between 5000 and 6000 years ago, and some may have had as many as 10,000 residents (some archeologists' estimates go even higher). Today these urban places are extinct, and careful excavations tell the story of their significant and sometimes glorious past. Mesopotamia's cities had their temples and shrines, priests, and kings; there were also wealthy merchants, expert craftsmen, respected teachers and philosophers. But Mesopotamia was no unified political state. Each city had a hinterland where its power and influence prevailed, and while there were sometimes alliances among cities, there was more often competition and conflict. This was *feudal* society, a society in which hostility and strife marked political relationships. But Mesopotamia made progress in political spheres as well as other areas, and regional unification eventually was achieved during the fourth millenium B.C. (i.e., between 5000 and 6000 years ago) in at least two early states named Sumer and Elam.

The early states were centered on cities, and they were *city-states*. It was a principle that had equivalents in other regions of the world where early states developed, and it proved to be a persistent phenomenon too: even today there remain some small, modern versions of these city-states. Singapore is such a modern city-state. Singapore was a part of Malaysia, but its leaders were often in conflict with the people who ruled the Malaysian nation. So Singapore—little more than the city with its immediate surroundings—broke off and became a city-state.

Another area that witnessed very early cultural and political development was Egypt. Possibly Egypt's evolution started even earlier than Mesopotamia's, but Egypt certainly possessed urban centers 5000 years ago, and there are archeologists who believe that even older remains of urban places may lie buried beneath the silt of the Nile Delta. Actually, the focus of the ancient culture hearth of Egypt lay above the Delta and below the Nile's first cataract, and this segment of the Nile Valley lies surrounded by rather inhospitable country. The region was open to the Mediterranean, but otherwise it was quite inaccessible by overland contact. In contrast to Mesopotamia, which was something of a marshland, the Nile Valley was a natural fortress of sorts. There, the ancient Egyptians converted the security of their isolation into progress. The Nile waterway was the area's highway of trade and association, its lifeline. It also sustained agriculture by irrigation, and the cyclic regime of the Nile River was a great deal more predictable than that of the Tigris and Euphrates. By the time ancient Egypt finally began to fall victim to outside invaders, from about 1700 B.C. onward, a full-scale, urban civilization had emerged, whose permanence and continuity are reflected by the massive stone monuments its artist-engineers designed and created. The political practices and philosophies of Pharaoic Egypt were diffused far and wide, especially into Africa. Egypt survived as a political entity longer, perhaps, than any

other state (China is its only rival); in the process, the state changed from a theocratic to a militaristic one, eventually to fall to colonial status, now to rise again as a modern nation. Ancient Egypt's armies were well disciplined and effective, and the cities were skillfully fortified. Where Egypt's armies ranged, peoples were subjugated and exploited for the state's benefit. Egypt far outlasted its Mesopotamian contemporaries.

Egypt lies to the west of Mesopotamia, and the Indus valley, still another Southwest Asian culture hearth, lies to the east of the land of Babylon. Here, in what is today Pakistan, arose a third Southwest Asian civilization with an urban tradition and a distinct religious-political ideology. This, too, was a literate society, and its major cities, Harappa in the north and Mohenjo-Daro in the south, were founded well before the beginning of the second mil-

Figure 18-2

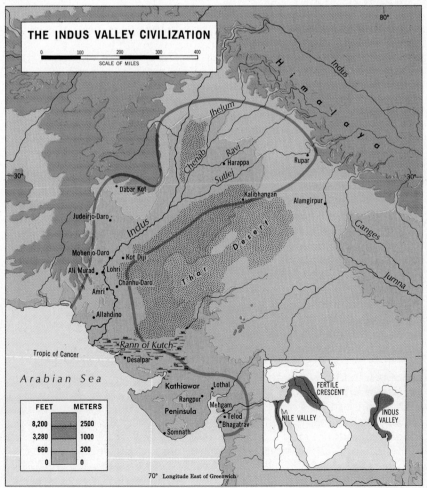

THE INDUS VALLEY CIVILIZATION

lenium B.C. Eventually they became the urban foci for a politically organized region that extended as far east as the upper Ganges Valley (in present-day India) and as far south as the Kathiawar Peninsula (Fig. 18-2). It is believed that influences from Mesopotamia reached the Indus region, stimulating development there.

It has long been postulated that the next urban tradition arose in China, chronologically not long after that of the Indus region, and that Mesopotamian innovations were received there as well. Thus the source of Chinese culture lay in the area where the Hwang Ho (Yellow River) and the Wei river flow together, and the first urban, literate society in China emerged during the second millenium B.C., between 3000 and 4000 years ago. But we should not conclude, as some scholars have, that the "idea" or urbanized life that first developed in Mesopotamia was simply transferred and adopted in such regions as the Indus and North China. Certainly some aspects of urban life were diffused even as far away as China, but the emergence of Chinese urban society was probably quite spontaneous. Southwest Asian ideas undoubtedly touched China, but China's urban-political emergence was self-propelled, not copied from the Middle East.

You will note that the rise of early states of dimensions larger than had prevailed before was a process intimately related to the growth of urbanism. The surpluses generated by more productive systems of agriculture made possible not only the agglomeration of people within a

Ancient Timbuktu (now in Mali) was a major administrative, intellectual, and trade center centuries ago. Today, none of its old glory remains.

small urban area and the emergence of a hierarchy of organizers and rulers: it also enabled the urban-based elites to assemble, arm, and sustain military forces. These armies were used not only to defend the cities and to attack rival places: they also policed the extraction of tribute and taxes from the countryside. While human populations were scattered in small villages, groups would take to arms to defend themselves or attack encroaching neighbors. But once the urban spiral had begun, the concept of the standing army had arrived. And states' competitive positions could be measured in terms of their military capacity, something we still do today.

So it was in West Africa, still another region of early urban tradition and ancient, durable states. Between the forests along

the West African coast and the desert of the interior lay a region astride the Niger River whose locational advantages were translated into urban growth and strength, and regional political integration. West Africa's savanna cities were in position to control the trade between the peoples of forest and desert, whose products and requirements were quite complementary. From the very beginning, perhaps even before the first millenium A.D., these cities—Timbuktu, Gao, Niani, and others no longer on the map—were centers of trade and exchange as well as political power. From the Nile Valley the savanna cities' rulers received ideas about the divine kingship, about the power inherent in a monopoly over the use of iron, and about the employment of military forces to exact tribute, enlarge the hinterland, and maintain control. Thus the cities of savanna West Africa produced city states of impressive strength and longevity. Ancient Ghana survived for about 10 centuries, welding many diverse peoples into a stable, durable political unit centered on a large, busy, cosmopolitan capital city. Ghana's successors, including Mali (Melle) and Songhai, were similarly cohesive and enduring.

Despite the efforts and adventures of researchers who have tried to prove by deed as well as scholarship that the ancient Middle Easterners could have sailed the Atlantic Ocean to American shores, the rise of indigenous American cities and states still appears to be a case of spontaneous invention and achievement. It happened in Middle America much later than it did in Southwest Asia, but perhaps on an even grander scale. In Yucatan during the first millenium A.D., Mayan societies built cities dominated by huge, often pyramidal structures of ceremonial purpose, but with living quarters for thousands of people in some cases. This first phase of development produced Teotihuacan. As Professor René Millon describes it in the June, 1967 issue of *Scientific American*, Teotihuacan

. . . had risen, flourished, and fallen hundreds of years before the conquistadors entered Mexico. At the height of its power, around A.D. 500, Teotihuacan was larger than imperial Rome. For more than half a millenium it was to Middle America what Rome, Benares or Mecca have been to the Old World: (at once a religious and cultural capital and a major economic and political center . . .

Hundreds of years later the Aztecs built, just 25 miles (40 kilometers) from Teotihuacan, an equally impressive capital for their vast Mesoamerican empire. Tenochtitlan probably had well over 100,000 inhabitants, rivaling its predecessor, and it was the headquarters for a powerful state that covered much of central Mexico. Mayan society had been theocratic, governed by priest-kings; Aztec power lay in the military, and Aztec armies ranged far and wide, well beyond the frontiers of the state, securing a constant flow of tribute and a continuous supply of human beings for the sacrifices that marked Aztec religious ceremonies.

The Aztec state was the pinnacle of organization and power in Middle America. Its origins are thought to lie in the late thirteenth or early fourteenth century A.D., following the breakup of an earlier political unit, that of the Toltecs. Tenochtitlan soon grew from a small, fortuitously located village into a major center of commerce. Positioned on a small island in one of the many lakes that lie in the Valley of Mexico, Tenochtitlan had advantages of easy defense, efficient communications (goods were moved across the lakes by

canoe), and centrality. As Tenochtitlan grew and prospered, so did the Aztec state. Through alliance and conquest, the Aztecs strengthened their political position, organizing their territory into provinces with their respective governors and district commissioners. Each province was assigned a certain task in the production of food crops, and in the capital a huge and complex administrative bureaucracy developed. Systems of tax collection, law enforcement, a postal service by messenger, and other features of a state emerged. A system of secondary central places, also cities of substantial size, was served by a network of permanent transport routes. Canals were dug to link the lakes of the Valley of Mexico. By canoe on the inland waters, by coastwise transport, and on the backs of women and men, goods streamed to the cities: not only foodstuffs but also gold, cotton, leather goods, and many other items of trade. And all the time the ceremonial buildings in Tenochtitlan grew larger, the religious, sun-god worshipping hierarchy expanded, the human sacrifices multiplied. The world had seen nothing like it—anywhere (Fig. 18-3).

The Aztec state was not the only major political entity in the Americas of its time. Also during the fourteenth century, the Incas achieved major political unification over a large region of the Andes Mountains in South America. This was no easy task, for the Andean terrain is among the most rugged in the world, and communciation and contact—so easy in the lake-dotted

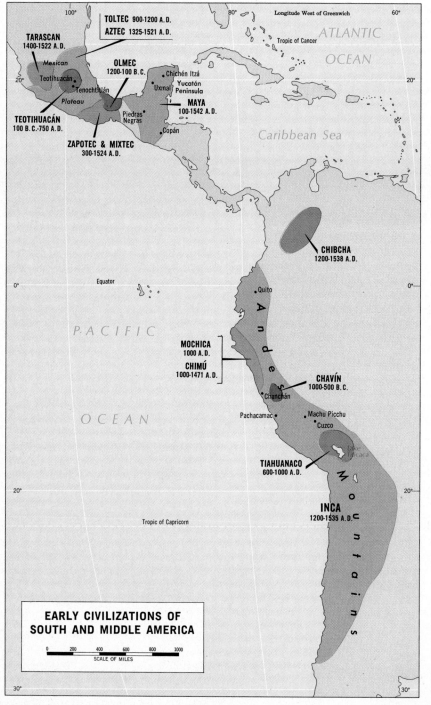

TARASCAN
1400-1522 A.D.

TOLTEC 900-1200 A.D.
AZTEC 1325-1521 A.D.

Mexican

OLMEC
1200-100 B.C.

Chichén Itzá

Teotihuacán

Uxmal

Yucatán
Peninsula

Tenochtitlán

Plateau

MAYA
100-1542 A.D.

TEOTIHUACÁN
100 B.C.-750 A.D.

Piedras
Negras

ZAPOTEC & MIXTEC
300-1524 A.D.

Copán

Caribbean Sea

CHIBCHA
1200-1538 A.D.

Quito

PACIFIC

MOCHICA
1000 A.D.

CHIMÚ
1000-1471 A.D.

CHAVÍN
1000-500 B.C.

Chanchán

OCEAN

Pachacamac

Machu Picchu

Cuzco

Lake
Titicaca

TIAHUANACO
600-1000 A.D.

INCA
1200-1535 A.D.

ATLANTIC

OCEAN

Tropic of Cancer

Longitude West of Greenwich

Equator

Tropic of Capricorn

A n d e s

M o u n t a i n s

**EARLY CIVILIZATIONS OF
SOUTH AND MIDDLE AMERICA**

0   200   400   600   800   1000
SCALE OF MILES

heartland of the Aztecs—were
very difficult. The Incas developed their civilization in high-
elevation *altiplanos*, basins
between the towering Andean
mountain ranges. On the map of
modern Peru you will find the
city of Cuzco located in such an
Andean valley; from this inter-
montane basin they expanded
and proceeded to conquer, occupy, and unify the peoples of
other *altiplanos*, and peoples
along coastal Peru as well. Eventually the Incas had created an
empire that extended from
Ecuador in the north, across the
length of Peru, into Northern Bolivia and Chile to the south.

Inca society was not as urbanized as was that of the
Aztecs, nor was it as far advanced
in literacy or mathematics.
The Incas were superb administrators, engineers, and architects, and unlike the Aztecs they
brought stability and peace to
most of the areas they conquered and attached to their far-
flung empire. But the Incas had
not progressed as far as some
other ancient cultures in such
fields as literacy and record
keeping; consequently, they
were at a disadvantage in their
codification of law, religion, administration, and other cultural
traditions. Cuzco was a large
city, and there were other substantial population agglomerations in the Inca empire, but the
absence of a large literate elite inhibited the evolution of the state
system in a number of ways.
The urban and political development of the early states went
hand in hand, and the invention
of writing was an indispensable
ingredient in both.

360

Figure 18-3

The European Model

The Incas' Machu Picchu, a lasting monument to the ancient people's ingenuity and ability.

When the Spanish invaders landed in Middle America in the early sixteenth century and pushed into the Aztec state, they reported with admiration and awe on much of what they saw. Tenochtitlan as a city exceeded in many ways what the Iberians were familiar with: it was a great, bustling, architecturally monumental metropolis. There in the Valley of Mexico two cultures in full flower came face to face, one European, the other American. Hernán Corteés and his 500 men actually saw, alive and functioning, a culture now extinct and the subject of archeology.

We have no similar eyewitness accounts of the cultures and political states of ancient Mesopotamia, the Nile Valley, the Indus region, or China. While they flourished, Europe's territorial integration had yet to begin. When Europe's time came, during the first millenium B.C., European political philosophy borrowed heavily from the experience of the Middle East.

The sequence of events that led to the emergence of the European state system began in pre-Christian times. The advanced states of the Middle East and North Africa required an increasing volume and variety of raw materials, and in their search for metals, textiles, oils, and other products they made contact with the peoples living on the Mediterranean shores of Southeast Europe. Soon Greek traders were active in Egyptian towns; Phoenician ships linked Aegean and Mediterranean Middle Eastern shores. To Southwest Asia and North Africa, Europe was merely a distant supplier of copper, tin, and other necessities. But those Middle Eastern states made a return contribution to Europe too: their ideas, innovations, and inventions, organizational, political, and scientific concepts spread to European shores as the trade grew.

During the first millenium B.C. the ancient Greeks created what, in many respects, is the foundation of European civilization. As the map shows, Greece and its Mediterranean surroundings consist of rugged countryside, narrow peninsulas, numerous islands, and few areas of level land in river valleys and along coasts. The early Hellenic city-states perched on the most suitable of these areas, but overland contact was always difficult. Communication by sea was generally more effective. As the strength of the city-states grew, so did their rivalries, and soon groups of cities began to associate in *leagues*. Such cities as Athens, Sparta, and Thebes each headed powerful and competing leagues.

That the ancient Greeks were able to consolidate their fragmented realm politically is testimony to their capacity to organize and administer effectively. During Greek times, political philosophy and public administration became sciences, pursued by the greatest of practitioners. Plato (428–347 B.C.) and Aristotle (384–322 B.C.) are two famous philosophers of this period, but surrounding them was many other contributors to the greatness of ancient Greece. What they wrote has influenced government and politics ever

In the center of Greece's ancient culture hearth: the Parthenon of Athens.

since, and the constitutional concepts that emerged at that time are still viable today.

For centuries the ancient Greeks held sway over much of the Mediterranean and the Middle East, and when Greek power finally began to wane, another Mediterranean power arose in what is today Italy: the Roman Empire. The Romans had an advantage never enjoyed by the Greeks, for their national territory was contiguous and unified in the truest sense of the word, and focused on one unrivaled city, Rome. Initially Rome was only one city among many small, fortified centers that lay on the Italian Peninsula, but Rome had locational advantages that contributed to its emergence as the area's leading urban center. As Rome grew, so did its regional influence, and the Romans soon set out to consolidate that advantage. As early as the third century B.C. there was a Roman Federation that extended from near the Po Valley in the north to the still Greek-occupied south.

The Romans ultimately ousted the Greeks, not only from the Italian Peninsula but from their power position in the whole Mediterranean region. But if the Greeks were forced to recognize Roman superiority, they nevertheless made a major contribution to Roman civilization. In fact, Roman civilization really was a Roman-Hellenic culture, for the Romans diffused many elements of Greek culture throughout their huge empire. And that empire was of unprecedented dimensions: by the second century A.D. it extended from Britain to the Persian Gulf and from the Black Sea to Egypt. In such fields as law, public administration, military organizations, and land communications the Romans made enormous progress. The Empire was the first truly interregional political unit in Europe, and it was indeed the first true empire my modern criteria, with outlying dependencies and diverse racial groups under its control. Centuries of comparative peace and stability permitted the Romans to organize their domain, promote its economic development, and disseminate the Roman language and other attributes of Roman culture (Fig. 18-4).

The Roman image in Lebanon. The Romans had red granite, the building stone of the Temple of Bacchus, brought from Aswan in upper Egypt to Baalbeck in Lebanon.

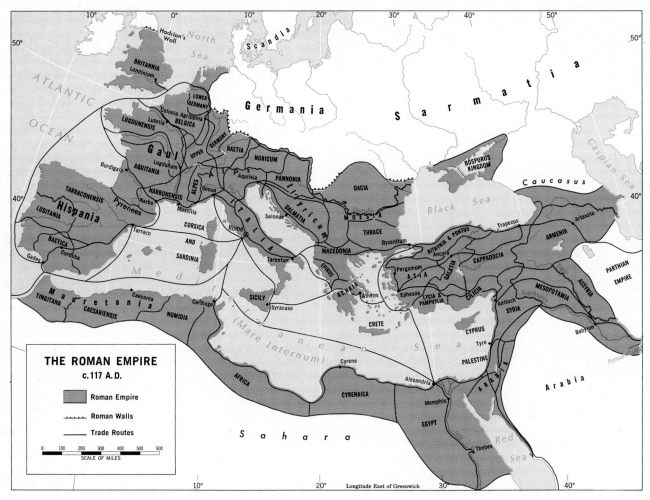

Figure 18-4

Certainly the roots of the European state system lie in ancient Greece and Rome, but there was to be no simple transition from Roman to modern times. The collapse of the Roman Empire involved the loss of centuries of progress in many spheres. Under Roman rule, judicial processes had protected individual rights to a greater extent than ever before, but in the feudal Europe that succeeded the Roman era, such niceties were largely abandoned. Fragmented Europe was ruled by kings, barons, and dukes, and once again Europe looked more like an amalgam of city-states of old rather than a stable, progressive, somewhat democratic state. The kings ruled by their version of divine right, by private law, personal power, influence, and wealth. Their agents and representatives (barons, dukes, and counts) in the kingdom's districts held control over practically every aspects of people's lives, from the peasantry to the military. When a larger political unit disintegrated through the death of a king, a weak successor, or a neighbor's invasion, the feudal barons and dukes were quick to assert complete hegemony over their local domains, including all the land and people within them. Europe had become a set of isolated pockets; Roman connectivity was largely lost.

A number of developments brought about a renewal of European progress in political (as well as other) spheres. The Norman invasion of England, in 1066, is perhaps the most prominent benchmark: the Normans invaded, destroyed the Anglo-Saxon nobility, created a whole new political order and achieved great national strength under William the Conqueror. On the European mainland, the continuity of dynastic rule and the strength of certain rulers began to produce national cohesiveness in the more stable domains. In Germany, France, and Spain sizable states existed, and some of the trespass lines of the twelfth century were to become modern-day political boundaries (e.g., the border between France and Spanish Aragon along the Pyrenees). At the same time, Europe experienced something of an economic revival, and internal as well as foreign trade increased. Ports and other cities came to life after lengthy dormancies, and while the wealth went to the nobility and the rich merchants, more people than ever were drawn from a subsistence lifestyle into the new economic order. Now the Moslem invaders in Southern Spain could be repelled, and Crusades to the Middle East could be financed. The Dark Ages were over, and a new Europe was emerging.

It may be appropriate to mark the year 1492—the year of Columbus' first arrival in the New World—to signal the beginning of Europe's rebirth. In Western Europe, the strong, prevailing monarchies began to represent something more than mere authority; increasingly they became centers of an emerging national consciousness and pride. At the same time Europe's chronic political fragmentation was reversed. The strengthening of central authority led to the recapture of breakaway feudal territories; royal alliances and marriages consolidated national territories. The aristocracies, which had strongly opposed monarchical rule, were placed under control. Parliamentary representation of the general population reappeared, albeit in modest terms. Renewed interest in Greek and Roman achievements in politics as well as the sciences prevailed. It was, indeed, Europe's *Renaissance*.

But Europe's rebirth would not be painless. The new political nationalism was paralleled by policies of economic nationalism we know as *mercantilism:* the promotion of the acquisition of wealth through plunder, colonization, and the protection of home industries and foreign markets. Rivalry and competition, in Europe as well as abroad, intensified. And superimposed on these conflicts was a series of religious wars that constituted a reaction to the new secular values of the Renaissance, and which ravaged Europe for many years. Catholicism and Protestantism, Reformation and Counterreformation fired the conflicts that devastated not only Europe's towns and cities but

also the parliaments and assemblies that had become a part of political life. In the end, the monarchies benefited most, and absolutism emerged once again, a despotism reminiscent of the Dark Ages. Louis XIV of France was the personification of this despotic rule; the numerous nobility were returned to the privileged status they had lost. All the while, the confrontation between organized religion and the state continued to erode society.

Ultimately, Europe's growing economic power proved to be the undoing of monarchical absolutism and its system of patronage. It was the city-based merchant who gained wealth and prestige, not the nobleman. Money and influence were concentrated more and more in the cities, and the traditional measure of affluence —land—began to lose its relevance in that changing situation. The merchants and businessmen demanded political recognition and began to exert pressure to get it. In the 1780s a series of upheavals commenced that would change the sociopolitical face of the continent. Overshadowing these events was the French Revolution (1789–1795), but this momentous event was only one in a series. The consequences of Europe's political revolution were felt by every monarchy on the continent, and the revolution continued into the twentieth century. It may not be over even now.

While Europe was in intermittent turmoil, European countries were nevertheless able to secure large colonial empires, for in the quest for overseas riches there was considerably more unanimity. England, benfiting from its political stability and its maritime power, gained an empire that spanned the world. France acquire huge spheres of influence in Africa and Southeast Asia. The Netherlands consolidated its hold on what is now Indonesia. Belgium's King Leopold II got control over the (then) Congo, and his hegemony there was ratified in 1885 by the Belgian parliament. Germany entered the colonial scramble late, but before the turn of the century the German world empire included large territories in West, South, and East Africa. The technological advantages that accrued from the Industrial Revolution, the wealth and power that had accumulated in Europe over several centuries of acquisition, and the insatiable colonial fervor and energy that drove European expansionism transformed the map of the world.

The European states that emerged from several centuries of revolutionary change have several characteristics in common, but there are also significant differences. Some, such as France and Italy, have eliminated the old monarchies altogether. Others, such as the United Kingdom and the Netherlands, are parliamentary democracies, but the Crown remains as the titular head of the state, and the king or queen still opens parliament and performs other ceremonial functions. In still other countries the role of the monarch is still not finally settled, as in Greece (where the royal family was ousted just a few years ago) and Spain (where the royal successor to Franco revived a monarchy in 1975). In the sphere of popular representation in government, Europe during the twentieth century has also shown great diversity. While democratic systems survived in Scandinavia and Britain, dictatorial, authoritarian regimes took control at various times in Germany, Italy, Spain, and Portugal.

Europe's national states did acquire certain common qualities, as we will note in more detail in Chapter 19: they unified and nationalized substantial populations; defined and delimited their national territories by demarcating and sometimes fortifying their boundaries; they achieved perhaps unprecedented organization in numerous spheres including administration and government, education, the military; and they came to possess a certain measure of power that was expressed in their capacity to acquire colonial realms and in their relationships in Europe itself.

European states, like Rome 2000 years ago, also have their philosophers and students of public administration. While they colonized much of the world, the Europeans set about introducing their concepts of statecraft into a world where those concepts were often inappropriate. In some cases transplanted European populations themselves modified European ideals and made them fit local conditions, as the Americans and the Australians did. But elsewhere the European colonial powers revealed in their colonies the prominent features of their own politicoterritorial systems. The British, for example, introduced an enormous civil service bureaucracy in Nigeria, India, and other colonies of the United Kingdom; an incorruptible, efficient civil service is an ideal of British home administration. The French goal of centralization, so clearly reflected by Napoleon's reorganization of France's territory, was transplanted to Africa and Asia. German military effectiveness and ruthlessness were no less evident in German South West Africa and East Africa than in German's European wars.

Thus European models of statecraft were superimposed on and welded to traditional forms of rule in the world beyond Europe and the West. Frontiers disappeared, to be replaced by our familiar world boundary jigsaw—not because this was everywhere essential under local conditions, but because it had been done in Europe and the West. Gleaming, skyscrapered capital cities arose in the most poverty-stricken countries—but London and Paris were symbols of power and progress, and so the new national capitals in the underdeveloped world should be. The European state became the world model.

19 Spatial Expressions of the State Systems

All states are not alike. In the preceding chapter we traced the evolution of state systems over time, and concluded that even within relatively small Europe, states had at least as many different qualities as they had characteristics in common. Now we turn our attention to the spatial properties of the world's states, and the map tells us to expect greater contrasts still. We live in a world where one state (the Soviet Union) swallows up more than 8.5 million square miles (22 million square kilometers) of the living space, while some others, such as Luxemburg and the Maldives, have less than 1000 square miles of it. China has as many as 900 million citizens, more than four times the population of the United States; Iceland has fewer than 250,000 inhabitants, the population of a small Midwestern city.

The state is an infinitely complex system of many interacting parts. It is far more than a piece of the earth's territory and a number of people: it is a region of cities, towns, and hinterlands; railroad and road networks; administrative subdivisions; schools; and hospitals. It is a maze of circulation and movement: of people, raw materials, finished products, foodstuffs, and newspapers. It exists for the people, demands their taxes, their adherence to the law, and often their service in the armed forces. To succeed, it must foster a sense of national unity and pride. The system functions to serve the nation.

We often use the terms *state* and *nation* interchangeably. Nearly all the states of the world, for example, are represented in an organization called the United Nations. But the incorporation of an aggregate of people within a political boundary does not automatically make these people members of a nation. The term *nation* should imply much more than a collection of people existing within a political state. You can prove the point by checking some major dictionaries of the English language for definitions of the term: you will find that they seek to convey a sense of unity, commonality,

369

and homogeneity to characterize the nation. Sometimes specific cultural attributes are mentioned, such as a common language, shared religious beliefs, and similar ancestry. But there is more to the concept of nation than that. Those definitions say little or nothing about an intangible but vitally important quality of a nation: the people's attitude, their emotional posture toward the state and what it stands for. Pride in an honorable history, appreciation of artistic accomplishments, collective drive for greater productivity, and revolutionary fervor are some of the strands that can bind a nation together.

When we view the world map, it is indeed possible to identify states whose boundaries enclose true nations. France is often cited as a nation-state; Poland, Japan, Egypt, and Uruguay are others. But the jigsaw of boundaries we see on the map is no guide to the world distribution of nations by whatever definition. Often the boundaries of states divide rather than unify national groups. A substantial number of residents of Northern Ireland feel themselves more closely related to the Irish nation than to the United Kingdom whose citizens they are. Hundreds of thousands of Somali live in Ethiopia, across the border from the Somali Republic, their national home. The Turks and Greeks on embattled Cyprus look to Turkey and Greece for protection of their respective interests in their island state. A complete list would be long indeed.

The breakdown of nation: civil strife in Northern Ireland, a part of the United Kingdom. Religious conflict lies at the roots of the failure of the national fabric here. The photo shows the aftermath of a conflict between Catholics and British troops in Londonderry.

Iconography

What makes one country appear and "feel" different from another? What goes into the creation of the "cultural atmosphere" that is so noticeable as you travel from one European country to another? The political geographer J. Gottmann tried to capture these realities in the term *iconography*, the essence of regional distinctiveness. Said Gottmann: " . . . boundaries exist because each country *feels* it is different from the other . . . this spirit (of each nation) is always made up of many components." What are some of these components that distinguish the political region? Gottmann argues that they include "a strong belief based on some religious creed, a certain social viewpoint, a pattern of political memories. Thus regionalism has what might be called an *iconography* as its foundation: each community has found for itself or was given an icon, a symbol slightly different from that cherished by its neighbors. For centuries the icon was cared for, adorned what whatever riches and jewels the community could supply. In many cases such an amount of labor and capital was invested that what started as a belief, or as a cult or even the memory of a military feat, grew into a considerable economic investment around which the interest of an economic region united." (from *A Geography of Europe*, 1969). Gottmann adds that, in the Old World, stubborn regionalisms of this kind have evolved toward nationalism in modern times, causing ever more intense partitioning of the land. It is one of the tasks of political geographers to identify the strands and interwoven patterns that make up regional-political iconographies.

The political boundaries of states divide otherwise homogeneous national groups in many instances; in other cases the state incorporates two or more distinctly different peoples. All continents contain such states. Canada is a bilingual state, the United States has a multiracial population, Mexico has peoples with Iberian, Indian, and mixed ancestries. The boundaries imposed on Africa by the European colonizers threw together peoples of different heritage and outlook, as in Nigeria, a true *plural* society with three dominant nations and numerous smaller minorities. Asia, too, has emerged from the colonial period with patchwork states such as India and Malaysia. The Soviet Union is a multinational state as well, and Europe's states include bilingual and bicultural Belgium, trilingual Switzerland, and multinational Yugoslavia.

We should also recognize that there are peoples who consider themselves to be a nation but who are presently without a national or state territory. The Palestinians now living in several Middle Eastern countries lost a homeland during the decolonization and partitioning of Palestine following World War II. The Kurds, a homogenous people numbering more than seven million but forming minorities in Turkey, Iraq, Iran, Syria, and Soviet Armenia, have from time to time rebelled against the governments of the countries in which they are minority populations, but they have never achieved a national state.

Comparatively few states, then, are nation-states on the European model: Europe itself has its exceptions. But a majority of states today possess all four of the European model's essential ingredients: a clearly defined territory, a substantial population, certain organizational accomplishments, and a measure of power. We now examine these elements in turn.

No state can exist without territory. Within the state's territory lie the resources the state must develop: soils for agriculture and minerals for industry and trade. This is the space that must be organized and exploited to best advantage. When we examine the political map of the world, two aspects of territory present themselves immediately: size (i.e., total area), and shape (sometimes called morphology).

Size

It is tempting to assume that the more territory a state owns, the better off it is in all respects. But that is not necessarily the case. True, a very large state has a greater chance that a wide range of environments and resources exist within its borders than a small state. But much depends also on location with reference to the earth's known mineral resources. Then there is the question of population distribution and size as it relates to areal dimension. A very large territory may be a liability rather than an asset if the population is too small to organize and exploit it. A government must be able to exercise effective national control over the state's total area; areas that lie beyond the reach of its administration and influence can produce problems. In the first place they are not productive, and second, such areas may come to harbor elements hostile

to the national government. Neighboring states may even seek to lay claim on such isolated reaches of territory. In recent decades the government of Brazil, for example, has been trying to "open up" the Amazonian interior and other lands west of that country's coastal heartland. Brazil is larger than the coterminous United States, but its population is less than half as large. And that population is far more strongly concentrated in the east than that of the United States. The Brazilian government even went so far as to create a whole new capital 400 miles into the interior, to draw national attention westward. And now attempts are being made to build a trans-Amazonian highway. Brazil wants to integrate its entire territory into a state that, for all intents and purposes, has been confined to its eastern periphery.

The range of sizes among the world's 150 states is so great as to defy generalization. At one extreme is the Soviet Union, a state larger than the whole continent of South America, whose more than 8.5 million square miles constitute one sixth of the entire land surface of the globe. At the other extreme are states so tiny that they are referred to as *microstates*. Between these extremes are continent-size countries such as Australia, Canada, the United States, Brazil, and China (whose areas average over 3 million square miles), states in a class with India, Argentina, and Zaire (around 1 million), and states of smaller dimensions such as the United Kingdom (under 100,000), the Netherlands (13,000), and Lebanon (4,000). From these data it is obvious that size alone does not mean a great deal: consider the respective roles in the modern world of the United Kingdom and a state more than 30 times as large, Brazil.

Shape

A second quality of states' territories that is evident from the world political map is their shape, or spatial form. Some states, such as the Philippines, lie on a group of islands, their territories broken by extensive waters. Other states, for example, Chile, consist of a long, narrow strip of land. When at first we look at the map, there appears to be so many different kinds of territorial forms that classification seems impossible. But when the states of the world are examined carefully, a typology does emerge. The Philippines and Chile suggest two types, and there are others.

Many states—Belgium, Uruguay, Kenya, and Cambodia among others—have territories

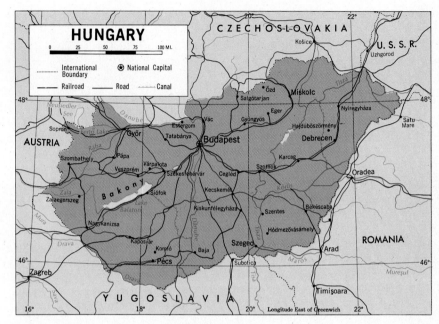

Figure 19-1

shaped somewhere between round and rectangular. There are no islands, peninsulas, or major indentations such as bays or estuaries. These states' territories are *compact*, which means that the distance from the geometric center of the area to any point on the boundary does not vary greatly (Fig. 19-1). The compact state encloses a maximum of territory within a minimum length of boundary, an obvious asset. Quite the opposite

situation prevails in the case we mentioned, the Philippines, and in Indonesia, Japan, and Malaysia. In those states the territory is *fragmented* into numerous pieces, and it is possible to go from one part to the other only by water or by air (Fig. 19-2). We can recognize three different kinds of fragmented states: those whose national territory lies entirely on islands (Japan, the Philippines); those whose territory lies partly on a continental landmass and partly on islands (Malaysia, Italy) and those whose major territorial units lie

373

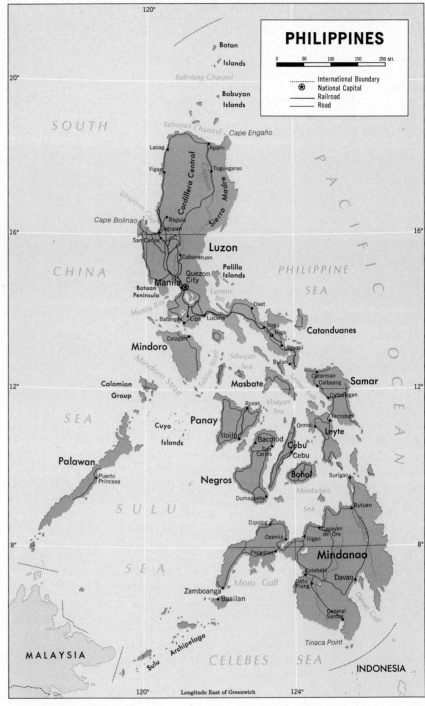

Figure 19-2

374

on the mainland, separated by the territory of another state (the United States, whose state of Alaska cannot be reached overland from the coterminous states except through Canada).

Fragmented states have problems of internal circulation and contact, and often suffer from the friction of distance. Far-flung Malaysia, for example, was incapable of accommodating the strong forces of secession in Singapore. After years of rising tension, East Pakistan broke away from the West. The government of Indonesia is based on the most populous island of that state, Djawa (Java), and it has had difficulties pacifying distant islands. The state of the Philippines has faced similar problems: the capital is on Luzon, the country's largest island, but there is a Moslem minority on Mindanao, another major island far to the south. The government has found it difficult to cope with the sporadic opposition mounted in Mindanao.

Quite a different spatial form is represented by Chile, Norway, Malawi (Africa), and Vietnam. The territory of these states is *elongated*. Such elongation (or *attenuation*, as it is sometimes called) also presents certain difficulties. If a state has a large territory, or if it lies astride a cultural transition zone, its elongated shape may associate it with contrasting life styles. An example is Togo in Africa, not a very large state but extending from the west coast, across the forest and savanna, to the Moslem-influenced interior. In Italy, which is an elongated as well as a fragmented state, there are north-south contrasts that

are related to the different exposures of those two regions to European mainstreams of change. In Norway, the distant, frigid north, inhabited by Laplanders, is another world from the south, where the capital city and the country's core area are positioned. And Chile, of course, provides the classic example of environmental—if not cultural—contrasts (Fig. 19-3). Northern Chile is desert country, the barren Atacama prevailing there. Central Chile has a large area of Mediterranean climatic conditions, and here the majority of the people are clustered. Southern Chile is dominated by Marine West Coast conditions, and by rugged topography. The effects of distance and isolation are very evident in the far, desert north and in the remote south. In many ways Chile *is* that central area between the two, the rest of the country still awaiting effective integration in the state.

Figure 19-3

Two faces of elongated Chile. The desert reaches the coast in the Atacama region (above); luxuriant vegetation marks the landscape near Santiago in the country's mid-section (right). The Andes loom in the background on both photos.

An entirely different situation is presented by Thailand. Thailand would be a compact state, except for one peculiarity: from its main body of territory there extends a long peninsula, several hundred miles southward to the boundary with Malaysia (Fig. 19-4). In fact, Thailand's neighbor, Burma, has the same feature, except that its southward extension is a bit shorter. This spatial form is called *prorupt*, and any time you see such a situation on the map a little investigation is warranted. Proruptions often have noteworthy histories. They also create special problems: in the case of Thailand, those border areas near Malaysia are 600 miles away from the capital, Bangkok, farther than any other area is removed from the government's headquarters. But at least there is a railroad along the Thai proruption. Not so in Burma: the railroad southward from the capital ends 300 miles short of the southern limit and for the last 150 miles, there is not even a good all-weather road!

One other spatial form should be mentioned, although its significance hardly matches that of the other four. In rare instances the territory of a state completely surrounds that of another state. That state, then, is *perforated* by the surrounded country. A look at the map of

Figure 19-4

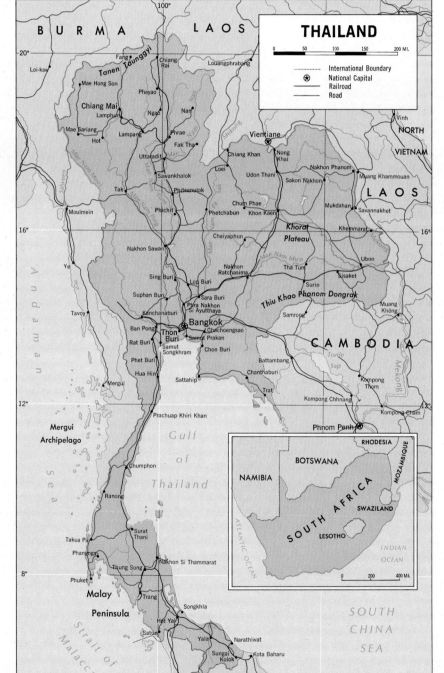

Population

South Africa will make this clear: the country of Lesotho (Basutoland on older maps) is entirely surrounded by South Africa. Lesotho is about the size of Belgium, so it takes a substantial piece of territory out of the heart of South Africa. Elsewhere the perforators are smaller, as in the case of San Marino, which perforates Italy. But only the South African case really has importance in political geography, for Lesotho is an independent black state and South Africa remains white controlled. In other cases, perforation is a curiosity rather than a vital aspect of territorial morphology.

The size and shape of national territories takes on more meaning when we view them in association with their respective populations. As we noted earlier, there is great variety in the size and character of states' populations. The largest state in the world, by population numbers, is China—now with 900 million persons and, some time during the 1980s, destined to become the state of one billion. At the other end of the spectrum are states with populations of less than a half million. It would be impossible to say just what the minimum number of people is that can constitute a nation; conditions vary too greatly. For example, among Iceland's 220,000 there may be more persons with specialized education and particular skills than in an underdeveloped country with 10 times the number of inhabitants. The capacities of the nation as well as its size are relevant.

In Chapter 2, we discussed some of the problems related to the interpretation of data on population density. Averages for individual states are not very meaningful, unless we know something about the agglomeration, the clustering of the people. Consider again the example of Brazil: with the overwhelming majority of that state's 100 million inhabitants concentrated in the eastern margins of the territory we might easily misinterpret the statement that the average density of people per square mile there is 29. Thus we want to know not only the total population of a nation state, but the way this population is distributed over the national territory. When we have this input, then our knowledge of states' spatial forms takes on more meaning. For example, we know that Burma and Zaire are both prorupt states. In the case of Burma, a state of 30 million people, the core area lies on the main body of territory, and the extension of area that forms the proruption is one of the least effectively integrated parts of the country. Zaire is a much larger state territorially, but with a population of about 20 million. When, however, we consider the distribution of population in Zaire, we realize that the two proruptions of that state are no mere extensions of area, but vitally important, productive regions. The southeastern proruption constitutes the Katanga, the famous copper producing area centered on Lubumbashi. The western proruption connects the vast Zaire interior to the ocean—it is the state's sole outlet to the sea. On that western proruption lie the capital city, Kinshasa, the major port, Matadi, a developing transport network, a substantial population cluster, and much more. In Burma, there may some day be problems with the isolation, the remoteness of the proruption that lies on the Malay Peninsula. In Zaire the

Organization

problem is not so much the proruptions—it is the vastness of the intervening Zaire (Congo) Basin itself. The distribution of the two states' populations tells much of this story.

When, therefore, we see a compact state, our next query ought to be whether the advantages inherent in this particular spatial form have been realized, or whether the population has concentrated along one of the margins, leaving a poorly integrated, frontierlike interior. Perhaps more than one population cluster exists, separated by zones that are barriers to contact. Nigeria is a compact state with three such clusters—two of them in the European-influenced, colonized south and one in the more remote, Moslem-traditional north. South and north long looked in different directions, but independence drew them together in a new state system. The system did not work well, and before long one of the clusters—Biafra—sought to secede from the rest. Nigeria's advantageous territorial morphology hardly counted in a situation where three population clusters lay so separated that they might as well have been islands. The map of territorial morphology must be viewed in the context of population distribution.

The state, we noted, is a system, with innumerable subsystems. From transport networks to education systems, national health plans to tarriff barriers, tax collection methods to the armed forces, the state has a multitude of organizational arms. The taking of a census, the calling of an election, and the distribution of funds to the elderly all evince the effectiveness of organization in the state.

In political geography, the most obvious manifestation of organization in the state is administrative. Except for some of the smallest microstates, all states are divided into subunits such as provinces, states, departments, or other designations. In the Soviet Union and China, complex hierarchies of such subdivisions were created following the appearance of the new orders. In the U.S.S.R., each of 15 Soviet Socialist Republics broadly corresponds to one of the major nationality groups in the huge state. Most Republics include smaller clusters of people with some cultural identity, and for them, autonomous Soviet Socialist Republics were created—republics *within* republics. Several lower levels of subdivision exist, even in nearly empty Siberia. It does not take long to realize that the complicated Soviet political map was created (1) to give Russia preeminence, (2) to permit culturally distinctive people to retain their identity while providing them with avenues for representation

in Moscow, and (3) to organize population and territory in such a manner that state control over the resource base and the means of production would be effective. The Chinese system was modeled after that of the Soviet Union, also with the aim to give the minority peoples certain measures of identity and autonomy. Three levels of administrative area exist. Interestingly, municipalities (such as Peking), the 22 provinces, and five autonomous regions (such as Tibet, Sinkiang, and Inner Mongolia) are all at the top level. The second and third levels exist for minority peoples.

All this seems very complex compared to the system in the United States, where the states are divided into counties, and the counties are subdivided into townships, parishes, or incorporated municipalities. But then, the whole U.S. map, with its many straight-line boundaries, looks quite unlike that of the U.S.S.R. or China. So is its genesis.

Unitary and Federal States

When Napoleon rose to power in France, swept the old administrative framework away and created an entirely new one, he envisaged a *unitary* French state, a state that would be one and undivided. Many European

Centrifugal and Centripetal Forces

Political geographers use the terms *centrifugal* and *centripetal* forces to identify forces that, within the state, tend—respectively—to pull the system apart and to bind it together. *Centrifugal* forces are divisive forces. They cause deteriorating internal relationships. Religious conflict, racial strife, linguistic division, contrasting outlooks are among major centrifugal forces. During the 1960s the Indochina war became a major centrifugal force in the United States, one whose aftermath will be felt for years to come. Newly independent countries find tribalism a leading centrifugal force, sometimes strong enough to threaten the very survival of the whole state system, as the Biafra conflict did in Nigeria. *Centripetal* forces are those that tend to bind the state together, to unify and strengthen it. A real or perceived external threat can be a powerful centripetal force, but more important and lasting is a sense of commitment to the system, a recognition that it constitutes the best option. This commitment is sometimes focused on the strong charismatic qualities of one individual, a leader who personifies the state, who captures the popular imagination. (The origin of the word *charisma* lies in the Greek, where it means "divine gift.") At times such charismatic qualities can submerge nearly all else; Peron's lasting popularity in Argentina is a case in point.

The degree of strength and cohesion of the state depends on the excess of centripetal forces over the divisive centrifugal forces. It is difficult to measure such intangible items, but some attempts have been made in this direction, for example, by determining attitudes among minorities, and by evaluating the strength of regionalism as expressed in political campaigns and voter preferences. When the centrifugal forces gain the upper hand and cannot be checked (even by external imposition): the state will break up—as Pakistan did in the early 1970s.

Centrifugal forces emerged strongly in the United States during the Indochina War. The prosecution of the war and a rising tide of opposition heavily damaged national unity and trust. The photo was taken at one of thousands of anti-war demonstrations.

states today are unitary states: Spain, Italy, Austria, and Sweden for instance. But in the New World and in colonial areas elsewhere, another idea took hold. There the idea was not so much unity, but voluntary association—*federation*. The United States, Canada, Brazil, and Australia are among states that were forged from diverse units that agreed to yield some sovereignty to a central government while retaining certain powers for themselves. Unitary and federal forms of politicoterritorial administration reflect different systems of government and, therefore, different ways of organizing the state's living space and its people.

The economic organization of the state is a vital link in the total system. All states have resources; some have very few, others have a wide range. Even location can be a resource: centuries ago, the Swiss found themselves positioned near the Alpine passes through which Venice and the north of Italy had to trade with Flanders and neighboring areas. The Swiss controlled the transit of goods, and bounded a state in the process—a state spawned, in large measure, by the Alps' relative location. How has the state managed to mobilize its resources—natural, spatial, and human? Probably the most dramatic example of economic

reorganization as a state-building process comes from Japan. The archipelago that is Japan does not have very large or varied resource base. There were mineral resources to sustain the handcraft and home-workshop industry, but the modernization envisaged by the leaders of the Restoration required the acquisition of far greater stores. The first step had to be at home: the reorganization of the handcraft industries. Then Japanese goods would have to be sent to world markets, there to undersell competing products. With the funds gained, investments were made in the industrial sector—and in another area of state organization, the military. Soon the military was capable of driving into neighboring territories (Korea, Manchuria), where resources needed in Japan were located and where goods made in Japan could be sold. The same Japan that lay isolated and remote some decades earlier now was an aggressive colonial power. For Japan, the European model did its work.

National power is an ingredient of the state system. Power is a product of organization in the state, and it is expressed not only in military terms, but also in the overall strength of the state politically, economically, and otherwise. A state's capacity to police and protect national interests is a measure of its power.

Power cannot be measured exactly, and so the subject of state power is a subject of much speculation. Obviously small states such as Luxemburg or Iceland do not have the strength larger states possess, but when it comes to closer matches, the differences are much less clear. Is present-day France stronger than the United Kingdom? Do Japan's economic strength and proven capacity for military organization outweight China's much greater territorial size and population? These are the sorts of questions students of power analysis try to answer. This is done by allotting a quantitative measure to every feature of the state that is deemed to have an effect on its strength and power: size of the armed forces, quantity of military equipment, industrial production, length of roads and railroads, availability of energy, and much more. But even these calculations must take into account some intangibles, such as the technical efficiency of the population, its "morale," the potential food supply in times of crisis.

Recent calculations place the United States and the Soviet Union in a tie for first place, but with the Soviet Union gaining more rapidly; China, Japan, the United Kingdom, West Germany, and France follow. But speculation continues to play a major role, for information of this sort often is of uncertain validity.

Power, whatever its measure, comes from organization. In his book, *The Might of Nations*, Professor J. G. Stoessinger defines power as "the capacity of a nation to use its tangible and intangible resources in such a way as to affect the behavior of other nations." Again, this does not mean solely or even primarily by military presence or threat; rather, it involves possessing and producing in economic spheres. A state can win concessions or reciprocal agreements with other states through its economic strength. It can outbid other states in the competition for exploitation rights in the territories of less developed countries by being able to offer superior conditions. Growth and development require organization; organization generates power.

Military might in Red Square, Moscow. Soviet power has risen markedly over the past three decades.

The Limits of the State

The politicogeographical map of the world today shows a veritable maze of boundaries—not surprising when our limited habitable space is chopped up into more than 150 states. Whenever we look at a globe, an atlas map, or a map in a newspaper or magazine to illustrate a story, we see boundaries as our frame of reference. When we refer to a country or an area where some important event is occurring, we bring to mind the layout of that country or area, defined by its boundaries. The United States is two coasts with a straight-line border with Canada between the Pacific and the Great Lakes, and the Rio Grande separates it from Mexico. We could all draw it fairly accurately, we have seen it so many times.

But boundaries are more than meets the eye. For every mile of amicably negotiated boundary there is a mile of strongly contested border. As we know too well, the contests are not over yet. In Middle and South America (Guyana-Surinam for example), in Asia (Kashmir), in the Middle East (Israel-Egypt), in Africa (Ethiopia-Somalia) the disputes continue. Boundaries are under pressure in many parts of the world, and even in Europe with its old and apparently stable states numerous changes have taken place in the last 50 years alone. The boundary that now divides Germany into an East and a

The Berlin Wall, a superimposed boundary, divides the city into Western and Communist sectors. It was erected in 1961 as a steady stream of refugees left East Germany through West Berlin's "window."

West appeared on the map in 1945. The city of Berlin was also divided after World War II, but the division was strengthened by the building of the Wall between the Eastern and Western sectors in 1961. Poland's boundaries changed after the war also, and there were adjustments along the Dutch-German and French-German borders as well.

The boundary framework with which we are familiar in the 1970s, then, is the result of innumerable modifications made over centuries of time, and although the broad outlines of this framework are likely to remain intact, every decade

brings changes of detail. Still, what we see on the map today is a far cry from the situation of just one century ago. In 1875 Bolivia still possessed the northern Atacama (and thus an outlet to the sea); there was no Pakistan; the whole African jigsaw was just beginning to develop. The ill-defined "sphere of influence" was a different reality in the nineteenth century than it is today.

Frontiers and Boundaries

Sometimes the terms boundary and frontier are used interchangeably, as synonyms.

But there is a difference, and an important one. The frontier throughout history served as a zone of separation, an area between states, and a territorial "cushion" to keep rivals apart. Such a frontier might have been a dense, vast, almost impenetrable forest, or a swampland, or a disease-infested river basin, or a range of mountains. Sometimes a frontier was defined by distance as much as by inaccessibility. The world map of the mid-nineteenth century was full of frontiers, in the Americas, in Africa, in Asia and Australia, even in Europe. But then the effects of Europe's technological and political revolutions, the colonial scramble, explosive population growth, and the rush for resources and empires combined to produce competition for even the most remote frontier areas. Before long the frontiers disappeared, divided and parcelled out among states and colonial acquisitions.

Thus the frontier has *area*; it is a spatial phenomenon. The boundary, on the other hand, should be thought of as a vertical plane separating two states, it is *linear* on the ground. It appears on our maps as a line, but it also separates airspace above the ground and the rocks and resources below. Today, though, only one frontierlike land area remains: Antarctica, where several states claim areas of preeminence, some of them overlapping (Fig. 19-5). But Antarctica today is mainly a region of research and investigation, and the claims have not yet led to serious conflict. A major discovery of some critical resource could change that picture considerably, however.

Boundaries, then, are the limits of states. They mark the extent of the state's territory, the limit of jurisdiction. They separate state from state, but they are also the place where states make territorial contact. This dual function—of separation and association—has led geographers to investigate the ways boundaries have come about, how they function and how those functions have changed in modern times), and how they might be usefully classified.

Boundary Evolution

In ideal circumstances, boundaries evolve through three stages. Imagine a frontier area, about to be divided between two states. First, agreement is reached on the rough positioning of the border. Then the exact location is established through the process of *definition*, whereby a treatylike, legal-sounding document is drawn up in which actual points in the landscape are described (or, where a

Figure 19-5

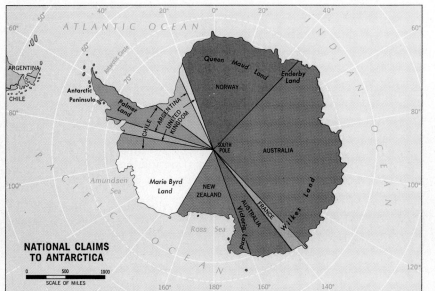

NATIONAL CLAIMS TO ANTARCTICA

straight-line boundary is involved, points of latitude and longitude). Next, cartographers, using large-scale maps and referring to the boundary line as defined, put the boundary on the map in a process called *delimitation*. And, if either or both of the states so desire, the boundary is actually marked on the ground, by steel posts, concrete pillars, fences (sometimes even a wall!) or some other visible means. That final stage is the *demarcation* of the boundary. By no means are all boundaries on the world map demarcated—there are thousands of miles where you could cross from one state into the other without ever knowing it. Demarcating a lengthy boundary by any means at all is expensive, and it is hardly worth it in inhospitable mountains, vast deserts, frigid polar lands, or other places where there is virtually no permanent human population.

Peoples have sought to demarcate their territories for thousands of years. The Romans built walls in northern Britain to mark the limits of their domain, the Chinese Wall is still one of the wonders of the world, the pre-Inca Peruvian Indians used stone lines to confirm their territorial claims. More often, linear physiographic features such as rivers and mountain chains became trespass lines in practice, then boundaries in fact. Until as recently as World War II, boundaries were viewed as viable lines of defense. The French in the late 1930s fortified their northeastern boundary with Germany,

called it the Maginot Line, and hoped that it would withstand the German onslaught. Modern warfare has more or less eliminated by this function of the boundary, except in places where guerilla warfare occurs. There, a river or a mountain range may still present some strategic advantages. But the concept of the boundary as the state's ultimate and practical line of defense no longer applies.

In the Old World especially, but also in Middle and South America and in Africa, boundaries seem to zigzag endlessly and, it would seem, pointlessly. Why are all boundaries not like those between the United States and its neighbors—along a major river, through the middle of lakes, or along a line of latitude? The answers are many: from Roman times on Europe's cultural and political patterns have changed almost continuously. In places (such as along the Pyrenees between Spain and France) a fairly stable and rather permanent boundary evolved, but elsewhere states and nations fought over territory time and time again, and boundaries were defined, altered, defined once more, wiped out, reestablished. Even boundaries in mountainous areas and along rivers were subject to pressure; in the mountains there would be argument over the sources of river water and control over watersheds, in the rivers there would be conflict over who would own the banks, the navigable channel, the river mouth. There is a piece of historical geography attached to almost every one of those bends and turns

you see boundaries make on maps. And yet today, after all those centuries of adjustment and readjustment, there are still Italian-speaking people in France, Italian speakers in Switzerland, Dutch speakers in Belgium, Hungarians in Rumania, and Germans in Poland.

If that is the situation in crowded and culturally complex Europe, what about the Americas, where the population numbers are so much less, or Africa, where external powers lay down boundaries with impunity? In the Americas, as the daily press will confirm, the appetite of states for their neighbors' territory is far from satisfied. Numerous Central and South American states consider sections of their boundaries temporary and subject to future redefinition. Venezuela has a potential dispute with Guyana, Guyana has a claim in Surinam, Guatemala has thinly veiled hopes for the absorption of a whole country, Belize. Panama wants to acquire the Canal Zone and take control of the U.S.-held corridor that renders it a fragmented state. And in Africa the colonial powers negotiated with each other and in only very few places actually contested their empires' borders, but they created some boundaries that may prove to be untenable in the future. African states have been busy trying to organize and survive following the colonial period, but as they gain strength it is likely that they will begin to contest the borders with which they were endowed. Already the Somali Republic has indicated that it wants the boundary with Ethiopia redefined (there are hundreds of thousands of Somali in Ethiopia). Uganda has expressed a desire to acquire a land corridor to the sea through northern Tanzania, and has laid claim to Western Kenya from the Rift Valley to the Uganda border.

And so we can watch the very adjustments that result in so tortuous a maze as we see on the map. Israel acquires a small piece of Syria called the Golan Heights. Pakistan and India struggle over a snowy, mountainous area in Kashmir. China redefines its boundary with Burma and starts an argument with India over the Simla Conference, where many decades ago the China-India border was defined. Cold, desolate country can provoke some hot, intense confrontations.

Functions

If boundaries today (with a few exceptions) no longer serve in a defensive context, how do they serve the modern state system? Boundaries may not be trespass lines any longer, but they do serve as the symbol of state inviolability. They are a factor in the development of that intangible emotional bond of national consciousness a regional iconography, especially if contrasts between societies and cultures on opposite sides are strong. States display maps of their national territories on the front pages of newspapers, on school books, on stamps, even on flags. A real or even an imagined threat to the boundary can be used to arouse national feeling.

But there are many states whose relationships with their neighbors across the boundary are such that the boundary hardly functions as a separator. People move across with only a minimum of control—some even commute across, daily. Social and economic conditions on the two sides are so similar that the boundary seems an unnecessary impediment. The U.S.-Canadian boundary comes to mind, and the boundaries between the Netherlands and Belgium, Norway and Sweden, Austria and Switzerland.

Even these boundaries (note that they are *within*, not *between* culture realms) still have important functions. One of these is obvious enough: the whole state system, with all its parts—education, taxation, law, conscription, and so on—is built within this framework. The boundary marks the limit of state jurisdiction in all these and countless more spheres. The boundary signifies the limit of sovereignty; weakening its role implies yielding of some of that sovereignty. As we will see, a number of states in the postwar period have proved themselves willing to do just that: to reduce the divisive functions of the boundary in order to join with other states in economic, political, and strategic "blocs."

Even though boundaries no longer provide the protection of fortification to states, they still serve to shield the state in another practical way: against illegal traffic in contraband goods. To prevent or inhibit such movement, boundaries are sometimes fenced and policed; at sea a cushion of "territorial waters"

is similarly guarded. States that want to prevent the movement of people into or out of their territories may create a belt of empty "no man's land" through which it is difficult to cross undetected.

This brings up to the most important function of the state boundary in modern times: its role in commerce and economics. A state can erect a tariff wall against goods that try to compete on the domestic market, and that wall coincides with the state's political boundary. Such a tariff wall makes foreign goods expensive and helps local producers sell theirs at an advantage—but at a price. The price, of course, is retaliation: the local producers may find that they face the same obstacle when they export their goods to the country where the foreign goods are made. And so states use their boundaries and the markets they enclose to compete and negotiate. Sometimes a group of states discovers that there is much to be gained *not* by creating economic barriers at their mutual boundaries, but by dropping many of them and joining in an economic union. After World War II this happened in Western Europe, where six states—France, the Federal Republic of Germany, Italy, Belgium, the Netherlands, and Luxemburg formed the European Economic Community—the Inner Six, or the *Common Market* as this bloc became known. Later, seeing the advantages involved, other states (Denmark, Ireland, even the United Kingdom) joined. But in so doing, all those states had to give up some of their sovereignty, some of their power to make decisions inside their borders, in order to share in the resultant benefits.

Thus we see boundaries functioning in many different ways: some states are still strengthening and confirming their borders (notably those states that have recently become independent), some still seek to move their boundaries outward to acquire part of their neighbors' territory, while other states can afford the luxury of reducing the divisiveness and absoluteness of their borders in order to open ways to—and participate in—a wider, international economic and political sphere.

Capital Cities

The capital city is the focus of the nation-state, its headquarters, its center of gravity. As the center of national life, the capital city is often used by name to identify a nation-state. "The reaction from London is . . ." or "Peking asserts that . . ."

The capital city is the pride of the state, and its layout, prominent architectural landmarks, and monuments and shrines reflect the nation's values and its aspirations for the future. Sometimes these values are rooted in history, but the map of world capital cities (Fig. 19-6) indicates certain emergent states that are in the process of relocating their national capitals. This represents a break with the colonial past and an assertion of national independence. Thus the map of world capital cities reveals changing national aspirations, notably in Brazil, Tanzania, and Pakistan, but in several other countries as well.

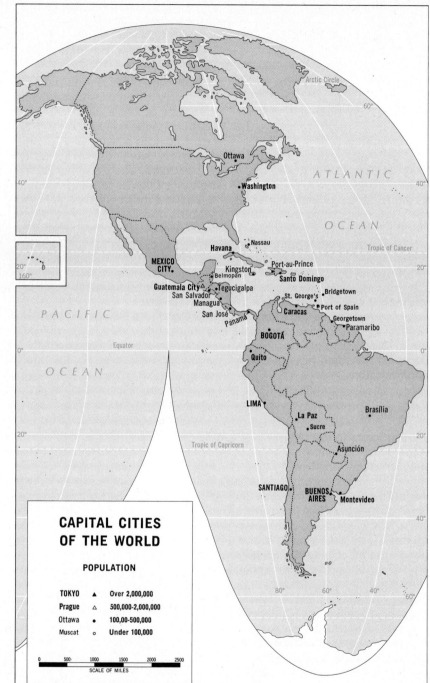

Figure 19-6

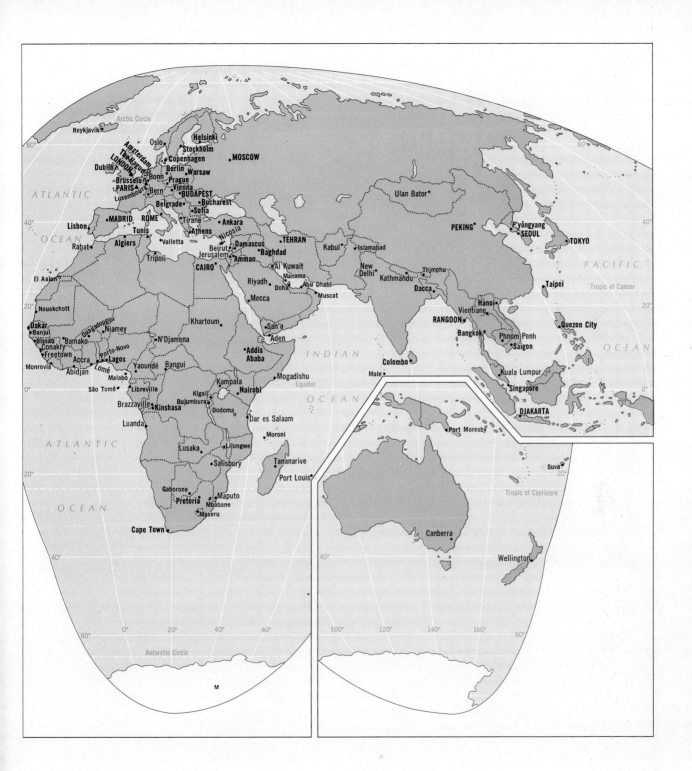

Arctic Circle

Reykjavík

Oslo
Helsinki
Stockholm
Amsterdam
The Hague
Copenhagen
MOSCOW
LONDON
Berlin
Dublin
Bonn
Warsaw
Brussels
Prague
PARIS
Vienna
Luxembourg
Bern
BUDAPEST
Belgrade
Bucharest
Ulan Bator
Sofia
MADRID
ROME
Tirane
Ankara
Lisbon
Athens
Nicosia
PEKING
P'yŏngyang
SEOUL
OCEAN
Tunis
Beirut
Damascus
TEHRAN
Kabul
Islamabad
TOKYO
Rabat
Algiers
Valletta
Jerusalem
Baghdad
New
Delhi
Tripoli
Amman
Al Kuwait
Thimphu
Taipei
El Aaiun
CAIRO
Manama
Kathmandu
Tropic of Cancer
Riyadh
Abu Dhabi
Dacca
Nouakchott
Doha
Muscat
Mecca
Hanoi
Dakar
Khartoum
Vientiane
Quezon City
Banjul
Ouagadougou
Niamey
RANGOON
Bissau
Bamako
N'Djamena
San'a
Bangkok
OCEAN
Conakry
Porto-Novo
Aden
Phnom Penh
Freetown
Accra
Lagos
INDIAN
Saigon
Monrovia
Abidjan
Lomé
Malabo
Yaoundé
Bangui
Addis
Ababa
Colombo
Kuala Lumpur
São Tomé
Libreville
Mogadishu
Equator
Male
Singapore
Kampala
Nairobi
OCEAN
DJAKARTA
Brazzaville
Kigali
Bujumbura
Kinshasa
Dodoma
Luanda
Dar es Salaam
Port Moresby
Moroni
Lusaka
Lilongwe
Tananarive
Suva
Salisbury
Port Louis
Tropic of Capricorn
Gaborone
Maputo
Pretoria
Mbabane
Maseru
Canberra
Cape Town
Wellington

ATLANTIC

OCEAN

PACIFIC

ATLANTIC

OCEAN

Antarctic Circle

M

389

A 350,000-ton deepwater platform, more than 500 feet (150 meters) tall, at the start of its 250-mile (400-kilometer) voyage to its marine destination.

20 The Scramble for the Last Frontier

Living space on this earth is at a premium. The continents have been appropriated by about 150 tightly packed states, and while there is territory under dispute, none is unclaimed. But the continental landmasses that must accommodate all those political entities constitute less than 30 percent of the surface area of the globe as a whole. Over 70 percent of our planet's total area is water, most of it salty and undrinkable. The human drama has been played out, mainly, on the earth's solid ground. Wars were fought over land territory, over land boundaries, over resources and riches in and under the soil. When people learned to navigate the waters and nations' fleets engaged in combat on the waves, the ultimate objectives lay not at sea, but on land. For thousands of years the oceans and seas functioned as frontiers: they were penetrated and traversed, and comparatively small sections were claimed and appropriated: if there were resources they were taken by whoever was able to do so. But most of all the oceans remained open, free, and unattached.

Until today, that is. We are witness to the final phase of the territorial expansion of states, and the spiral has begun. The last frontier on our planet is presently falling victim to one of the salient qualities of the state system: its insatiable appetite for expansion. Soon the atlas you have before you today, with its huge expanses of unbounded blue to mark the open oceans, will be as outdated as the African map before 1885. The technology that brought minerals thousands of feet below the surface within our reach is now beginning to unlock the ocean floors and all that lies beneath them. The seas and oceans are being converted into states' spheres of influence. It is not difficult to discern the next step. In some regions it is already being taken.

391

The Oceans

Aside from references to the seas and oceans as routes to distant regions and as sources for protein in human diets, we have had little occasion to focus our attention on the water areas of our globe. For obvious reasons the bottoms of the oceans and seas were never as well known as the exposed surfaces of the continents, and even today the ocean floors still hold many unsolved mysteries. But we know a great deal more today than we did just a decade ago, and the flow of information is constantly growing.

Perhaps the most remarkable of all the features of the ocean basins is that they presently overflow onto the margins of the continents. When gently sloping continental land surfaces such as the coastal plain of the Southeastern United States reach the water's edge, they continue their slight decline under the water until they reach a depth of about 100 fathoms (about 600 feet or 200 meters). There, rather suddenly, the submerged surface drops off more steeply to the deeper ocean floor (Fig. 20-1). Thus the continental landmasses are substantially larger than they appear on our familiar maps, but during present geologic times their edges are inundated by ocean water that is too large in volume to be contained by the ocean basins proper. Should an ice age come about, then much of the ocean water will be frozen in the larger ice caps and the

Figure 20-1A

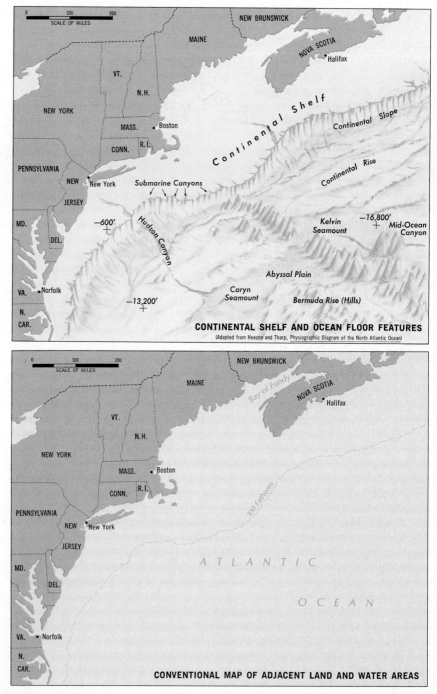

CONTINENTAL SHELF AND OCEAN FLOOR FEATURES
(Adapted from Heezen and Tharp, Physiographic Diagram of the North Atlantic Ocean)

CONVENTIONAL MAP OF ADJACENT LAND AND WATER AREAS

Figure 20-1B

water level of the oceans will drop, exposing the continental margins.

The present situation has several significant side effects. Since the submerged edges of the continents consist of the same rocks that make up the entire landmass, they also yield the same minerals. In addition, these inundated margins are covered by a relatively thin layer of water, so that mineral exploitation there presents fewer problems than it does in the deeper ocean basins. The *continental shelves*, as they are called, consequently have substantial economic value, especially since oil and natural gas occur in these areas and energy sources command a high price. But Figure 20-2 indicates that the continental shelf is not everywhere of the same dimensions. The most extensive shallow shelf lies off Eastern Asia's land areas from Japan to Indonesia; Australia and New Zealand also have wide continental shelves.

Figure 20-2

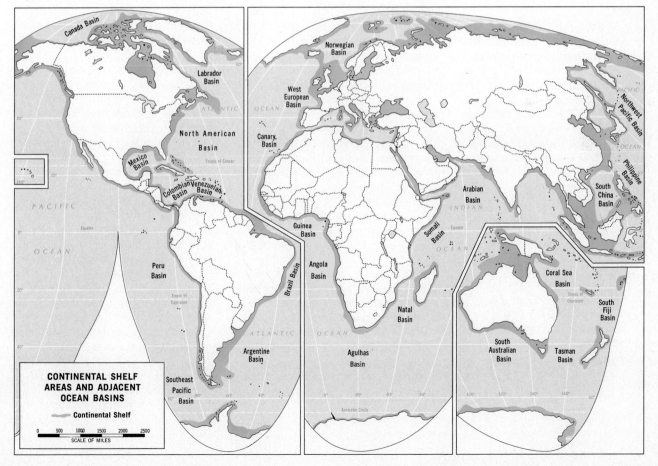

CONTINENTAL SHELF AREAS AND ADJACENT OCEAN BASINS

Continental Shelf

0 500 1000 1500 2000 2500
SCALE OF MILES

On the opposite side of Eurasia, a wide shelf lies off Europe and the British Isles. North America's eastern continental shelf is wider than that extending along the west coast. In South America, Argentina fronts the major shelf region, and while there is a large continental shelf along the north coast of South America, the west coast has only narrow shelves. Neither is Africa as well endowed as some other world regions. Off South Africa and along parts of the West African coast lie modest continental shelves.

Where the continental shelf ends and the sea bottom drops off more steeply to the ocean floor lies the *continental slope*, the appropriately named, "real" edge of the continental landmass. The ocean floor itself, at depths of 10,000 to 20,000 feet (3300 to 6600 meters), has a surface that is much less smooth and gentle than the continental shelf. The landscape of the ocean floor has hills and mountains, ridges and valleys; some of the mountains are high enough to protrude above the surface of the water and form islands.

Coastlines, where landsurface and ocean water make contact, display an enormous variety of spatial forms. You can find stretches of coast in the Southeastern United States where tens of miles of nearly ruler-straight, gently sloping, wide, sandy beaches are touched gently by waves reduced to ripples by the shallowness of the water, and where you can wade out for hundreds of yards. But travel north to New England and Eastern Canada, and you can hear the roar of white-capped waves smashing into cliffs and stacks even before you can see the shoreline itself. In Western Ireland you can stand and look out over thousands of miles of Atlantic Ocean; in Spain there are places where you can see the coastline of North Africa. In the morphology of the shore, the power of the waves, the force of the tides, the depth of the water, the width of the sea beyond, the world's coastlines present limitless variety.

People have been possessive about waters near their homes for thousands of years. The first fishermen probably waded out into shallow water and gathered shellfish; they probably would not let fishermen from another village do so. There is ample evidence that the ancient Greeks considered their bays and estuaries, and the waters separating their islands and peninsulas, as much their national domain as the land on which Athens and Sparta were built. Later the Romans made the Mediterranean an inland sea: their empire surrounded Mediterranean waters almost completely. But those ancient claims were never defined with any real precision, and there were no buoys or other marine markers to warn potential tresspassers.

The formalization of national claims to adjacent waters began during the Middle Ages, when Western European states from Scandinavia to Iberia emerged from their doldrums and their competition and rivalry intensified. European coastlines vary from the deep, narrow fiords of Norway to the gently curving beaches of Southern France, and European waters include large estuaries, narrow straits, and bays of every dimension. The European states' governments were aware that it would be difficult if not impossible to arrive at a formula that would define territorial boundaries at sea and which would fit all this diversity, even if all the parties would agree to the principle. So Norway's rulers, in the thirteenth century, simply announced that no foreign vessel would be permitted to sail north of the latitude of Bergen without a Norwegian royal license. An Italian scholar proposed in the fourteenth century that states should be awarded sovereignty over a

While segments of the world's coastlines are smooth and straight, many miles look like this—rugged and irregular. The measurement of seaward boundaries from such coastlines can present problems.

strip of water adjacent to their national territories—the first recorded instance of the concept of a *territorial sea*. This proposal led to a lengthy legal debate over the appropriate width for such a strip: should it be some specified distance from shore? To the horizon as seen by someone standing on the beach? To a line midway between countries facing opposite sides of a sea? To a line marking the distance a shore-based cannon could fire a cannonball? Famous European legal experts participated in this debate, including Bodin, a French scholar, Grotius and Van Bynkershoek, the Dutch lawyers, and Plowden and Selden for Britain. The argument raged for several centuries and produced some impressive legal treatises, some of which are still quoted on occasion today.

While the legal debate continued, the kings made their own decisions on behalf of their particular spheres of interest. The Danes acquired Norway and Iceland and, in the late sixteenth century, they reached Greenland; they proceeded to claim control over the entire North Atlantic Ocean. Denmark was a powerful imperial force in the region, and while the Danes did issue fishing licenses to applicants from other countries, they reserved zones of territorial waters along Danish and Icelandic coasts as exclusive fishing grounds for their own nationals. The decree of 1598 claims such a continuous zone, two leagues wide, or 8 nautical miles. During the seventeenth century, Danish claims ranged to as high as eight leagues (32 nautical miles). Other countries claimed narrower territorial seas based on various criteria, and of course the differences led to conflict. Warships were sent by Britain and the Netherlands to protect trading and fishing interests in the North Atlantic; the French and the Russians also put pressure on the Danes. Eventually Denmark was compelled to reduce its maritime claims.

While the Danes were negotiating their widening maritime claims, the British thought of another way to secure large areas of adjacent waters. Instead of measuring a zone of water along the coast, a zone whose outer limit would reflect the curves and bends of the coastline the British drew lengthy *baselines* from one coastal promontory to another, thus cutting off for their own use huge stretches of sea. Any territorial waters, they announced, would be measured not from the shoreline, but from those baselines. For some time the British legal position and national preference was for closed seas; the British preferred to divide the waters of the seas up between coastal countries. The Dutch position was exactly opposite, for Dutch maritime power had proved the usefulness of free and open seas.

The Nautical Mile

Measurements at sea are normally given as *nautical* miles, which differ from the *statute* miles used on land (and now giving way to the metric system). The statute mile equals 5280 feet. Its origins lie in Roman times, a measure amounting to 1000 paces, each 5 feet in length. Around the beginning of the sixteenth century, the division familiar to us, into 5280 feet, was adopted. European countries eventually abandoned the measure and went to the metric system and the kilometer.

The nautical mile is calculated by dividing the circumference of the earth into 360 degrees and each degree into 60 minutes. Thus one nautical mile equals the distance of one such minute on the earth's surface. There is just one problem: the circumference of the globe is not the same in all directions, because the earth is not a perfect sphere. Therefore international agreement had to be reached on the exact length to be used, and it was determined as 6076.12 feet. This means that the nautical mile equals about 1.15 statute miles.

References to miles in the present chapter are to *nautical* miles.

Early Compromise

The Europeans achieved a compromise of sorts during the eighteenth century. As the English fleet grew in size and capacity, the British realized that a general application of their closed-sea concept would adversely affect their interests. In due course they shifted their position toward that of the Dutch and agreed that a narrow belt of maritime sovereignty would be preferable than massive closures achieved by lengthy baselines and exorbitant claims. But now another issue arose. Should such a (comparatively narrow) belt be continuous, as the Danes and the Swedes had devised, or should the zone exist only where shore-based cannon could enforce it?

The Dutch jurist Van Bynkershoek suggested just such a solution, arguing in 1702 that no state should be permitted to claim adjacent waters over which it had no control by force of arms. Then Van Bynkershoek introduced another principle, one that still has relevance today. This is the concept of "intended and continuous occupation." Van Bynkershoek argued that any state should be allowed to claim permanently any part of the sea or ocean where it could establish a permanent presence and continuous control. In his day, that would have meant the assignment of a fleet, but in modern times, "intended and continuous occupation" can be achieved by the construction of

steel structures such as offshore drilling rigs and platforms, and strategic artificial islands.

One result of the Van Bynkershoek proposals was the limitation of national claims. The Netherlands, Britain, France, and several Mediterranean countries preferred the three-mile limit (three miles was a standard measure in Southern Europe). The Danes agreed to observe a continuous zone of just one league (four nautical miles) in 1745, and this became the standard Scandinavian measure. For a time, scholars believed that the three-mile limit was the result of measurement of the reach of an eighteenth-century cannon, but no cannon could shoot that far. The three-mile limit, therefore, was not the "cannon-shot rule" it was once believed to be. But the three-mile limit had the twin advantage that it was a standard measure in much of Europe *and* would put ships beyond the range of shore-based guns. So when the Italian expert, Galiani, proposed in 1782 that the three-mile limit become the standard width for territorial seas, this compromise was generally adopted. The United States indicated its approval as well.

If you consider the expanses of water involved, these were very modest claims, even when several Mediterranean countries increased their territorial

"Intended and continuous occupation." Van Bynkershoek would have recognized the situation pictured here (in Venezuela's Maracaibo Gulf) as constituting national occupation.

waters to a width of six miles. The Scandinavian countries generally adhered to their four-mile limit, and other European states claimed three nautical miles—a zone thinner than the line marking the coastline on your atlas map. The freedom of the seas during the eighteenth century appeared confirmed. And when, during the nineteenth century, the era of colonization brought European settlement and control on other continents, the European precedent seemed to secure world order. Japan, Australia, Canada, and numerous other countries and territories adhered either to the three-mile limit or to the limit set by the European colonial power, which never exceeded six miles.

Ironically it was an effort to codify and standardize world practice that proved that the compromise of the eighteenth century would not last. In 1930 a conference was held at The Hague, Netherlands, whose objective was to confirm the three-mile limit in international law and to define the method of delimitation to be used by all coastal countries. The 47 states in attendance represented a very large percentage of the world's coastal ownership, for the major colonial powers of the time were present. But agreement could not be reached. Several Mediterranean countries were unwilling to yield their six-mile claim; the Soviet Union similarly refused to abide by a three-mile limit.

Neither was the 1930 Conference able to adopt a standard method for the delimitation of territorial seas (whatever their width), although there was informal agreement on the issue. The ships approaching a coastline should be able to determine, by a fairly simple triangulation, whether they are within or outside the territorial sea of a coastal state. This requires agreement on baselines and other lines of closure, and on these matters the conference could not reach an accord.

Coastlines, we noted earlier, display enormous variety. When the first attempts were made to establish rules for the delimitation of territorial seas, numerous problems arose. Coastlines are subject to tidal fluctuations. The 1930

conference agreed that measurement should be from the point of low water during spring tide; a later conference held at Geneva in 1958 changed that stipulation to mean low water. This conforms to the practice used in the preparation of marine charts, which give depths based on mean low water. In addition, there is the problem of the low-tide elevation. This is a sandbar that is submerged during high tide, but exposed during low tide. The conference agreed that countries may measure their territorial waters from such low-tide elevations, provided that these lie within the territorial waters as measured from the mean low water mark. But on baselines, the definition of bays, fishing privileges, and many other matters the 1930 conference could not agree, and this doomed its hopes for a worldwide standard for territorial waters. Several countries demanded special rights in so-called historic waters (seas of particular importance and location to the state) and strategic waters (where military facilities are concentrated and naval equipment is tested). The longer the list of exceptions and special privileges, the more difficult became the task. Eventually it was abandoned.

It was not long before states, perhaps made aware of the issues and potentials by the The Hague conference, began to expand their claims over adjacent waters.

The postwar process of decolonization also produced increased
claims, for the newly independent, decolonized countries of
Africa and Asia frequently decided to decree a wider territorial
sea than their colonial ruler had
done previously. In 1950, the 3-
mile limit was still claimed by
some 40 countries, while only 9
countries had territorial waters
wider than 6 miles. In 1975, only 24
countries still adhered to the 3-
mile limit, nearly 60 states claimed
12 miles of territorial sea, and 10
countries demanded sovereignty
over 100 to 200 miles of adjacent
water!

International conferences
were unable to stem this tide of
expanding claims. The 1958 and
1960 U.N. Conferences on the
Law of the Sea, convened in
Geneva, failed to produce the
necessary consensus although
agreement was reached on certain specific items involving the
maximum length of baselines,
the disposition of particular historic bays, and low-tide elevations. Again, a conference held
in Caracas in 1974, attended by
no less than 148 interested countries, achieved only a general
consensus that the maximum
allowable width for the territorial
sea would be 12 miles (there

Table 20-1 Some Examples of Expanding Maritime Claims,
by Country and Date

Brazil	3 (1940);	6 (1966);	12 (1969);	200 (1970)
Cameroun	3 (1933);	6 (1962);	18 (1967)	
Ecuador	3 (1930);		12 (1951);	200 (1956)
Gabon	3 (1933);		12 (1963);	100 (1972)
Gambia	3 (1878);	6 (1968);	12 (1969);	50 (1971)
Guinea	3 (1933);			130 (1964)
Nigeria	3 (1964);		12 (1967);	30 (1971)
Panama			12 (1958);	200 (1967)
Peru	3 (1934);			200 (1947)
Uruguay	3 (1914);	6 (1963);	12 (1969);	200 (1969)

Source: J. V. R. Prescott, *The Political Geography of the Oceans*, New
York, Halsted/Wiley, 1975, p. 72.

was no unanimity on this); it was
decided to reconvene the conference at Geneva in 1975. Predictably, the 1975 conference failed
as well to stop states from unilat-
erally declaring sovereignty over
ever wider territorial waters. The
only diminishing quality was the
restraint of the interested parties
(Table 20-1). At the New York
1976 conference, the concept of
a 200-mile "economic zone"
gained currency. This would
reserve for the use by coastal
states a zone 200 miles wide,
eliminating the need for the
series of zones shown on
Figure 20-3.

Offshore Zones

During the course of the development of states' maritime territorial claims a set of zones evolved, among which the territorial sea is but one. Today it is possible to identify five such zones, each with a greater or lesser degree of general acceptance among interested states (Fig. 20-3):

Internal Waters. When a state establishes a baseline across a bay or an estuary, it thereby makes that estuary or bay an *internal* water body, not a part of the territorial sea. Such a bay or estuary has the same sovereign status as a river or lake.

Territorial Waters. This is the zone of sea or ocean water whose outer edge legally constitutes the maritime boundary of the state. Presently some states still claim only 3 miles of territorial sea; others claim 200 miles. Within the territorial waters the state possesses essentially the same sovereign rights it holds over its land territory. Foreign vessels do have the right of innocent passage, but offenses committed within the territorial sea come under the coastal state's jurisdiction.

Contiguous Zone. The contiguous zone is recognized under international law as a zone within which states can excercise certain powers, including pollution control and customs inspection. At present only states claiming less than 12 miles of territorial sea may claim a contiguous zone; territorial waters and contiguous zone should not be wider than twelve miles combined.

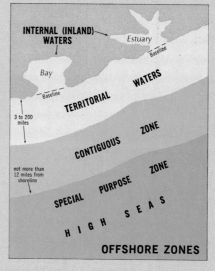

Figure 20-3

Special-Purpose Zone. Less clearly defined even than the contiguous zone, this zone was established to permit states to carry out naval manoevers, test new weaponry, pursue suspected smugglers, or perform some other activity deemed to be in the national interest. This zone has no standard width and its existence can be decreed as the need arises.

High Seas. Those waters so far unclaimed by coastal states are high seas. If the 200-mile territorial sea principle were to be adopted by all coastal states, the area of the high seas would be reduced by 30 percent. The 12-mile limit has already eliminated high-sea passages from dozens of straits and channels around the world.

Motives

What drives coastal states to expand their sovereignty over adjacent waters? It is usually a combination of objectives and circumstances. States still guard their fishing privileges in nearby waters as jealously as the Danes did centuries ago, especially since the fleets of technologically advanced countries can now appear anywhere in the world. The Icelanders, who depend almost totally on their fishing industry, do not want Japanese (or British, or Dutch) fishing fleets in their best fishing grounds. If those grounds must be protected by enlargement of the territorial waters, then the national interest prevails and such action is taken—no matter what preferences may be expressed at international conferences. A more modern concern involves the increasing pollution of the oceans. As ever larger oil tankers ply the seas, oil spills occur in greater numbers as a result of accident or deliberate carelessness. Huge oil spills have damaged beaches and destroyed wildlife in many parts of the world in recent years, and many of these spills resulted simply from tankers cleaning out their holds while at sea. A wider territorial sea provides a state with a protective cushion and some legal recourse against the companies and countries causing spills within territorial waters.

Still another basis for the expansion of territorial waters lies

Salmon fishing fleet near port off Vancouver Island, British Columbia, Canada.

401

The Soviet floating fish factory ship Vostok carries 14 fishing boats, one of which is seen being lowered into the water. Each of these 14 fishing boats has a crew of 5 and can harvest 300 tons of fish daily. Helicopters are carried on the 43,000-ton Vostok's decks for the purpose of locating large schools of fish. In one six-month trip, the Vostok produces 5 million cans of fish and fish flour.

Two British trawlers fish the waters of the North Atlantic off the coast of Iceland, under the protection of a British Navy destroyer. Disputes over the 200-mile fishing limit have produced confrontations and skirmishes in several areas.

in national security. As our technological age produces more sophisticated equipment for long-range spying, countries become more concerned over intelligence operations by other states, carried out by ships lying just outside the maritime boundary. With the 3-mile limit in effect, such spy ships, often disguised as fishing trawlers, lie within sight of beaches, coastal towns, ports, and various installations. A widening of the territorial sea pushes those ships away from the coast. Another advantage to the state involves the control of smuggling. While the United States in 1790 agreed to adhere to the 3-mile limit, it announced even then that it would reserve the right of customs inspection as far from the coast as 12 miles. During the period of prohibition, the United States also signed a number of "liquor treaties" with other countries, whereby the United States was permitted to search ships that were within one hour's sailing time from shore. In 1935 Congress approved the Anti-Smuggling Act, which authorized the President to establish, in the event that it should become necessary, customs-control points located up to 50 miles beyond the customary 12-mile customs zone. The intensification of drug smuggling in the past decade has led to the implementation of these contingencies.

Undoubtedly the era of decolonization played its role in complicating the situation as well. Countries that had long suffered colonial occupation and had been forced to adhere to colonial stipulations could make their own decisions after independence. Not unnaturally many of them concluded that if narrow territorial waters were advantageous to the colonial powers, then wider territorial seas would serve their own interests better. They were encouraged in this by the Soviet Union and by China, both countries claiming 12 miles when 3 miles was still the general rule.

403

But the strongest motive for the seaward expansion of states has had more to do with what lies *under* the territorial waters than with the sea itself. Beneath the territorial waters lies the continental shelf, and below the seabed lie valuable resources. States want to protect their interests in the adjacent continental shelf; they do not want to see the exploitive equipment of other states right on their doorstep, on the continental shelf just outside their territorial waters. One solution: expand the claim to territorial waters, thus protecting all that lies below. Or alternatively: claim not only a territorial sea, but specifically the continental shelf as well, as far out as it extends from the coastline, even if the distance is over 100 miles. States have done both, and there can be no doubt about it; as more of the continental shelf came within reach of mining equipment of the technologically advanced countries, coastal states' maritime claims leapfrogged. When several South American states found themselves with very narrow continental shelves, they compensated for their misfortune by claiming 200 miles of territorial waters.

The continental shelf, as we noted previously, is the submerged extension of the landmasses on which we live. In a sense, as we get to know more of the contents of this area of the world, it is as though we are discovering a new continent. Exploration intensifies; formerly impenetrable areas are becoming accessible. States are aware that their self-interest is involved in their participation in this maritime venture, just as colonial powers during the nineteenth century secured spheres of interest as much to obstruct their rivals' designs as to obtain wealth for themselves. Only this time, weak states have a chance as well as powerful ones. Peru's acquisition of 200 miles of territorial waters compensates for the absence of a wider shelf and protects its fishing industry; Peruvian gunboats have confirmed Peru's primacy in these waters by arresting trespassers. Other countries, unable to exploit their maritime resources themselves in the absence of capital and technical know-how, can at least deal with states whose technological advantage does make exploitation possible, securing a substantial share of the benefits involved.

Even today, we do not know the full potential of the continental shelf. In 1976, nearly one fifth of the world's oil production came from reserves in the continental shelf, and exploration for additional offshore oil sources was continuing. Indonesia and Thailand mine tin from deposits in the continental shelf, and major diamond fields lie off the coast of Namibia (South West Africa). Coal seams are known to continue under the continental shelf, and an increasing volume of natural gas now comes from offshore sources (about 15 percent of the world total in 1975). It is likely that just about ever mineral we find on land will also be found under the sea, but their development must await advances in marine mining technology.

We can catch a glimpse of what lies ahead when we read about the technological developments now taking place, soon to have an effect on maritime mineral exploitation. Oil wells are being drilled in excess of 20,000 feet (6600 meters); and for the first time, minerals have been taken *not* from the continental shelf, but from the depths of the ocean floor itself, far beyond the limits of the shelf. Among minerals on the ocean floor are manganese nodules, potato-sized concentrations of a valuable mineral. An American ship was able to "mine" these nodules by lowering a pipe, 16 inches in diameter (40 centimeters), to depths in excess of 12,000 feet (4000 meters), and sucking them to the surface. Before this venture began, it was estimated that the world supply of manganese, at current rates of consumption, would last less than 100 years. Now, when one square mile of ocean floor yields 60,000 tons of nodules, the supply is estimated to be enough for a half million years of use. Scientists are equally optimistic that minerals such as copper, nickel, aluminum, iron, lead, zinc, and cobalt will also supplement mainland reserves. Thus, significantly, the deeper ocean basins also appear to have resource potential, and if this is so, then states will soon begin to extend their marine-territorial demands beyond the edge of the continental shelf. Efforts to reach international agreement limiting national offshore interest to the continental shelf may be doomed before they succeed.

As the world's land-based states expand into the last frontier, their claims are beginning to meet and, in some cases, overlap. It is one thing for Chile, Peru, and Ecuador to claim 200 miles of territorial waters; their frontage faces the huge Pacific Ocean. No such claim could be made by European countries. If Denmark claimed 200 miles, that would include not only the surrounding waters but also much of Sweden and Norway!

And so maritime claims converge and meet, and the high seas cease to be free and open. The North Sea, on the continental shelf of Europe, proved to be more than a rich fishing ground: beneath it lie productive fields of oil and natural gas. As countries and companies scrambled to explore and exploit, the need for the territorial allocation of the

The Truman Declaration

The United States played a major role in precipitating the expansion of claims over the continental shelf. In 1945, President Harry S. Truman signed a Declaration that stated, in part:

. . . the Government of the United States regards the natural resources of the subsoil and seabed of the continental shelf beneath the high seas but contiguous to the coasts of the United States as appertaining to the United States, subject to its jurisdiction and control . . .

Soon afterward, countries in South and Middle America also laid claim to their adjacent shelf areas, as did states elsewhere in the world. The scramble had begun.

405

North Sea and its subsoil soon became evident. Thus the map of Europe today shows the North Sea still partially high seas, but the continental shelf below it is allocated to coastal states (Fig. 20-4). It is likely that this map will ultimately apply to the superjacent waters as well as the continental shelf, for the waters of the North Sea have become the scene of intense economic activity beyond that already generated by the fishing industries. Huge drilling platforms and storage facilities protrude above the waters, pipelines lead to coasts, and oil- and gas-related water traffic multiplies on already crowded waters. Van Bynkershoek would recognize it all as "intended and continuous occupation."

Is it reasonable to assume that states will continue to adhere to boundary systems in which the boundary lies 12 (or more) miles offshore, then extends along the surface of the continental shelf, to mark the state's limits along the upper edge of the continental slope? Not likely. Again the similarity to the invasion of land frontiers is striking: states would establish footholds in colonial areas, establish administrative boundaries around such footholds, and then expand into a surrounding sphere of influence where economic gains were secured, at first without political control. In the Congo (now Zaïre), various colonial powers had economic interests, but none had political responsibility until Belgium's King Leopold II acquired the region—and then, in recognition of the open, competitive economic situation there, it was

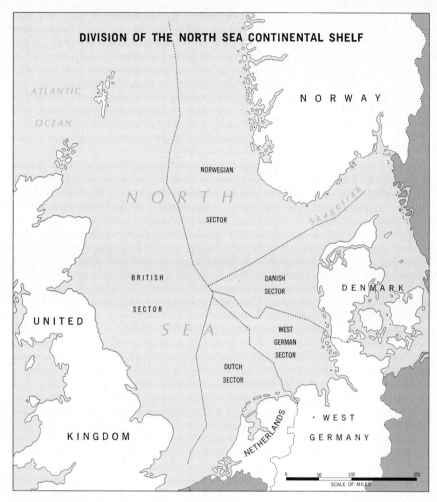

Figure 20-4

called the Congo Free State! Today we see countries still willing to limit their territorial seas to 12 miles (some even less), but none is prepared to relinquish its primacy over continental shelves extending far beyond the 12-mile limit. The "free" state of the high seas will become an anachronism in a world of intensifying competition for the resources that lie below.

The North Sea is by no means the only world region where national states face limited water areas. The situation in the Caribbean Sea and the Gulf of Mexico is perhaps even more complicated, and the Southeast Asian continental shelf also is an area of potential problems of jurisdiction. The map of the Gulf of Mexico and the Caribbean Sea (Fig. 20-5) suggests the results of an application of United Nations-approved principles of maritime boundary delimitation.

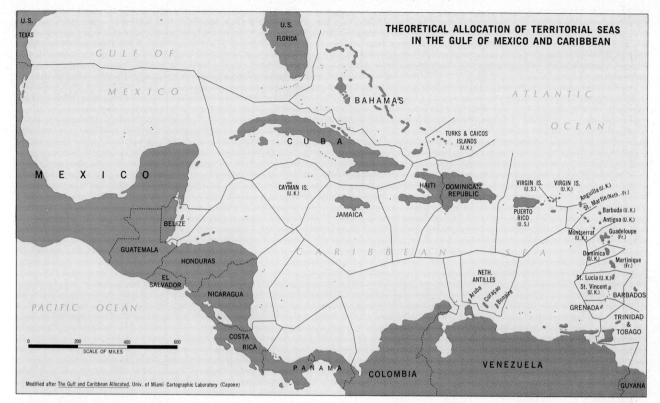

THEORETICAL ALLOCATION OF TERRITORIAL SEAS
IN THE GULF OF MEXICO AND CARIBBEAN

Figure 20-5

You will note that while some countries would acquire major shares of the region allocated, other states do not fare as well, and the potential for conflict is great. But we should expect this, for such conflicts also arose when land frontiers were finally absorbed and delimited into colonial possessions.

When problems of overlapping spheres of influence and uncertain boundaries arose in Africa during the last quarter of the nineteenth century, the competing states agreed to meet at a conference in Berlin (1884–1885), to create a boundary framework, and to adhere to the decisions made there. Out of that conference came, essentially, the boundary framework of modern Africa. Will the time come when such a conference will again be needed—this time to avert conflict over the seas and oceans and to establish the allocation of the world's last frontier?

The march on Spanish Sahara, 1975. Some 350,000 Moroccans massed on the border with Spanish Sahara to support King Hassan's claim to the colonial territory as Moroccan soil. It was an impressive display of national solidarity toward an objective with which virtually all Moroccans could identify.

21 The State and Collective Behavior

A German political geographer named Friedrich Ratzel (1844–1904) once suggested that political states are like biological organisms, passing through stages of growth and decay. Just as an organism requires food, Ratzel reasoned, so the state needs space. Any state, to retain its vigor and to continue to thrive, must have access to more space, more territory, the essential, life-giving force. Only by acquiring greater area, and through the infusions generated by the newly absorbed cultures, could a state sustain its strength. The acquisition of frontier areas with their resources and populations would renew the state's energies, Ratzel argued. But boundaries he viewed as dangerous straightjackets, quite capable of administering the death knell to the state.

Ratzel a century ago was grappling with a problem that still keeps political geographers and political scientists occupied today: what are the sources of national character, and how are the attitudes of a nation of people translated into the behavior of a state? Ratzel believed that a nation, being constituted by an aggregate of organisms (human beings, that is), would itself behave as an organism capable of birth, growth, maturity, and death. His excessively environmentalist *organic theory* was only one answer to the question of what governs the life cycle of states (how many scholars have tried to account for the rise and decline of the Roman Empire?), and the problem still defies solution today. States do experience distinct stages in their existence, and it appears as though the people's drive, energy, and fervor varies from one such stage to another. Japan is a case in point. For centuries prior to 1868 Japan had been a tradition-bound, isolated, aloof country whose rulers resisted European and other alien influences. Only during the 1850s and early 1860s did superior European and American technology (in the form of steel ships and unprecedented firepower) force entry into Japan's island fortress. But then, in 1868, a revolution occurred that overthrew the old rulers and brought to power a group of reformers whose objective was to modernize Japan as fast as possible, and to make the state a competitor, not a colonial prize for the powerful Europeans.

What happened in Japan after 1868 is the kind of miracle that keeps political geographers guessing. The whole nation was mobilized; there was hardly anyone in Japan who did not take part in the national effort. And Japan's success was soon written on the map. Even before the end of the nineteenth century a Japanese empire was in the making and the country was ready to defeat encroaching Russia. Japan set out on the kind of colonial conquest Ratzel's theory holds to be essential: Taiwan was taken from China in 1895, Korea was colonized in 1910, a sphere of influence was established in Manchuria, and a large number of island possessions were acquired in the Pacific Ocean (Fig. 21-1). Then in World War II Japan proved that in little more than a half century it had acquired the capacity to wage war with the world's most powerful states. The United States was unable to protect the Philippines; Japan's war machine occupied most of China, all of Southeast Asia, and even the northern two thirds of Australian-administered New Guinea. It was evidence of just how far Japan's modernization had gone: airplanes, tanks, warships, guns, and ammunition all were produced by Japanese industries and they were a match for their Western counterparts. Japan, we know, was ulti-

mately defeated by superior American power (two cities were devastated by atomic bombs), but this defeat coupled with the loss of its prewar as well as its wartime empire still has failed to halt or even diminish the state's progress. Japan has rebounded with such vigor that its overall economic growth rate in recent years has been the highest in the world. Whatever the sphere into which the Japanese pour their energies, the forward drive succeeds.

Ratzel may not have intended it, but his organic theory of state evolution, purely an academic speculation, became a matter of practical politics in the hands of some of his students and successors. In Germany a school of *geopolitics* developed whose practitioners were political geographers less in the business of objective scholarship than involved in advising governments on the best way to acquire that essential *lebensraum* (life space) and to break real and imagined "encirclements" of the German state by powerful enemies. It was not difficult to persuade political leaders that the acquisition of more territory could do a state no harm. During Ratzel's lifetime Europe's colonial era reached its climax, and European rivals saw Britain and France acquire enormous overseas empires. England, the far-away Roman colony, had gained control over Wales, Scotland, and Ireland; British armies had fought successfully on the European mainland, British fleets dominated the oceans, and now, during the second half

of the nineteenth century, Britain controlled an empire that spanned the world. Germany itself acquired large colonies in Africa, Belgium was in the process of discovering the real riches of the Congo, and the strength of the Netherlands was in no small measure due to the contributions of its East Indian dependency. Ratzel never said that the territory a state should seek to absorb should be contiguous to that state, and it is easy to see why.

The question to ask, of course, is whether expansionism such as colonialism is a stage that must occur in the life cycle of every state—and if so, whether that stage is predictable. A political geographer in the United States, Van Valkenburg, thought so. In the 1930s he proposed a *cycle theory* of the development of states, which held that states can be "born" and go through stages of youth, adolescence, maturity, and old age. This was no mere recapitulation of the organic theory, however. Van Valkenburg suggested that the earliest stage of a state's evolution would involve internal consolidation and organization. There would be little pressure on its boundaries, no major invasion of any available frontier. Next, during adolescence, the state attains great dynamic qualities, and can expend its energies aggressively. Expansionism prevails, conflicts with

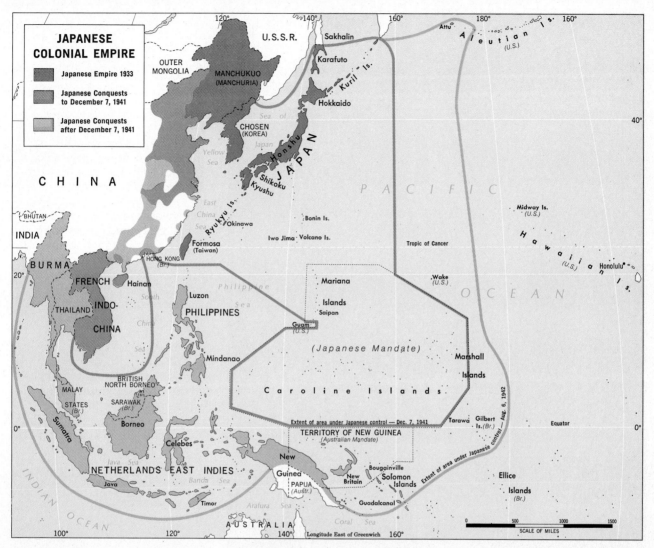

Figure 21-1

neighbors may arise, colonial occupation of distant territories occurs. These conflicts may serve to arouse unprecedented nationalism and patriotism, and national prestige becomes a matter of personal concern to large numbers of the population. Eventually these energies wane, and the state enters a period of maturity, a stabilizing period. There may be introspection over past national behavior, even attempts to correct previous mistakes. The state may seek security through participation in international organizations, and it may yield territory acquired during the adolescent stage. And finally, Van Valkenburg argued, states can slip into old age, a kind of national senility, decline, even internal disintegration.

Van Valkenburg suggested that the cycle, after completion, could renew itself, and that it could also be interrupted at any time and brought back to a previous stage. France, for example, has gone through several cycles; during the past 200 years it atrophied under the kings of Versailles, went through a renewal and brief organizing stage during Napoleon's first years, then set out on campaigns of expansion that brought it a European as well as a world empire, fought and lost disastrous wars, and eventually stabilized during the postwar era, abandoning the bulk of its colonial empire and joining in Europe's Common Market.

But do not expect to be able to fit all states into some stage of the Van Valkenburg model, and

Renewal of the cycle? For many months Lebanon has been convulsed by a civil war that has all but eradicated the old order but failed to generate a new stability.

then to predict what will happen next. Many of the world's 150 states may never have the luxury of excess energy to expend on territorial expansion (and may limit themselves to huge claims to territorial waters). The Ratzel and Van Valkenburg models were based on precedent in a politicogeographical world that has changed enormously since then. Today far more than a century or even a half century ago, national behavior is modified by the balances and pressures of the world at large. Just one example lies in the attitude of the majority of people, nearly everywhere, toward colonialism. In the nineteenth century, colonialism was viewed, generally, as an honorable, positive practice, a productive national policy, even a "civilizing" mission. Today, for numerous reasons, colonialism is held in very low esteem, and a majority of people in both former colonies and former colonial powers view it negatively because it is deemed wrong for one people to dominate another, it is exploitive, destructive of traditional societies—or simply impractical in the modern world. This does not mean that the phenomenon has disappeared: various forms of neocolonialism still exist. Powerful states still dominate weaker ones. What *has* changed is the overt behavior of states in the world arena.

Even though the colonial era is receding, we should examine some of the geographical expressions of the former colonial powers' national policies in their dependencies, for these expressions reveal much about the qualities and aspirations of the European states themselves. After the rush to gain their empires, the colonial powers began to organize and integrate their often heterogeneous possessions, and to bring to these areas the imprint of their home cultures.

France, for example, viewed its overseas domains as just that: *France d'Outre Mer.* Overseas France would be shaped as much like metropolitan France as possible. A French-acculturated elite was developed, many of whose number were educated in Paris itself. The use of the French language was encouraged in the colonies, and in the educational system, children in the colonial dependencies learned more of the geography and history of France than they learned of their own countries. The cities were adorned with French architectural styles; communications in the colonies were laid out to promote the centrality of the major cities and to facilitate exploitation for the benefit of the homeland. Several million French citizens went to the colonies to farm (as many did in Algeria), for business to teach in the schools and universities built by the colonial governments, to act as missionaries of Christian faiths, and to tend the sick. For decades it appeared that the colonial relationship between France and its overseas empire would be long lasting if not permanent, and the process of "assimilation" as the French called it was expected to take many generations of interaction. When times changed and independence approached quite rapidly, the French intensified their efforts to leave their dependencies with as strong a French heritage as possible. Every attempt was made to leave a committed, French-oriented elite in power. In the universities and schools, in music and poetry, in local cuisine and in the highest of life-styles, France's impress would be permanent (Fig. 21-2).

Against the background of the sometimes armed hostilities and bitter enmities that attended French withdrawal from such places as Algeria and Vietnam, the French attempted at acculturation must be viewed as a considerable cultural and ideological success. France (before the United States entered the arena) fought one of its most costly colonial wars in Vietnam, but during and after the war of the 1960s both North and South Vietnam looked to France for assistance,

413

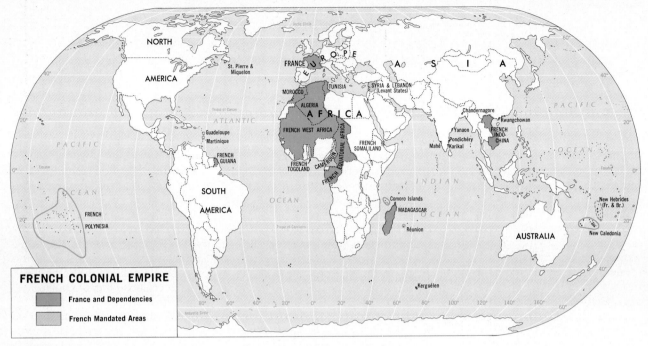

Figure 21-2

support, and even refuge; significantly the parties at the peace conference met in Paris. From Martinique to Madagascar, from Togo to Tahiti the French imprint remains pervasive. It is true even in regions long beyond French control and absorbed into other cultures. Visit Quebec and be convinced; seek it out in New Orleans and discover the durability of French influence in our own melting pot.

The British, in their worldwide colonial realm, never sought to create a second England in the manner of the French. British institutions were

exported, certainly, but so was the concept of flexibility and adjustment. As we noted previously, the British tried to duplicate their efficient and incorruptible civil service, a source of national pride, in the empire from Nigeria to India. British governments were well acquainted with the problems of regionalism (in the United Kingdom, dominated politically by England, the regions of Wales, Scotland, and Northern Ireland have strong, distinct identities), and throughout their empire the British experimented with various systems of government and administration to adjust to regional diversity. Thus while Ghana became a unitary state with a government (at

independence) based substantially on the Westminster model, Nigeria, also a West African state, was endowed with a federal system of government. Other federal states that formerly were British dependencies include India, Uganda, and Pakistan; but in each, the move has been toward greater centralization of authority. Britain's federal experiments did not prove very durable, but neither did governmental structures patterned on the British system survive the transition to independence without modification. Many African states became one-party states after the suppression of

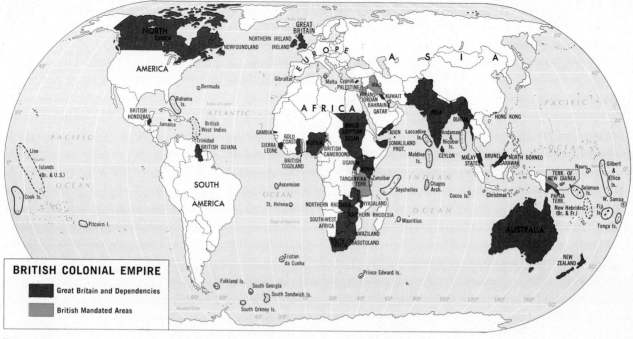

Figure 21-3

parliamentary opposition; military government eventually took over in Nigeria and Uganda (Fig. 21-3).

A visit to a formerly British-developed city in Middle America (say Kingston), West Africa (Lagos), East Africa (Nairobi), or Asia (Bombay) will bring far fewer reminders of Britain than the French colonial cities do of France. The British cultural imprint has been less overt, less pervasive than that of the French, and if there are remnants of a French cultural landscape from Vietnam to Senegal,

you will discover no British equivalent. But this is more than compensated by the British contributions to government and administration, education, sports (the West Indies have, for decades, fielded a powerful cricket team, as have India and Pakistan), and other institutions.

Portugal's centuries of colonial empire ended in tragedy and chaos during the 1970s. Portugal acquired small dependencies in Asia (Macao off China, Timor, in Indonesia, Goa in India), but its major empire, after the early loss of Brazil, was in Africa. In Angola and Mozambique the Portuguese possessed

ample cheap labor, exploited especially harshly in Mozambique, and rich mineral resources, mostly in oil-producing Angola. Good farmland also attracted a sizable Portuguese settler population, which came to exceed 100,000 in Mozambique and approached 500,000 in Angola. In their colonies, the Portuguese sought to entrench Portuguese culture in every way. Luanda and Lourenço Marques, the two capitals, were given a strong Portuguese flavor complete with inlaid sidewalks, meticulously manicured gardens, and plentiful monuments to notables of Portuguese history and culture. The Roman Catholic faith was encouraged as a matter of colonial policy, and local people could achieve "civilized" status by attaining certain prescribed standards of competence in various areas including language and history. If education in the French colonies was oriented to France, Portuguese education (albeit minimal quantitatively) was even more exclusively focused on Portugal and things Portuguese.

Portugal in Europe has had a long tradition of authoritarian government, and that tradition, too, was imposed on the colonies. Portugal's colonial practices gained worldwide notoriety even before colonialism became subject to worldwide disapproval. Forced labor, compulsory cropping, and other excesses produced profit for European Portugal, but they also sowed the wind that would harvest the storm of the 1970s. During the period of decolonization in other parts of Africa, armed resistance to Portugal's rule in both Mozambique and Angola broke out and a costly African war followed, overshadowed in the international scene by the Vietnam conflict but a war of major proportions nevertheless, with hundreds of thousands of casualties. The African campaign resulted in a political crisis at home, and Portugal quite suddenly announced its intention to grant independence to both Mozambique and Angola in 1975. In Mozambique where the conflict had raged most heavily, the transition was made with minor problems only. But in Angola, three African power groups fought a bitter civil war, each with the support of external interests. A mass exodus of white residents attended this conflict, and the tenuous infrastructure of the country was demolished.

In the Belgian administration of the Congo (Zaïre), too, we can discern some of that European country's outstanding cultural qualities. After rescuing the Congo from the grip of King Leopold II and his murderous adjudants, the Belgian government viewed its colonial task essentially as a paternal one. While the Belgians never envisaged on "overseas Belgium" in the Congo, they did treat the Congolese more or less as children, to be brought slowly and at the same, equal pace to desirable levels of "civilization." This, it was reasoned, would require many generations, and so there was no rush here to create an acculturated elite, no universities, no Belgianization. Perhaps mindful of Belgium's own strong cultural fragmentation, the Belgians laid out an administrative structure in the Congo that fused diverse sectors of the country together into several provinces.

Belgium found itself with less time than it had envisaged. The system of administration had favored the mineral companies by providing ample cheap labor, the Catholic Church by providing it primary responsibility for education and primacy in the missionary effort, and the Belgian state by producing maximum returns from the exploitation of the Congo's considerable resources. Thus the Congo in the 1950s was as unready for the wind of change as any African colony, and Belgium departed amid chaos unmatched until the Angola of 1975.

The Dutch in Europe have for centuries been known for their efficiency and their capacity to organize. The map of the Netherlands, with its large areas reclaimed from the sea, is testimonial to these qualities. In their organization and exploitation of their colonial territories, the Dutch confirmed these traits as well. In Java, the most populous island of the former Dutch East Indies, the Dutch introduced a concept known as the culture system, which involved a combination of forced cropping and forced labor and was designed to extract the maximum profit from the people and soil of the island. The system required the cultivation of stipulated crops on predetermined acreages; people who had no land to cultivate were forced to make themselves available as laborers in the service of the state. Professor J. E. Spencer, in his book *Asia, East by South*, reports that the system turned Java into one great farm estate. The profits were huge: sugar, coffee, and indigo were the leading exports and they brought Holland its famous Golden Age. But Dutch efficiency translated into colonial ruthlessness. Harsh and cruel methods were used to keep the system going at maximum productivity, and throughout Java the principal incentive to comply was fear. Lands that should have been producing rice and other staples were placed under cash crops, and people went hungry. There were differences between the various colonial powers, but one common quality was their greed.

It is strange that the Netherlands, known in Europe for its liberal character and frequently a haven for political, religious, and intellectual refugees, should have spawned so oppressive a colonial administration. It was not until 1870 that the culture system was abandoned, following an outcry about the issue in Holland itself. Still the Dutch con-

tinued a form of forced cropping for coffee until 1917, and the Dutch presence in what is now Indonesia increased considerably during the first half of the twentieth century because settlers were attracted to the region's opportunities. When the Netherlands was defeated and occupied by Germany, the Japanese made use of the opportunity to take the Dutch East Indies from their colonial masters. Following the defeat of Japan, the Dutch were unable to reestablish themselves in the face of Indonesian opposition, and the colonial era there ended before midcentury.

The European colonial powers acquired their dependencies principally for their actual and potential productive capacity, but they also hoped to enlarge their cultural spheres, secure the commitment of diverse peoples, spread what they regarded as the true religion, and, ultimately, endow their colonies with the fundamentals of statehood and nationality. Now, less than a century after the colonial powers gathered in Berlin to carve Africa into colonial jurisdictions, the colonial era is ending (at least by some definitions: in Eastern Europe it may just be starting). The Third World carries some powerful imprints from the First.

When a state achieves a certain degree of maturity, we noted earlier, it may be prepared to give up a certain amount of sovereignty (i.e., its independence of action) in order to participate in a larger community, bloc, or group of states. Actually, this phenomenon is not new (the old Greek city-states banded together for common advantage), and we argue that it is not only the mature state that will behave this way. Even individual cities have been known to form alliances, as did the towns of what is today Northern Germany during the thirteenth to the fifteenth centuries, the heyday of the Hanseatic League. Nevertheless, this process of multistate grouping has been a hallmark of the twentieth century, and it has involved, in one way or another, nearly all the states of the world.

The modern beginnings came with the conferences that followed the end of World War I. The concept of an international organization that would include all the nations of the world became a flawed reality in 1919 with the League of Nations: the United States was among countries that did not join this organization. In all, 63 states participated in the League, although the total membership at any single time never did reach 63. Costa Rica and Brazil left the League even before 1930; Germany departed in 1933, shortly before the Soviet Union joined (1934). The League was born of a worldwide desire to repudiate any future aggressor, but the failure of the United States to join dealt the organization a severe blow. Then the League had its big opportunity to stand on its principle when Ethiopia's Haile Selassie made a dramatic appeal for help in the face of an invasion by Italy, a member state until 1937. The League failed to take action, and in the chaos of the beginning of World War II, it collapsed.

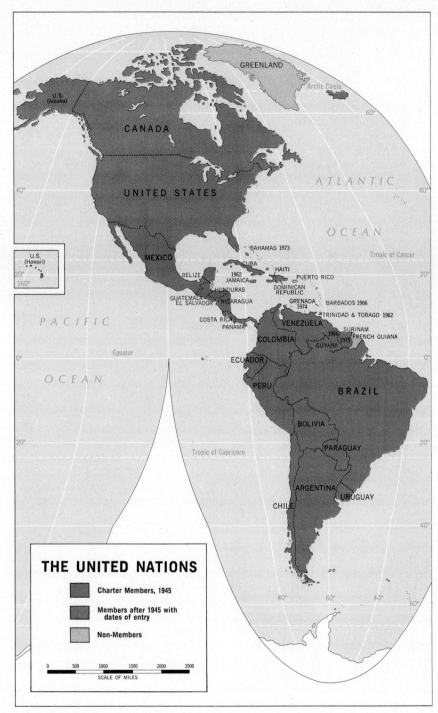

Figure 21-4

418

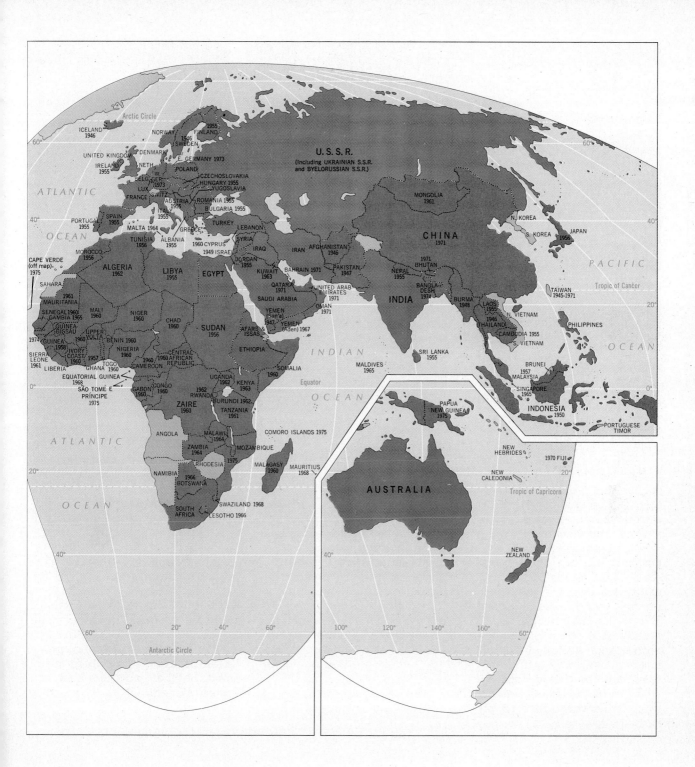

ATLANTIC

OCEAN

ICELAND
1946

NORWAY 1946
SWEDEN

FINLAND
1955

Arctic Circle

60°

UNITED KINGDOM
IRELAND
1955

DENMARK
NETH.
BEL.
GER.
LUX.
1973
SWITZ.
FRANCE

E. GERMANY 1973

POLAND

CZECHOSLOVAKIA
HUNGARY 1955
YUGOSLAVIA
AUSTRIA
ROMANIA 1955
BULGARIA 1955

U. S. S. R.
(Including UKRAINIAN S.S.R.
and BYELORUSSIAN S.S.R.)

60°

40°

PORTUGAL
1955

SPAIN
1955

ITALY
1955

MALTA 1964
GREECE
TURKEY
LEBANON

ALBANIA
1955
CYPRUS
1960
SYRIA
1949 ISRAEL
JORDAN
1955
IRAQ

IRAN

AFGHANISTAN
1946

MONGOLIA
1961

N. KOREA

S. KOREA

JAPAN
1956

40°

CAPE VERDE
(off map)
1975

TUNISIA
1956

MOROCCO
1956

ALGERIA
1962

LIBYA
1955

EGYPT

KUWAIT
1963

BAHRAIN 1971

QATAR
1971

UNITED ARAB
EMIRATES
1971

SAUDI ARABIA

PAKISTAN
1947

NEPAL
1955

1971
BHUTAN

CHINA
1971

BANGLA-
DESH
1974

INDIA

BURMA
1948

TAIWAN
1945-1971

LAOS
1955

Tropic of Cancer

PACIFIC

SAHARA

MAURITANIA
1961

SENEGAL 1960
GAMBIA 1965

MALI
1960

NIGER
1960

CHAD
1960

SUDAN
1956

YEMEN
(San'a)
1947 YEMEN
(Aden) 1967

OMAN
1971

N. VIETNAM
1946
THAILAND

CAMBODIA 1955

PHILIPPINES

20°

OCEAN

GUINEA-
BISSAU
1974 GUINEA
1958

UPPER
VOLTA
1960

BENIN 1960

NIGERIA
1960

CENTRAL
AFRICAN
REPUBLIC

ETHIOPIA

AFARS &
ISSAS

INDIAN

SRI LANKA
1955

S. VIETNAM

OCEAN

SIERRA
LEONE
1961

IVORY
COAST
1960

LIBERIA

GHANA 1960

TOGO
1960

CAMEROON

EQUATORIAL GUINEA
1968

SÃO TOMÉ E
PRÍNCIPE
1975

GABON
1960

CONGO
1960

UGANDA
1962

RWANDA

ZAIRE
1960

KENYA
1963

SOMALIA
1960

MALDIVES
1965

Equator

BRUNEI
1957
MALAYSIA

SINGAPORE
1965

0°

ATLANTIC

OCEAN

20°

40°

ANGOLA

NAMIBIA

BURUNDI 1962

TANZANIA
1961

MALAWI
1964

ZAMBIA
1964

RHODESIA

1962

1975

MALAGASY
1960

COMORO ISLANDS 1975

MOZAMBIQUE

MAURITIUS
1968

1966
BOTSWANA

SOUTH
AFRICA

SWAZILAND 1968

LESOTHO 1966

0°

20°

40°

60°

Antarctic Circle

INDONESIA
1950

PORTUGUESE
TIMOR

PAPUA
NEW GUINEA
1975

NEW
HEBRIDES

NEW
CALEDONIA

1970 FIJI

0°

20°

AUSTRALIA

Tropic of Capricorn

NEW
ZEALAND

100°

120°

140°

160°

40°

60°

419

The League of Nations as it met in Geneva in September, 1924.

The Emperor Haile Selassie appeals to the League of Nations in 1936 on behalf of his country (at the time known as Abyssinia), then being overrun by Italian military forces. The appeal was ignored.

Still the interwar period witnessed significant progress in the area of interstate cooperation. The League of Nations produced other international organizations, and a prominent one was the Permanent Court of International Justice, created to adjudicate legal issues between states (e.g., disputes over fishing rights.) After the end of World War II, the international community once again formed an organization designed to foster international security and cooperation: the United Nations. And just as the United Nations in many ways was a renewal of

the League of Nations, so its International Court of Justice succeeded the Permanent Court of the interwar period.

The representation of states in the United Nations has been more nearly universal than that of the League (Fig. 21-4). A handful of states, for various reasons, had not joined the United Nations by the mid-1970s, but the admission of China in 1971 gave the organization

unprecedented constituency. And again, the U.N.'s General Assembly and Security Council, the newsmaking units, overshadowed the cooperative efforts of numerous less visible but enormously productive subsidiaries such as the FAO (Food and Agricultural Organization), UNESCO (United Nations Educational, Social, and Cultural Organization), and WHO (World Health Organization). The membership in these organizations is less complete than in the parent organization, but their work has been of world benefit.

The U.S. Delegation to the United Nations accuses the USSR in the Security Council of placing missiles in Cuba (1962). The maps and photographs are in evidence, and the Cuban Missile Crisis is on.

Considering the pressures of the period through which the world has gone since the creation of the United Nations in 1945, it is something of a miracle that the organization has survived. The confrontations over Berlin, Korea, Vietnam, the Suez Canal, and Cuba, the assertion of Soviet power in Hungary and Czechoslovakia, and several major regional crises (notably in the Middle East) put severe strain on the United Nations, but it survived. In 1975 the greatest threat to the United Nation's representativeness appeared to be the collective efforts by certain groups of states to oust a common adversary. Arab states were seeking the ouster of Israel, and African states succeeded in suspending South Africa from General Assembly participation.

The League of Nations and the United Nations constitute manifestations of a twentieth-century phenomenon that is expressed even more strongly at the regional level. This century has been a period of cross-national ideologies, growing cultural-regional awareness and assertiveness, and intensifying economic competition. States have begun to join together to further their shared political ideologies, their economic objectives, and their strategic goals. In 1976 more than 40 such organizations existed, many of them with subsidiaries designed to focus on particular issues or areas. Today interstate cooperation is so widespread around the world that a new era has clearly arrived.

The first major experiments in interstate cooperation were undertaken in Europe. Three small countries—the Netherlands, Belgium, and Luxemburg—led the way. It had long been thought that all three might benefit from mutual agreements that would reduce the divisiveness of their political boundaries. And certainly they have much in common. Northwest Belgium speaks Flemish, a language very close to Dutch. Luxemburg speaks French, like Southeast Belgium. But even more importantly, the countries have considerably economic complementarity. Dutch farm products sell heavily on Belgian markets. Belgian industrial goods go to the Netherlands and Luxemburg. Would it not be reasonable to create common tariffs, to eliminate import licenses and quotas? Representatives of Benelux (as the organization came to be called) thought so, and even before the end of World War II they met in London to sign an agreement of cooperation. Other European countries watched the experiment with great interest, and soon there was talk of larger, more comprehensive economic unions.

Out of the reconstruction of postwar Europe, aided so greatly by the infusion of U.S. support through the Marshall Plan, several economic blocs emerged. The most successful and effective among these is EEC, the European Economic Community, also known as the Common Market. Initially the EEC included the three Benelux countries, plus France, Italy, and the Federal Republic of (West) Germany. This group, as the map indicates, substantially makes up Europe's core area, and so it became known as the "Inner Six." The experiment was successful, and the EEC became an economic force of world proportions. Eventually the United Kingdom joined, as did Denmark and Ireland; in 1976 the short name for the Common Market had become "The Nine" (Fig. 21-5).

As anyone who has visited there recently is aware, Europe has been transformed by its economic successes of the 1950s and 1960s. Mobility is greater than ever before: Italians work in Amsterdam, Frenchmen go to live and work in Germany, Belgian capital invests in Italy. Moving across an international border to live and work in another member country is easier than ever. License plates bearing the exhortation "Europa!" can be seen on automobiles from Rotterdam to Rome. And behind the EEC's overall structure stand several supplementary cooperative unions: the European Atomic Energy Community, the European Coal and Steel Community, and more.

Does this mean that we may see the emergence of a United States of Europe? It is still doubtful. The lesson of Europe is that economic cooperation is achieved more easily than political unification. Ever since 1948, a Council of Europe has existed, a sort of experimental European parliament. But as an embryo government of a future-unified Europe, the Council has barely begun to make progress comparable to that of the continent's economic unions. Nevertheless, there is talk of selecting a "capital of Europe," and the hope is often expressed that the Council may indeed turn out to be a forerunner of a government for a United States of Europe. In 1974 at its Paris meeting, the representatives of The Nine agreed that their heads of government would henceforth meet three times each year as a European Council (not to be confused with the older Council of Europe), and that a European passport should signify membership in a European Union. After many centuries of rivalry, conflict, and war, Europe has witnessed a remarkable 30 years.

But Europe has no monopoly over interstate cooperation (or *supranationalism*, as the phenomenon is sometimes called). Of course, the world's most powerful states have formed unions that are essentially in their interest and in which they dominate affairs, as the Soviet Union does

EUROPEAN SUPRANATIONALISM

European Economic Community (EEC or Common Market); European Coal and Steel Community (ECSC); European Atomic Energy Community (EURATOM)

Council for Mutual Economic Assistance (CMEA or COMECON)

Figure 21-5

in the Warsaw Pact and the United States in the Organization of American States. But elsewhere states are associating at various levels and for different purposes. The Organization of African Unity convenes its member states annually to discuss efforts to terminate the remnant colonialism in Africa, to bring majority rule to countries where white minorities still are in control, and to assist member states in settling current conflicts. But behind the scenes, the OAU also works to improve health

and education in Africa, to solve refugee problems, and to mediate long-standing issues. In and near the Middle East, the countries of the Arab world have founded the Arab League. Again, the primary unifying issues for Arab League states are the position of Israel in the Middle East and the best use that can be made of the power inherent in the region's oil pro-

The 1975 North Atlantic Treaty Organization summit meeting in Brussels.

duction. But the Arab League can make important contributions also in less volatile areas.

Some international unions have not done as well as others. The British Commonwealth has to sustain the bonds first forged during the colonial period among states where English became the lingua franca and where sterling was the currency, but the Commonwealth today has lost much of its early strength and status. The French Community, envisaged by De Gaulle as a permanent bond for the French-speaking world, also has weakened much since its inception. Japan's projected East Asian Co-Prosperity Sphere foundered with Japan's defeat in

Corporative Behavior

World War II. Nevertheless, from Central America to East Asia, from NATO to OPEC, states are joining in common efforts, and state systems will of necessity enter still another phase in their complicated life cycles.

We have discussed the behavior of states as though the governments of these states can control and direct the relationships of their countries in the international arena. But this is not always the case, and not merely because some states are less powerful than others. In recent decades a whole new element has entered the international scene: the so-called multinational corporation. Today there are corporations—oil companies, industrial concerns—that are so powerful that they can influence the behavior of national states and their governments. In the boardrooms of those corporations in New York or Tokyo or London sit small groups of directors who control far more money and who can exercise much more power than the governments of many entire countries. They have representatives in cities all over the world who control, on behalf of the corporate headquarters, the industries of foreign countries. It is another kind of example altogether of the interstate phenomenon and, in the view of some scholars of economic affairs, an alarming one.

It is customary to call these huge organizations *multinational* corporations, but in fact they are hardly multinational. Generally there is neither a genuine partnership among countries in which the corporation functions nor are the citizens of other countries greatly involved in the decision-making and actual directing of corporate affairs. Of the 10 largest multinational corporations in 1976, 8 had their headquarters in the United States. Every one of these corporations had a total production that was larger than the total national product of half of the world's countries. Together, these multinational corporations had subsidiary industries in perhaps two thirds of the world's countries, but the people in charge of those distant industries tended to be United States citizens, not citizens of the other nations in the "multinational" scheme.

It has been estimated that perhaps as much as two thirds of the investment by multinational corporations takes place in developed countries, but the remaining one third (spent in the underdeveloped countries) has an enormous impact on weaker economies and governments. In a country where there is limited industrial development, the ownership of factories by multinational corporations can impair the government's ability to control domestic industry; the corporations might even begin to dictate to the government. In the early 1970s a major multinational corporation, International Telephone and Telegraph Corporation, was accused of trying to initiate and fund a CIA opera-tion designed to sabotage the government of Chile, where ITT interests were threatened by the Allende regime. That incident was neither the first nor the best-concealed case of its kind, and in many countries the public began to demand that their government guard against the growing power of multinational corporations represented there. A U.N. committee was appointed to study the role of multinational corporations in individual countries, and its report, *Multinational Corporations in World Development* (1972) stressed the ability of the corporations to dominate the affairs of individual countries, especially underdeveloped countries.

On the positive side, the multinational corporations can speed the diffusion of technological advances across otherwise inhibitive political boundaries, they can provide capital and employ labor where none of this might otherwise have occurred. But on the negative side, these powerful corporations can throttle local competition, could develop worldwide monopolies at the expense of the consumer, and might use improper methods to achieve their objectives—political or economic. For the first time in world history,

truly global organizations have emerged complete with financial power to implement decisions made in the corporate headquarters, disseminated through corporation-owned communications networks, and carried out by representatives in cities and towns around the world. It is not altogether inconceivable that such global corporations (for that is what they are better called) might use their capital strength not merely to buy off the necessary politicians but also to develop their own armed strike forces to protect their interests. The era of the multinational corporation has just begun, and its impact on the world politicogeographical scene is yet incalculable.

The emergence of supranationalism and the global, power-wielding corporation, the rise of nationalist movements in long-stable states such as the United Kingdom's Scotland and Wales, the breakdown of the system in countries such as Lebanon and Ethiopia, and other symptoms (including our own disaffection with "Washington") suggest that the national state is in demise, inadequate to the pressures of the modern world. In part this may be so because Western models of state organization have proved incompatible to the traditions of non-Western cultures and societies; Western countries themselves reel under the impacts of diminished influence and power, more expensive resources, declining economic growth, persistent inflation, and regionally-expressed political dissatisfactions. Is it all inevitable, as Ratzel suggested? Can we trace the source of the trouble?

The preceding discussion has touched on concepts of community, territory, influence, and power—all in the context of the national state. But all the associated behavior, as Ratzel said, has its roots in the individual, in the aspirations and desires of people who make up communities and nations. And while we have learned to eschew the sort of determinism Ratzel espoused, we still do not have complete answers to the questions Ratzel raised.

Urban Graffiti

Territorial behavior manifests itself in many ways. In a recent article entitled "Urban Graffiti as Territorial Markers," D. Ley and R. Cybriwsky discuss the "turf" or area of control held by rival inner-city gangs. Members of the gangs use graffiti to announce their territory's ownership. The authors report:

> The mastery and occupation of space might well be a behavioral primitive. Climbing mountains, descending to ocean depths, landing astronauts on the moon who leave their own territorial marker, colonial adventures, riding the freeway, possessing a home on a large lot—middle-income Americans have ample opportunity to sublimate their territorial needs, but many of these options are closed to the inner city dweller. Territorial graffiti . . . (ascribe) a proprietary meaning to space.

In their study of graffiti in Philadelphia, Professors Ley and Cybriwsky found that the incidence and content of graffiti may delineate zones of tension and contested space and form indicators of gang violence; it is not difficult to extrapolate to the behavior of states in confirming their presence in areas divided by a contested boundary. And in other ways as well our cities are microcosms of the wider world: there are the wealthy and the poor, exploiters and exploited, powerful and weak, empires and colonies, boundaries and buffer zones, even competing governments. To the questions to be raised about states, the answers in part lie in the cities.

Graffiti on a wall in New York City: territorial markers in the inner city.

The dominant theme in human history involves territory—people's attempts to wrest it from others and, once acquired, to defend it against outsiders who are perceived to covet it. In the competition for domain lies a binding agent, a national objective. As individuals we are possessive about our personal space and do not like to be encroached on. We fence off our yards and will argue with a neighbor over the narrowest of strips of land. Collectively, on a small scale, occupants of wealthier subdivisions build walls and gates and hire private police forces to protect their properties. On a larger scale there are few issues that can arouse national passion to the extent that a violation of territorial sovereignty can. The principle is used by rulers to foster national objectives: in February, 1976, President Amin of Uganda declared that his country is the rightful owner of most of western Kenya, and rallies were held throughout Uganda to disseminate that aim. In Kenya, the government seized the opportunity to unite a divided people on an issue on which almost everyone could agree: a repudiation of Uganda's claim. It is unlikely that King Hassan II of Morocco could have mobilized 300,000 citizens for anything other than the famous march into Spanish Sahara. If Guatemala has a national objective, it is its acquisition of Belize, its weak eastern neighbor.

A number of scholars have suggested that, to understand this behavior, we would do better to study the individual and the small community rather than the state. R. Ardrey ascribed our attitude toward territorial space to instinct: man, he said, is a territorial animal, individually and collectively. This suggests, of course, that our human sense of territoriality as an instinctive drive is a greater determinant of our political-territorial accommodation and organization then what we have learned through social and cultural evolution. But critics of this idea doubt that it is appropriate to make inferences about group behavior from research dealing mainly with the behavior of individuals, and they also wonder whether it is appropriate to equate human behavior with animal behavior.

Still there can be no doubt that personal attitudes toward space vary from culture to culture, and that national positions sometimes seem to be extensions of individual behavior. Scholars have begun to study personal attitudes toward space and individual behavior involving territory in new and interesting ways. Anthropologist E. T. Hall reports on some of the early results, and speculates quite freely, in *The Silent Language* (1965) and *The Hidden Dimension* (1966). He points out that people have a sort of envelope of territory that is carried about, and which they do not like to see invaded. This "personal space" is in effect an extension of ourselves, and it seems to exist in all cultures—but it is not the same in different cultures. We Americans, for example, are far less able to

tolerate invasion of our personal space than many other peoples. For this phenomenon Hall invented the term *proxemics*. Other social scientists are working on the concept of *dominance behavior*, which relates territorial adjustment to power. Dominance behavior can be observed among individuals (even children); it can also be seen to exist among groups. In an African country, where the population may be divided into as many as a dozen or more discrete peoples, one people may dominate the national scene (as, for example, the Kikuyu do in Kenya). When groups of people migrate from rural to urban areas and there must accommodate and adjust to available residential locations, the national situation is duplicated: the people who have the power in the state also tend to acquire the most favorable locations available in the city, and the weakest get the least. It is not difficult to extrapolate to dominance behavior among states.

The behavior of states, and especially the interaction among states, are topics perhaps too complex to interpret systematically, and certainly prediction in these contexts can only be guesswork. But our lives are daily affected by states' multifaceted competition and, as the Cuban missile crisis of 1961 proved, even threatened. While we work toward greater understanding through research on behavior, we should remain alert to the fortunes of the state system in this rapidly changing world.

Reading

The article by R. Millon, "Teotihuacán," appeared in *Scientific American*, Vol. 216, June, 1967. For several articles on ancient cities and their roles in developing early civilizations, see *Cities: Their Origin, Growth, and Human Impact*, introduced by K. Davis (W. H. Freeman, San Francisco, 1973). H. E. Driver's edited volume, *The Americas on the Eve of Discovery* (Prentice-Hall, Englewood Cliffs, N.J., 1964) contains much information on cultural origins on these continents. Still a good source is R. E. Sullivan's *Heirs to the Roman Empire* (Cornell, Ithaca, 1963). Also see C. G. Starr, *Rise and Fall of the Ancient World* (Rand McNally, Chicago, 1960). "Urbanization of the Classical World," an article by N. J. G. Pounds, appeared in the *Annals* of the Association of American Geographers, Vol. 59, March, 1969.

On the development and decline of nation states, see J. H. Herz, "The Rise and Demise of the Territorial State," World Politics, Vol. 9, July, 1957. The volume by J. G. Stoessinger, *The Might of Nations*, was published by Random House, New York, in 1961, J. R. V. Prescott focuses on *The Geography of Frontiers and Boundaries* (Aldine, Chicago, 1965), and an excellent source in a number of related contexts is A. Sheikh, *International Law and National Behavior* (Wiley, New York, 1974). Also see S. D. Brunn, *Geography and Politics in America* (Harper & Row, New York, 1974).

On the scramble for the last frontier, see J. V. R. Prescott, *The Political Geography of the Oceans*, Halsted/Wiley, New York, 1975, a book that provides a substantial background on this topic. The United Nations Organization publishes reports on its Law of the Sea Conferences, and the Office of The Geographer, Department of State, publishes information on maritime (as well as terrestrial) boundary questions. Also see L. M. Alexander, editor, The Law of the Sea: Offshore Boundaries and Zones (Ohio State, Columbus, 1967). The subjects of colonialism and supranationalism are covered in chapters of introductory texts such as N. J. G. Pounds, *Political Geography* (McGraw-Hill, New York, 1972) and H. J. de Blij, *Systematic Political Geography* (Wiley, New York, 1973).

On multinational corporations and their impact, see R. J. Barnet and R. E. Müller, *Global Reach: the Power of the Multinational Corporations* (Simon and Schuster, New York, 1974). The September, 1972 issue of the *Annals of the American Academy of Political and Social Science* (Vol. 403) is devoted entirely to this matter. The United Nations reports include *Multinational Corporations in World Development* (1973) and *The Impact of Multinational Corporations on Development and on International Relations* (1974).

E. T. Hall's *Silent Language* (Premier Books, New York, 1965) was followed by *The Hidden Dimension* (Garden City, New York, 1966). In the same area see R. Sommer, *Personal Space: the Behavioral Basis of Design* (Prentice-Hall, Englewood Cliffs, N.J., 1969) and O. Newman, *Defensible Space* (Macmillan, New York, 1972). The article by D. Ley and R. Cybriwsky entitled "Urban Graffiti as Territorial Markers" appeared in the *Annals of the Association of American Geographers*, Vol. 64, December, 1974. Relevant in these contexts is S. Greenberg's *Politics and Poverty* (Wiley/Interscience, New York, 1974, as is K. R. Cox, *Conflict, Power, and Politics in the City* (McGraw-Hill, New York, 1973).

Photo Credits

searchers. 228: (top) Ken Heyman; (bottom) Bernard Pierre Wolff/Photo Researchers. 229: (top) Russ Kinne/Photo Researchers; (bottom) Charles E. Rotkin/PFI. 230: (top) S. Trevor/Bruce Coleman (bottom) Georg Gerster/Rapho-Photo Researchers. 231: (left) Georg Gerster/Rapho-Photo Researchers; (right) C. Bonington/Woodfin Camp. 232: (top) E. Boubat/Photo Researchers; (bottom) Hubertus Kanus/Rapho-Photo Researchers. 233: Victor Englebert/Photo Researchers. 234: Von Meiss-Teuffen/Photo Researchers. 235: (top) Frank Siteman/Stock, Boston; (bottom) John Lewis Stage/Photo Researchers. 236: (top) Hubertus Kanus/Rapho-Photo Researchers; (bottom) Tom Hollyman/Photo Researchers. 237: Peter Vandermark/Stock, Boston. 239: Georg Gerster/Rapho-Photo Researchers.

CHAPTER THIRTEEN Opener: Charles E. Rotkin/PFI. 245: Burt Glinn/Magnum. 247: Diane Rawson/Photo Researchers. 248: (top) Gerg Gerster/Rapho-Photo Researchers; (bottom) Yan/Rapho-Photo Researchers. 250: George E. Jones III/Photo Researchers. 253: Courtesy French Government Tourist Office.

CHAPTER FOURTEEN Opener: Harm deBlij. 263: John S.

Shelton. 271: Georg Gerster/Rapho-Photo Researchers. 273: Chicago Aerial Survey. 274: Daniel D. Sullivan/Photo Researchers. 279: (top) Harm deBlij; (bottom) Ira Kirschenbaum/Stock, Boston.

CHAPTER FIFTEEN Opener: Arthur Tress/Magnum. 285: M. Shostak/Anthro Photo. 286: Irven DeVore/Anthro Photo. 287: Georg Gerster/Rapho-Photo Researchers. 290: George Rodger/Magnum.

CHAPTER SIXTEEN Opener: Grant Heilman. 305: Harm deBlij. 308: Georg Gerster/Rapho-Photo Researchers. 309: (top) Carl Frank/Photo Researchers; (bottom) Bernard Pierre Wolff/Photo Researchers; 312: George Gerster/Rapho-Photo Researchers. 314: Almasy.

CHAPTER SEVENTEEN Opener: Charles E. Rotkin/ PFI. 324: Stephen L. Feldman/Rapho-Photo Researchers. 328: Tom Hollyman/Photo Researchers. 329: Ken Heyman. 331: Robert Mottar/Photo Researchers. 335: Georg Gerster/Rapho-Photo Researchers. 337: Howard Sochurek/Woodfin Camp. 338: Lowell J. Georgia/Photo Researchers. 341: Marc Riboud/Magnum. 343: Paolo Koch/Rapho-Photo Researchers. 347: Ken Heyman.

CHAPTER EIGHTEEN Opener: Farrell Grehan/Photo Researchers. 358: Georg Gerster/Rapho-Photo Researchers. 361: Carl Frank/Photo Researchers. 362: Lucile Nix Rybakov/Photo Researchers. 363: Diane Rawson/Photo Researchers.

CHAPTER NINETEEN Opener: René Burri/Magnum. 370: Jim Anderson/Woodfin Camp. 376: Georg Gerster/Rapho-Photo Researchers. 377: H.W. Silvester/Rapho-Photo Researchers. 381: Jim Anderson/Woodfin Camp. 383: Jerry Cooke/Photo Researchers. 384: Ken Heyman.

CHAPTER TWENTY Opener: John Moss for EXXON Corporation. 395: Pierre Berger/Photo Researchers. 397: Georg Gerster/Rapho-Photo Researchers. 401: John Running/Stock, Boston. 402: TASS from Sovfoto. 403: Philippe Achache-Gamma/Liaison Agency.

CHAPTER TWENTY ONE Opener: Bruno Barbey/Magnum. 412: Claude Salhani/Sygma. 420: (left) Culver Pictures; (right) Wide World Photos. 421: Wide World Photos. 424: Henri Bureau/Sygma. 427: Margot Granitsas/Photo Researchers.

index

Information found in maps, diagrams, or photographs is indicated by **boldface** page numbers.

435

443

Ural Mountains, 108
  region, 338
Uranium, 126
Urbanism, 243–246, 252–260, 345
  functions of, 261–264
  graffiti, 427
  industrial cores, 304
  renewal, 277
  settlements, 240
  stresses, 244
  world distribution, 267–270
Uruguay, 44, 345, 370
USSR (see Soviet Union)

Vaccination, 63, 73, 133
Values, 142
van Bynkershoek, 395, 397, 406
Van Valkenburg, 410, 412
Vectored diseases, 74, 76–79
Vegetables, 314
Vehicles, 74
Venereal diseases, 74, 83
Venezuela, 132
  boundary dispute, 386
  nutrition, 44
Venice, 249, 252
Versailles, 211
Vietnam, 20, 22, 375
  France and, 413
  migration, 104–105
  nutrition, 45
Villages, 227–241, 260, 264, 265
Violence, 244
Viruses, 74, 76
Vitamins, 41, 45, 64
  shortages, 162
Vladivostok, 108
Volcanos, 102

Volga region, 338
Voltaic language, 182
Voluntary migration, 101
von Humboldt. Alexander, 2–3
Von Thünen, J. H., 12, 300–303, 304. See
  also Thünian zones

Wales, 268, 410
  language, 186
  mining, 330
  urbanization, 255
Walled villages, 241
Walloon, 186
Walls, 113
Warsaw, 249
  Pact, 423
Washington, D.C., 22, 212, 267
Water, 127. See also Oceans
Watermelon, 288
Wattle houses, 236
Watusi, 163
Wegener, Alfred, 4
Wei River, 249, 288
  culture hearth, 355, 358
Wes Kos, 183
West Africa, 22, 73
  agriculture, 288
  cities, 249
  culture hearth, 145, 355, 358
  language, 182–183
West Asia, 167
West Germany, 106
Wheat, 51, 58, 314–315
Whittlesey, D., 143, 144
WHO, 420
Wholesale cities, 261
Wildlife migrations, 287

Windbreaks, 231, 233, 234
Witwatersrand, 107, 270
Women, 60
  migration and, 106
Wood, 234–235
Woodstock, **221**
World Food Conference, 53
World Health Organization, 79, 82, 420
World Population Conference, 17, 18
World War II, 158, 159, 214, 420
Writing, 177, 355

X, Malcolm, 06
Xhosa language, 186

Yams, 288, 317
Yangtze River, 22
  district, 342–343
Yellow fever, 66, 76–77
Yellow River, see Hwang River
Yokohama, 270
Youngstown, Ohio, 267
Yucatan, 249
  culture hearth, 355

Zadkine, Ossip, 214
Zaire, 58, 64, 406, 416
  migration, 107
  population, 379
  stature in, 163
Zambia, 107
Zero population growth, 34
Zimbabwe, 238
Zinc, 405
Zionism, 202
Zoroastrianism, 202
ZPG, 34